A Cruising Voyage Round the World

FIRST TO THE SOUTH-SEAS, THENCE TO THE EAST-INDIES, AND HOMEWARDS BY THE CAPE OF GOOD HOPE. BEGUN IN 1708, AND FINISH'D IN 1711.

By Captain Woodes Rogers

THE NARRATIVE PRESS

TRUE FIRST-PERSON HISTORICAL ACCOUNTS

To the Worthy Gentlemen my surviving Owners, the Worshipful Christopher Shuter Esq; Sir John Hawkins Kt. John Romsey Esq; Capt. Philip Freake, Mr. James Hollidge, Francis Rogers, Thomas Goldney, Thomas Clements, Thomas Coutes, John Corsely, John Duckinfield, Richard Hawksworth, William Saunders, John Grant, Laurence Hollister, and Daniel Hickman, Merchants in Bristol.

Gentlemen,

As you did me the Honour to approve my Proposals for the following Voyage, and generously fitted out two Ships, in which you gave me the principal Command; I no sooner resolv'd to publish my Journal, than I determin'd to chuse you for my Patrons: and thereby to take an opportunity of expressing my Gratitude to you, who had the Courage to adventure your Estates on an Undertaking, which to Men less discerning seem'd impracticable.

I heartily congratulate you on the Success and Profit of this Long and Hazardous Voyage; which might have been greater, but the following Sheets will show it was not my fault.

I shall only add on this Head, that I used my utmost Endeavours to promote your Interest, which was always prefer'd to my own.

I make no doubt, it will be to your lasting Honour, that such a Voyage was undertaken from Bristol at your Expence; since it has given the Publick a sufficient Evidence of what may be done in those Parts, and since the Wisdom of the Nation has now agreed to establish a Trade to the South-Seas, which, with the Blessing of God, may bring vast Riches to GREAT BRITAIN.

I wish you intire Health and Happiness, and am,

Gentlemen,

— Your most Humble Servant,
Woodes Rogers

This edition is a reproduction of an early original, printed for *A. Bell* at the Cross-Keys and Bible in *Cornhil*, and *B. Lintot* at the Cross-Keys between the two Temple-Gates, *Fleetstreet*, London. MDCCXII.

The Narrative Press LLC.
2041 East A St., Torrington, WY 82240 U.S.A.
Telephone: (800) 315-9005 Web: www.narrativepress.com

ISBN 1-58976-238-X (Paperback)
ISBN13 978-1-58976-238-1 (Paperback)
Produced in the United States of America

CONTENTS

An Introduction

CONCERNING THE SOUTH-SEA TRADE.

The *Spaniards* were always so jealous of this Commerce, that they wou'd never allow the least share of it to any other Nation, but oppos'd them with Force whenever they attempted it. Their Inclination to engross all the Trade of the *West-Indies* to themselves, was so very great, that they have depopulated their own Country to people *that*; and in their Treaties with foreign Princes they were so very cautious as not to allow their Ships so much as to touch on those Coasts, but in cases of extreme Necessity, and even then under very severe Restrictions. Thus till this War began, the vast Wealth of the *Spanish West-Indies* ran in a constant Channel by their own Flota and Galleons to *Cadiz*, where most of the trading Nations of *Europe* had more or less benefit by it. Our *English* Manufactures, *etc.* were annually shipt off in their Galleons, either in the name of *Spanish* Factors, or sold at *Cadiz* to the *Spanish* Merchants, who sent them to the *Indies* on their own accounts; and in Returns we had Gold, Silver, and other valuable Commodities. This was the Course of our publick Trade with that Country, while possess'd by the House of *Austria*. Besides, there was also a private Trade by way of *Jamaica* to their Coasts on the *North Sea*; which was carry'd on with great advantage to the few who thought fie to venture it, but was liable to very great Dangers, because the *Spanish* Guard-Ships made Prize of all they could, and our Men were made Prisoners, or rather Slaves; and their own Subjects, who traded with us, were forc'd to do it by stealth for fear of incurring the severe Penalties of their own Laws. Yet as we were able to furnish them this way with better Commodities, and at easier Rates than they had by their own Galleons; not only their Merchants, but even their Guards did often willingly trade with us in this private manner, when they could do it with safety.

Thus things continu'd till the second Grand Alliance in 1701. when the *French* King, in the name of his Grandson the Duke of *Anjou*, usurp'd the Crown of *Spain*; and the House of *Austria* not being able to recover it themselves did enter into an Alliance with us and the *Dutch*: and in consideration of our Assistance, it was wisely stipulated by King *William*, That for the Enlargement of Navigation and Commerce, it should be lawful for us and the *Dutch* to seize by force what Lands and Cities we could of the *Spanish* Dominions in *America*, and to possess them as our own. The *French* soon after the Peace of *Reswick* seem to have foreseen such an Article, and resolv'd to be beforehand with us. Thus they sent from *Rochelle* in 1698. two Ships under the Command of M. *Beauchesne-Gouin* of *St. Malo* to the *South-Sea*, with a Cargo of Goods, to try what could be done in a Trade there; as appears by his Journal, of which I have a Copy. They have so improv'd his Discovery, and carry'd on such a vast Trade in those Seas ever since, that there have been in the *South-Sea* in one Year seventeen *French* Ships of War and Merchant-Men, with all sorts of Goods: and the Advantage they made by it was so great, that I was inform'd by several Merchants whom we took in those Seas, that by a modest Computation the *French* in the first Years of that Trade carry'd home above 100 Millions of Dollars, which is near 25 Millions

Sterling; besides the Advantages they make by trading to the *North-Sea*, when they convoy the *Spanish* Galleons and Flota to and from the *West-Indies*. By this means they are now absolute Masters of all that valuable Trade, which has enabled their Monarch hitherto to carry on the War against most of the Potentates of *Europe*, which otherwise he could not have done.

'Tis not for me to enquire why the beforemention'd Article of the second Grand Alliance has not been more improv'd, or whether it was practicable to make a national Settlement in the *South-Sea* when the War commenc'd; but that the Thing is practicable in it self, I dare boldly affirm from my own Experience. Had there been a proper Force there when I was in the *South-Sea*, we might easily have settled in many places, where we could have commanded Provisions, without those Difficulties to subsist which we met with. Had a Trade thither been promoted at the beginning of the War, we might not only have prevented the *French* from bringing thoie vast Soms outof *America*, but have brought, much greater our Selves, since we are better provided with Commodities for that Trade, and have a stronger Naval Force to carry it on.

Necessity has frequently put private Men on noble Undertakings; and I think it can't be deny'd that our Nation is now under a necessity to make an extraordinary Effort for settling a Trade there. That we are concern'd to do it for the Preservation of our Liberty and Religion, is evident enough from what has been said already; and that we are likewise oblig'd to do it for the Recovery of our sinking Trade, will be evident from what follows. Our *Spanish* Commerce, which formerly supply'd us with Bullion, yields us so little now, that our Mony must insensibly ebb out of the Nation, whilst it flows into the Enemies Country thro a new Channel, of which he alone is Master; for the *French* not only supply the *South-Seas*, but carry all sorts of Goods, with Negroes, to *Portobello*, *La Vera Cruz*, *Carthagena*, and *Buenos-Ayres*: so that they have outed us both of the publick and private Trade that we formerly had with the *Spanish West-Indies*, which must necessarily stop the Fountain of our Bullion, and affect all the other Branches of our Trade thro the World. Therefore I hope every true *Briton* will approve my Zeal in proposing a way how those threatning and imminent Dangers may be prevented, and cordially join in supporting a Trade to the *South-Sea*, and other parts of the *Spanish West-Indies*, under such Regulations and upon such Encouragements as the Wisdom of the Nation has granted, or may yet think sit to grant.

I am sorry to hear so noble a Design talk'd of with so much Indifference by some, and exploded as impracticable by others; whilst the *French* carry on a Trade thither with so much Success, to the Enriching of themselves and Impoverishment of us: as if 'twere enough to call our selves Masters of the Sea, without proving to the World we are so, on such an important occasion. I find that the want of Success in other Expeditions to *America* has created a mean Opinion in some People of this. I shall not pretend to enquire into the Reasons why those Expeditions have miscarry'd; but I will venture to say, that with the Divine Assistance, this might succeed, if undertaken by Men of Experience and Integrity, under such Regulations as may prevent their disagreeing abroad. This Expedition being altogether new, and of such vast consequence to our Nation, it ought to be adjusted with all the Care and Precaution possible; for I very much doubt, if our first Attempt should miscarry, whether ever we should make a second. I have consider'd all the Objections against it, and find the chief of them to be, *First*, The Difficulty of any number of Ships to keep company so far. *Secondly*, That it won't be easy to furnish Provisions and Stores to carry us thither and back again, if we should not succeed. *Thirdly*, The Improbability of getting thither with Men enough to maintain a Settlement, or to find a proper Place for one, where the adjacent Country can furnish Provisions enough to Subsist 'em. *Fourthly*, That we shall not be able to hinder the *French* from Trading there, or succeed in that Trade our selves.

To these Objections I answer in brief thus: *First*, I found by my own Experience, that with Care it is practicable for Ships to keep company round the World; and 'tis very well known, that considerable numbers of Ships keep company together to and from the *East-Indies*, which is farther. To the second and third, I answer, That our two Ships were much fuller of Men than usual for Vessels of their Burden, and yet we carry'd Provisions that serv'd us sixteen Months; which puts it beyond all dispute that Men of War and Transports may conveniently go on this Expedition, well fitted with Men, and carry twelve months Provisions at least for each Ship. Besides, for every Man of War or Transport that carries considerable Numbers of Men, a proportionable Victualler may be allow'd, with no more Men than are enough to sail her; so that she may carry eight or ten months Provisions more or the other Ships which embark the Men. Thus a sufficient Number fit for a Settlement may be carry'd, and fully victual'd for 22 months, which is time enough, and to spare, to go and return from the South-Seas. And if any Ship should lose company, there's little danger of their meeting again at places appointed for Rendezvous. 'Tis true, the Distance from home is great; but the Ships that have traded thither find it an easy Passage in a proper Season, and their Men continue more healthful than those that trade to the West-Indies by the North-Seas. The general Distemper in such long Runs is the Scurvy; and the Methods to prevent the ill Effects of it are so well known, that they may easily be provided against. The Ships may likewise refresh by the way, first at the Cape de Verd Islands, and then at Brazil, betwixt which and the South-Sea is the longest Passage, and that in all probability cannot exceed ten weeks at Sea; so that when they arrive at Chili, the Climate is so wholesom, and agrees so well with European Constitutions, that such as are sick do speedily recover. Then as to proper Places for a Settlement where Provisions abound, there are so many of them on the Coast of Chili, &c. that a Body of Men well-disciplin'd, and under good Commanders, may easily settle there. Our taking of Guiaquil with a Handful of raw undisciplin'd Men, is a sufficient proof of this; and they may soon fortify themselves so, as no Power that can be brought against them shall be able to dislodg them. The whole Spanish Force in that Sea consists but of three small Ships, and their Land-Troops are so little accustom'd to War, that they are not able to look a Body of disciplin'd Men in the face; as we our selves, and others, have found by experience. Besides, the Natives of Chili, who are a brave People, have such an aversion to the Spaniards because of their Cruelty and Oppression, that when they find the Mildness of an English Government, they will readily join us, in order to be freed from that intolerable Servitude under which they have groan'd so long.

By all this it appears, that we have no Enemy to dread but the *French*; and since we are Superior to them by Sea, there's no doubt but our Government, who countenances this Settlement, will take due care to protect any Colony till it be able to defend it self.

To the last Objection I answer, That as we are capable to furnish that Country with better Commodities, and at cheaper Rates than the *French*, there's no doubt of our carrying the Trade, or at least that we shall have the best share of it. And that we shall find a Trade there, is evident, considering what a great Vent the *Spaniards* had for *European* Commodities by way of *Portobello, Carthagena,* and *Panama*; and what a Vent the *French* do now meet with for such Commodities in the *South-Seas*; which are brought to them so much cheaper than by the old way, that the *Spanish* Trade by the Flota and Galleons from *Old Spain* will be lost.

What I have said here, is on the supposition that the War may continue; but when there's a Peace, we cannot doubt but the Government will take care to remove all those Impediments, which are the natural Result of a War, by the Treaty, and get those Restraints taken off, which the *Spaniards* have hitherto laid upon our Trade to those parts; and in that case, the Inhabitants of the *West-Indies*, who have a very great aversion to the *French*, will be more willing to trade with us than ever they were to deal with them But whether we have War or Peace, there is no carrying on a fix'd Trade without a Settlement; which, if we have a Peace, must be granted us; and if we have War, may easily be taken by Force. But I doubt 'tis scarce possible in time of a Peace to bring the Course of Trade on the same foot as in King *Charles* It's time; for 'tis very much to be fear'd, if King *Philip* continue possess'd of *Spain* and the *Indies*, the *French* will still have as great an Interest in *Old Spain* to make us trade there at a disadvantage, as they have already done in *France*, and at the same time continue the carrying on of a *South-Sea* Trade underhand, now they have found the vast Advantage of it. And since the Government there is wholly in their Interest already, and will be more confirm'd in it when *Philip* is left Master of the Country by Treaty, we cannot be upon an equal footing with them: for the two Crowns of *France* and *Spain* being in one Family, whose Ambition for an Universal Monarchy has hitherto broke thro all Treaties, 'tis too much to be dreaded, that if King *Philip* be left in possession of *Spain* and the *Indies*, we shall not have an equal Advantage of Trade with *France*; who, I cannot but doubt, will still have the same Advantages they now have, which must endanger the Liberty of all *Europe*. And therefore 'tis my humble Opinion, we have little probability that ever a Trade can be settled to and from *Spain* and the *Indies* as formerly, whilst there's a *French* Monarch in *Spain*. So that all our Pretensions of a Trade to the *South-Sea*, unless settled in our possession during the War, and confirm'd by a Peace, are little to be depended upon.

I ought to beg pardon for meddling with Politicks, which is none of my Province; but having been on the spot, I think it a Duty which I owe to my Country to hint what occur'd to my own Observation, that due Precautions may be taken to prevent the Dangers that threaten our Settlement there or Trade thither; which I have only hinted, and leave the Improvement to those whose business it is, and are more capable Judges.

I am sensible that a great deal more is to be said upon this Head, and that the Matter might have been better digested; but my Hurry and the Pressure of my particular Affairs have been such since my Return home, that I must reserve my self to another opportunity, to enlarge and explain what I have here but glanc'd at.

So much at present for a Trade to the *South-Sea*; that which follows is what I ought to say by way of Preface to the Voyage it self, which by the Blessing of God we perform'd.

I was not fond to appear in Print; but the Solicitations of my Friends who had read my Journal, and the mistaken Reports that were spread abroad of our Voyage, prevail'd with me at last to publish it.

I know 'tis generally expected, that when far distant Voyages are printed, they should contain new and wonderful Discoveries, with surprising Accounts of People and Animals; but this Voyage being only design'd for cruising on the Enemy, it is not reasonable to expect such Accounts here as are to be met with in Travels, relating to History, Geography, etc. Something of that however I have inserted to oblige the Booksellers, who persuaded me that this would make it more grateful to some sort of Readers: But I have confin'd my self to those parts which are most likely to be frequented for Trade, and quoted my Authors from whom I had the Collections; which I did not insert at random, but when I found them to agree with the Relations of those who had been in the places, or with the Accounts of the Natives, with whom I had opportunities to converse. The rest is from my own knowledg, being a Description of those Places we were at, with such Remarks as occur'd to my Observation, and that I thought might be useful to them who may hereafter trade to those parts. I had not time, were it my Talent, to polish the Stile; nor do I think it necessary for a Mariner's Journal.

'Tis usual for such Undertakings to be much talk'd of, which raises Mens Expectations beyond what the Performance can possibly answer, and occasions Censures on the Persons concern'd, if they happen to fall short of those mighty Ideas that People are apt to conceive.

'Tis also a particular Misfortune which attends Voyages to the *South-Sea*, that the Buccaneers, to set off their own Knight-Errantry, and to make themselves pass for Prodigies of Courage and Conduct, have given such romantick Accounts of their Adventures, and told such strange Stories, as make the Voyages of those who come after (and cannot allow themselves the same liberty) to look flat and insipid to unthinking People. Therefore I make it my Request to the candid Readers, that they would be favourable in their Censures when they peruse this Journal, which is not calculated to amuse them, but barely to relate the Truth.

I must add concerning these Buccaneers, that they liv'd without Government; so that when they met with Purchase, they immediately squander'd it away, and when they got Mony and Liquor, they drank and gam'd till they spent all; and during those Revels there was no distinction between the Captain and Crew: for the Officers having no Commission but what the Majority gave them, they were chang'd at every Caprice, which divided them, and occasion'd frequent Quarrels and Separations, so that they cou'd do nothing considerable; and for any thing I could learn, they scarce shew'd one Instance of true Courage or Conduct, tho they were accounted such fighting Fellows at home.

It was to avoid such Disorders as these, that the following Constitution was prudently agreed on by our Owners.

The Constitution of a Council, for directing the Affairs of the Ships Duke and Dutchess in their Voyage to America.

FOR the better Government and Regulating of Affairs of the present Voyage, we whose Names are underwritten, Owners and appointed Directors for the Ships Duke and Dutchess, do hereby appoint and constitute Capt. Woodes Rogers Commander, Capt. Tho. Dover second Captain and Captain of the Marines, Capt. William Dampier Pilot, Mr. Garleton Vanbrugh Owners Agent, Mr. Green chief Lieutenant, Mr. Frye second Lieutenant, Mr. Charles Pope, Mr. Glendal, Mr. Ballet, and Mr. Wasse, all Officers on board the Duke, to be Council on board the said Ship: and Capt. Stephen Courtney, Capt. Cook his second Captain, Mr. William Stretton Lieutenant, Mr. Bath Owners Agent, Mr. John Rogers, Mr. White, and the Master-Officers on board the Dutchess, to be the Council on board the said Ship, in case they should be separated from each other: but when in company, the Officers of both Ships abovenam'd are conjunctly at the Summons of the Captains Rogers, Dover, and Courtney, or any two of them, to come on board either Ship, and be the Council refer'd to in our general Orders, to determine all Matters and Things whatsoever, that may arise or be necessary for the general Good, during the whole Voyage.

In cafe of Death, Sickness, or Desertion of any of the above Officers of either Ship, the rest that are of the Council appointed as aforesaid for the Ship, shall Convene on board their own Ship, and chuse another fit Person into that Office and Council.

We farther require and direct, that all Attempts, Attacks, and Designs upon the Enemy, either by Sea or Land, be first consulted and debated on in the general Council, if together; and as the Majority thereof shall conclude how or when to act or do, it shall be indispensably, and without unnecessary Delay, put chearfully in execution.

In cafe of any Discontents, Differences, or Misbehaviour among the Officers and Men, which may tend to the disturbance of the good Concord and Government on board either, the Men or Persons may appeal to the Captain to haw a Hearing and Decision by a Council, or the Captain shall call a Council, and have it heard and decided, and may prefer or displace any Man according to Desert. All Decisions and Judgments of this Council shall be finally determin'd by the Majority of Voices; and in case of an Equality, Capt. Dover is to have the double Voice, as President of the Council; and we do accordingly order him to be President.

All Matter transacted in this Council shall bi register'd in a Book, by the Clerk appointed for that purpose. Dated in Bristol, July 14. 1708.

John Batchelor, Christ. Shuter, James Hollidge, Thomas Goldney, Francis Rogers.

But several of these Officers were alter'd, and their Names fill'd up by others, to the number of sixteen in all, before we left Ireland; of which nine were allotted to be Council aboard the Duke, and seven in the Dutchess. I have omitted the rest of our Orders, as being not so remarkable, but common in all such Cases.

In pursuance of this Constitution, we held frequent Councils to make such Agreements as Occasion requir'd, that the Officers who sign'd them might see them put in execution; for without this method we could never have perform'd the Voyage, nor kept together.

Privateering at so great a distance is but an indifferent Life at best, especially with so small a Force as ours, and when oblig'd to depend upon Chance or the Enemy's Courtesy for Provisions.

Another Inconveniency we labour'd under, was the want of Power to try Offenders, as aboard her Majesty's Ships of War; which oblig'd us to connive at many Disorders, and to be mild in our Punishments: but which was still worse, there was no sufficient Power lodg'd in any one hand to determine Differences amongst our chief Officers; which was a great Omission, and might have prov'd of dangerous Consequence, because of the Divisions which happen'd among us.

I should not have mention'd this, neither here nor in my Journal, had not more of it been already publish'd than I think was convenient, since the knowledg of our petty Differences do no way concern the Publick: but since a part has been publish'd, I thought my self oblig'd in Justice to my own Reputation, and for the Information of my Friends, to write what I have done; tho I have only touch'd it where I could not avoid it, and as softly as possible, keeping strictly to the Truth, in which I am not afraid of any Contradiction worth notice.

As the first Command lay on me, I had also the Care and Trouble to propose and draw up almost every Resolution and Agreement; which if they be not exactly according to Form, I hope will be readily excus'd, being such as the Necessity of our Affairs oblig'd us to make from time to time: and the Law being none of my Study, I was oblig'd to do the best I could in this cafe, where all must be voluntary; for we had no power of Compulsion, nor any other Rule to direct us but our Owners Instructions, which 'twas impossible to accommodate to all Emergencies in an Undertaking of this nature, and at so great a distance. The Reader may perhaps think I took too much upon me, since Capt. *Dover* was President of our Council, and had two Voices: To which I answer, That tho he had that Office in Council, yet he was but third in Command in other respects, according to the Instructions given me by our Employers.

Others may possibly object against the relating of so many particular Incidents: but my Design in it was to confirm the Truth of my Journal, and to satisfy the Curious by what methods 'twas we perform'd the Voyage, and kept together under so many Difficulties; which may be of use to others that hereafter undertake the like.

From our first setting out, I took the best method to preserve an unquestionable Relation of the Voyage, by having a daily Account kept in a publick Book of all our Transactions, which lay open to every one's View; and where any thing was reasonably objected against, it was corrected. This Method we observ'd during the whole Voyage, and almost in the fame manner as you have it in the following Relation.

Memorandum.

Since I advertis'd my publishing this Book, the Booksellers have thought it their Interest to hurry out a Continuation of *Cook's* Voyage; in which they have attempted at the Views of several Harbours and Sights of

Land in the *South-Sea*: which tho not done so effectually as I intended in mine, yet it has prevented my Intention of Engraving the Harbours; which, on second Consideration, may at a proper time be better publish'd separate in a Coasting-Pilot-Book for that Trade.

Chapter I

THO others, who give an Account of their Voyages, do generally attempt to imitate the Stile and Method which is us'd by Authors that write ashore, I rather chuse to keep to the Language of the Sea, which is more genuine, and natural for a Mariner. And because Voyages of this fort have commonly miscarry'd, 'tis necessary that I should keep to my Original Journal; that the Methods we took to succeed in our Designs, may appear from time to time in their native Light: Therefore without any disguise I shall publish the Copies of all our material Regulations and Agreements, and keep to the usual Method of Sea-Journals, omitting nothing that happen'd remarkable to our selves, or that may serve for Information or Improvement to others in the like Cafes. Every day's Transactions begin at the foregoing Day about twelve a Clock, and end at the same Hour the following Day carrying that Date.

Since Custom has likewise prevail'd for Sailors to give an Account of such Countries upon whose Coasts they touch or pass by, I shall so far comply with it, as to give a Description of those that occur'd in the Course of my Navigation, especially of such as are or may be of most use for enlarging our Trade; wherein I have consulted the best Authors upon the Subject, and the Manuscript Journals of others, as well as inform'd my self by Inquiry upon the Spot, and from those that have been in the respective Countries I treat of.

August 2. Yesterday about four in the Afternoon we weigh'd from *Kingroad* near *Bristol*, on board the *Duke-Frigot*, whereof Capt. *Woodes Rogers* was Commander, in Consortship with the *Dutchess*, Capt. *Stephen Courtney* Commander; both private Men of War, bound to *Cork* in *Ireland*, and thence to the Southward a cruising; the *Duke* Burden about 320 Tuns, having 30 Guns and 117 Men; and the *Dutchess* Burden about 260 Tuns by Measure, 26 Guns and 108 Men: both well furnish'd with all Necessaries on board for a distant Undertaking.

We had in Company the Scipio, Peterborough-Frigot, Prince Eugene, Bristol-Galley, Berkely-Galley, Beecher-Galley, Pompey-Galley, Sherstone-Galley, and Diamond-Sloop. At ten at night having little Wind, we made the Signal for the Fleet to anchor, between the Holms and Minehead. We lay near two hours, and about twelve we fir'd a Gun, and all came to sail, a fine Gale at S E. and E S E. We ran by Minehead at six in the morning, having stem'd the Flood from the place we anchor'd at. We came up with a Sloop about ten a clock; but she could not hold way with the Fleet, being all light and clean Ships, and good Sailors.

August 3. The Wind veer'd to the N E. and E N E. Our Ship and the *Dutchess* did not sail so well as the major part of the Gallies, our Masts and Rigging being all unfit for the Sea, our Ships out of trim, and every thing in disorder, being very indifferently mann'd; notwithstanding our Number, we had not 20 Sailors in the Ship, and it's very little better on board the *Dutchess*; which is a Discouragement, only we hope to get some good Sailors at *Cork*. We saw a Sail at five list night, the Dutchess gave chase, and came near her; she seem'd a large Ship, but we lost sight of her at eight a clock. Being inform'd at *Bristol* that the *Jersy*, a *French* Man of War carrying 46 Guns, was cruising betwixt *England* and *Ireland*, it oblig'd us to keep our Hammocks up, and a clear Ship for a Fight, all night. About two this morning the rest of the Fleet that lay a-stern of us came up, and we kept an easy Sail, with a Light out all Night; but when Day came, we saw nothing, so that this prov'd a false Alarm: which happen'd well for us, since had it been real, we should have made but an indifferent Fight, for want of being better mann'd.

Aug. 4. The *Bristol-Galley*, *Berkley-Galley*, *Prince Eugene*, and the *Beecher-Galley*, being bound to the Westward, left us at six in the Evening; little Wind at E S E. and Smooth Water.

Aug. 5. We Saw the Land, and finding we had overshot our Port, came to an anchor at twelve a clock off of the two Rocks call'd the *Sovereigns Bollacks* near *Kinsale*, being calm.

Aug. 6. About eight last night we weigh'd with the Flood, a small Gale at East; it came on to blow, and veer'd to the Northward. We had a *Kinsale* Pilot on board, who was like to have endanger'd our Ship, it being dark and foggy. Before day he would have turn'd us into the next Bay to the Westward of *Cork*, had not I prevented it; which provok'd me to chastise him for undertaking to pilot a Ship, since he understood his Business no better. The rest of our Company, except the *Diamond* and *Sherstone-Galley*, got into *Cork* before us; only our Consort staid in the Harbour's Mouth till we came up with her.

Aug. 7. Yesterday at three in the Afternoon we came to an anchor with our Consort in the Cove, Wind at N N E.

Aug. 8. Came in the *Arundel* a Queen's Ship, and order'd us to strike our Pendant; which we immediately did, all private Commission Ships being oblig'd by their Instructions to pay that Respect to all her Majesty's Ships and Fortifications.

Aug. 9. Yesterday Afternoon came in the *Hastings* with the Fleet Under her Convoy, which we left in *Kingroad*: as also the *Elizabeth*, a Merchant-Ship of 500 Tuns, about 26 Guns, and well mann'd, with a Fleet under her Convoy from *Leverpool*, bound to the Westward, with us and the *Hastings*, &c. Fair Weather, the Wind Southerly.

Aug. 10. We were well pleas'd with the Men Mr. *Noblett Rogers* got for us at *Cork*; upon which we clear'd several of those brought from *Bristol*, and some of 'em run away, being ordinary Fellows, and not fit for our Employment.

Aug. 11. It blow'd fresh and dirty Weather; we had four Lighters from *Cork* to discharge our Ships, that we might have them well stow'd, and the Provisions in the bottom when they came aboard us. We lengthen'd our Mizen-Mast four Foot and a half, by placing it on a Step on the Gun-Deck; got our Fore-Mast forward, and did what we could in order to be in a better trim than before, against we had better Men to work the Ship, who lay all ready to come aboard from *Cork*.

Aug. 12. Blew fresh, and dirty Weather; we clear'd and run near forty of our fresh-water Sailors. The *Shoreham*, Capt. *Saunders*, came hither to convoy a Fleet back to *Bristol*.

Aug 16. Continu'd dirty Weather, so that we could not have an Opportunity to heel our Ship and clean her Bottom; and were forc'd to keep our Provisions cover'd in the Lighter, and Men to watch 'em. This Morning about ten, one Boat loaded with Men came down from *Cork* to us. The Fellows appear'd to be brisk, but of several Nations; and I sent to Mr. *Rogers* to stop the rest till we were ready, our Ships being pester'd.

Aug. 28. Nothing happen'd worth notice since the 16th, but that we had good Weather to clean and tallow our Ships five Streaks below the Water-Line, and to take in our Provisions and Men, &c. This Morning we fell down to the *Spit-end* by the *Hastings* Man of War, as our Consort did the night before. When I came without the *Spit-end*, I saluted the *Hastings* with seven Guns; they return'd five, and I three for Thanks. We had now above double the number of Officers usual in Privateers, and a large Complement of Men to each Ship. We took this Method of doubling our Officers to prevent Mutinies, which often happen in long Voyages, and that we might have a large Provision for a Succession of Officers in each Ship, in case of Mortality. Our Ship was now so full, that we sent our Sheet-Cable and other new Store Cordage to Mr. *Noblett Rogers* at *Cork*, to make room for our Men and Provisions; having three Cables besides, and being willing rather to spare that, than any thing else we had aboard. Our Crew were continually marrying whilst we staid at *Cork*, tho they expected to sail immediately. Among others there was a *Dane* coupled by a Romish Priest to an *Irish* Woman, without understanding a word of each other's Language, so that they were forc'd to use an Interpreter; yet I perceiv'd this Pair seem'd more afflicted at Separation than any of the rest: The Fellow continu'd melancholy for several days after we were at Sea. The rest understanding each other, drank their Cans of Flip till the last minute, concluded with a Health to our good Voyage, and their happy Meeting, and then parted unconcern'd.

I think it necessary to set down here the Names of all the Officers in both Ships, with the Number of our Men; because it is proper, that the Persons whom this Journal concerns, should be known.

Officers of the Duke.

Woodes Rogers, Captain, a Mariner; *Thomas Dover*, a Doctor of Physick, second Captain, President of our Council, and Captain of the Marines; *Carleton Vanbrugh*, Merchant, now our Owners Agent; *Robert Fry* a Mariner, chief Lieutenant; *Charles Pope*, Second Lieutenant; *Thomas Glendall*, third Lieutenant; *John Bridge*, Master; *William Dumpier*, Pilot for the *South-Seas*, who had been already three times there, and twice round the World; *Alexander Vaughan*, chief Mate; *Lanc.*

Appleby, Second Mate; *John Ballet*, rated third Mate, but design'd Surgeon, if occasion; he had been Captain *Dampier's* Doctor in his last unfortunate Voyage round the World; *Samuel Hopkins* being Dr. *Dover's* Kinsman and an Apothecary, was both an Assistant to him, and to act as his Lieutenant, if we landed a Party any where under his Command during the Voyage; *George Underhill* and *John Parker*, two young Lawyers design'd to act as Midshipmen; *John Vigor*, a Reformado, to act as Capt. *Dover's* Ensign when ashore; *Benj. Parsons* and *Howel Knethel*, Midshipmen; *Richard Edwards*, Coxswain of the Pinnace, to receive Midshipmens Pay; *James Wasse*, Surgeon; *Charles May*, his Mate; *John Lancy*, Assistant; *Henry Oliphant*, Gunner, with eight Men call'd the Gunner's Crew; *Nath. Scorch*, Carpenter; *John Jones*, his Mate, with three Assistants; *Giles Cash*, Boatswain; and *John Pillar*, his Mate; *John Shepard*, Cooper, with two Assistants; *John Johnson, Thomas Young, Charles Clovet*, and *John Bowden*, all four Quarter-Masters; *John Finch*, late wholesale Oilman of *London*, now Ship's Steward; *Henry Newkirk*, Sail-maker; *Peter Vandenhende*, Smith and Armourer; *William Hopkins*, Ship's Corporal, Capt. *Dover's* Serjeant, and Cook to the Officers; *Barth. Burnes*, Ship's Cook.

Officers of the Dutchess.

Stephen Courtney, Captain, a Mariner; *Edward Cook*, second Captain; *William Stretton*, chief Lieutenant; *John Rogers*, second Lieutenant; *John Connely*, third Lieutenant; *William Bath*, Owners Agent; *George Milbourn*, Master; *Robert Knowlman*, chief Mate; *Henry Duck*, second; *Simon Hatley*, third; *James Goodall*, fourth; and *William Page*, fifth Mate: With all other inferior Officers much the same as aboard the *Duke*. Most of us, the chief Officers, embrac'd this Trip of Privateering round the World, to retrieve the Losses we had sustain'd by the Enemy. Our Complement of Sailors in both Ships was 333, of which above one Third were Foreigners from most Nations; several of her Majesty's Subjects on board were Tinkers, Taylors, Hay-makers, Pedlers, Fidlers, etc. one Negro, and about ten Boys. With this mix'd Gang we hop'd to be well mann'd, as soon as they had learnt the Use of Arms, and got their Sea-Legs, which we doubted not soon to teach 'em, and bring them to Discipline.

Sept. 1. We took failing Orders, the better to keep Company with the *Hastings* and Fleet: and after having agreed with our Consort, Captain *Courtney*, on Signals between us, which are so common that I need not insert them here, and appointed places of Rendevouz in case of Separation, and how long to lie for each other at every place; about ten this Morning, we came to sail with the *Hastings* and about 20 Merchant Ships, bound to the Southward and Westward, Wind at N by W. We should have fail'd yesterday, but could not weigh and cast our Ships clear of the rest; some at that time drove, and the *Sherstone-Gally* run quite ashore on the *Spit*: in the night it grew moderate Weather, and Captain *Paul* got her off to sail with us. Our Holds are full of Provisions; our Cables, a great deal of Bread, and Water-Casks between Decks; and 183 Men aboard the *Duke*, with 151 aboard the *Dutchess*: so that we are very much crouded and pester'd Ships, not fit to engage an Enemy, without throwing Provision and Stores over-board.

Sept. 2. We and our Consort stood out of the Fleet to chase a Sail we saw to Windward: Our Ships sail'd as well as any in the Fleet, not excepting the Man of War: so that we began to hope we should find our heels, since we go so well tho deep loaden and pester'd. We found the Chase to be a small Vessel coming into the Fleet from *Baltimore*, one *Hunt* Master, call'd the *Hope-Gally*, a small *French*-built Snow belonging to Mr. *James Vaughan* of *Bristol*, bound for *Jamaica*, Wind at N by W. Moderate Weather.

Sept. 3. The Wind very veerable from the W S W. to the N W, blow'd strong with Squalls, so that we reef'd often, and our Ship was a little leaky in her upper Works.

Sept. 4. It blew fresh this Morning, but not so much Wind as Yesterday, and the Water smoother. Captain *Paul* made a Signal for me, Capt. *Courtney*, and Capt. *Edwards* Commander of the *Scipio*; and after speaking with him, he sent his Boat for us, being larger than ours. We with Capt. *Dover* and Mr. *Vanbrugh* went in her, and din'd with Capt. *Paul* aboard his Ship, where we were very handsomly treated. He propos'd to me and Consort when he left the Fleet, which would be very soon, to cruise a few days together off Cape *Finister*, after having ask'd us what we wanted that he could supply us with.

He gave us Scrubbers, Iron Scrapers for our Ships Bottom, a speaking Trumpet, and other things that we wanted: but he would accept nothing from us, because our Voyage would be long; but told us, he should be well pleas'd if our Owners return'd him the same Necessaries for his Ship when he return'd. Wind from the N N W. to the N W by W. moderate.

Sept. 5. We came from on board Capt. *Paul* to our own Ships, yesterday at six in the Afternoon; and now thought it fit to discover to our Crew whither we were bound, that if any Disorders should have risen upon it, we might have exchang'd our Malecontents whilst in Company with one of her Majesty's Ships. But I found no Complaint on board the *Duke*, except from one Fellow who expected to have been. Tything-Man that year in his Parish, and said his Wife would be oblig'd to pay Forty Shillings in his Absence: but seeing all the rest willing, he was easily quieted, and all Hands drank to a good Voyage. I and Capt. *Courtney* writ to our Owners, Alderman *Bachelor* and Company, in the same Letter, a Method we design'd to continue in the whole Voyage, for all things that related to it. A brisk Gale and clear Weather.

Sept. 6. The *Hastings* and we parted at six last night. The reason why we did not keep him longer Company, was our Ships being very full, and our Consort unwilling to lose time so near home; so that we were oblig'd to break Measures with Capt. *Paul*. I excus'd it to him, and saluted him, which he answer'd, and wish'd us a prosperous Undertaking. Wind N by W. and clear Weather. Our Ship does not sail so well as she did two days before. The *Crown-Gally* of *Biddiford* keeps us Company bound for the *Maderas*. Wind from N N W. to N by E.

Sept. 8. Every thing now begins to come into Order, we having been hitherto in some Confusion, as is usual in Privateers at first setting out. We had a good Observation. Moderate Weather, Wind at W N W. Lat. 40.10. N. This day the chief Officers din'd on board me, and the next day on board the *Dutchess.*

Sept. 9. Now we begin to consider the Length of our Voyage, and the many different Climates we must pass, and the excessive Cold which we cannot avoid, going about Cape *Horne*; at the same time we had but a slender Stock of Liquor, and our Men but meanly clad, yet good Liquor to Sailors is preferable to Clothing. Upon this we held our first Committee, to debate whether 'twas necessary for us to stop at *Madera*, as follows.

At a Committee held on Board the *Duke Frigate*, resolv'd by the General Consent of the following Persons:

> *THAT both the Ships Duke and Dutchess do touch at Madera, to make a larger Provision of Liquors, the better to carry on our long Undertaking, being but meanly stor'd for so large a Number of Men as are in both Ships; and in case of Separation between this Place and Madera, then to meet at the Island St. Vincent, one of the Cape de Verd Islands, to wood and water our Ships. But if we miss of one another at that Island, or that the first Ship finds it inconvenient for stopping, then to proceed to Praia on St. Jago, another of the same Islands; to wait at both these Islands fourteen Days: And then if the missing Ship does not appear, the other to proceed to the Isle of Grande, in Latitude 23 deg. 30 m. S. on the Coast of Brazil, there to wait three Weeks; and then if we don't meet, let the single Ship pro-*

ceed on the Voyage, according to the Orders given from cur Owners. This is our Opinion this 9th day of September, 1708.

Tho. Dover President, Stephen Courtney, Woodes Rogers, Edward Cooke, William Dampier, Robert Frye, Charles Pope, Carleton Vanbrugh, Tho. Glendall, John Bridge, John Ballet.

Sept. 10. At six in the Morning we saw a Sail; after speaking with our Consort, we both chas'd. I gave the *Dutchess* about a mile start of us, in order to spread the more. It blew fresh, with a great Sea; and the Chafe being to Windward, we crouded extravagantly. Wind at N W.

Sept. 11. At three yesterday Afternoon we came up with the Chase, who bore down right upon us, shewing *Swedish* Colours. I fir'd twice at her before she brought to, then went aboard her with my Yall, Captain *Courtney's* Boat being just before me. We examin'd the Master, and found he came round *Scotland* and *Ireland.* We suspected he had Contraband Goods on board, because some of the Men, we found drunk, told us they had Gunpowder and Cables; so we resolv'd to examine her strictly, put 12 Men on board her, and kept the *Swedes* Master and 12 of his Men on board our Ships. This Morning, after we had examin'd the Men, and search'd the Ship, we found it difficult to be prov'd whether she was a Prize: And not willing to hinder time to carry her into any Harbour to examine her farther, we let her go without the least Embezelment. The Master gave me two Hams, and some rufft dry'd Beef, and I gave him a dozen Bottles of Red-streak Cyder. They saluted us at parting with four Guns: She belong'd to *Stadt* near *Hamburg*, and was a Frigate built Ship of 22 Guns, about 270 Tuns. While I was on board the *Swede* yesterday, our Men mutiny'd, the Ringleaders being our Boatswain, and three other inferior Officers. This Morning the chief Officers having kept with me in the afterpart of the Ship, we confin'd the Authors of this Disorder, in which there was not one Foreigner concern'd. We put ten of the Mutineers in Irons, a Sailor being first soundly whip'd for exciting the rest to join him. Others less guilty I punish'd and discharg'd, but kept the chief Officers all arm'd, fearing what might happen; the Ship's Company seeming too much inclin'd to favour the Mutineers, made me the easier forgive some beg'd Pardon, and others I was forc'd to wink at; however, they began to find their Design frustrated, which was to make a Prize of the *Swede*, who they alledg'd had much Contraband Goods aboard, tho we could see none; yet they obstinately insisted, that we apparently gave away their Interest, by letting her go without plundering her. I labour'd to convince them of the necessity of our making Dispatch, and that if we could make her a Prize, it would unman our Ships too much to send her into any Port, besides other Disadvantages it might procure to our selves and Owners should we be mistaken; which pacify'd the major part. Our Consort's Men were at first very uneasy, but finding the Malecontents quell'd aboard our Ship, they all kept quiet.

Sept. 12. Yesterday the Wind was very little and veerable, and we had an Observation, 34 deg. 30 min. N.

Sept. 13. Those in Irons discover'd others who were Ringleaders in the Mutiny, whom we also punish'd, and consist'd one of them in Irons with the rest. *Alexander Wynter* was made Boatswain instead of *Giles Cash*, one of the Mutineers. Fair pleasant Weather, little Wind at N W by W.

Sept. 14. I agreed with the Captain of the *Crown-Galley* to carry my Boatswain (who was the most dangerous Fellow among the Mutineers) in

Irons with him to *Maderas*. I did not at his first Confinement think of fending him off; but this day a Sailor came aft to the Steeridg Door, with near half the Ship's Company or Sailors following him, and demanded the Boatswain out of Irons. I desir'd him to speak with me by himself on the Quarter-Deck, which he did, where the Officers assisted me, feiz'd him, and made one of his chief Comrades whip him. This Method I thought best for breaking any unlawful Friendship amongst themselves; which, with different Correction to other Offenders, allay'd the Tumult; so that now they begin to submit quietly, and those in Irons beg Pardon, and promise Amendment. This Mutiny would not have been easily lay'd, were it not for the number of our Officers, which we begin to find very necessary to bring our Crew to Order and Discipline, which is always very difficult in Privateers, and without which 'tis impossible to carry on any distant Undertaking like outs. Fine pleasant Weather, and moderate Gales.

It being little Wind, and contrary, we agreed to pass by *Maderas*, and cruise a little amongst the *Canary* Islands for Liquor, to prevent Loss of time: So we took leave of the *Crown-Galley*, who was bound into *Madera*.

Sept. 15. Last night we sent *Giles Cash* aboard her in Irons, with several Letters by the Commander at large to our Owners. We parted at twelve a Clock at night. Fair Weather, very little Wind from W N W. to N by E. had a very good Observation. Latitude 31 deg. 29 min. N.

Sept. 16. I discharg'd the Prisoners from their Irons, upon their humble Submission, and strict Promises of good Behaviour for time to come. While they continu'd in Irons, they had Centries over them, and were fed with Bread and Water. Those that were Officers we restor'd to their Places, and every body was order'd to obey them; *John Pillar* the Boatswain's Mate was advanc'd to be Boatswain, so that we are all quiet again. About eight this morning we saw Land, and found it to be *Salvage's* Island, bearing S.S.W. distant eight Leagues, Latitude 29 deg. 45 min. Wind very little, and veerable, with fair clear Weather.

Sept. 17. Moderate Gales of Wind; the *Salvages* at a distance is not unlike the Island *Lundy* in *Bristol* Channel, about two miles long, a high Island. This Morning we saw the Rock, that appear'd to us a good League to the S W. of the Island, and took it to be a Sail till we came near it. Little Wind between the N N E. and the West.

Sept. 18. At four yesterday in the Afternoon we came in fight of *Pico Teneriff*, bearing S W by W. distant about eight Leagues; steer'd S S E. and S E by S. for *Grand Canaries*. This Morning b bout five a clock we spy'd a Sail under our Lee Bow, between the Islands of *Grand Canaries* and *Forteventura*; we chas'd her, and at 7 came up with her. Our Consort being a little a Head, fir'd a Gun, and made her bring to; she prov'd a Prize, being a *Spanish* Bark about 25 Tuns, belonging to *Oratava* on *Teneriff*, and bound to *Forteventura* with about 45 Passengers; who rejoic'd when they found us *English*, because they fear'd we were *Turks*. Amongst the Prisoners were four Fryars, and one of them the Padre Guardian for the Island *Forteventura*, a good honest old Fellow. We made him heartily merry, drinking King *Charles* the Third's Health; but the rest were of the wrong sort. We us'd them all very well, without searching them, etc. Fresh Gales and fair Weather, Wind from the N N E. to the E S E.

Sept. 19. After we had took the Prize, we stood to the Westward for *Teneriff*, in order to have her ransom'd; where our Agent Mr. *Vanbrugh* press'd to go ashore with some of the Prisoners. At eleven last night the Wind being at N E. when we were very near the Shore, we could hardly weather Cape *Nago*, the Eastermost part of *Teneriff*, till the Wind veer'd to the Northward. We stood off till Day: In the Morning it prov'd moderate, so we stood in for *Oratava*, and sent the *Spanish* Master of the Bark to it in his Boat, being mann'd with some of the Prisoners. Mr. *Vanbrugh* still insisting to go ashore, I consented, tho against my Judgment, and he went with them to treat for the Ransom of the Hull of the Bark; her ьmall Cargo, which consisted in two Butts of Wine, and one Hogshead of Brandy, and other small matters, we design'd for our own use in both Ships, the Agents of each being to take an account of it the first Opportunity. Fresh Gale of Wind at N E.

Sept. 20. About eight this Morning came a Boat off from *Oratava* with a Flag of Truce, and brought a Letter signifying that unless we would immediately restore the Bark and Cargo, Mr. *Vanbrugh* should be detain'd. I sent to Capt., *Courtney*, who agreed with me on an Answer. We stood in with our Ships within a League of the Town, to tow in the Boat for Dispatch, and about eleven they went ashore again. Wind at N E by E. very fresh.

The Letter sent us was as follows:

Capt. Rogers and Capt. Courtney;

Gentlemen, Port Oratava, 20 Sept. 1708.

Your Lieutenant coming ashore, and having given an account to our Governor of your having taken a Boat belonging to this place bound to Forteventura: we must inform you that her Majesty is graciously pleas'd to allow a Trade between her Subjects and the People of these Islands, whereof we suppose you are not ignorant; and that it is approv'd of not only by his Catholick Majesty, but also by the most gracious Christian King, who has sent express Orders unto his Consul here, that none of his Men of War or others shall molest any Ship trading to these islands: and there has been actually an Example of a Ship belonging to the Subjects of her Britannick Majesty, which was taken by a French Privateer, and upon due Application to the French Consul, the Ship was restor'd. Wherefore we are all of Opinion, that there can be no room for your making a Prize of this Spanish Bark; for it will be extremely prejudicial to her Majesty's Subjects that reside here, and likewise to those in England trading hither, by prohibiting of all future Trade, by masking more than sufficient Reprisal upon our Effects here, and perhaps on our Persons, by reason of the evident Breach on our part of the stipulated Trade which has been concerted with us. Wherefore we must once more desire you to restore the Spanish Bark, as you will answer the contrary before her Majesty, who has so far approv'd of the private Trade, that she was pleas'd to allow of two Men of War (viz. the Dartmouth Capt. Cock, and the Greyhound Capt. Hariot) the last year, who had express Orders to molest in no manner of way any Vessel belonging to the Spaniards; which accordingly they observ'd. Wherefore as you have a due Regard to what is so much the Interest of her Majesties Subjects, we expect at the return of this Boat, that you will make Restitution of the said Bark, otherwise Mr. Vanbrugh will not be permitted to go off, and there will be extravagant Reprisals made upon our Estates and Persons, which we expect you will take into your Consideration: and we cannot omit to let you know, that there is now a Spanish Bark actually in England, which is daily expected with other English ships to load Wine, which they will not be admitted to do, in case you don't restore this Bark. We don't doubt but the People here out of Complaisance will make you some acknowledgment of a Refreshment.

Gentlemen,

Your very humble Servants,

J. Pouldon, Vice-Concul, J. Crosse, Bernard Walsh, G. Fitz-Gerald.

Pray excuse Haste, that we have not time to transcribe. The rest of the Merchants are in the City where our Governor generally resides, being about six Leagues hence.

Our Answer was thus:

On board the Duke-Frigat, Sept. 20.

Gentlemen,

We have yours, and observe its Contents; but having no Instructions given us with our Commission relating to Spanish Vessels trading amongst these Islands, we can't justify the parting with this Bark on your single Opinions. It was Mr. Vanbrugh's misfortune to go ashore; and if he is detain'd, we can't help it. To have convinc'd us satisfactorily of what you say, you ought to have sent us a Copy of her Majesty's Orders or Proclamation; but we doubt there's no such thing in this case. If Mr. Vanbrugh is unjustly detain'd, we'll carry the Prisoners we have on board to the Port we are bound to, let the Consequence be what it will. We are requir'd to be accountable no farther than we are oblig'd by our Instructions, which we have given sufficient Security already to follow, and don't fear a Premunire when we comply with them.

We know Fishing-Boats are excus'd on both sides, and all trading Vessels from Rio la Hache to the River of Chagre in the Spanish West-Indies. We admire the Master and Passengers should be so ignorant of a thing so necessary to be known by 'em, for we never had the least word or intimation from them of what you write. The Example you give us of a Trade here allow'd by the French King and Duke of Anjou, we don't admire at, because it is for tire Benefit of the Spaniards; and we know the English Ships are protected no farther than in Anchor-Ground: and since we took this Vessel at Sea, we shan't part with her unless on our own Terms. If you are positive in what you wrote us, and conscious what detriment it will be to the English Trade, you have no way to prevent it, but immediately to ransom this Bark; and if it be her Majesty of Great Britain's Pleasure, and we are better inform'd in England, then we can justify our Conduct to the Gentlemen that imploy'd us, and you will be again reimburs'd. We shall wait but a short time for an Answer, having Water and Provisions for our selves and Prisoners to the English Settlements, where we are bound. We are apprehensive you are oblig'd to give us this Advice to gratify the Spaniards; and with Respect are,

Gentlemen, Your Humble Servants,

Woodes Rogers, Stephen Courtney.

If you send us Mr. Vanbrugh, and the Man with him, we'll send you the Prisoners; but we'll not part from the Bark, unless ransom'd: tho the Value is not much, we will not be impos'd on. We desire you to use all manner of Dispatch without loss of time, which we can't allow, nor answer it to our Employers.

Sept. 21. At six last night the *Spanish* Boat came again to us with dilatory Answers to our last, insisting on behalf of the *Spaniards*, that the Goods should be return'd 'em, tho they consented to ransom the Bark. To which we immediately return'd an Answer; for we were angry at their Tediousness and our ill Treatment, our time being precious, because we were inform'd that they expected every hour a small Privateer that usually cruis'd off of *Madera*, as also a *Spanish* Ship from the *West-Indies* design'd for *Santa Cruz*: So that it look'd like a Design, to keep us here in suspense till these Ships might get safely in, on the other side of the Island. Our Answer was to this effect: That had it not been out of respect to our Officer on shore, we would not have staid one minute, but would now stay till Morning for their Answer, and take a Cruise among the Islands some time longer than we intended, in order to make a Reprisal; and tho we could not land our Men, would visit the Town with our Guns by eight next morning: adding, that we hop'd to meet with the Governor's Frigat, and should repay his Civility in his own way, but wonder'd that they being *Englishmen* should trifle with us. The Letter had its effect; for this Morning at eight a clock we stood in close to the Town, and spy'd a Boat coming off, which prov'd to be one Mr. *Crosse* an *English* Merchant, and Mr. *Vanbrugh* our Agent with him, with Wine, Grapes, Hogs, and other Necessaries, for the Ransom of the Bark. Upon his coming up, we immediately went to work, discharg'd the Bark, and parted the small Cargo between our two Ships. We treated Mr. *Crosse* as well as we could, and at his desire gave the Prisoners back as much as we could find of what belong'd to their Person's; particularly to the Fryars their Books, Crucifixes, and Reliques. We presented the old *Padre* Guardians with a Cheese, and such as were strip'd, with other Clothes. So that we parted, very well satisfy'd on all sides. Mr. *Crosse* told us the *Spaniards* ashore were very inquisitive whither we were bound; and understanding by the Prisoners that our Ships were sheath'd, and so full of Provisions, they suspected we design'd for the *South-Sea*: and he inform'd us that four or five *French* Ships from 24 to 50 Guns fail'd thence about a month before on the same Voyage. But we did not think fit to own there, that we were bound to any other place than the *English West-Indies*. These Islands being so well known, I need not add any Description of them. We saw the Pike of *Teneriff* plain but once while there, it being generally clouded; you may often see the Top above the Clouds, when the rest is all cover'd with them. Now we are indifferently well stock'd with Liquor, and shall be the better able to endure the Cold when we get the Length of Cape *Horn*, which we are inform'd has always very cold bad Weather near it.

Sept. 22. Last night just as we had finish'd with Mr. *Crosse*, and deliver'd the *Spaniards* their Bark, we Spy'd a Sail to the Westward of the

Island between three and four in the Evening. We immediately made what Sail we could, and steer'd W by N. along the Shore. At eight a clock we were in sight of *Gomera* bearing S S W. distant three Leagues, *Palma* W by N. distant five Leagues. We lost sight of the Sail before Night, spoke with our Consort, and agreed to keep between *Palma* and *Gomera* in our Voyage; it being uncertain to meet with the Chase the next day, since last night she was near five Leagues from us, so that we believ'd she might get into a place of safety, if an Enemy, before we could see her. Besides, there came on a stiff Gale, which put us quite out of hopes of seeing her again to advantage. Fair Weather, fresh Gales at N E by N.

Sept. 23. About five yesterday in the afternoon, when at least 36 Leagues distant, we saw the *Pico Teneriff* very plain. Fine pleasant Weather, fresh Gales with smooth Water, Wind at N E by E.

Sept. 24. We sent our Boat for Capt. *Courtney*, Capt. *Cock*, Mr. *Stratton*, and Mr. *Bath* their Agent, who staid and din'd with us; and whilst they were aboard, we held a Council, the Result of which was as follows.

At a Committee by Desire of Capt. Woodes Rogers, Capt. Thomas Dover, and Capt. Stephen Courtney, held on board the Duke.

WE have examin'd all Letters and Proceedings that happen'd at and after the taking the Spanish Bark, and the Reason of both Ships stay off of Teneriff and amongst the Canary Islands; and we do approve of all that was transacted and wrote: the major part of us having at the time when 'twas done advis'd the Commanders to it. Witness our Hands,

Tho. Dover, Steph. Courtney, Woodes Rogers, Will. Dampier, Edward Cook, Carl. Vanbrugh, William Bath, Pres. William Stratton, Robert Frye, Charles Pope, Thomas Glendal, John Bridge, John Ballet.

Whilst the Committee were together, Mr. Vanbrugh complain'd I had not treated him as I ought: upon which I offer'd to refer it to all present, that we might not have needless Misunderstandings at the beginning of our Voyage; and they came to the following Resolution.

WHERE AS there has been some Difference between Capt. Woodes Rogers and Mr. Carleton Vanbrugh the Ship's Agent; it being refer'd to the Council, we adjudged the said Mr. Vanbrugh to be much in the wrong. In witness whereof, we have set our Hands, the 24th of Sept. 1708.

Tho. Dover, Pres. William Bath,

Stephen Courtney, Charles Pope,

William Dampier, Thomas Glendal,

Edward Cook, John Bridge,

Robert Frye, John Ballet, William Stratton.

Sept. 25. This day, according to custom, we duck'd those that had never pass'd the Tropick before. The manner of doing it was by a Rope thro a Block from the Main-Yard, to hoist 'em above half way up to the Yard, and let 'em fall at once into the Water; having a Stick cross thro their Legs, and well fastned to the Rope, that they might not be surpriz'd and let go their hold. This prov'd of great use to our fresh-water Sailors, to recover the

Colour of their Skins which were grown very black and nasty. Those that we duck'd after this manner three times, were about 60, and others that would not undergo it, chose to pay Half a Crown Fine; the Mony to be levy'd and spent at a publick Meeting of all the Ships Companys, when we return to *England*. The *Dutch* Men and some *English* Men desir'd to be duck'd, some six, others eight, ten, and twelve times, to have the better Title for being treated when they come home. Wind N W by W. and veering to the Northward and Eastward.

Sept. 26. Yesterday in the Afternoon we fold the loose Plunder of the Bark amongst the Sailors by Auction. Fair Weather, moderate Gales at N NE. had a very good Observ. Lat. 21. 33. N.

Sept. 29. Betwixt nine and ten at night, a Sailor going up to furl the Main-Top-Gallant Sail, fell suddenly without any noise from the Main-Top over board, occasion'd as I suppos'd by a Fit. At nine this morning we saw Land, and suppos'd it to be *Sal* one of the Cape *De Verd* Islands, bearing S E by S, distant about 12 Ls. At twelve a clock at noon it bore E S E. dist. 4 Ls. fair Weather, smooth Water, fresh Gales at N E. Lat. 17.5. N. Long. W. from *London*, 23. 16.

Sept. 30. After being satisfy'd the Island was *Sal*, we stood from it W and W by N. for *St. Vincent*. At four a clock *Sal* bore E by S. ¼S. dist. 10 Ls. At six *St. Nicholas* bore S W by W, dist. 8 Ls. We went with an easy Sail till four this Morning, and lay by to make the Islands, because we had none aboard either Ship that was acquainted with 'em. When day broke, we saw the Islands all in a range, much as is laid down in the Draughts. At ten a clock we anchor'd in the Bay of *St. Vincent* in five fathom Water. 'Tis a fine Bay: The Northmost Point bore North near a mile dist. and the Westermost Point bore West dist. about two miles: *Monk's* Rock, which is like a Sugar-Loaf, high and round, and bold on every side, lies almost in the Entrance of this fine sandy Bay on the Westside of the Island: But nearest the North Point of the Bay, Sailors must be careful as they come in, not to run too near under the high Land of the North Point, for fear of being becalm'd, and sudden Flaws coming every way upon 'em. There being a small Shoal about three Ships length almost without the Point, but giving it a small birth it's bold enough: We ran within two Cables length of the first round Point, next to the long sandy Bay, and came to an anchor in clean sandy Ground. *Monk's* Rock bore N W by N. dist. ¾ Mile; the Body of the Island *St. Antonio* bore NW ½ N. dist, nine Miles.

This is a fine Bay and good Landing, but the best at the Northermost Point. The Wood lies in the middle of the sandy Bay, and the Water between the North Point and the place where we anchor'd. There is good Anchoring all over the Bay, and the *Monks*-Rock will direct any Stranger into it, there being no other like it about this Island on the side opposite to *St. Antonio*. It blows here a constant Trader-Wind betwixt the E by N. and the N N E. except in the Months of *October*, *November*, *December*, and *January* it sometimes blows Southerly with Tornadoes and Rain.

October 1. We clear'd our Ship yesterday, but it blow'd too hard to row our Boat-Loads of empty Butts ashoar; and we could do but little to Wooding and Watering, till this morning we were forc'd to get a Rope from the Ship to the watering-place, which is a good half-mile from our anchoring-place, and so haul'd our empty Casks ashore by Boat-loads, in order to have 'em burnt and clean'd in the Inside, being Oil-Casks; and for want of cleaning, our Water stunk insufferably. I borrow'd a Cooper from the *Dutchess*, and having five of my own, made quick dispatch.

Octob. 3. We sent our Boat over to *St. Antonio*, with *Joseph Alexander* a good Linguist, and a respectful Letter to the Governour, who accounts himself a Great Man here, tho very poor, to get in Truck for our Prize-Goods what we wanted; they having plenty of Cattel, Goats, Hogs, Fowls, Melons, Potatoes, Limes, ordinary Brandy, Tobacco, Indian Corn, etc. Our People were very meanly stock'd with Clothes, and the *Dutchess*'s Crew much worse; yet we are both forc'd to watch our Men very narrowly, and punish several of 'em, to prevent their selling what Clothes they have for Trifles to the Negroes, that came over with little things from *St. Antonio's*. The People at all these Islands rather chuse Clothing or Necessaries of any sort than Mony, in return for what they fell. The Letter sent by the Linguist to the Governour of *St. Antonio's*, Senior *Joseph Rodriges* was as follows:

> *Honourable Sir,*
>
> *THE Bearer hereof is one of our Officers, whom we have sent to wait upon your Honour with our due Respects, and to acquaint you with our Arrival in the Bay of St. Vincent; and further, that being Subjects and Servants of her Majesty the Queen of Great Britain, a High Ally and Confederate of his Sacred Majesty the King of Portugal, and having several Necessaries which we suppos'd the Inhabitants of your Island may want, and supposing they can accommodate us per contra, we are desirous of an immediate Traffick with them. We arriv'd three days ago, but being Strangers were unacquainted in these parts, and not sooner inform'd of your Honour's Residence in the neighbouring Islands; else we had been earlier with our Respects: and if not too great a Favour, we should be proud to see your Honour on board. Our Stay cannot exceed two days more, so that Dispatch is necessary. We have Mony or Goods of Several kinds, to pay or exchange for what they bring. The Bearer can inform your Honour of the publick Occurrences of Europe, and the great Successes of the Confederate Arms against the French and Spaniards; which, no doubt must Soon be follow'd with a lasting Peace, which God grant. We subscribe our selves with much Respect,*
>
> *Your Honour's most Obedient Humble Servants,*
>
> *Woodes Rogers, Stephen Courtney.*

Octob. 4. Our Boat return'd this Morning; but the Landing-place being far from the inhabitable part of *St. Antonio*, they brought nothing but a few Limes and Fowls, and left our Linguist behind to get what we wanted. We struck two of our Gun-room Guns into the Hold, being useless in their place, and the Ship having too much top-weight, and not very stiff. We had plenty of Fish here, but not very good. Wind at N N E.

Octob. 5. Our Boat went to *St. Antonio* to see for our Linguist, according to appointment. We heel'd and clean'd our Ships, and got a great deal of Wood and Water aboard. Wind at N E. fine Weather.

Octob. 6. Our Boat return'd with nothing but Limes and Tobacco, and no News of our Linguist. But soon after there came another Boat belonging to that part of the Island where the Governour lives, with his Deputy-Governour, a Negro, who brought Limes, Tobacco, Oranges, Fowls, Potatoes,

Hogs, Bonanoes, Musk and Water-Melons, and Brandy, which we bought of him, and paid in such Prize-Goods as we had left of the Bark's Cargo cheap enough. They are poor People, and will truck at any Price for what they want, in such Payments as they can make.

Octob. 7. We sent our Boat at Three this Morning to See if our Linguist was return'd. The Deputy-Governour told us he promis'd him to wait at the Water-side all that night where we put him ashore, and that there were Cattel for us if we would fetch 'em. We were ready to fail: A good Wind at N E. and a fresh Gale.

Octob. 8. Our Boat return'd yesterday in the Afternoon with two good black Cattel, one for each Ship, but no News of our Linguist; upon which we consulted with the Officers of both Ships, and all unanimously agreed, that we had better leave him behind, than to wait with two Ships for one Man that had not follow'd his Orders. We held a Committee on board the *Dutchess* to prevent Embezlements in Prizes, and to hinder Feuds and Disorders amongst our Officers and Men for the future, because the small Prize had shew'd us, that without a Method to be strictly observ'd in Plunder, it might occasion the worst of Consequences to both Ships, and such Quarrels as would not easily be laid. So with the Consent and Approbation of the Officers appointed for a Committee, we unanimously agreed on it, to prevent those Mutinies and Disorders amongst the Men of both ships, who were not yet reconcil'd since the taking the small *Canary*-Prize. They all insisted there was never any Privateer's Grew hinder'd from Plunder, so that we were forc'd to agree on the following Instrument of a Dividend, when we should meet with any Prize. And that the things we deem'd to be Plunder, according to custom in Privateering, should tend as little as possible to the disadvantage of the Owners, we did for that end take care by the second Article in the said Instrument and Agreement with the Men, to reserve the Power of adjudging what should be deem'd Plunder, unto the superior Officers and Agents exclusive of the Crew, etc. For we found it would be next to a miracle to keep the Men in both ships under Command, and willing to fight resolutely on occasion, if we held 'em to the Letter of Agreement with the Owners, which was not duly consider'd of at home. We had a particular Regard however to the sentiments of the Owners, deliver'd on this head in Discourses at several times with divers of the Committee, as my self, Capt. *Dover,* Capt. *Courtney,* Mr. *Robert Frye,* and Mr. *Carleton Vanbrugh*; and particularly in *Kingroad* to the Men, at the time of signing of their Instrument. By all which we judg'd that the Owners could not but approve of the Measures that we took on this occasion, and that the good effects of 'em would abundantly answer our Intentions. Altho the Officers and Men did voluntarily allow Capt. *Courtney* and me 5 *per Cent.* each, out of the Value of all Plunder, it was much less than our Due; and we would have been glad to have let all alone, provided we could with the Advice of our chief Officers in both Ships have contriv'd any other Method to be safe in the Prosecution of our Designs with our Men, and have kept them to their Duty on all occasions, at so great a distance from home: without their being easy, we must unavoidably have run into such continual Scenes of Mischief and Disorder, as have not only tended to the great Hindrance, but generally-to the total Disappointment of all Voyages of this nature, that have been attempted so far abroad in the Memory of Man. The Agreement we made was as follows.

At a Committee held on board the Dutchess the 8th of October, 1708. it is agreed by the Officers and Men of both Ships to the sundry Particulars following.

1. THAT all Plunder on board each Prize we take by either ship, shall be equally divided between the Company of both Ships, according to each Man's respective whole Share, as ship'd by the Owners or their Orders.

2. That what is Plunder shall be adjudg'd by the superior Officers and Agents in each Ship.

3. That if any Person on board either Ship do conceal any Plunder exceeding one Piece of Eight in value, 24 hours after the Capture of any Prize, he shall be severely punish'd, and lose his Shares of the Plunder. The same Penalty to be inflicted for being drunk in time Action, or disobeying his superior Officer's Commands, or concealing himself, or deserting his Post in Sea or Land-Service; except when any Prize is taken by storm in Boarding, then whatsoever is taken shall be his own, as followed: A sailor or Landman 10l. Any Officer below the Carpenter 20l. A Mate, Gunner, Boatfwain, and Carpenter 40l, A Lieutenant or Master 80l. And the Captains 100l. over and above the Gratuity promis'd by the Owners to such as shall signalize themselves.

4. That publick Books of Plunder are to be kept in each Ship attested by the Officers, and the Plunder to be apprais'd by Officers chosen, and divided as soon as possible after the Capture. Also every Person to be sworn and search'd so soon as they shall come aboard, by such Persons as shall be appointed for that purpose: The Person or Persons refusing, shall forfeit their shares of the Plunder as above.

5. In corsideration that Capt. Rogers and Capt. Courtney, to make both ships Companies easy, have given the whole Cabin-Plunder (which in all probability is the major part) to be divided as aforesaid; we do voluntarily agree, that they shall have 5 per Cent, each of 'em, over and above their respective Shares, as a Consideration for what is their Due of the Plunder aforesaid.

6. That a Reward of twenty Pieces of Eight shall be given to him that first sees a Prize of good Value, or exceeding 50 Tuns in Burden.

7. That such of us who have not sign'd already to the Articles of Agreement indented with the Owners, do hereby oblige our selves to the same Terms and Conditions as the rest of the Ships Company have done; half Shares and half Wages, &c.

To which Articles of Agreement we have set our Hands, as our full Intent and Meaning, without any Compulsion.

Sign'd by the Officers and Men of both ships.

Octob. 8. At seven in the Evening (after having put the Deputy-Governour ashore, where he must lie in a Hole of the Rocks, there being no House on that part of the Island) we came to sail: our Confort got before us, and lay with a Light for us. There were several Negroes on the Island, that came from *St. Nicholas* and *St. Antonio* to make Oil of Turtle, there being very good green Turtle at this time of the Year, which I sometimes gave our Men to eat. They have like-wise wild Goats, but in no great plenty; wild Asses, *Guinea-*

Hens and Kerlews, and abundance of Sea-Fowls. Capt. *Dampier*, and others aboard each Ship, that had formerly stopt at *St. Jago*, another of these Cape *de Verd* Islands, told us, that tho this Island is not often frequented by Ships, yet it is preferable to *St. Jago* for stopping outward, because 'tis a much better Road for Ships, and more convenient for Water and Wood, and has better Landing. The Island is mountainous and barren, the plainest part lies against this sandy Bay where we rode. The Wood that grows in it is short, and for no use but Firing. They have very large Spiders here, which weave their Webs so strong betwixt the Trees, that 'tis difficult to get thro 'em. Where we water'd, there's a little Stream that flows down the Hill from a Spring, and is very good, but in other parts 'tis brackish. This Island was formerly inhabited, and bad a Governor, but is now only frequented in the Season for catching Tortoises by the Inhabitants of the other Islands, who are for the most part Negroes and Mulattoes, and very poor. The Stock of wild Goats in this Island is almost destroy'd by the People of *St. Nicholas* and *St. Antonio*. The Heats are excessive to us who came newly from *Europe*, so that several of our Men began to be sick, and were blooded. Some of our Officers that went ashore a hunting, could meet no Game but a wild Afs, which after a long Chafe they got within shot and wounded; yet he afterwards held out so as to tire them, and they return'd weary and empty-handed.

These Islands are so well known, that I need not say much of 'em. They are ten in number, Of which *St. Jago, St. Nicholas Bonavist, St. Antonio, Brava Mayo*, and *Fuego* are inhabited: The latter is so nam'd from a *Volcano*. *St. Jago* is much the largest and best, and the Seat of the chief Governour. It produces a small matter of Indico, Sugar and Tobacco; which, with their Goat-Skins and others, they send to *Lisbon*, The Capital is of the same Name, and the See of a Bishop. There is also a Town call'd *Ribera Grande*, which is said to consist of 500 Houses, and has a good Harbour towards the West. The Air of this Island is not very wholesom, and the Soil uneven. Their Valleys, produce some Corn and Wine. Their Goats are fat and good Meat, and the she ones are said to bring three or four Kids at a time once in four months. *St. Nicholas*, is the best peopled next to *St. Jago*. The Island *Mayo* has a great deal of Salt naturally made by the Sun from the Sea-Water, which is left from time to time in Pits on shore: It's known they load many Ships with that Commodity in a Year, and are able to furnish some thousands, had they Vent for it. The fine *Marroquin* Leather is made of their Goats-Skins. The other inhabited Islands afford more or less of Privations. They have their Name from Cape *Verd* on the *African* Coast, from whence they lie about 160 Leagues to the Westward. The *Portuguese* settled here in 1572. We had very hot Weather here. On the 8*th* a brisk Gale at E N E. At nine last night *St. Antonio's* bore N W. –by N. dist. 3 Ls. from whence we took our Departure for the Isle of *Grande* in Brazile.

Octob.9. Fair Weather, brisk Gale of Wind at N E. We saw abundance of flying Fish. At 12 a clock being near the Lat. 14 N. we hal'd up S E. by S. to get well to the Eastward, expecting as usual to meet with Southerly Winds, when near the Equinoctial Had an Observ. Lat. 12.. 53.

Octob. 10. Fair Weather, moderate Gales of Wind at. N E by E. These 24 hours we met with several great Riplings as if a Current, which had it been calm we would have try'd.

Octob. 11. Wind and Weather as, before till seven last night, when we had much Lightning follow'd by a hard Shower of Rain, and a Calm enfu'd. Such Weather is customary as we draw near the Line.

Octob. 14. Cloudy Weather, with moderate Gales from the S S W. to the S W by W. all last night; but this morning cloudy Weather, with hard Showers of Rain. This day we put up the Smith's Forge, and he began to work on such things as we wanted.

Octob 21. Yesterday I din'd on board Captain *Courtney.* Nothing remarkable happen'd since the 14th, but veerable Winds and frequent Showers of Rain, with Calms. We agreed with our Consort, if possible, to stop at the Isle *Trinidado,* and not to water and refresh at *Brazile,* for fear of our Mens deserting, and losing our time.

Octob. 22. Close cloudy Weather all night, with Squalls of Rain. At ten this morning it clear'd up: Capt. *Courtney* came aboard of us, and sent back his Boat for Capt. *Cook,* with Orders to bring Mr. *Page,* Second Mate, with him, to be in the room of Mr. *Ballett,* that we exchang'd out of our Ship. *Page* disobeying Command, occasion'd Capt. *Cook,* being the superior Officer aboard, to strike him; whereupon *Page* struck him again, and several Blows past: but at last *Page* was forc'd into the Boat, and brought on board of us. And Capt. *Cook* and others telling us what Mutiny had pass'd, we order'd *Page* on the Fore-Castle into the Bilboes. He begg'd to go into the Head to ease himself; under that pretence the Corporal and the rest left him for a while: upon which he leapt over board, thinking to swim back to the *Dutchess,* it being near calm, and the Captains out of the Ship. However, the Boat being along side, we soon overtook him, and brought him on board again. For which and his abusive Language he was lash'd to the Main-Geers and drub'd; and for inciting the Men to Mutiny, was afterward confin'd in Irons aboard the *Duke.*

Octob. 28. At five last night we were on the Equinoctial, and spv'd a Sail about 4 Leagues dist. to Windward, bearing S by E. and thinking she had not Seen us, we lay by in her way from six a clock till half an hour past ten, hoping to meet her if bound to the *West-Indies;* but it growing dark, and the having, as we suppose, seen us before night, and alter'd her Course, we saw no more or her. This day we began to read Prayers in both Ships Mornings or Evenings, as Opportunity would permit, according to the Church of *England,* designing to continue it the Term of the Voyage. Cloudy Weather, moderate Gales at S E by S.

Octob. 29. This Morning I let Mr. *Page* out of Irons on his humble Submission, and acknowledging his Fault, with Promises of Amendment; Fair pleasant Weather, with a fresh Gale.

*Novemb.*1. This Morning between one and four a clock the Sea Seem'd to be in a Breach as far as we could See, being a Moon-light Night. The Watch being surpriz'd, call'd me up; for they Suppos'd it to be something extraordinary, and hove the Lead: but finding no Ground, were all easy, and afterwards believ'd that it was the Spawn of Fish floating on the Water. Fair Weather, with moderate Gales.

Novemb. 2. This Morning two Persons being accus'd of concealing a Peruke of the Plunder in the *Canary* Bark, two Shirts, and a Pair of Stockings; and being found guilty, I order'd them into the Bilboes: After which they begg'd pardon, promis'd Amendment, and were discharg'd. Pleasant

Weather and moderate Gales of Wind from E S E to S E by S. Had an Observ. Lat. 7.50. S.

Nov. 4. Yesterday about four in the Afternoon we spoke with our Consort, and agreed to bear away for the Island of *Grande* in *Brazile*, it being uncertain to fetch the Island of *Trinidado*; and besides, by the time we could get the length of it, being generally close Weather, and the Sun in the Zenith, we might miss so small an Island; which would prove a great loss of time to us. Close Weather, with a fresh Gale of Wind at S E by E.

Nov. 13. Nothing remarkable since the fourth. We have had the Winds very veerable. Now we draw near the Land, the Wind veers to the Northward, and often strong Gales with hazy Weather. About eleven last night we made a Signal to our Consort and both lay by, thinking our selves to be near the Land. This morning came on moderate Weather, and we made sail again. Wind at N by E.

Nov. 14. This Morning at five we made the Land of *Braile* very plain, bearing N W. We had several Soundings on the Sand call'd in the Maps *Bonfunda* from 28 to 50 Fathom Water; brown fair Sand, with grey Stones amongst it. We had several Showers of Rain with very little Wind from N N E. to N by W. Lat. 22. 9. S.

Nov. 15. At ten a clock last night we had a heavy Turnado with Lightning, which fell as if it had been liquid. While this Storm held, which was not above an hour, we had all our Sails furl'd; yet the Ship lay along very much, Wind at S W. but afterwards calm, and little Wind. The Sun being near the Zenith here at this time, occasions such Weather. As Soon as Day appear'd, we saw the Land bearing West about 7 Ls. dist, a small Breeze at N N W. We stood in with it, but could not be certain what Land it was: we had sundry Soundings from 40 to 50 Fathom Water, coarse Sand.

Nov. 16. Yesterday Evening having a brave Breeze at E. we stood in with the Land, and suppos'd it to be the Island of Cape *Frio*. It makes the Southernmost Land of several other Islands; is high and uneven. This Island appears in two Hills to the Southward: The least looks like a Saddle, and appears at a distance like two Islands, but as you draw near it, you see that it joins.

Nov. 17. This Morning, the Weather being calm, our Pinnace went ashore with Capt. *Dampier* into a sandy Bay about two Leagues off; they brought aboard a large Tortoise which our People eat. The Tortoises on this Coast have a strong Taste. Foggy Weather, and very little Wind from the East to the S W. sometimes calm.

Nov. 19. Yesterday in the Afternoon we came to an anchor in 22 Fathom Water. The East End of the large Island, which we took to be *Grande*, bore W S W dist, about 4 Ls. and there's a high wooing Point at the West end of the low sandy Bay, which at last we run by, about one League and a half from us. We sent our Pinnace ashore well-mann'd to this Point, with Capt. *William Dampier*, in order to be certain whether it was the Entrance of *Grande* between the two Lands. The Boat return'd about ten a clock at night, with a Confirmation that it was the Island of *Grande*, as we had suppos'd: So we immediately weigh'd with a small Breeze; but it soon falling calm, we came to anchor again: then weigh'd with another small Breeze, and row'd and tow'd; by the help of which, at twelve a clock we came to an anchor in the middle of the Entrance of the Island of *Grande* in 11 Fathom water. The

Entrance goes in W by S. a remarkable white Rock on the Larboard side of the Bay bore S E. about a mile and a half. 'Tis a long Entrance near 5 Leagues from the place we anchor'd at.

Nov. 20. Yesterday at one a clock in the Afternoon we sent our Boats in, with a Lieutenant in one Boat, and Capt. *Dampier* in the other, to found all the way to our watering-place, and fee if no Enemy lay there. I borrow'd the *Dutchess* Yall, and kept her a-head sounding; but having a Breeze against us, we got little ground. This morning at four we weigh'd again, with the Wind at N E. and got both into the Bay on the West side of the Isle of *Grande*, but could not reach the Cove where we design'd to water: heavy Showers of Rain took us. At eleven we row'd and tow'd into the Cove, where our Consort had been an hour before us: A *Portuguese* Boat came from a small Cove on our Starboard side as we came in, and told us they had been rob'd by the *French* not long before.

Nov. 21. Yesterday Afternoon it rain'd so hard that our Men could not work. At four a clock Capt. *Courtney* put eight of his Men in Irons for dis-obeying Command; and knowing 'em to be Ringleaders, was willing to secure them whilst here, where they could run away. About six a clock it began to clear up, and our Pinnace with Capt. *Cook* and Lieutenant *Pope* went to *Angre de Reys*, as it's call'd in Sea-Draughts, but the Portuguese call it *Nostra Seniora de la Conception*, a small Village about three Leagues dis-tant, to wait on the Governour, and acquaint him with our Arrival, with a Present of Butter and Cheese, to procure his Friendship if any of our Men should, run away. The Boat return'd at twelve at night, and told us that when they came near the Town it was almost dark; that the People suspecting they were *French*, fir'd on 'em several times, but did no hurt, and when they came ashore begg'd their pardon. The Fryars invited them to the Convent, and told 'em they were often plunder'd by the *French*, or they should not have been so ready to fire at 'em. The Governour was gone to *Riojancro*, a City about 12 Ls. distant, but expected back every day. This morning our Men went in our Boat to hall our Fishing-Net, and caught some very good Fifh much better than those at *St. Vincent*.

Nov. 22. Yesterday Afternoon we got our empty Casks ashore, and sent our Carpenter with a *Portuguese* to look out Wood for Trusle-Trees; our Main and Fore Trusle-Trees being both broke: but the Weather prov'd so wet and Sultry, that we could do little or nothing. Here are abundance of Graves of dead Men; and the *Portuguese* tell us, that two great *French* Ships home-ward bound from the *South Seas*, that water'd in this same place about nine months before, had bury'd near half their Men here; but God be thank'd ours are very healthy. At this place the *French South-Sea* Ships generally water both out and homewards. This Morning we had Several Canoes from the Town, with Limes, Fowls, *Indian* Corn, etc. to exchange for such things as we could spare. We treated 'em all very civilly, and offer'd a Gratuity to such as would secure our Men if any of 'em run away: they all promised to give us good Information, and assist us in searching after 'em.

Nov. 23. This was a fair pleasant Day, but violent hot. We heel'd the *Dutchess* both sides by us, we had a great deal of Wood cut, caught excellent Fish with our Lines, and had Several Canoe from the Town, which inform'd us of a Brigantine at an anchor in the Entrance where we came in. I sent our Pinnace mann'd and arm'd to know what she was, and found her a *Portu-guese* laden with Negroes for the Gold Mines. Our Boat return'd and brought a Present, being a Roove of fine Sugar and a Pot of Sweet-meats from the Master, who Spoke a little *English*, and had formerly fail'd with 'em. The Way that leads to these Gold Mines is not far from this Place by Water, but the *Portuguese* say they lie several days Journy up in the Country; and some will tell you 'tis ten or fifteen days, others a month's Travel from the Town of *Sanetas*, which is the Sea-Port; for they are cautious how they discover the Truth: but there is certainly abundance of Gold found in this Country. They told us, the *French* often Surprize their Boats, and that at one time when the *French* staid to water, which could not exceed a month, they took of Gold above 1200 *l.* weight (in Boats from the Mines bound to *Rio-Janero*, because the Way is not good by Land.)

Nov. 24. Yesterday in the Afternoon we clean'd one side by the *Dutchess*, and this Morning the other side, gave the Ships great Lists; and having Men enough, whilst our Ship was cleaning, we let the Pinnace with Capt. *Dover*, Mr. *Vanbrugh*, and others, go to take their pleasure, but to return by twelve a clock, when we should want our Boat. When they return'd, they brought with them a monstrous Creature which they had kill'd, having Prickles or Quills like a Hedghog, with Fur between them, and the Head and Tail resembled those of a Monkey. It stunk intolerably, which the *Portuguese* told us was only the Skin; that the Meat of it is very delicious, and they often kill'd them for the Table. But our Men being not yet at very short Allowance, none of 'em had Stomach good enough to try the Experiment: so that we were forc'd to throw it overboard, to make a sweet Ship. Soon after came several Canoes with *Portuguese* in 'em, whom we treated very civilly.

Nov. 25. This Day was fair, but very hot. We had three or four Canoes aboard, one of which had three Fathers belonging to the *Franciscan* Convent at *Angre de Reys*. We had got a great deal of Water and Wood aboard, with new Trusle-Trees fix'd to the head of the Fore-Mast.

Nov. 26. Yesterday Afternoon we rigg'd the Fore-Mast again, and got almost all our Water on board. Last night one *Michael Jones* and *James Brown*, two *Irish* Landmen, run into the Woods, thinking to get away from us; tho two such Sparks run away the 25th from the Dutchess, and in the night were so frighted with Tygers, as they thought, but really by Monkeys and Baboons, that they ran into the water, hollowing to the Ship till they were fetch'd aboard again. About four this Morning the Watch on the Quarter-Deck spy'd a Canoe, and call'd her to come on board; but they not answering, and trying to get away, made us suspect they had either got our Men that run away last Evening, or were coming by Agreement' to fetch 'em off the Island, which was uninhabited. We immediately sent the Pinnace and Yall after 'em; the Pinnace coming up near the Canoe, fir'd to stay 'em, but to no, purpose; at last they wounded one of the *Indians* that row'd in the Canoe. He that own'd and steer'd her was a Fryar, and had a Quantity of Gold which he got at the Mines, I suppose by his Trade of confessing the Ignorant. The Fryar had just ran the Canoe ashore on a little Island full of Wood as our Boats landed, and afterwards told us he hid some Gold there. A *Portuguese* that would not run away with the Father, because he had no Gold to hide, knew our People to be *English*, and call'd the Father back. The Man that was wounded could not move, and was brought by our Men, with the Father and several Slaves that row'd the large Canoe, on board our Ship, where our Surgeon dress'd the wounded *Indian*, who died in two hours time. I made the Father as welcome as I could, but he was very uneasy at the Loss of his Gold and the Death of his Slave, and said he would seek for Justice in *Portugal* or *England*.

*Nov.*27. Yesterday in the Afternoon the Dutchess weigh'd, and tow'd out of the Cove about a mile, and came to anchor to wait for us: Their Boats returning to the Cove to fetch what was left, they spy'd two Men waiting under the side of a Wood by the Shore, for a *Portuguese* Canoe to get 'em off; but our Boats landed on each side of the Point, where they were not seen, found 'em to be the Men that left us the Evening before, and brought 'em to us. I order'd 'em both to be severely whip'd, and put in Irons.

This Morning Capt. *Courtney* and I, with most of our Officers, except those which we left to do what little remain'd unfinish'd on board the Ships, went in our Boat to *Angre de Reys*, it being the Day kept for the Conception of the Virgin *Mary*, and a high Day of Procession amongst these People. The Governour Signior *Raphael* de *Silva Lagos*, a Portuguese, receiv'd us very handsomly. He ask'd us if we would see the Convent and Procession: we told him our Religion differ'd very much from his. He answer'd we were welcome to see it, without partaking in the Ceremony. We waited on him in a Body, being ten of us, with two Trumpets and a Hautboy, which he desir'd might play us to Church, where our Musick did the Office of an Organ, but separate from the Singing, which was by the Fathers well perform'd. Our Musick play'd, *Hey Boys up* go *we!* and all manner of noisy paltry Tunes: and after Service our Musicians, who were by that time more than half drunk, march'd at the head of the Company, next to them an old Father and two Fryars carrying Lamps of Incense with the Host, next came the Virgin *Mary* on a Bier carry'd on four Mens shoulders, and dress'd with Flowers and Wax-Candles, etc. After her came the Padre Guardian of the Convent, and then about forty Priests, Fryars, etc. Next was the Governour of the Town, my self, and Capt. *Courtney*, with each of us a long Wax-Candle lighted: Next follow'd the rest of our Officers, the chief Inhabitants, and junior Priests, with every one a lighted Wax-Candle. The Ceremony held about two hours, after which we were splendidly entertain'd by the Fathers of the Convent, and then by the Governour at the Guard-House, his Habitation being three Leagues off. It's to be noted, they kneel'd at every Cross-way, and turning, walk'd round the Convent, and came in at another Door, kneeling and paying their Devotion to the Image of the Virgin and her Wax-Candles. They unanimously told us, they expected nothing from us but our Company, and they had no more but our Musick.

The Town consists of about sixty low Houses built of Mud, cover'd with Palmetto Leaves, and meanly furnish'd. They told us they had-been plundered by the *French*, or perhaps they hid their Plate and other best Movables, because they were in doubt whether we were Friends or Enemies. They have two Churches and a *Franciscan* Monastery tolerably decent, but not rich in Ornaments: They have also a Guard-house, where there are about 20 Men commanded by the Governour, a Lieutenant, and Ensign. The Monastery had some black Cattel belonging to it, but the Fathers would sell us none.

The Fish we saw in the Road were Sharks, so well known that I need not describe them. 2. Pilot-Fishes, so call'd because they commonly attend the Sharks, find out their Prey for 'em, and are never devour'd by 'em. 3. The Sucking-Fish, so call'd because of a Sucker about two inches long on the top of their Heads, by the Slime of which they stick so fast to Sharks and other large Fish, that they are not easily pull'd off. 4. Parrot-Fish, So nam'd because their Mouths resemble the Beak of a Parrot. 5. A Rock-Fish, which is very good, and much like our Cod. 6. Silver-Fish in great plenty: 'tis a deep-body'd bright Fish, from 12 to 18 inches long, and very good Meat: But there are so many sorts of good Fish here, that we can't describe 'em all.

Nov. 28. Yesterday in the Afternoon we left *Angre de Reys*; when we got aboard, we found the Main-Mast rigg'd, with every thing ready. This Morning we got our Ship out by our Consort, and the Wind being out of the way, and but little, we went with our Boat to the Town, to get Liquors for the Voyage, and bring the Gentlemen of the Town aboard our Ships, where we treated 'em the best we could. They were very merry, and in their Cups propos'd the Pope's Health to us; but we were quits with 'em, by toasting that of the Archbishop of *Canterbury*: to keep up the Humour, we also propos'd *William Pen's* to them; and they lik'd the Liquor so well, that they refus'd neither. We made the Governour and the Fathers of the Convent a handsom Present of Butter and Cheese from both Ships, in consideration of the small Presents and yesterday's Favours from 'em, and as a farther Obligation on 'em to be careful of our Letters, which we took this opportunity to deliver into their own hands. I shall say no more of our Letters, but that they contain'd every thing material since my coming out, with two Postscripts wrote by Capt. Dover and Capt. Courtney, to put it out of doubt amongst all those concern'd, that we join'd heartily in prosecuting our long Undertaking, and that oar Officers behaved themselves to satisfaction; which may clear up some Difficulties started amongst the Gentlemen at home before we sail'd, that were a great Hindrance and Discouragement to us in the beginning, because Mismanagement and Misunderstanding amongst the Officers never fail of ill Effects to the Voyage, and of spoiling the Men; which is an irrecoverable Loss.

Nov. 29. Yesterday in the Afternoon our Yall went to Town to get Necessaries for our next long Voyage, because we were to run near 2000 Leagues before we could expect any Recruit of Liquors, unless by extraordinary good fortune. In the Evening it came on blowing with thick Showers of Rain, which prevented the Governour and the rest from going ashore that night. This Morning the Governour and Company were carry'd ashore: at parting we saluted 'em with a Huzza from each Ship, because we were not over-stock'd with Pouder. After which all the Officers of the Committee met on board the Dutchess, where we enquir'd into the true Cause of the aforesaid *Indian's* Death, and protested against Mr. *Vanbrugh* (who was the Occasion) for commanding our Ships Pinnace as he did in chafe of the Canoe unknown to me, and without my Order. At the fame time I desir'd to have the Committee's Hands, if they approv'd what I had transacted since my leaving the *Canary Islands*, which they very readily sign'd, as also the Protest against Mr. *Vanbrugh* unadvis'd Management; for I was sensible that good Order and Discipline in Privateers was the only Method to support my self and the other Officers, and keep up our Authority, which is so essential towards acting with Success and Vigour on all occasions. This made it highly necessary in the Infancy of out Undertaking to prevent Innovations in Command, which inevitably confound the most promising Designs, Therefore I thought it a fit time, now to resent ignorant and wilful Actions publickly, and to shew the Vanity and Mischief of 'em, rather than to delay or excuse such Proceedings; which would have made the Distemper too prevalent, and brought all to remediless Confusion, had we indulg'd conceited Persons with a liberty of hazarding the fairest Opportunities of Success. The above-mention'd Resolves of the Committee follow.

At a Committee held on board the *Dutchess* riding at the Island Grande on the Coast of *Brazile*, by Request of Capt. *Tho. Dover* President, Capt. *Woodes Rogers*, and Capt. *Stephen Courtney*, 29 *Novemb*. 1708.

WE have examin'd, and do approve of all the Proceedings and Transactions since our being at the Canary Islands, both as to the punishing of Offenders, and acting in all cases for the best of our intended Voyage, and that we found it actually necessary to sell part of the Goods taken in the Prize amongst the Canary Islands here, to purchase some Liquor and other Necessaries for our Men as they go about Cape Horn, they being very meanly clothed, and ill provided to endure the Cold; and we have and do hereby desire the Agent of each Ship to take particular Cognizance of what such Goods are sold and dispos'd of for; and agree that all possible Dispatch hath been made both here and at St. Vincent., In, acknowledgment of which we have for our Hands the Day and Year above-written.

Tho. Dover, Pres. William Dampier, Woodes Rogers, Edward Cook, Stephen Courtney, Robert Frye, Carleton Vanbrugh, John Rogers, William Stratton, John Connely, William Bath, Geo. Milbourne, Charles Pope, John Ballet.

Memorandum, That on the 26th Day of November, 1708. a little before break of Day, a Canoe coming near the Ship Duke, as she rode at Anchor at the Island of Grande on the Coasts of Brazile; they hal'd her, she not answering, they hal'd at her; upon which she row'd away, and the Captain ordered the Boat to get ready and pursue her: And Mr. Carleton Vanbrugh, Agent of the said Ship, putting of the Boat, without the Order of his Captain, or before any Commanding Officer was in pursuit of her, fir'd, or ordered to be fir'd, at her federal Muskets at a distance: But coming nearer, he ordered the Men to fire into the Boat; and the Corporal string, as we have reason to believe, kill'd an Indian, and took the Canoe, and sent her away with two of the Duke's Men, the Corporal and a Padre, and afterwards brought the rest of the People in the Ship's Pinnace; since which time we are informed by the Padre Master of the dead Indian, that he lost a quantity of Gold to the Value of 200 l. which he says he carry ashore, and hid in hopes to preserve (he taking them for Frenchmen by their firing and chasing) which could not afterwards be sound, also, he says, be does verily believe it was not taken by any of the Ships People, but alledges it was lost by means if their chasing And surprizing him. Whatever Damages may arise from the abovemention'd Action on the account of killing the Indian, or Loss of the Gold that the Padre Jays he has lost, We the Commanders and Officers of Ship Duke and Dutchess Consorts, do in behalf of our selves, and the rest of the Ships Company, Protest against the unadvis'd Actions of the aforesaid Mr. Carleton Vanbrugh, for proceeding without any Order from the Captain of the same Ship, and acting contrary to what he was ship'd for. In witness whereof we have set our Hands the 29th day of November, 1708.

Tho. Dover, Pres. William Stratton,

Woodes Rogers, William Bath,
Steph. Courtney, John Rogers,
Will. Dampier, Thomas Glendal,
Edward Cook, John Connely,
Robert Frye, Geo. Milbourne,
Charles Pope, John Ballet.

Nov. 30. The Wind continuing out of the way, last night we held a Committee on board the *Dutchess*, and agreed to remove Mr. *Carleton Vanbrugh* from the Ship *Duke*; which Agreement is as follows:

Memorandum, This 30th of Novemb. 1708. We the underwritten Officers belonging to the Ships Duke and Dutchess, pointed as a Committee by the Owners of both Ships, do find it necessary for the Good of our intended Voyage, to remove Mr. Carleton Vanbrugh from being Agent of the Duke Frigate, to bi Agent of the Dutchess, and to receive Mr. William Bath Agent of the Dutchess in his Place. This is our Opinion and Desire, in acknowledgment of which we have hereunto set our Hands in the Port of the Island of Grande on the Toast of Brazile, the Day above-written.

Tho. Dover, Pres. Robert Frye, Woodes Rogers, Charles Pope, Stephen Courtney, Tho. Glendall, William Dampier, John Bridge, Edward Cooke.

Chapter II

Nov. 30. About ten this morning we both weigh'd, in order to go out on the other side of *Grande*, which I think is the fairest Outlet, tho they are both very large, bold and good. We went out E S E. the Wind at N E. and in two hours came to an Anchor again, it proving calm, and a Current against us.

Dec. 1. Yesterday at twain the Afternoon we weigh'd again, with a Breeze at N E. but at five a Gale came up at S S W. and blew very strong with Rain, insomuch that we were forc'd to bear away, and come to an Anchor close under the island of *Grande*, in fourteen Fathom Water. It rain'd hard all night, but towards morning little Wind. About ten this morning we weigh'd Anchor, and steer'd away SW, At twelve it was calm, and we anchor'd again. Just before we anchor'd, we spy'd a small Vessel close under the Shore, near the West-End of *Grande*. We sent our Boat to examine her, and found it to be the same Brigantine our Boats were aboard of six days before, and from whence I had the Present. I gave the Master an Half-hour Glass, and other small things of little Value, for which he was very thankful

Dec. 2. I wrote a long Letter to my Owners, which Captain *Dover* and Captain *Courtney* also underwrote, and gave it the Matter of this Brigantine, who promis'd to forward it by the first Conveyance for *Portugal*; *so* that now I had sent by four Conveyances. At ten this morning we fail'd, Wind at W NW. row'd and tow'd till twelve and came to au Anchor to the Southward of Grande, our Men continuing healthy.

Dec. 3. Yesterday in the afternoon we fail'd with a brisk Gale of Wind at E by N. At six a clock in the Evening, the S W Point of *Grande* bore W N W. distant five Leagues. The small Three-*Hummock* Island without Grande, which is seen as you go in both ways to it, bore N E N. dist. 5Ls. the Westermost Point of the Main bore W by S dist. 9 Ls. from whence we departed for the Island of *Juan Fernandez*,. The rest of these 24 hours a good Gale from E by N. to the E S E. This I observ'd when we came from Cape *Frio to Grande*, more than I have yet noted: About 13 Leagues to the Eastward of the Isle of: *Grande* is a high round Rock, a good League without the Land, as it appear'd to us; within it is high mountainous Land, which we are inform'd is the Entrance to *Rio-Janeiro*: and as we came to the Westward, we open'd a Sandy Bay with low sandy Land in the middle, and high Land on each side clear to the Points; it's about 3 Leagues over, and deep. Next to this Bay, as we came to the Westward, open'd another low Sandy Bay, not quite so deep, but above twice as wide. The Westermost Point is indifferent high, and full of Trees, which makes the Easternmost Point as we enter'd Grande; from whence it runs in West and Northerly about 4 Ls. There is no such Bay to the Eastward as Rio-Janeiro between that and Cape Frio. This is a certain Mark not to miss *Grande*, which might easily be done by a Stranger, the Latitude being near the Tame for 40 Leagues within Cape *Frio*; but *Grande* lies cut near two Points farther Southerly, as you come to it from the Eastward, than any other Land between that and Cape *Frio*. We kept but an indifferent Account of the Ship's Way from Cape *Frio*, being nothing but fluttering Weather; but the *Portuguese* Master told me it is not less than 34 Ls. We kept continual Soundings, and had always Ground from one League to ten off the Shore, from 20 to 50 Fathom Water: Very even and gradual Soundings, with soft blue clayish Sand, till we got the Length of Grande; then we said harder

Ground, mix'd with small Stones and red Sand. The Shore runs hither nearest West.

The Island *Grande* is remarkable high Land, with a small Notch, and a Tip standing up on one side in the middle of the highest Land, easy to be seen if clear; and there's a small Island to the Southward without it, which rises in three little Hummocks; the nearest Hummock to the Island *Grander* the least. As we came in and out, we saw it, and it appears alike on both sides: there is also a remarkable round white Rock that lies on the Larboard side nearest to *Grande*, between it and the Main at the Entrance going in. On the Starboard side there are several Islands, and the Main is much like Islands, till you get well in. The best way, when you open the Coves that are inhabited on the Starboard side going in, is to get a Pilot to carry you to the watering Cove within *Grande*; otherwise fend in a Boat to the fresh-water Cove, which lies round the inner Westermost Point of the island, and near a League in: the Passage is between small Islands, but room enough and bold; it's the second Cove under the first high Mount and round, behind the first Point you see when you are in between the two Islands. This is die Cove where we water'd. There are two other Coves very good, with some Shoal- Banks between them, but no Shoal-Ground before we come to this Cove. We founded all the Passage in, and seldom found lest than ten Fathom Water, but had not time to know or sound the rest of the Coves. The Town bears N E. about 9 LS. dist. from this Cove. The Island of *Grande* is near about 9 Ls. long high Land, and so is the Main within it. All you lee near the Water-side is thick cover'd with Wood. The Island abounds with Monkeys and other wild Beasts, has plenty of good Timber, Fire-wood, and excellent Water, with Oranges and Lemons, and Guavas growing wild in the Woods. The Necessaries we got from the Town were Rum, Sugar, and Tobacco, which they fell very dear, tho not good to smoke, 'tis so very strong. We had also Fowls and Hogs, but the latter are Scarce; Beef and Mutton are cheap, but no great quantity to be had; *Indian* Corn, Bonanoes, Plantanes, Guavas, Lemons, Oranges, and Pine-Apples they abound with; but have no Bread except Cassado (the same sort as is eaten in our *West-Indies)* which they call *Faranadepau, i. e.* Bread of Wood. They have no kind of Salleting. We had sine pleasant Weather most of the time we were here, but hot like an Oven, the Sun being right over us. The Winds we did not much observe, because they were little and veerable; but commonly between the North and the East.

We clear'd an ordinary *Portuguese* here, call'd *Emanuel de Santo*, and shipt another, whose Name was Emanuel *Gonsalves*.

I had *Newhoss's* Account of Brazile on board, and by all the Enquiry and Observation I could make, found his Description of the Country, its Product and Animals, to be just; particularly of that Monster call'd *Liboya*, or the Roebuck-Serpent, which I enquir'd after, thinking it incredible till the *Portuguese* Governour told me there are some of them 30 foot long, as big as a Barrel, and devour a Roebuck at once, from whence they had their name. I was also told that one of these Serpents was kill'd near this place a little before our Arrival. Tygers are very plenty here on the Continent, but not So ravenous as those in India.

The Product of Brazile is well known to be Red Wood, Sugars, Gold, Tobacco, Whale-Oil, Snuff, and several sorts of Drugs. The *Portuguese* build their best Ships here: The Country is now become very populous, and the People delight much in Arms, especially about the Gold Mines, where those of all sorts resort, but mostly Negroes and Molattoes. Tis but four years Since they would be under no Government, but now they have Submitted: some Men of Repute here told me the Mines increase very fast, and that Gold is got much easier at these Mines than in any other Country.

This is all I can affirm from my own Observation concerning this Country, which was discover'd first by the famous *Americus Vespucius, Anno* 1500. when he call'd it *Santa Cruz*; but the *Portuguese* afterwards nam'd it Brazile, from the red Wood of that name which grows here. It s situate in the Torrid Zone, and extends from the Equinoctial to the Lat. of 28 South. The Extent from East to West is uncertain, therefore I can determine nothing concerning it. The Portuguese divide it into fourteen Districts or Captainships, fix of which, being the Northern part, were subdu'd by the Dutch about the Year 1637. and a Peace concluded, allowing it to be call'd Dutch Brazile, which extended from North to South about 180 Leagues: And since it is not usual for the Dutch to lose their Settlements abroad, it mayn't be a miss to give a brief Account how they were outed; of this profitable Country. In 1643. the Face of the *Dutch* Affairs there began to alter for the worse, the Magazines of their *West-India* Company were exhausted by several Expeditions against Angola, etc. and receiving no Supplies from *Holland* as usual, the great Council at the *Receise*, their Capital in *Brazile*, was forc'd to make use of what was due to the Company, for paying the Garisons and Civil Officers, and by consequence to force their conquer'd Debtors the *Portuguese* to prompt Payment. This oblig'd the Debtors to borrow Mony at 3 or 4 *per Cent*, per Month, which impoverish'd them so in a little time, that they were neither able to pay Principal nor Interest. The *Portuguese* immersed themselves in Debt to the Company, because of their hopes that the Fleets coming from *Portugal* would quickly subdue the *Dutch*, and pay off all scores. Besides, there happen'd a great Mortality among the *Portuguese* Negroes, which they purchas'd from the *Dutch* at 300 Pieces of Eight per head. This completed their Ruin; which, together with their Hatred to the *Dutch* on account of Religion, made them resolve on a general Revolt.

The *Dutch* at the same time were engag'd in a War with *Spain* at home, and Count *Maurice*, who was Governour of *Dutch Brazile*, was recall'd just in the height of the Plot. The *Dutch* had several Discoveries of it, and an account of *Portuguese* Commissions, importing that this Revolt was undertaken for the Honour of God, the Propagation of the Roman Faith, the Service of the King, and common Liberty. They complain'd of this to the *Portuguese* Government in Brazile, who told them they would cultivate a good Correspondence with them, according to the Orders of the King their Master; and wrote so to the *Dutch* Council, yet still carry'd on the Conspiracy, till at last the Rebellion broke out. The Dutch renew'd their Complaints, but the *Portuguese* Government deny'd their having any hand in it, till in 1645 they openly invaded the *Dutch*, on pretence at first of appealing the Revolts of the *Portuguese* in the *Dutch* Provinces, according to the Tenour of the Peace; but afterwards when they had got footing, they alledg'd the Dutch had murder'd many of the *Portuguese* in cool Blood; and then carry'd on the War till 1660, when the *Dutch* were forc'd to abandon *Brazile* on the following Conditions: That the Crown of Portugal should pay the States Eight hundred thousand Pounds in Mony or Goods, and that the Places taken on each side in the *East-Indies* should remain to the present Possessors; and that a free Trade should be allow'd the *Dutch* in *Portugal*, and at their Settlements in *Africa* and *Brazile*, without paying any more Custom than the *Portuguese*. But other Agreements have been since made between the two States, and the *Portuguese* remain in full possession of this fine Country, without allowing the *Dutch* to trade to it. This they fancy makes them sufficient amends for the Loss of their large Conquests in India, taken from them by the *Dutch East-India* Company; the *Portuguese* being now the least Traders thither, after enjoying the whole *East-India* Trade for above one hundred Years.

Newhoff, who gave the best Account of *Brazile* at that time, assigns the following Causes for so easy a Reconquest of it by the *Portuguese*: 1. The *Dutch* took no care to have sufficient Colonies of their own Natives, nor to keep strong Garisons in the Country. 2. They left the *Portuguese* in possession of all their Sugar-Mills and Plantations, which hinder'd the *Dutch* from getting any considerable Footing in the open Country. 3. The Plantations and Sugar-Mills that fell into their hands by Forfeiture or otherwise, they sold at such excessive Rates, and laid such Taxes on the Product, that the *Dutch* did not care to purchase them. 4. The States of *Holland*, instead of reinforcing the Garisons of *Brazile*, according to Prince *Maurice's* Advice, reduced them lower, notwithstanding all the Remonstrances of the Company to the contrary; for they were so intent upon their Conquests in the *East-Indies*, that they seem'd willing to be rid of *Brazile*, which is now a vast and populous Country, and employs a great number of large Ships yearly from *Portugal*, who carry home an immense Treasure of Gold, besides all other Commodities of that Country.

Whilst Prince *Maurice* was in *Brazile*, the *Dutch* sitted Ships thence for *Chili*, which arriv'd there: but wanted a sufficient Force to withstand the *Spaniard*, while they could be recruited, or gain an Interest amongst the Natives, which they might have easily done, could they have settled, because at that time the *Spaniards* had not conquer'd the *Indians* of *Chili*; so the *Dutch* being too weak, were forc'd to return without effecting any thing. I shall conclude this Head with a brief Account of the Natives of *Brazile* from *Newhoff* whose Authority, as I have said already, I found upon Inquiry to be very good. They are divided into several Nations, and speak different Languages. They are generally of a middling Size, well-limb'd, and their Women not ill-featur'd. They are not born black, bat become so by the Heat of the Sun. They have black Eyes, black curl'd Hair, and have their Noses made flat when young. They come soon to Maturity, yet generally live to a great Age, without much Sickness; and many *Europeans* live here to above a hundred Years old, which is ascrib'd to the Goodness of the Climate. The *Portuguese* cut off such multitudes of 'em, that they perfectly hate that Nation, but were civil enough to the *Dutch* because they treated them kindly. Such as live next the Europeans, wear Shirts of Linen or Callico, and the chief of 'em affect our Apparel; but those within Land go for the most part naked, covering their Privities slightly with Leaves or Grass fasten'd about them with a string, and the Men exceed the Women in Modesty. Their Hutts are built of Stakes, and cover'd with Palm-tree Leaves. Their Dishes and Cups are made of *Calabasses*, being the Shells of a sort of Pompions. Their chief Furniture is Hammocks of Cotton made like Network, and these they fasten to sticks, and use them for Beds; and when they travel, tie them to Trees. The Wives follow their Husbands to War and elsewhere, and carry their Luggage in a Basket, with a Child hung about them in a piece of Callico, a Parrot or an Ape in one hand, and leading a Dog by a string in the other; while the idle Lubber carries nothing but his Arms, which are Bows and Arrows, Darts or Wooden Clubs. They know nothing of Arithmetick, but count their Years by laying by a Chesnut in the Season. Those who inhabit the inland Parts know scarce any thing of Religion; yet they have a sort of Priests, or rather Conjurers, who pretend to foretel what's to come. They have a Notion of a Supreme Being more excellent than the rest; some reckon this to be Thunder, and others *Ursa Minor*, or some Constellation. They fancy that after Death their Souls are transplanted into Devils, or enjoy all sorts of Pleasures in lovely Fields beyond the Mountains, if they have kill'd and eat many of their Enemies; but those that never did any thing of moment, they say are to be tormented by Devils. These People are much afraid of Apparitions and Spirits, and make Offerings to pacify 'em. Some of 'em are mightily addicted to Sorcery, to revenge themselves upon their Enemies; and they have others who pretend to cure those that are so bewitch'd. The *Castilians* converted some of 'em, but the *Dutch* Ministers were more successful, till they were hinder'd by the Revolt of the *Portuguese*. The *Brazilian* Women are very fruitful, have easy Labour, retire to the Woods where they bring forth alone, and return after washing themselves and their Child; the Husbands lying a bed the first 24 hours, and being treated as if they had endur'd the Pains.

The *Tapoyars*, who inhabit the inland Country on the West, are the most barbarous of the Natives, taller and stronger than the rest, and indeed than most *Europeans*. They wear little Sticks thro their Cheeks and tinder-Lips, are Man-eaters, and use poison'd Darts and Arrows. They change their Habitations according to the Season, and live chiefly by Hunting and Fishing. Their Kings and Great Men are distinguish'd by the manner of shaving their Crowns, and their long Nails. Their Priests are Sorcerers, make them believe that the Devils appear to 'em in form of Infects, and perform their diabolical Worship in the night, when the Women make a dismal howling, which is their chief Devotion. They allow Polygamy, yet punish Adultery by Death; and when young Women are marriageable, but courted by no body, their Mothers carry 'em to their Princes, who deflower 'em; and this they reckon a great Honour. Some of these People were much civiliz'd by the *Dutch*, and very serviceable to them, but still kept under Subjection to their own Kings. For the extraordinary Animals, Plants, *etc.* of *Brazile*, I refer to *Newhoff*; being sensible that the Descriptions of such things are not my Province, but I thought it convenient to give this Hint for the Diversion of such Readers as may relish it better than a Mariner's bare Journal.

The River of the *Amazons* being the Northern Boundary of *Brazile*, I shall describe it here.

According to most Geographers it rises in the Mountains of *Peru*, and is compos'd at first of two Rivers, one of which begins about Lat. 9. S. and the other about 15. The Sansons call the latter *Xauxa* or *Maranhon*, which communicates its Name to the other. 'Twas call'd *Amazons*, not because of any Nation of Virago's, who as some fancy are govern'd by a Queen, and have no Commerce with our Sex; but at certain times, when they make an Appointment with the Males of neighbouring Nations, and if they prove with Child, keep the Daughters and fend away the Sons, as the *Greeks* fabled of their *Amazons*. But the true Reason of the Name is, that the *Spaniards*, who first discover'd it, were told of such a terrible barbarous Nation of Women by some of the Natives, on purpose to frighten them, and that they did actually on several places of this River find their Women as fierce and warlike as the

Men; it being their Custom to follow their Husbands, *etc.* to War, on purpose to animate them, and to share in their Fate, as we find was antiently practis'd by the Women of *Gaul*, *Germany*, and *Britain*.

But to return to the Course of the River. The *Sansons* give us a Map of it from the Discoveries of *Texeira*, who sail'd up and down the same in 1637, 1638, and 1639. The River, he says, begins at the foot of a Chain of Mountains nam'd *Cordelera*, about 8 or 10 Ls. East of *Quito* in *Peru*. It runs first from West to East, turns afterwards South; and then after many Windings and Turnings holds its main Course East, till it falls into the *Atlantick* Sea. Its Fountains and Mouth are very near under the Equator, and the main of its Stream is in the 4th and 5th deg. of S. Lat. The Rivers which fall into it on the North side, rise about one or two deg. N. Lat. and those on the South side, some of them begin in 10, some in 15, and others in the 21st of S. Lat. Its Channel from *Junta de los Reyos* about 60 deg. from its Head, till it is join'd by the River *Maranhon*, is from one to two Leagues in breadth. From thence, say the *Sansons*, 'tis from 3 to 4, but grows larger as it advances towards the Atlantick, into which it falls by a Mouth from 50 to 60 Leagues broad, betwixt Cape *Nort* on the Coast of *Guaiana*, and Cape *Zaparara* on the Coast of *Brazile*. Its Depth from *Junta de to Reyos* to Maranhon is from 5 to 10 fathom, from thence to *Rio Negro* from 12 to 20, and from thence to the Sea from 30 to 50, and sometimes a great deal more. 'Tis always of a good depth near the Shore, and has no Sand-Banks till it come towards the Sea. Its running in a continu'd Descent from West to East, makes the sailing down it very easy; and the East Winds, which last most part of the day, are very commodious for those who sail up this River. From the Fountain to its Mouth 'tis 8 or 900 Leagues in a direct Line, but the Windings and Turnings make it about 1200. Some compute it at 1800, and others 1276; but then they derive its Source from the Lake *Lauricocha* near *Guanuco* in *Peru* about Lat. 10. Authors differ whether this River or La Plata be the greatest, which I shall not take upon me to determine. The Rivers which run into it on the right and left, have their Courses from 100 to 600 Leagues in length, and their Banks are well inhabited by multitudes of People of different Nations, not so barbarous as those of *Brazile*, nor so polite as the Natives of *Peru*. They live chiefly upon Fish, Fruit, Corn and Roots; are all Idolaters, but pay no great Respect to their Idols, nor perform any publick Worship to them, except when they go upon Expeditions.

Texeira and his Fellow -Discoverers say, that most of those Countries enjoy a temperate Air, tho in the middle of the Torrid Zone. This is probably owing to the multitude of Rivers with which they are water'd, the East Winds which continue most of the day, the equal Length of the Days and Nights, the great numbers of Forests, and the annual Inundations of the Rivers, which fructify this Country, as that of the *Nile* does *Egypt*. Their Trees, Fields, and Flowers are verdant all the Year, and the Goodness of the Air prevents their being infested so much with Serpents and other dangerous Insects as *Brazile* and *Peru*. In the Forests they have Store of excellent Honey, accounted very medicinal. They have Balm good against all Wounds. Their Fruit, Corn, and Roots, are not only in greater plenty, but much better than any where else in *America*. They have vast number of Fish of all sorts in the Rivers and Lakes; and among others, Sea-Cows, which feed on the Banks, and Tortoises of a large Size and delicate Taste. Their Woods abound with Venison, and afford Materials for building the largest Ships. They have many Trees of five or fix fathom round in the Trunk, and inexhaustible Stores of Ebony and *Brazile* Wood, Cocoa, Tobacco, Sugar-Canes, Cotton, a Scarlet Dye call'd *Rocon*, besides Gold and Silver in their Mines and the Sand of their Rivers.

The Nations who inhabit about this and the other Rivers that run into it, are reckon'd by Sanson and others 150, and their Villages so thick in many places, that most of 'em are within Call of one another. Among those People, the *Homagues* who live towards the Head of this great River, are mostly noted for their Manufactures of Cotton; the *Corosipares* for their Earthen Ware; the *Surines* who live betwixt Lat. 5 and 10. and Long. 314 and 316, for their Joyners Work; the *Topinambes* who live in a great Island of this River, about Lat. 4. and Longit. 320. for their Strength. Their Arms in general are Darts and Javelins, Bows and Arrows, with Targets of Cane or Fish-Skins. They make war upon one another to purchase Slaves for their Drudgery, but otherwise they treat them kindly enough.

Among the River's that fall into it on the North side, the *Napo*, *Agaric*, *Putomaye*, *Jenupape Coropatube*, and others, have Gold in their Sands. Below Coropatube there are Mines of several sorts in the Mountains. In those of *Yagnare* there are Mines of Gold; in Picora there are Mines of Silver; on the River *Paragoche* there are precious Stones of several sorts; and Mines of Sulphur, *etc.* near other Rivers. Those of Putomaye and Cigars large Rivers: the latter is divided into two Branches; one falls into the *Amazons* River, by the name of *Rio Negro*, which is the largest on the North side; and the other, call'd *Rio Grande*, falls into the *Oronoko*. The chief Rivers that fall into it on the South side, are *Maranhon*, *Amarumaye*, *Tapy*, *Catua*, *Cucignate*, *Madere* or *Cayane* and many other large ones.

The *Sansons* add, that on this River, about 200 Leagues from the Sea, there is a Bosphorus or Strait of one mile broad; that the Tide comes up hither, so that it may serve as a Key to all the Trade of thole Countries; But the *Portuguese* being already possess'd of *Para* on the side of *Brazile*, *Corupa* and *Estero* on the side of *Guaiana*, and *Cogemina* an Island at the mouth of it; they may, by fortifying the Island of the *Sun*, or some other place in its chief Outlet, be Masters of all the Trade.

William Davis a *Londoner*, who liv'd in this Country some time, gives us this further Account of it, and of the Inhabitants about this River. They have Store of excellent Wild-Fowl in their Woods, and among others, Parrots as many as we have Pidgeons in *England*, and as good Meat. Their Rivers and Lakes abound with Fish, but such as catch them must be upon their guard against Crocodiles, Alligators, and Water-Serpents. The Country is subject to frequent and violent Storms of Rain, Thunder, and Lightning, which commonly hold 16 or 18 hours; and the Inhabitants are terribly pester'd with Muskettoes. There are abundance of petty Kings, who live upon their particular Rivers, on which they decide their Quarrels with Canoes, and the Conqueror eats up the Conquer'd; so that one King's Belly proves another's Sepulcher, The Regalia by which they are distinguish'd, is a Crown of Parrots Feathers, a Chain of Lion's Teeth or Claws about their Necks or Middles, and a Wooden Sword in their hands. Both Sexes go quite naked, and wear their Hair long; but the Men pluck theirs off on the Crown. He says 'tis a question whether the Womens Hair or Breasts be longest. The Men thrust pieces of Cane thro the Foreskin of their *Pudenda*, their Ears and Under-Lips, and hang Glass-Beads at the Gristle of their Noses, which bob to and fro when they speak. They are thievish, and such good Archers, that they kill

Fish in the water with their Arrows. They eat what they catch without Bread or Salt. They know not the Use of Mony, but barter one thing for another, and will give twenty Shillings worth of Provisions, etc. for a Glass-Bead or a Jews-Harp.

I come next to the Discovery of this River. When *Gonsales Pizarro*, Brother to *France* that conquer'd *Peru*, was Governour of the North Provinces of that Country, he came to a great River where he saw the Natives bring Gold in their Canoes to exchange with the *Spaniards*. This put him upon a compleat Discovery of that River from its Fountains to its Mouth. In order to this, he sent out Capt. *Francisco de Orellana* in 1540., with a Pinnace and Men: Some say he went also himself, and sail'd down the River *Xauxa* or *Maranhon* 43 days, but wanting Provisions, commanded *Orellana* to go in quest of some down the River, and to return as soon as he could; but *Orellana* being carry'd down 200 Leagues thro a desert Country, the Stream was so rapid, that he found it impracticable to return, and therefore sail'd on till he came to that which is properly call'd the River of the *Amazons*. He had spent all his Provisions, and eat the very Leather on board; so that seven of his Men died of Want. In January that Year, after sailing 200 Leagues further, he came to a Town on the Bank of the River, where the People were afraid of him, but at last furnish'd him with Provisions; and here he built a large Brigantine. He set out again the 2d of *Febr.* and 30 Leagues further was almost cast away by the violent Stream of a River which run into that of the *Amazons* on the right side. He sail'd above 200 Leagues further, and was invited ashore in the Province of *Aparia*, where he discover'd several of their Caciques, who forewarn'd him of his Danger by the *Amazons*. He staid here 35 days, built a new Brigantine, and repair'd the other. He sail'd again in *April* thro a desert Country, where he liv'd upon Herbs and toasted *Indian* Wheat. On the 12th of May he arriv'd at the populous Country, of *Machiparo*, where he was attack'd by many Canoes full of Natives arm'd with long Shields, Bows and Arrows; but fought his way thro them till he came to a Town where be took Provisions by Force, after two hours fight with some thousands of the Natives whom he put to flight, and had 18 of his Men wounded, but all recover'd. He put off again, and was purSu'd two days by 8000 *Indians* in 130 Canoes, till he was past the Frontiers of that Country. Then he landed at another Town 340 Leagues from *Aparia*, which being abandon'd by the Natives, he rested there three days, and took in Provisions. Two Leagues from hence he came to the mouth of a great River with three Islands, for which he call'd it Trinity-River. The adjacent Country seem'd very fruitful, but so many Canoes came out to attack him, that he was forc'd to keep the middle of the Stream. Next day he came to a little Town, where he took Provisions again by force, and found abundance of curious earthen Ware finely painted, and several Idols of monstrous shapes and sizes. He also saw some Gold and Silver, and was told by the Inhabitants that there was abundance of both in the Country. He sail'd on 100 Leagues further, till he came to the Land of *Pagnana*, where the People were civil, and readily furnish'd him with what he wanted.

On *Whitsunday* he pass'd by a great Town divided into many Quarters, with a Canal from each to the River. Here he was attack'd by Canoes, but soon repul'd them with his Fire-Arms. He afterwards landed, and took Provisions at several Towns. He met with the Mouth of a River, the Water as black as Ink, and the Stream so rapid, that for 20 Leagues it did not mix with that of the *Amazons*. He saw several small Towns in his Passage, enter'd one by force, which had a Wall of Timber, and took abundance of Fish there. He pursu'd his Voyage by many great Towns and well-inhabited Provinces, by which time the River was grown so wide, that they could not see the one side from the other. Here he took an *Indian*, by whose Information he suppos'd this to be the proper Country of the *Amazons*. He sail'd on by many other Towns, and landed at one, where he found none but Women. He took abundance of Fish there, and resolv'd to have staid for some time; but the Men coming home in the Evening, they attack'd him, so that he ship'd off, and continu'd his Voyage He saw several great Towns with pav'd Roads between Rows of Fruit-Trees into the Country and landed for Provisions. The Inhabitants oppos'd him; but their Leader being kill'd, they fled and left him at liberty to carry off Provisions. From hence he sail'd to an Island for Rest, and was inform'd by a Female he had taken Prisoner, that there were Men like themselves in that Country and some white Women, whom he conceiv'd to be *Spaniards*: she told him they were entertain'd by a Cacique. After several days sail, he came to another great Town, near which the *Indians* told him those Whites did live. He kept on his Course, and after four days came to another Town, where the Natives were civil, furnish'd him with Provisions; and here he saw abundance of Cotton Cloth, and a Place of Worship hung with Weapons and two *Mitres* resembling those of a Bishop. He went to a Wood on the other fide in order to rest, but was soon dislodg'd by the Natives. He saw several large Towns on both sides the River, but did not touch at them. Some days after they came to a Town where he got Provisions. After doubling a Point, he saw other large Towns, where the People flood ready on the Banks to oppose him. He offer'd 'em Toys in order to please them, but in vain. He continu'd his Voyage, and on the Banks saw several Bodies of People. He stood into them, and landing his Men, the Natives fought with great Resolution, ten or twelve being white Women of an extraordinary Size, with long Hair and all naked but their Pudenda, who seem'd to be their Commanders. They were arm'd with Bows and Arrows; and seven of 'em being kill'd, the rest fled. *Orellana* had several Men wounded; and finding that multitudes of the Natives were marching against him, he sail'd off, reckoning that he had now made 1400 Leagues during his Voyage, but still did not know how far he was from the Sea, He afterwards came to another Town, where he met with the like Opposition: several of his. Men were wounded, and. his Chaplain lost an Eye. Here he observ'd several Woods of Oak and Cork-Trees: He call'd this Province by the name of St. John's, because he came to it on that Saint's Day. He sail'd on till he met with some Islands, where he was attack'd by 200 Canoes with 30 or 40 Men in each, abundance of Drums, Trumpets, and Pipes, etc. but he kept them off with his Fire-Arms. These Islands appear'd to be high, fruitful, and pleasant, and the largest of 'em about 50 Leagues long; but he could take in no Provisions, because the Canoes continually pursu'd him.

When he came to the next Province, he perceiv'd many large Towns on the Larboard side of the River: Multitudes of Natives came in their Canoes to gaze on him, and his *Indian* Prisoner inform'd him that these Countries abounded with Gold and Silver. *Orellana* was here oblig'd to barricado his Boats to cover his Men, because one of 'em was kill'd by a poison'd Arrow. As he sail'd on, he came to inhabited Islands, and perfectly discern'd the Tide. Here he was attack'd by multitudes of Canoes, and lost some more Men by poison'd Arrows. There were many Towns on the Starboard side of the

River, and he found other inhabited Islands, where he got Provisions, but was attack'd and beat off when he landed on the Continent, till he came near the mouth of the River, where the People readily furnish'd him. He sail'd 200 Leagues among the Islands, where he found the Tide Strong, and at last in *August* that Year found a Passage to the Sea of about 50 Ls. wide, where the Tide rises five or six fathom, and the fresh Water runs 20 Leagues into the Sea; Esquire *Harcourt*, in his Voyage to *Guiana*, says 30 Ls. and that the fresh Water there is very good. He was mightily distress'd for want of Rigging and Provisions till he came to the Island of *Cubagua*, from whence he went to *Spain* to give the King an Account of his Discovery. The Manuscripts taken by Capt. *Withrington* say that *Orellana* was about a Year and half upon this River.

When he reported his Discoveries, the King of *Spain* sent him back with a Fleet and 600 Men to take possession of this River in 1544, some say 1549. but the Project came to nothing: for the Captain himself, after he had sail'd up 100 Ls. died with 57 of his Men by the Unhealthiness of the Air; and some of them sail'd 60 Ls. higher, where they were friendly entertain'd by the Natives, but being too few to pursue the Discovery, they return'd to the Island *Margarita*, where they found *Orellana's* Lady, fays *Heerera*, who told them that her Husband died of Grief for the Loss of so many of his Men by Sickness and the Attacks of the *Indians*. And thus they return'd *re insecta*: so that Orellana receiv'd no other Advantage for his Danger and Expence, but the Honour of the first Discovery, and having the River call'd by his name in some Authors. *Ovalle* Says that he lost half his Men at the *Canaries* and Cape *Verd*, and his Fleet was reduc'd to two large Boats before he came back to the River; so that he was too weak to attempt a further Discovery.

The Manuscripts taken by Capt. *Withrington* say the second Person who attempted it was *Leus de Melo* a *Portuguese*, by order of his Sovereign King *John* III. to whom the Country from the mouth of this River to that of *La Plata* belong'd, according to the Partition agreed on betwixt the *Portuguese* and the *Spaniards*. He had ten Ships and 800 Men, but lost eight of his Ships at the mouth of the River; so that he went to the Island *Margarita*, from whence his Men were dispers'd all over the Indies. Two or three Captains from the Kingdom of *New Granada* attempted it afterwards by Land, but without Success.

In 1560. those of *Peru* try'd it another way. The Viceroy sent *Pedro de Orsua*, a Native of *Navarre*, with 700 Men to the Head of this River, where he built Pinnaces and Canoes; and having furnish'd himself with Provisions, and taken 2000 *Indians* with many Horses on board, he imbark'd on the River *Xauxa* or Maranhon. He sail'd till he came to a plain Country, where he began to build a Town: but his Men not being us'd to such Labour, and fatigu'd by the hot and rainy Seasons, they murmur'd, tho they had Provisions enough, and a great prospect of finding Store of Gold. The Mutineers were headed by *Lopez, de Agira* a *Biscayner*, who had been an old Mutineer in *Peru*; and being join'd by *Ferdinand de Guzman* a *Spanish* Soldier, and one *Saldueno* who was enamour'd on *Orsua's* beautiful Lady, they murder'd him when asleep, with all his Friends and chief Officers. Then they proclaim'd *Guzman* their King, but 20 days after he was also murder'd by *Lopez*, who assum'd the Title to himself. Being a Fellow of mean Birth, he murder'd all the Gentlemen in company, lest any of them should rival him; and having form'd a Guard of Ruffians about him, he became so jealous of his new Dignity, and was so conscious of what he deserv'd, that when any of the Men talk'd together, he concluded they were plotting against him, and sent his Ruffians, to murder them. Abundance of the rest and the Women falling sick, he barbarously left them to the mercy of the Natives, and sail'd to the Island *Margarita* with 230 Men. He was well entertain'd by the Governour, who took him to be one of the King's Officers; but this ungrateful Villain did speedily murder him and his Friends, ravag'd the Island, forc'd some Soldiers to go along with him, and pretended to conquer the *Indies*; but was defeated, taken and hang'd by the Governour of *New Granada*. The Wretch murder'd his own Daughter that she might not be insulted by his Enemies, and then attempted to murder himself, but was prevented. Thus concluded that fatal Expedition.

The *Sansons* say the next Attempt was by those of *Cusco* in 1566. but it came to nothing; for their Leaders fell out and fought with one another, which made the rest a Prey to the Natives: so that only *Maldonado* one of their Captains and two Priests escap'd to carry home the News. Two of the Generals of *Para* and Governours of *Maranhon* were the next that renew'd the Attempt by the King's Command, but met with so many cross Accidents that they could not effect it.

In 1606. two Jesuits set out from *Quito*, thinking to reduce the Country on this River by their Preaching; but one of them was kill'd by the Natives, and the other narrowly escap'd, says *Ovalle*. The next Discovery was by Capt. *John de Palacios*. Authors differ as to the time; but most agree 'twas in 1635. He set out from *Quito* with a few arm'd Men and *Franciscan* Fryars, sail'd down the River till he came to *Annete*, where he was kill'd in 1636. and most of his Companions return'd, except two Monks and five or six Soldiers, who sail'd down in a little Vessel as far as *Para* the Capital of *Brazile*; where they acquainted *Texeira* the *Portuguese* Governour with their Discovery: who upon their Information sent 47 Canoes with 70 *Spaniards* and 1200 *Indians* to sail up the River under *Texeira* the Sailor. He set out in *October* 1637. and met with several Difficulties, which occasion'd many of the *Indians* to forsake him; but he went on, and sent a Captain with eight Canoes to make Discoveries before him. This Captain arriv'd *June* 24. 1638. at a *Spanish* Town built at the Conflux of the Rivers *Huerari* and *Amazons*, and dispatch'd a Canoe to acquaint *Texeira* with it. This encourag'd him to proceed till he came to the Mouth of the River *Chevelus*, where it falls into the *Amazons*, and there he left part of his Men under a Captain, and the rest at *Junta de los Rios* under another; while himself with a few went forward to *Quito*. The other Captain arriv'd there some time beforehand both were well receiv'd by the *Spaniards*, to whom they reported their Discovery in *September* 1638. The Men he left behind were well entertain'd by the Natives at first, but quarrelling with them afterwards, suffer'd much for want of Provisions, and had little but what they took by force.

Upon the News of this Discovery, the Count de *Chinchon* Viceroy of *Peru* sent Orders from *Lima* to furnish *Texeira* with all Necessaries for his Return down the River, and appointed Father *d'Acugna*, Rector of the College of *Cuenca*, and another Jesuit, to attend him and carry the News to *Spain*. They set out in *February* 1639. and arriv'd at *Para* in *December* following; from whence *d'Acugna* went to *Spain*, and publish'd his Account of this River in 1640.

The Sum of his Discovery, besides what has been mention'd already, is as follows. There's a Tree on the Banks of this River call'd *Andirova*, from whence they draw an Oil that is a Specifick for curing Wounds. There's plenty of Iron-Wood, so nam'd because of its Hardness, Red-Wood, Log-Wood. *Brazile*, and Cedars so large, that *Acugna* says he measur'd some that were 30 Span round the Trunk. They have Timber enough to build ships, make Cordage of the Barks of Trees, and sails of Cotton, but want Iron. They make Hatchets of Tortoise-shells, or hard Stores ground to an Edg; and Chizzels, Plaines and Wimbles of the Teeth and Horns of wild Beasts. Their chief Directors are Sorcerers, who are the Managers of their hellish Worship, and teach them how to revenge themselves on their Enemies by Poison and other barbarous methods. Some of them keep the Bones of their deceas'd Relations in their Houses; and others burn them with all their Movables, and Solemnize their Funerals first by mourning, and then by excessive drinking. Yet the Father says they are in general good-natur'd and courteous, and many times left their own Hutts to accommodate him and his Company. Some of these Nations, particularly the *Omaguas*, whose Country is 260 Leagues long, and the most populous on the River, are decently clad in Rayment of Cotton, and trade in it with their Neighbours. Some of the other Nations wear Plates of Gold at their Ears and Nostrils; and their Joiners are so expert, that they make Chairs and other Haushold Furniture in the shapes of several Animals with great Art.

The Jesuits of *Quito* in *Peru* have engrav'd a Map of this River, in which they give the following Account, *viz*. That 'tis the greatest in the known World: That tho it be call'd by the same of *Amazons* or *Orellana*, its true name is *Maranhon*: That it rises from the Lake *Lauricocha*, as we have mention'd already, runs 1800 Leagues, and falls into the North Sea by 84 Mouths: That near the City *Borja* it is pent up by a Strait call'd *El-Pongo*, not above 13 Fathom wide and 3 Ls. long; where the Stream is so rapid, that Boats run it in a quarter of an hour. The Truth of this must be submitted to the Judgment of the Reader, but it seems very improbable, since none of those who fail'd up and down this River describe it thus: besides, 'twere impossible to sail up against so rapid a Stream without a Tide, which the *Sansons* say comes up to this Strait; but they make it a mile broad, and by consequence not so rapid. The Jesuits add, that both Banks from the City *Jaen* in the Province of *Bracamoros*, where it begins to be navigable, down to the Sea, are cover'd with Woods of very tall Trees, among which there's Timber of all colours, abundance of *Sarsaparilla*, and the Bark they call Cloves, which is us'd by Dyers and Cooks. In the neighbouring Woods there are many Tygers, wild Boars, and Buffaloes, etc. The Jesuits began their Mission upon this River in 1638. have their Capital at the City of *St. Francis* of *Borja* in the Province of *Manos*, 300 Leagues from *Quito*; and their Mission extends along three other Rivers as far as the Province of the *Omaguas*, whither they make sometimes long and dangerous Voyages in Canoes. They give an account of eight of their number that have been murder'd by the *Barbarians*, the last of them in 1707. Besides *Borja* and its Dependencies, they have 39 Towns founded mostly by their own Labour and Charge, but we shan't insist on their Names. Their Converts they reckon at 26000, and the Missionaries about 18. They add, that they have contracted Amity with several numerous Nations, whose Conversion they hope for.

The *Portuguese* have some Towns at the Mouth of this River, and a Fort on *Rio Negro*; so that of late years they have traded much upon it, and, as several *Spaniards* inform'd me, during the last Peace they extended their Commerce as far as *Quito* and many other Places in *Peru*. I have insisted the longer on this River, because it is of so great Fame, and may be of mighty Advantage for Trade.

The River of *La Plata* being the South Boundary of *Brazile*, within the Limits of the *South-Sea* Company, and lying conveniently for opening a great Trade from the North-Sea with *Peru*, *Chili*, and other vast Countries; I shall give a Description of it here, from the best Authors.

The first European who discover'd it, seems to have been *Juan Dias de Solis*, who sailing from *Spain* in 1512. some say 1515. run along the Coast of *Brazile* till he came to this River, says *Ovalle*. With him agree the Manuscripts taken on some *Spanish* Priests in this River by Capt. *Withrington*, publish'd in *Harris's* Collections; where we are told, *De Solis* obtain'd the Government of this River, but was murder'd by the Natives with most of his Men in 1515. The next who came hither was *Sebastian Cabot* in 1526. but his Men being mutinous, he had not the desir'd Success, tho he sail'd 150, some say 200 Leagues up this River; and purchasing many Pieces of Gold and Silver Plate from the Natives, who call'd this River *Parama*, he call'd it the River of Plate, because he thought it to be the Product of the Country, which was afterwards found to be a Mistake. Yet upon his Report, in 1530. when he return'd, the Emperor *Charles* V. sent Don *Peter Mendoza*, one of his chief Grandees, with 2200 Men besides Mariners, to plant a Colony here in 1535. and they had so great hopes of finding Mines of Gold and Silver, that above thirty Heirs of noble Families went on the Expedition; and sailing 50 Leagues up the River, where the Air was good, he founded a Town, which from thence was call'd *Buenos-Ayres*.

They built a Fort, and enlarg'd the Town; but as they were carrying on their Work, the Natives attack'd them, and overpowering them with Numbers, kill'd 250, among whom were several of the chief Men. This oblig'd the *Spaniards* to keep within their Fort, where they suffer'd much by Famine. *Mendoza* return'd towards *Spain*, but died miserably, with many of his Companions, for want of Provisions by the way. His Deputy-Governour *Oyola* sail'd up into *Paraguay*, in quest of a Country said to abound with Gold and Silver; but was treacherously slain by the Natives, with all his Followers.

Irala who was his Deputy, and left at *Buenos-Ayres*, contracted a Friendship with some of the Natives call'd *Guaranians*. In 1538. he built *Assumption* in their Country, which is now the Metropolis of *Paraguay*, and left *Buenos-Ayres* for a time. *Assumption* lies on the Banks of the River *Paraguay*) in S. Lat. 2 5. 240 Leagues from the Sea, and 40 from the Mouth of the River *Paraguay*, where it falls into *La Plata*. These Rivers after they join continue their natural Colour for several miles, *La Plate* being clear, and *Paraguay* muddy. The latter is by much the most considerable River, and the adjacent Country abounds with Mines of Gold and Silver, and is navigable above 200 Leagues. The River *Vruquay* falls into *Paraguay* on the right side, and runs a Course of 300 Leagues, according to Sepp the Jesuit, who in his Voyage says 'tis as big as the *Danube* at *Vienna*. In short, as to this River *La Plata*, Authors are not agreed. some of the Jesuits who are Missionaries in those Countries think it to be the same with that call'd *Paraguay* higher up in the Country, and that it has a Communication with the North-East Coast of

Brazile by the River *St. Meary*, which rises out of the same Lake, and runs N E, as *Paraguay* or *Plata* runs S. and afterwards to the S E. when it falls into the Sea. Be that how it will, here are many Rivers which fall into the same Channel on both sides. But that which is commonly call'd *La Plata*, begins near the Town of that Name about S. Lat. 19. and after running N. a little way, takes its Course S E. till it join the River *Paraguay*, So that I chuse rather to trust to the Account given us by Mr. *White* our Linguist, who having dwelt long in that Country, told me this River derives its Name from the Town of La Plata, a sort of Metropolis to which there lies an Appeal from other Jurisdictions. He adds, that 'tis a pretty Town, has fourteen Churches with a Cathedral, and four Nunneries, and lies North-west from *Buenos-Ayres* about 500 Leagues, which requires commonly two months and a half's Travel.

All are agreed that *La Plata* is very large at the Mouth, where some account it 50, and others 30 Leagues broad. The Mouth of it is dangerous because of Sands, and therefore requires Pilots. *Knivet* in his Description of the *West-Indies*, says, the best way to avoid those Sands is to keep near the North Shore till you come to a high Mountain white at top; and then to sail 4 Ls. South, to another small Hill on the North side, near which you must sail. This brings you into a fair Bay, where you must still keep along shore: and after pasting the West Point of this Bay, you come to the River *Maroer*, and then there are no more Shoals between that and *Buenos-Ayres*.

La Plata runs into the Sea about S, Lat. 35. and sometimes overflows the Country for several miles, when the Natives put their Goods into Canoes and float about till the Inundation assuages, and then they return to their Habitations. *Ovalle* gives the following Account of this River, viz. That it runs with such a mighty Stream into the Sea, as makes it fresh for a great way: That the Water of this River is very sweet, clears the Voice and Lungs, and is good against all Rheums and Defluxions: That the People who dwell about it have excellent Voices, and are all inclin'd to Musick: That it petrifies the Branches of Trees, and other things which fall into it; and that Vessels are naturally form'd of its Sand, which are of various Figures, look as if they were polish'd by Art, and keep Water very cool. It breeds great store of excellent Fish of divers Sorts, and most beautiful Birds of all kinds are seen on its Banks. *Sepp* informs us, that this River and *Vraguay* abound so with Fish, that the Natives catch great numbers of them without any other Instrument than their Hands: one of the choicest, call'd the Kings-Fish, is small without Bones, and taken only in Winter. Our Author, says he never saw any *European* Fish in this latter, except one that the *Spaniards* call *Bocado*; and that the Fish are larger here than ours, of a dark or yellow colour, and well tasted; which he ascribes to the nature of the Water, that tho drunk in great quantities even after raw Fruit, helps Digestion, and never does any hurt. The Plains about this River are so large and even, without any Obstruction to the Sight, that the Sun seems to rife and set in them. Their way of travelling in those Plains is by high Carts cover'd with Hoops and Cows-Hides like our Waggons, with Conveniency for Travellers to sleep in the bottom; which is so much the better, because they travel most by night to avoid the Heat. They are drawn by Oxen, which are frequently so pinch'd by Drought, that when they come towards any Water, which they smell at a great distance, they run furiously to it, and drink tip the very Mud which they raise with their Feet. This obliges Travellers to furnish themselves with Water and other Provisions for their

Journy; there being no Water to be had, except by Rain: so that Travellers are frequently as much distress'd for want of Water as the Oxen, and can scarce get any that's clear at the Watering-places, tho they send before-hand, because the Oxen run with so much haste to it that they make it all in a puddle: *Ovalle* says, that in this case Travellers are forc'd to stop their Noses and shut their Eyes when they drink it. The Journy thro these Plains is at least 14 or 20 days, without any place of shelter, or any Firing to dress their Victuals but the dry'd Dung of Cattle. Yet there are several Lakes and Ponds where Inns might be fix'd, but 'tis neglected because there's no fettled Trade that way.

It remains to give some account of the Towns upon the River *Plata* and on the Road to Potosi. 1. Buenos-Ayres lies upon the River 50 Leagues from the Sea, about Lat. 36. Our Linguist inform'd me that 'tis the Residence of a *Spanish* Governour, is defended by a Stone Fort mounted with 40 Guns, and is generally garison'd by 4 or 500 Men. The Harbour is pretty good, but troublesom in a N W. and W. Wind. The River is 7 Ls. broad there, and navigable by Ships 60 Ls. above the Town, but no further, because of a great Cataract. The Town has one Cathedral, and five other Churches: The *Portuguese* had a Settlement over against this Town, but were dislodg'd by the *Spaniards* at the beginning of this War; since which time the *French* drive a *Guinea* Trade hither for Negroes, who are sent over Land to *Peru* and *Chili*, and yield them vast Profit. The Trade from hence to *Spain* is in Hides and Tallow, Silver from *Peru*, and Gold and Silver from *Chili*. All *European* Goods yield a good Price here. They have plenty of Fruit-Trees about the Town of all kinds, both of the hot and cold Climates; and have store of Wheat and other *European* Grain, besides *Indian* Corn. Thousands of Cattel of all sorts run wild in the Neighbourhood, and they furnish *Peru* with 50000 Mules *per ann.* In short, this place lies very convenient for Commerce in Silver and Gold, and the other Commodities of *Peru* and *Chili*, which the *French* have now begun to engross. They sent three Ships to those parts and the *South-Sea*, under M. *de Beauchesne Gouin* of *St. Malo* in 1698. of whose Progress I shall give a further account from a Copy of his Journal, as I go on with my Description of the Coasts. Their Winter here is in *May, June,* and *July,* when 'tis cold by night, but warm enough by day, the Frost never being violent, nor the Snow considerable in those parts.

Father *Sepp*, who was here in 1691. tells us in his Voyage from *Spain* to *Paraquaria* or *Paraguay,* that *Buenos-Ayres* has only two Streets built crosswise; that there are four Convents, one of which belongs to the Jesuits; that their Houses and Churches are built of Clay, and not above one Story high; that the Jesuits have taught them of late to burn Lime, and make Tiles and Bricks, with which they now begin to build. The Castle is likewise of Clay, encompass'd with an earthen Wall and a deep Trench, and defended by 900 *Spaniards*; tho in cafe of necessity above 30,000 *Indian* Hone might be arm'd out of the several Cantons, where they have been train'd by the Jesuits: But this boasting Account I can't believe. They have in the Neighbourhood whole Woods of Peach, Almond, and Fig-Trees, which they propagate by putting the Kernels in the Ground: they grow so fast as to produce Fruit the first Year, and their Timber is us'd for Fewel. The adjacent Pastures are so fat and large, that many thousands of Beeves feed together; so that any one when he pleases goes into the Field, throws a Rope about their Horns, brings 'em home and kills 'em. They are very large, generally white, and being so numerous, are valu'd only for their Hides, Tallow, and Tongues; the rest being expos'd to the Birds and Beasts of Prey, which are very numerous, and frequently destroy the Calves. The Natives feed most on Beef half-raw without Bread or Salt, and in such quantities that they throw themselves naked into cold Water, that they may retain the natural Heat within their Entrails to help Digestion; and sometimes they He down with their Stomachs in hot Sand: but their Gluttony in devouring so much raw Flesh fills them so with Worms, that they seldom live till 50 Years old. There are such numbers of Partridges here, and so tame, that they knock them down with Sticks as they walk in the fields. The Missionaries, who are absolute Masters of the Natives in the neighbouring Cantons of *Paraguay*, etc. suffer none of 'em to come nearer *Buenos-Ayres* than two or three Leagues, on pretence that they would be corrupted by the ill Example of the *Spaniards*; and under that same pretence they won't suffer the Spaniards to fettle in their Missions, which extend above 200 Leagues up the River; nor do they allow Merchants who trade thither to stay above a few days: the true cause of which is, they are not willing that the Laity should be privy to the Wealth they heap up there, in a Country which abounds with Gold, nor be Witnesses to their splendid, or rather luxurious way of living. sometimes Complaints of this Procedure of the Jesuits have been made to the *Spanish* Governours, but they find a way to bribe them to silence. This I was inform'd of by those who have been among them, and am confirm'd in it by Father *Sepp*: He does not dissemble that the Missionaries have a Despotical Turn, Power over the Natives, tho he gives it another Turn, and pretends that 'tis necessary in order to convert and force them to work. He says the Jesuits are Captains, teach them the use of Arms, and how to draw up into Squadrons and Battallions; which he boasts they can do as well as the Europeans. The Jesuits obtain'd tins Power, on the specious Pretence of reducing those *Indians* to the Obedience of the *Spaniards*, which they would not submit to till within these few Years. This Management is so much the more easily carry'd on, because the Ecclesiastical Government there is lodg'd in the hands of one Bishop only and three Canons; and the Missionaries being compos'd of all Nations, few of them have any natural Affection to the *Spanish Government*. This is the more to be observ'd, because the Jesuits being an intriguing Society, and generally in the French Interest, it would seem to be the Concern of the Allies to recover the Trade of those Countries from the House of *Bourbon* with all possible speed, lest by making themselves Masters of the vast Treasures *of Peru* and *Chili*, they be enabled at last to compleat their Design of an Universal Monarchy. Father *Sepp* says, that Silver in 1691. was cheaper here than Iron; that for a Twopenny Knife one may have a Crown, for a Hat of two Shillings 10 or 12 Crowns, and for a Gun of ten or twelve Shillings 30 Crowns; that Provisions are so plenty here, that a fat Cow may be bought for the Value of 10d. or 12d. a good Ox for a few Needles, a stout Horse for about 2 *s.* that he has seen two given for a Knife not worth 6 d. and that he and his Company had 20 Horses for a few Trifles that did not cost them a Crown; being only a few Needles, Fish-Hooks, sorry Knives, Tobacco, and a little Bread. He mentions a Cataract in the River *Vruquay*, which he says Providence has plac'd here for the advantage of the poor Indians against the Avarice of the *Spaniard's*; who not being able to go further with their Vessels, have been hitherto confin'd to *Buenos-Ayres*, and could' not settle in those Cantons, tho very inviting, because of the vast Profit they might draw from them. This he reckons a great Happiness to the Natives, who being a simple People, would not only be soon infected with the Vices of the *Spaniards*, but enslav'd by 'em: for, says he, they make no difference betwixt Pagan and Christian Natives, but treat them promiscuously like Dogs. He adds, that this Province of *Paraquaria* or Paraguay exceeds in bigness *Germany, France, Italy*, and the *Netherlands* put together; (wherein I doubt he exceeds:) That they have no Cities, and are govern'd by 80 Colleges of Jesuits, in which there are no more than 160 Persons; and that these Colleges are from 100 to 600 Miles distant from one another. There's, one Plain of 200 Leagues long betwixt *Buenos-Ayres* and *Corduba* in *Tucuman*, without so much as a Tree or Cottage, and yet it contains the best Pastures in the World, fish'd with Cattel of all sorts which have no Owners.

He describes the Natives thus: The Men are not quite so tall as Europeans, but have thick Legs and large Joints. Their Faces are round, flattish, and of an Olive Colour; and their Arms are Bows and Arrows. Some of the strongest have many Scars on their Bodies, occasioned by Wounds which they gave themselves when young, that these Scars may be remaining Proofs of their Courage. Their Hair is black, long, and as strong as that of a Horse. The Women look more like Devils than rational Creatures, with their Hair loose over their Foreheads, and the rest twisted in Locks behind, which hang as low as their Hips. Their Faces are wrinkled, their Arms, Shoulders and Breasts naked; and their Ornaments are Fish-Bones made like Scales of Mother-of-Pearl about their Necks, Arms and Hands. The Wives of their Caciques or petty Princes wear a Sort of Triple Crowns of Straw. The Caciques wear Doe-Skins hanging over their shoulders; the rest only a piece of a Skin wrap'd about their middle, and hanging down before to their knees. The Boys and Girls are quite naked. They have holes in their Ears and Chins, in which they put Fish-Bones, or a colour'd Feather tied by a thred, and Feathers of several colours fasten'd to a string round their Necks. They wrap their Infants as soon as born in a Tyger's Skin, give them the Breast for a little while, and then half-raw Meat to suck. He fays, the Men at the death of their nearest Relations cut off a Finger of their own left Hand; and if it be a handsom Daughter, they make a Feast and drink out of her Skull. They live in Straw Hutts without Roofs, and their Utensils are a few Sticks for Spits, and Pumpkins hollow'd out, in which they eat their Meats. Their Beds are the Hides of Oxen or Tygers, spread on the ground; but the Caciques, and those of Note, lie in a Net fasten'd to two Poles for Hammocks, at some distance from the ground, being a Security against wild Beasts and Serpents. Our Author says that he sent well-boil'd Meat to several of them when sick, which they receiv'd thankfully; but afterwards gave it to their Dogs, because they lik'd their own Cookery better.

Chapter III

It is now time to see how the Missionaries live among those Flocks over whom they assume the Pastoral Care. Father *Sepp* tells us, that he and other new Missionaries were welcom'd by some of them with 20 Musicians in a Train, abundance of Boats equip'd like Galleys lin'd with Firelocks, and having Drums, Trumpets, and Hautboys on board. The Missionaries brought 'em Sweatmeats, and all sort of Fruit; and the *Indians* diverted them by wrestling in the Water, and Salvoes of their Fire-Arms, etc. They conducted them thro a green Triumphal Arch to the Church, where the Women were so earnest at their Devotion, that not one of them cast an eye upon our Father and his Companions: so that here were a Militant and a Triumphant Church both together. When the Devotion was over, the chief of the *Indians* welcom'd the Father and the rest of the Missionaries, by a short but very pathetick Speech; and one of the *Indian* Women did the like with wonderful Elegancy, says the Jesuit, who it seems is not against Womens Speaking in the Church. That and the next day they spent in Mirth and Jollity, and in the Evening were diverted by four Dances; 1. By Boys, who danc'd with Pikes and Lances. 2. By a couple of Fencing-Masters. 3. By six Seamen. 4. By six Boys on horseback, who afterwards gave them a kind of Tournament, the place being illuminated by Ox-Horns fill'd with Suet, for they have no Oil nor Wax. On Whitsunday, which happen'd soon after, the Missionaries went to Church, and return'd Thanks for so many Converts; as certainly they had reason, since they are such merry ones.

These Cantons, he says are 26, and have but one or two Missionaries apiece, tho they contain from 3000 to 6000 People each, and sometimes more; so that they must either have too much work, or perform it very slightly, especially if they be so ignorant, as our Father says, that if they be neglected one day, they scarce know how to make the Sign of the Cross the next: And besides all the Pastoral Work, the Missionaries must act the part of Clerks, and clean the Church-Ornaments and Plate; for these poor Wretches are uncapable of doing it. To be short, says he, the Missionary must be Cook, Nurse, Doctor, Architect, Gardiner, Weaver, Smith, Painter, Baker, Potter, Tile-maker, and every thing else that is necessary in a Commonwealth. This he supposes will appear incredible (and he's certainly in the right) but he says 'tis the naked Truth; the Natives being so stupid, that unless he plainly shew his *Indian* Cook how much Salt he must put in each Pot, he would put all into one, tho ever so much; and he must see them wash the Vessels, unless he would be poison'd: yet this Father, for all his other hard work, must look after his Garden, Orchard, and Vineyard, where he has all sorts of Flowers, Herbs, Roots and Fruits, and so many Vines as produce 500 large Casks of Wine in a Year, if not prevented by multitudes of Pismires, Wasps, Birds, or by the North Winds, which sometimes make Wine so dear, that a Cask yields 20 or 30 Crowns; and after all, 'tis not to be preserv'd from turning sour without a great mixture of Lime. The chief Distemper of the Natives is the Worms beforemention'd, the bloody Flux and spotted Fever, which frequently carry off great numbers. The Medicines which the Missionaries give against Worms, is a Vomit of Tobacco-Leaves; and after that, four Lemon-Juice with those of Mint and Rue put into Milk.

These Cantons or Towns, he says, are generally upon an Ascent near the Rivers *Uruguay* and *Paraguay*, and contain young and old from 6000 to 8000

Souls. Each Canton has a Church and a Square Market-place near it, the rest being divided into Streets of Clay-Hutts cover'd with Straw, only of late they begin to use Tiles. They have no Windows, Chimneys, or different Apartments; and over the Fire-place they hang their Beds at night. Their Doors are Ox-Hides; and since all lie together in one Room, with their Dogs, Cats, &c. the Missionaries are entertain'd with very ungrateful Scents, besides Smoke, when they go to visit them. He says, in the main they are very patient under Distempers, and the Death of Relations; that they seek after no Riches but a present Maintenance; that their young Women are marriageable at 14, and the Men at 16, when the Missionaries take care to match them, otherwise they will pair themselves. There are no Disputes here about Dowries, Jointures, or Marriage-Settlements; the Agreement consists only in two Articles, *viz.* The Woman promises to fetch what Water the Husband wants from the River, and he engages to provide the Kitchin with Fewel. The Missionaries furnish them with Hum, the Wedding-Clothes and Dinner. The Wedding-Suit is five yards of coarse woollen Stuff for each, the Dinner is a fat Cow, and the Bed some Ox-hides. He presents them also with a little Salt and a few Loaves, and then they trait their Parents. The Women court here, come to the Missionary, and tell him they have a mind to such a Man, if he will give his Consent; which if he do, the Match is made, and the Missionary is both Priest and Father.

How mean soever the Natives live, the Priests have enough of Splendor and Plenty. Their Churches and Steeples are lofty, have four or five Bells apiece, most of 'em a couple of Organs, Altars, and Pulpits richly gilt, Images well painted, plenty of Silver Candlesticks, Chalices, and other Church-Plate; and the Ornaments of the Priests and Altars are as rich as in Europe. They teach the Natives to sing and play on all Musical Instruments both for Devotion and War; so that according to the Jesuits they go now more merrily to Heaven than formerly they did to Hell, and the good Fathers divert themselves with Sets of Musicians on the Banks of the Rivers and in charming Islands. Nor can we wonder that they live so merrily, since they fare so well; for besides all Sorts of delicious Fruits and Preserves, they have plenty of Fowl, Fish, and Venison of all forts, as well as ordinary Butchers Meat; only the Tygers, which are very numerous, frequently put in for a share with them, invade their Flocks and their Followers: but if you'll believe our Father, they never attack the Clergy, they have such a Respect for their Cloth, and are so civil to *Europeans*, that they'l charge the *Indians* in their Company, and let them go scot-free; and the Serpents, which likewise abound here, are charm'd by *Ave Mary's* into the like Good-Manners. The Priests use Honey for their Sallets, for they have no Oil, so that they are very hard put to it. They had Silver in such plenty, says the Father, that old Shoes and Hats were much more valuable. And as if the Missionaries had not Work enough otherwise, Father *Sepp* tells us, the Natives when they kill their Cows bring 'em to the good Jesuits to allow each their share; and to be sure the Hides fall to the Missionaries, for he fays the three Ships which brought him and his Companions from *Spain*, carry'd back 300000 Ox-Hides, which they had for nothing, and each Hide he says would yield 'em fix Crowns at home. A good Horse-shoe he says is here worth six Horses, and the Bit of a Bridle worth three. An Ell of Linen is worth four or five Crowns; for they have no Hemp or Flax, but store of Cotton: and one Sheep, Lamb or Kid, is for the sake of the Wool worth three Oxen or Cows. Tho the Natives, he says, are so dull that they can't do the most frivolous thing without direction, yet they are so good at Imitation, that if you give them Models, they will make any thing very well. Thus he says the *Indian* Women after ripping a piece of Bone-Lace with a Needle, will make one by the same pattern very exactly; and so the Men do Trumpets, Hautboys, Organs, or Watches; and copy Pictures, Printing and Writing to admiration.

But they are so lazy that they must be forc'd to their work by blows, at the direction of the Missionaries, who tho they convert 'em themselves, make them cudgel one another. This they take very patiently, give no ill Language, but cry *Jesu Maria*! and thank the good Fathers into the bargain for taking such care of 'em; so that they have learnt Passive-Obedience to perfection. But to make them amends, our Author says the Missionaries teach their young ones to dance as well as to sing in the Church, when they are habited in rich Apparel: so that they are extremely taken with the Ornaments of our Religion, says he, which raises in them a high Esteem and Affection; and indeed 'twould be a wonder if it should not. The Missionaries do now take care to instruct both Sexes in all necessary Employments, Reading, Writing, etc. They have also taught 'em to make Images, epically of our Lady of *Ottingen*; and very good reason, for if we believe *Sepp*, she has done abundance of Miracles there. The Fathers wear Caps like a Bishop's, and black Linen Cassocks when they go abroad; and instead of Canes use Crosses, which have a peculiar Virtue to knock Serpents o' the head.

The Soil is so fruitful that it produces a hundred fold, tho sorrily manur'd. The Natives sow nothing but *Turky* Wheat, and scarce enough of that, they are so lazy: and are likewise such bad Husbands, that they would eat all at once, did not the Missionary force 'em to lay it up in his Barn, where he distributes it to 'em as they want, and so he does their Flesh. They have no Mills, but pound their Wheat in a Mortar, and make it into Cakes which they bake on Coals, or boil with their Meat. The Fathers have white Bread for themselves, which the Natives value so much, that they will give two or three Horses for a Loaf; and of there the Missionaries have good store, for they have always 40 or 50 Acres sow'd with Wheat for themselves: Land, Corn, Cattel, and every thing is theirs; so that they call all the People their Sons and Daughters, and perhaps there's just cause enough to give many of 'em that Title. These Lords Proprietors assign every Family their number of Cows and Oxen to till their Ground, and to eat; tho one would think they might have enough for the taking, without asking any body's leave: and yet our Father says he has been forc'd to chide his Parishioners for killing and eating their Oxen, and roasting them with their wooden Plows in the very Field while they were tilling the Ground; for which they pleaded in excuse that they and their Wives were hungry and weary: and yet there was no great reason for the latter, since their Plows, says our Author, don't enter above three inches into the Ground. They need no Hay for their Cattel, since they go up to the knees in Grass all the year. This is the way of living in those Cantons, which the Missionaries call Reductions, because, if you'll believe 'em, they have reduc'd them to Christianity by their Preaching, tho the *Spaniards* could never do it by their Arms.

Our Linguist told me that the Road from *Buenos-Ayres* to *Chili* is only passable in the Summer Months, when Commodities are purchas'd at that Town, and transported by Land to *Chili*.

On that Road about 100 Leagues N. W. from *Buenos-Ayres* lies the City of *Cordoua*, which is the See of a Bishop, has ten Churches, and an University. 'Twas founded in 1573. says F. *Techo*, by a Native of *Cordoua* in *Old*

Spain, when there were 60000 Archers reckon'd in its Territory, about 8000 of whom continu'd in Subjection, but the others revolted. 'Tis now the Metropolis of the Province, and the Jesuits have a Chappel in their College there, which for Riches and Beauty may vie with the best in *Europe*. The Natives of this Country were very barbarous, made use of Sorcery to satisfy their Revenge, and of Philtres of their own Blood to gratify their Lust. Both Sexes daub'd their Faces with strange Colours and each Village was govern'd by a Sorcerer, who pretended to be their Physician. To shew their Courage, they would draw Arrows thro the Skins of their Bellies, and they fought Duels with sharp Stones, standing foot to foot, and holding down their Heads to receive the Blows from one another by turns. He that struck first was reckon'd the most fearful: It was accounted disgraceful to dress their Wounds, and the Conqueror was applauded by hideous Shouts from the Spectators.

'Twas a long time before the Missionaries could reform those barbarous Customs.

Another Town on this Road is *Mendosa*, where they make large quantities of Wine, Brandy, and Oil.

So much for that part of this vast Country which lies toward *Chili* and *Brazile*: I shall next come to that part which lies towards *Peru*, and particularly the Road to *Potosi* and the Mines. *Santa-Fe* the next *Spanish* Settlement of note to *Buenos-Ayres*, from which it lies 80 Leagues N W. at the mouth of a River which fall into *la Plata*. The Country.betwixt this Town and *Buenos-Ayres* is fruitful, well inhabited by *Spaniards* and *Indians* and produces Wheat from forty to an hundred fold, and abounds with Cattel. The Town is encompass'd with a River, and built of Brick. Our Prisoners and Linguist: told us that there are Mines of Gold and Silver in the Neighbourhood, but the *Spaniards* don't care to open them, because the Conveniency of sailing up the River might encourage Enemies to invade and take them from 'em. This Town was built by the *Spaniards* when they first settled, for the Defence of this River.

St. Jago de l'Istero 200 Leagues N W. from *Santa-Fe*, is a pretty Town govern'd by a Corregidore, has three Churches, and lies on the River that runs down to *Santa-Fe*. Hither the Plate is brought from *Potosi* on Mules, because the Roads are bad; and from hence it is carry'd to *Buenos-Ayres* by Waggons. Next to this Town lies *St. Miquel de Toloman* 200 Leagues N W. Then *Salta* 150 Leagues. This Town contains fix Churches. Then *Ogui* 50 Leagues further, which has five Churches.

Potosi is next, lies N. of the Tropick of *Capricorn* about S. Lat. 21. Long. 73. Our Linguist tells us the City is large, has ten Churches govern'd by an Arch-Priest. The Town Stands at the bottom of that call'd *the Silver Hill* which is round like a Sugar-Loaf. There are 1500 or 2000 *Indians* constantly at work in the Mines here; they have two Reals a day, and are paid every Sunday. The Mines are a hundred fathom deep, and the Silver is grown much scarcer of late. Provisions are Scarce at this Town, and they have no Firing but Charcoal, which is brought from 30 to 50 Ls. distance. They have great Frosts and Snow here in *May, June*, and *July. Knivet* in his Remarks says, in his time they were well supply'd here with all things from the *South-Sea*, and that the Natives in the adjoining Country traffick'd in Gold and precious Stones; and hundreds of 'em ply'd upon the Road to carry Passengers from Town to Town in Nets fasten'd to Canes, and Supported by two or more Men; which was the easiest way of travelling, and they desir'd no other Reward but a Fish-Hook and a few Glass-Beads. They have also Sheep of all extraordinary Size, with large Tails, upon which they carry'd Jars of Oil and Wine. He fays the rich Oar when taken out of these Mines looks like Black Lead, then they grind it by certain Engines, and wash it thro sine Sieves into pav'd Cisterns. They make the *Indians* and other Slaves work quite naked in the Mines, that they mayn't hide any thing.

The Curious who would know more of the Manners of the Natives, or the History and particular Product of this large Country, may find it in *Gemelli*, Father *Sepp*, and Father *Techo*; but this is enough for my purpose, to shew what a vast Field of Trade may be open'd here, and how dangerous it may prove to all *Europe*, if the House of *Bourbon* continue possess'd of that Trade.

Some being of Opinion that our *South-Sea* Company may possess themselves, by virtue of the late Act, of the River *de la Plata*, as far up that River and Country as they please, either in the Provinces of Paraguay or *Tucuman*; I shall give a further Description of those large Provinces, after taking notice that according to several of our Draughts *Paraguay* lies both on the E. and W. fide of the River *La Plata*; according to others, entirely on the E. fide, and Tucuman on the W. side. The *Sansons* make *Paraguay* 720 miles from S. to N. and 480, where broadest, from. E; to W. and place it betwixt S. Lat. 14 &24. Long. 315 & 325. but the Breadth is not equal. Father *Techo* says the River *Paraguay*, which gives name to the Country, is one of the greatest in America, receives several other large Rivers, runs 300 Leagues before it falls into the *Parana*, about 200 from the Sea is navigable, and together with the *Parana* forms the River *La* Plata. The word *Paraguay* in the Language of the Country signifies the Crown'd River, because the Inhabitants wear Crowns of Feathers of several beautiful Colours, which they have from the Birds that abound in that Country. I shall not insist upon the several Nations that inhabit it, among whom the *Garanians* are the chief, and Submitted first to the *Spaniards*; but growing weary of the Slavery they subjected them to, revolted, and were with much difficulty subdu'd after their Leaders were cut off, about 1539. The chief Discovery of this Country is owing to *Dominick Irala*, who in the Reign of the Emperor Charles V. was sent by the Governour *Alvar Nunez*, *Cabeca de Vaca* with 300 chosen Men, and went 250 Leagues up this River, to endeavour a Communication with *Peru*, but was oppos'd by some of the Natives, of whom 4000 were kill'd, and 3000 taken in a Battel. The Governour went afterwards on the Discovery himself, and failing up the River, came to a delicious Island, which his Men call'd *Paradise*, and would have settled there, but he dissuaded them, and advancing to the Borders of *Peru*, found a large Town of 8000 Houses deserted by the Inhabitants, who were affrighted with the noise of the *Spanish* Fire-Arms. 'Tis said they found in this Town a great Marketplace, with a wooden Tower in form of a Pyramid built in the middle, and a monstrous Serpent kept in it by which the Devil pronounc'd Oracles: this Serpent they kill'd with their Fire-Arms. But a Difference happening betwixt the Officers and Soldiers about dividing the Booty, they return'd to *Assumption* without pursuing the Discovery any further.

This Province, till that of *Tucuman* was taken from it, contain'd all the Country betwixt *Brazil* and *Peru*. Our Author adds, that besides the Towns above-mention'd the *Spaniards* built here *Corientes* on the Conflux of the *Paraguay* and *Parana*, which is but a small Town, no way suiting the Dignity of those two Rivers: That 100 Leagues up the *Parana*, in the Province of *Guirana*, the Spaniards built two little Towns call'd *Villarica* and *Guaira*; that on the upper part of the *Paraguay* they built *Xeres* and another *Villarica*, to join *Paraguay* on that side to the further Provinces; and lastly, the City of Conception on the Marshes of the red River which falls into *Parana*, and was of great use to curb the fierce Nations in the Neighbourhood. He adds, that all these Towns were first planted by a Race of the noblest Families in *Spain*. He mentions an extraordinary Herb here call'd *Paraguay* by the name of the Country; it grows in marshy Grounds, and the Leaves being dry'd and powder'd, and mix'd with warm Water, the *Spaniards* and Natives drink it several times a day, which makes them vomit, and strengthens their Appetite. They look upon it as a sort of Gatholicon use it so much that they can't live without it; and this Custom has so much overspread the neighbouring Provinces, that the Inhabitants will sell any thing to purchase it, tho the excessive use of it occasions the same Distempers as the immoderate use of Wine. They did so fatigue the Natives to gather and powder this Herb, that multitudes of 'em died; and this, with other Slavish Employments, did much dispeople the Country. The Natives live mostly by Fishing, Hunting, and Shooting.

Tucuman is 300 Leagues long, but varies much in breadth. 'Tis inhabited by four Nations: The furthest South have no fix'd Dwellings, live by Fishing and Hunting, and carry about Mats to serve them for Tents. The North People live in Marshes, and feed most on Fish. The Southern People are the tallest, but the Northern the fiercest; and many of them live in Caves, but those nearest *Peru* in Villages. They are all very slothful, and have store of Brass and Silver, but make little use of them. They have large Sheep which carry their Burdens, and their Wool is almost as sine as Silk. They have many Lions, not so large and fierce as those of *Africa*, but their Tygers are fiercer than those of other Countries. Their two chief Rivers are *Dulce* and *Salado*, so call'd from the Sweet and Salt Taste of their Waters. They have multitudes of Springs and Lakes, some of which have a petrifying quality. The Country was formerly very populous, but their Numbers are much decreas'd since the *Spaniards* planted among them. They easily subdu'd this Country, which was govern'd by abundance of petty Princes continually at war with one another. This Province was first discover'd in 1530. by one *Cesar* a Soldier belonging to Sebastian Cabot, and three more, at the time when *Pizarro* took *Atabalipa* the Great *Inga of Peru*. In 1540. the Viceroy of Peru, *Vaca de Castro*, assign'd this Country to John *Rojas* as a Reward for his Services. He went thither with 200 Spaniards, but was kill'd on the Frontiers by a poison'd Arrow, and his Men under *Francis Mendoza* march'd thro to the River of Plate. *Mendoza* being kill'd as going up that River by Mutineers, *John Nunez*. *Prada* was sent hither by the Viceroy *Peter Gasca*, subdu'd the *Indians* built the Town of *St. Michel* on the Banks of the River *Escava*, and settled Fryars there. This Province was afterwards Subjected to *Chili*; and *France d'Acquire* being sent thither with 200 *Spaniards*, destroy'd St. *Michel*, and built St. *Jago*, now the Metropolis of *Tucuman*, on the River *Dulce*, in S. Lat. 28. says *Techo*, but others place it on the River *Salado*. 'Tis the same Town I have already describ'd In 1558. *Tarita* being made Governour of this Province, built the City of *London* near the Borders of *Chili*, about Lat. 29. calling it so out of compliment to Q. *Mary* of *England*, at that time marry'd to *Philip* II. of *Spain*. This Town serv'd to curb the Natives. *Tarita* did likewise rebuild

St. *Michel*, and reduc'd the Country so much, that 80000 *Indians* who submitted to Spain were muster'd in the Territory of *St. Jago*. The *Spaniards*, as was usual in those days, fighting with one another about the Command of the Provinces, *Tarita* was drove out in 1561. by *Castaneda*; so that most of the Natives revolted, till 1563. that *Francis d' Acquire* reduc'd 'em again, and built *Esteco* above-mention'd. But the *Spaniards* contending afterwards with one another about the Government, many of their Settlements were destroy'd; so that in *Techo's* time the chief Places remaining in this Country were *St. Jago, Cordoua, St. Michel, Salta* or *Lerma, Xuxui* or *St. Salvador, Rioja, Esteco* or *Nuestra Senora de Talavera, London*, and a few other small *Garisons*. He says that in this Country it does not rain in Winter, but in Summer they have thick Milts and Rains enough. The Jesuits are the chief Missionaries here, and settled in the principal Towns. He adds, that near the City *Conception*, which is ninety Leagues from *St. Jago*, the Natives were call'd *Frontones*, because they made the Fore-part of their Heads bald. Their Arms were a Club at their Girdle, Bows and Arrows, and Staves set with Jaw-bones of Fishes. They went naked, and painted their Bodies to make them look terrible. They were continually at War among themselves about the Limits of their Land, and they fix'd the Bodies of their slain Enemies in Rows to the Trunks of Trees, that others might be afraid of invading their Borders.

He adds, that the Country about *St. Michael* is well peopled, abounds with Woods, and all forts of *European* and other Fruits, so that it was call'd *The Land of Promise*; but they are much infested with Tygers, which the Natives kill with great dexterity. *Guaira* a Province of *Paraguay* is very hot, because for the most part under the Tropick of *Capricorn*; is very fruitful, but subject to Fevers and other Diseases: yet when the *Spaniards* came hither in 1550. they are said to have found 300,000 People in this Country, but they say there's scarce a fifth part of that number now; and the Natives very miserable, having no Meat but the Flesh of wild Beasts, nor Bread but what they make of the Root *Mandiosa*. There are Stones here which breed in an oval Stone-Cafe, about the bigness of a Man's Head. Our Author says, they lie under ground, and when they come to maturity, break with a noise like Bombs, and Scatter abundance of beautiful Stones of all colours; which at first the Spaniards took to be of great Value, but did not find 'em so. The other remarkable Product of this Country is a Flower call'd *Granadillo*, which the Jesuit says represents the Instrument of our Saviour's Passion, and produces a Fruit as big as a common Egg, the Inside of which is very delicious. 2. A Fruit call'd *Guembe*, which is very sweet, but has yellow Kernels, which if chew'd, occasions a sharp Pain in the Jaws. 3. Dates, of which they make Wine and Pottage. 4. Wild Swine which have their Navel on their backs, and if not cut off immediately when the Beast is kill'd, corrupts the whole Carcase. 5. Abundance of wild Bees, several sorts of which yield store of Honey and Wax. 6. Snakes which dart from the Trees, and twist themselves about Men or Beasts, and soon kill 'em if they be not immediately cut in pieces. 7. *Macaqua* Birds, so call'd because of an Herb which they eat as an Antidote when hurt by Snakes, which lie and watch for them in the Marshes. They frequently fight those Snakes, for which Nature has provided them with sharp Beaks for a Weapon, and strong Wings to serve them as a Buckler. Our Author mentions the River *Paranapan*, which runs thro this Country, is almost as large as the *Paraguay*, and falls into the Parana. Its Banks on both sides are cover'd with tall Trees, especially Cedars, of so vast a Bulk that they make Canoes out of a single Trunk, which row with twenty

Oars. The Jesuits built the Towns of *Loretto* and St. *Ignatius* and two more near the Conflux of this River and the *Pyrapus*, about 1610. and eleven more have since been built in that Province, where they have brought over many of the Inhabitants to their Religion. They kill'd many of the *Spaniards* at first, and then eat them. These Towns are plac'd by the *Sansons* about Lat. 22. and betwixt Long. 325, and 330.

Our Author not being distinct in describing the Provinces of *Paraguay* and *Tucuman*, but sometimes confounding one with the other, I shall only add a few things more relating to those Countries in general. He mentions a People call'd *Guaicureans* who live on the Banks of *Paraguay* near the City *Assumption*, maintain themselves by Fishing and Hunting, and eat all manner of Serpents and wild Beasts without hurt. They have Tents of Mats, which they remove at pleasure. They dawb one side of their Bodies with stinking Colours, scarify their Faces to make them look terrible, suffer no Hair to grow on their Bodies; and instead of a Beard fasten a Stone of a finger's length to their Chin, and make their Deformity the Standard of their Valour. Their chief Delight is in Drunkenness and War; and to acquire the Title and Dignity of. Soldiers, they must endure to have their Legs, Thighs, Tongues, etc. bored with an Arrow; and if they flinch in the least, are not allow'd that Quality: and therefore they inure their Children from their Youth to all forts of Hardship, and to run Thorns and Briars into their Flesh by way of Pastime. They honour their Commanders so much, that when they spit they receive it into their hands, stand about them when they eat, and observe all their Motions. They chose to fight by night, because they knew nothing of Order, but made their Onsets like Beasts. They either kill'd or fold their Prisoners, if at Man's Estate, and the young ones they bred in their own way. They lurk'd in Marshes and Woods by day, keeping Spies abroad; and thus they plagu'd the *Spaniards* for above a hundred years, till they were civiliz'd by some Missionaries. They would not allow their Women to paint with a Clay-colour till they had tasted human Flesh; and therefore when they kill'd Enemies, would divide them among the young Women, or give them the Corpse of their own Dead. They planted Trees over their Graves, adorn'd them with Ostrich Feathers, and met there at certain times, howling in a most barbarous manner, and performing many lewd and hellish Ceremonies. They worship Parrots as Gods, and have a sort of Bears call'd Ant-Bears: They have long Heads, Snouts much longer than those of Swine, and Tongues like Spears, which they thrust into the Ant-Hills, and lick up those Infects, which are as big as the top of one's finger, and being toasted over the fire, are eat by the Natives and *Spaniards* too as a Dainty.

Father *Techo* mentions another People nam'd *Calchaquins* in this Country, whom he supposes to have been of *Jewish* Descent, because when the *Spaniards* came first here, they found that many of them had *Jewish* Names, and something of their Habit and Customs. Our Author draws a Parallel in several Instances; but this, as well as his Arguments to prove that St. *Thomas* the Apostle planted Christianity in this Country, will scarce obtain Credit among the Learned. I refer the Curious who would know more of those things to our Author, who brings down what he calls the History of this Country as low as 1645. which is the latest Account we have yet printed, except Father *Sepp's* abovemention'd, which brings it to 1691. of which I have given the Substance already.

Before I go further, I shall give some account of the River *Aranoca* or *Oronoco*, which is the Northern Boundary of our *South-Sea* Company's Limits. The Head of it, according to our Maps, is about N. Lat. 3. and in Long. 77. It runs Eastward about 840 miles, about 60 miles N. of the Equator, then run's N. about 420. and turning N E. about 120, falls into the Sea about N. Lat. 9. So that its whole Course is about 1380 miles, including Turnings and Windings; for it runs almost the whole Breadth of that part of. America, since it rises within 160 miles of the *South-Sea*.

Mr. *Sparrey*, who was left in the adjoining Country by Sir *Walter Raleigh* in 1595. gives the following Account of this River. He says it is also call'd *Barequan*, is a great River, and others call it *Paria*. It falls into the Sea by sixteen Mouths, but according to *Sansons* Map, what *Sparrey* calls Mouths are a number of Islands which lie near the Shore at the Entrance of the River, and the chief of those Mouths nam'd *Capuri* lies furthest South. They say it has 9 foot water at full Sea, and but 5 at Ebb: It flows but a small time, when it rises apace, and the Ebb continues 8 hours. There are several other ways of entring this River, for which I refer to *Sparrey*; as also for the other Rivers which fall into it on both sides. He attempted a Passage to *Peru* this way, but in vain. He says that in this Search he enter'd the great River *Papemena*, which is six Leagues broad, and came to a pleasant Island call'd *Athul*, where the Climate is temperate, the Island is well water'd, and abounds with Fish, Fowls, and other Animals for Food. It has many Woods that abound with delicate Fruit all the Year. There's store of Cotton, Balsam, *Brazile* Wood, *Lignum Vita*, Cypress Trees, several Minerals and fine Stones, but for want of Skill he could not judg of the Value of 'em- This Island was not then inhabited, because of the Cannibals nam'd *Caribbes* in the Neighbourhood. He is of opinion, that Westward from *Oronoco* Gold might be found; but it was dangerous to go far into the Country, because the Natives were continually in Arms. He adds, that in the Country of *Curaa*, part of the Province of *Guiana*, which lies on the S. and E. of *Oronoco*, there was plenty of Gold; but it was dangerous seeking for it in the Sands of the Rivers, because of Crocodiles. He talks also of Pearl or Topazes found here, but dubiously. At *Camalaha* South of *Oronoco*, he says, there was then a Fair for Women Slaves, where he bought 8 for a coarse red-hafted Knife, the eldest of whom was not above 18 years old. The Inhabitants, he says, are generally swarthy. We have few modern Accounts of this River, because it is not much frequented for Trade; and therefore I shall say no more of it, but return to my Journal.

Chapter IV

Nothing remarkable happen'd till *Decemb.* 6. when we had close cloudy Weather, with Showers; Wind at E by N. We saw a large Bird call'd *Alcatros*, who spread their Wings from eight to ten foot wide, and are much like a Gannet.

Dec. 7. Rainy Weather, with Thunder and Lightning, a brisk Gale from E by N. to N E. This day I remov'd one of the Boatswain's Mates, and put *Rob. Hollanby* one of our best Sailors in his place.

Dec. 10. Yesterday I exchang'd *Benjamin Long*, one of the Boatswain's Mates, with *Tho. Hughes* Boatswain's Mate on board the *Dutchess*; he being mutinous there, they were willing to be rid of him.

Dec. 13. We had a strong Gale of Wind at SW. Yesterday in the Afternoon we reef'd our Main-Sail, which was the first time since we left *England*.

*Dec..*15. The Colour of the Water being chang'd very much, we founded, but had no Ground: so that this Change is probably occasion'd by the nature of the Ground at bottom. We find it much colder in this Lat. which is 43. 30 S. than in the like degree N. tho the Sun was in its furthest Extent to the Southward: which may be ascrib'd partly to our coming newly out of warmer Climates, which made us more sensible of the Cold; or 'tis probable the Winds blow over larger Tracts of Ice than in the fame Degrees of N. Latitude.

Dec. 18. Cold hazy rainy Weather. Yesterday in the Afternoon one of the *Dutchess's* Men fell out of the Mizen-Top down on the Quarter-Deck, and broke his Skull: They desir'd the Advice of our Surgeon, and I went on board with our two, where they examin'd the Wound, but found the Man irrecoverable; so that be died, and was buried next day. Brisk Gales from the W N W. to the W by S.

Dec. 19. Cold airy Weather: We saw several Crampusses, and a great number of uncommon fort of Porpusses, black on their Back and Fins, and white underneath, with sharp white Noses; they often leap'd a good height out of the Water, turning their white Bellies uppermost: they were much of the shape and bigness of our Porpusses. We also saw many Seals.

Dec. 20. This day, according to what our Committee agreed at *Grande*, we exchang'd Mr. *Vanbrugh* for Mr. *Bath* Agent of the *Dutchess*. Easy Gales of Wind, but very veerable. This morning at four we had a very thick Fog, when we were caught in Stays, and lost sight of the *Dutchess*, tho we made all the noise agreed on between us. At nine a clock it clear'd up, being very little Wind, and we were, within a League of them.

Dec. 21. Easy Gales of Wind, but very veerable. We have seen a deal of Rock-Weed for some days past, of a great length and generally round in large Branches., Lat. 48. 50. S.

Dec. 22. Fair Weather with Rain, Wind very Bearable. The Water is generally discolour'd. We had a good Observ. Lat. 49.32. S.

Dec. 23. At ten this morning we saw Land, bearing S S E. dist. 9 Ls. It appear'd first in three, afterwards in several more Islands. At twelve it bore S. 4 W. the West End dist. 6 Ls. a long Tract of Land. We saw most of that which appear'd at first to be Islands, join with the low lands. The Wind being

Westerly, and blowing fresh, we could not weather it; but was forc'd to bear away and run along Shore from 3 to 4 Ls. dist. It lay as near as we could guess E N E. and W S W. This is *Falkland's* Land, describ'd in few Draughts, and none lay it down right, tho the Latitude agrees pretty well. The middle of it lies in Latitude 51. 00. S. and I make the Longitude of it to be 61. 54. West from *London*. The two Islands extend about two Degrees in Length, as near as I could judg by what I saw.

Dec. 24. Last night we reef'd both Courses; it blowing strong, lay by from eight till three in the Morning, with our Heads to Northward, Wind at W by S. because we could not tell how far *Falkland* Islands ran to the Eastward. Between two and three a clock yesterday in the Afternoon we ran by a high round large white remarkable Rock, which appear'd by it self near 3 Ls. without the Land; which is not unlike Portland, but not so high, and the Rock like that call'd the *Fastneste* to the Westward of Cape Clear in *Ireland*. At four yesterday in the Afternoon the North-East End bore S E by S. 7 Ls. the white Rock bore S. 3 Ls. At fix the Easternmost Land in fight bore S E. 7 Ls. All this Land appear'd with gentle Descents from Hill to Hill, and seem'd to be good Ground, with Woods and Harbours. At three a clock we made sail, steering S E. Lat.52. S.

Dec. 25. Yesterday Noon we saw the Land again, and find it to trim away Southerly from the white Rock. A strong Gale of Wind at S W. At Six a clock in the Evening we loft fight of the Land, but could not come near enough to see if it was inhabited; and spy'd a Sail under our Lee-Bow bearing S E. from us, dist. about 4 Ls. We immediately let our Reefs out, chas'd and got ground of her apace: we kept sight till ten at night, when we loft her. We spoke with our Consort, and were both of opinion that the Chafe would, as soon as she lost fight of us, if homeward bound, bear away to the Northward; so we ran North till Dawning: then we stood to the Westward till it was light, and our Consort kept on with an easy Sail When it was full light we saw nothing, being thick hazy Weather: we bore away, and were with our Consort again by five a dock. Between six and seven it clear'd up: we few the Chase bearing about S by E. between 3 and 4 Ls. from us. It falling calm, we both got out our Oars, row'd and tow'd, with our Boats a-head, and made pretty good way; had a small Breeze at North, so we set all the Sail we could, and by twelve a clock had gain'd very much ground of the Chase. We had an Observ. Lat. 52.40.

Dec. 26. We kept on rowing and towing till about six in the Evening; and perceiving we approach'd her, I went in the Boat to speak with Capt. Courtney, and agree how to engage her, if a great Ship, as she appear'd to be; and also adjusted Signals, if either of us should find it proper to board her in the night. I return'd aboard as soon as possible, when we had a fine Breeze: we got in our Boats and Oars, and made all possible Sail after the Chafe, kept in sight of her till past tea a clock, bearing S S W. of us, when it came on thick again; we kept her open on the Larboard, and the *Dutchess* on the Starboard-Bow, and being short Nights, we thought it impossible to lose one Another. At one a clock this Morning my Officers persuaded me to shorten Sail, telling me we should lose our Consort if we kept on: I was prevail'd with to do so, and in the Morning had a very thick Fog, so that I could see neither our Consort nor Chafe till an hour after 'twas full Light. When it clear'd up, we saw our Consort on our Larboard-Bow; we fir'd a Gun for her to bear down, but immediately we saw the Chafe ahead of her about four miles, which gave us new Life. We forthwith hal'd up for them; but the Wind soon veering a-head, had a great disadvantage in the Chafe. We ran at a great rate, being smooth Water; but it coming on to blow more and more, the Chafe outbore our Consort: so she gave off, and being to Windward, came down very melancholy to us, supposing the Chafe to have been a *French* homeward-bound Ship from the *South-Seas.* Thus this Ship escap'd; which, considering that we always out-went her before, is as strange as our first seeing of her in this place, because all Ships that we have heard of bound out or home this way, kept within *Falkland's* Island. At twelve a clock we saw a little plain low Island, which bore W N W. dist. 4-Ls. not mark'd in any of our Charts. The Wind has been very veerable since six a clock last night, from the N N E. to the S. where it now is. Lat. 53.11. S.

Dec. 27. Strong Gales, with Squalls from the South to the West. The *Dutchess* put her Guns into the Hold again, that she took up in the Chase. Yesterday at two in the Afternoon we put about, and stood off to the Eastward from the little low Island: because we could but just weather it, we were not willing to come too near it. Lat. 54. 15. S.

Dec. 30. Fresh Gales of Wind at West, hazy Weather mix'd with small Rain. We had an Observ. Lat. 58.20.

January I. Fresh Gales of Wind from the W N W. to the W S W. with Fogs, but indifferent smooth Water. This being New-Year's Day, every Officer was wish'd a merry New-Year by our Musick; and I had a large Tub of Punch hot upon the Quarter-Deck, where every Man in the Ship had above a Pint to his share, and drank our Owners and Friends Healths in *Great Britain,* to a happy new Year, a good Voyage, and a safe Return. We bore down to our Consort, and gave them three Huzza's, wishing them the like.

Jan. 2. Fresh Gales from the W S W. to the N W. with Fogs. Clothes and Liquor were now an excellent Commodity amongst our Ships Company, who are but meanly stor'd: We had six Taylors at work for several weeks to make them Clothing, and pretty well supply'd their Wants by the spare Blankets and red Clothes belonging to the Owners; and what every Officer could spare, was alter'd for the Mens Use. The like was done on board the *Dutchess.*

Jan. 5. Just past twelve Yesterday it came on to blow strong: We got down our Fore-Yard, and reef'd our Fore-Sail and Main-Sail; but there came on a violent Gale of Wind, and a great Sea. A little before six we saw the *Dutchess* lowering her Main-Yard: the Tack flew up, and the Lift unreev'd, so that the Sail to Leeward was in the water and all a-back, their Ship took in a great deal of Water to Leeward; immediately they loos'd their Sprit-Sail, and wore her before the Wind: I wore after her, and came as near as I could to 'em, expecting when they had gotten their Main-Sail stow'd they would take another Reef in, and bring to again under a two-reef'd Main-Sail, and reef'd and ballanc'd Mizen, if the Ship would not keep to without it: but to my surprize they kept scudding to the Southward. I dreaded running amongst Ice, because it was excessive cold; so I fir'd a Gun as a Signal for them to bring to, and brought to our selves again under the same reef'd Main-Sail. They kept on, and our Men on the look-out told me they had an Ensign in their Maintop-Mast Shrouds as a Signal of Distress, which made me doubt they had an sprung their Main-Mast; so I wore again, our Ship working exceeding well in this great Sea. Just before night I was up with them again, and set our

Fore-Sail twice reef'd to keep 'em Company, which I did all night. About three this morning it grew more moderate; we soon after made a Signal to speak with them, and at five they brought to: when I came within haile, I enquir'd how they all did aboard; they answer'd, they had ship'd a great deal of Water in lying by, and were forc'd to put before the Wind, and the Sea had broke in the Cabin-Windows, and over their Stern, filling their Steerage and Waste, and had like to have spoil'd several Men; but God be thank'd all was otherwise indifferent well with 'em, only they were intolerably cold, and every thing wet. At ten we made sail, Wind at W N W. and moderate. Lat. 60. 58.

Jan. 6. Raw cold Weather, with some Rain. A great Sea from the N W. little Wind from the N N W. to the West. I and Capt. *Dampier* went in the Yall on board the *Dutchess*, to visit 'em after this Storm; where we found 'em in a very orderly pickle, with all their Clothes drying, the Ship and Rigging cover'd with them from the Deck to the Main-Top: They got six more Guns into the Hold, to make the Ship lively.

Jan. 7. Fresh Gales of Wind, with hazy Weather and some small Rain. Yesterday about three in the Afternoon *John Veale a* Landman died, having lain ill a Fortnight, and had a Swelling in his Legs ever since he left *Grande*. At nine last night we bury'd him; this is the first that died by Sickness out of both Ships since we left *England*. Several of the *Dutchess's* Men bad contracted Illness by the Wet and Cold. Wind from the N N W. to the W N W.

Jan. 10. Strong Gales of Wind, with Squalls of Rain and Hail, and a great Sea from the W. We lay by with our Head to the Southward till 12 last night, then came to sail under three-reef'd Courses, and sometimes the Main-top-Sail low set, Wind from the W. to the N. and thence to the N. W. We have no Night here. Lat. 61. 53. Long. W. from *Lond.* 79. 58. being the furthest we run this way, and for ought we know the furthest that any one has yet been to the Southward.

Jan. 14. Moderate Gales with cloudy Weather, Wind veerable. This day the *Dutchess* bury'd a Man that died of the Scurvy.

Jan. 15. Cloudy Weather, with Squalls of Rain, fresh Gales at S W. We had an Observ. Lat. 56. S. We now account our selves in the *South-Sea*, being got round Cape *Horne*. The *French* Ships that came first to trade in these Seas came thro the Straits of Magellan: but Experience has taught them since, that it is the best Passage to go round Cape Horne, where they have Sea-room enough; the Straits being in many places very narrow, with strong Tides and no Anchor-ground.

Chapter V

Here I think it proper to give an Account of the first Discovery of the South-Sea, of the Passage to it by the Straits of *Magellan*, of the chief of those who have pass'd those Straits, and a short Description of the Country on both sides of 'em.

An Account of the Discovery of the South-Sea, *and of the Straits of* Magellan, *etc. from* Ovalle *and other Authors.*

The first *European* who discover'd the *South-Sea*, was *Basco* or *Vasco Nunes de Balboa* a *Spaniard*, in 1513. He was the first who landed on the Isthmus of *Darien*, and made war with their Caciques or Princes; who not being able to resist his Fire-Arms, and perceiving that the chief Design of the *Spaniards* was to find Gold, one of the Caciques told *Vasco*, that since they were so fond of that which he and his Countrymen valu'd so little, he would conduct them over the Mountains to another Sea, upon which they might find a Country where the People had all their Utensils of Gold. This was the first notice the Spaniards had of the *South-Sea*. Vasco march'd on till he came near the top of the highest Mountain, where he order'd his Men to halt, because he would have the honour of first discovering that Sea himself: which having done, he fell down on his knees and thank'd God for his Success, and call'd it the *South-Sea*, in opposition to that on the other Side the Continent. Having pass'd these Mountains, he march'd down till he came to the Coast, and took possession of it in the name of the King *of Spain*. When here turn'd back, he found a new *Spanish* Governour, in *Darien* call'd *Pedrarias*; who being his Enemy because be envy'd the King's making him Governour and Admiral of the *South-Sea*, he falsly accus'd him. of Treason and cut off his Head, and sent *Caspar Morales* and *Francis Pizarro* to compleat the Discovery, with a good number of Men, and larger Dogs that were as terrible to the *Indians* vaster *Spaniards* Fire-Arms. Here they discover'd the Isle of Pearls, and forc'd the Natives to fish for them, and then discover'd the rest of the Coast. The first who found a Passage from the *North-Sea* was *Ferdinand Magaillans*, who in 1519. sail'd on purpose by Commission from the Emperor *Charles* V. to discover it. In Lat. 52.S. he found the Passage, which from him has been since call'd the Straits of *Magellan*, *Pigasetta* an *Italian*, who made the Voyage with him, says that in S. Lat. 491\2 at Port *St. Julian*, they found Giants whose Waste a middle-siz'd Man could scarce reach with his Head: they were clad with the Skins of Beasts as monstrous as themselves, arm'd with huge Bows and Arrows, and of a Strength proportionable to their Bulk, yet good-natur'd: One of them seeing him self in a Looking-Glass on board the Ship, was so frighten'd that he run backward, and tumbled down several Men that stood behind him. The Crew gave Toys to some of them, at which being mightily pleas'd, they suffer'd them to put Shackles about their Arms and Legs, which they took for Ornaments; but when they found themselves fast, bellow'd like Bulls. One of them, he says, made his Escape from nine Men, after they had got him down and ty'd his bands. Other Voyagers say they have seen such Giants in those parts, particularly Mr. *Candish*, *Sebald de Wert* in 1599. and *Spilberg* in 1614. but the Reader may believe of this Story what he pleases. *Pigasetta* says the Straits were 100 Ls. long, in some places very wide, and in others not above half a League over. *Magaillans* pass'd 'em in *Novemb.* 1520. and being overjoy'd, he call'd the Gape from whence he first saw the *South-Sea*; the *Cape of*

Desire. After rambling almost four months in the *South-Sea,* where he suffer'd extreme Want, and lost many of his Men, he sail'd to the *Ladrones* Islands, and foolishly engaging 7000 Natives in *Mathan,* which is one of them., he was kill'd. One of his Ships forsook him as he pass'd the Straits, and return'd to *Spain:* of the other four, only the Ship Victoria return'd to *St Lucar near Sevil,* under the Command of *John Sebastian Cabot,* who was nobly rewarded by the Emperor.

In 1539. *Alonso de Camargo* a *Spaniard* pass'd the same Straits, and arriv'd at the Port of *Arequipa in* Peru; but much shatter'd, having lost one of his Ships, and another leaving him, return'd to *Spain.* After him several other *Spaniards* pass'd the same way, and they planted a Colony and Garison at the North End, to block up the Passage to other Nations; but without success, the Garison being all starv'd or destroy'd by the *Indians.*

The 15*th* of *Novemb.* 1577. the famous Sir *Francis Drake* set out from *Plymouth* with five Sail, and having touch'd at several places by the way, enter'd the Straits the 21st of August following. He found them very dangerous, because of the many Turnings, contrary Winds, and sudden Blasts from high Mountains cover'd with Snow on both sides, and their Tops reaching above the Clouds, and no anchoring but in some narrow River or Creek. The 24th he came to an Island in the Straits, where there were so many Fowls call'd *Penguins,* that his Men kill'd 3000 in a day, which serv'd them for Provisions. The 6th of *September* he enter'd the *South-Sea,* where he met with dreadful Storms, and one of his Ships was drove back into the Straits, thro which she return'd to *England;* as Sir *Francis Drake* did July 24. 1580. being the first Sea-Captain that ever sail'd round the World, and brought his Ship home, which was accounted a great Honour to the *English* Nation.

July I. 1586. Mr. *Tho. Candish,* afterwards Sir *Thomas,* sail'd from *Plymouth* with three Ships, and the 6th of *January* after enter'd the Straits, having met with a severe Storm near the mouth of 'em. He took the Remainders of a *Spanish* Garison there, who from 400 were reduc'd to 23 by Famine; and those of King Philip's City, which had been built in the Straits, were in the same miserable Condition, so that they abandon'd the Place. They found Cannibals in tome part of the Straits, who had eat many of the *Spaniards,* and design'd the like to the *English,* had they not been kept off by their Guns. Mr. *Candish* was stop'd here a considerable while by a furious Storm and bad Weather, which reduc'd him to Want of Provisions, till the 24th of *February* that he got into the *South-Sea,* and bought Provisions of the *Indians.* Mr. *Candish* return'd to *England,* after having sail'd round the World, the 9*th* of *September* next Year. He again attempted the Passage of the same Straits in 1591. but without Success; as Mr. *Fenton* did in 1582. as *Floris* did at the same time; the Earl of *Cumberland* in 1586. Mr. *Chidley* in 1589. and Mr. *Wood* in 1596. Sir *Richard Hawkins* pass'd them in 1593. but was taken by the *Spaniards;* and Mr. *Davis* the Discoverer to the N W. pass'd and repass'd those Straits, but was forc'd back by contrary Winds. So that our Countrymen, tho they did not all succeed in the Attempt, yet have been the most fortunate in passing them, of any other Nation: for the *Dutch* pass'd them in 1597. with five Ships, of which only one return'd. Five other *Dutch* Ships pass'd them in 1614. when they lost one of them. In 1623. the *Dutch Nassaw* Fleet, so call'd because the Prince of *Orange* was the greatest Adventurer, attempted it with fifteen brave Ships, and 2 or 3000 Men; but were repuk'd, wherever they came to land, by the *Spaniards*, so that they could not settle there.

Other Nations attempted it likewise, and particularly Don *Garcia de Loaisa*, a Knight of *Malta*, and a *Spaniard*, with seven Ships and 450 Men; and tho he pass'd the Straits, he died himself, and all his Ships were afterwards taken by the *Portuguese* or others. *Vargas* Bishop of *Placentia* sent 7 Ships to attempt it, one of which only succeeded, went to *Arequipa* a Port on the *South-Sea*, and discover'd the Situation of the Coast of *Peru*; but went no further. *Ferdinand Cortex*, the Conqueror of *New Spain*, sent two Ships and 400 Men in 1528. to discover the way to the *Moluccas* thro the Straits, but without success. Two *Genoese* Ships were the first that attempted it in 1526. after *Magellan*, but could not effect it. *Sebastian Cabot* try'd it also by Commission from Don *Emanuel* King of *Portugal*, twit could not do it. *America Vespusius* was sent by the same Prince, but could neither find the Straits nor the River of *La Plata*. *Simon Alcasara* a *Spaniard* attempted it likewise with several Ships and 440 Men, but came back without performing it, his Men having mutiny'd. All these Attempts by the *Spaniards*, &c. happen'd before Sir *Francis Drake* perform'd it.

In the Reports made of those Straits upon Oath to the Emperor *Charles V*. those who attempted this Passage give the following Account, *viz.* That from the Cape of 11000 *Virgins* at the Entrance of the North Sea, to the Cape of *Desire* at the Entrance of the South-Sea, is 100 *Spanish* Ls. that they found in this Strait three great Bays of about 7 Leagues wide from Land to Land, but the Entrances not above half a League, and encompass'd with such high Mountains, that the Sun never shines in them, so that they are intolerably cold, there being a continual Snow, and the Nights very long: That they found good Water with Cinamon-Trees, and several others, which tho they look green burnt in the Fire like dry Wood: That they found many good sorts of Fish, good Harbours with 15 fathom Water, and several pleasant Rivers and Streams: That the Tides of both Seas meet about the middle of the Straits with a prodigious Noise and Shock; but some of the *Portuguese*, who had pass'd the Straits, say they are only high Floods which last about a month, rise to a great height, and sometimes fall so low and ebb so fast, that they leave Ships on dry ground. The Reader may find more of this in *Herrera's* History: but others differ in their Accounts, and particularly *Spilberg* a *Dutchman*, who mentions a Port here that he call'd *Famous*, by way of Eminency, the adjacent Soil producing Fruit of various Colours and excellent Taste, and affording Brooks of very good Water. He mentions 24 other Ports besides those that he did not see, and particularly the *Piemento* or Pepper-Harbour, so call'd because of the Trees which grow there of an Aromatick Smell, whose Bark tastes like Pepper, and is more hot and quick than that of the *East-Indies*. The *Spaniards* having brought some of it to *Seville*, it was sold there for two Crowns a pound.

The last of our Countrymen who pass'd them, was Sir *John Narborough*, who set out from the *Thames*, *May* 15. 1669. with two Ships. He had K. *Charles* II's Commission, was furnish'd out at his Majesty's Charge, and enter'd the Straits *October* 22. following. He says, that from the Entrance of this Strait to the Narrow there's good Anchorage, and not much Tide, but in the Narrow the Tide runs very strong. The Flood sets into the Straits, and the Ebb out, keeping its Course as on other Coasts. It rises and falls near 4 Fathom perpendicular, and it is high Water here on the Change of the Moon at eleven a clock. When he came to the Narrow, he found the Tide very Strong, which endanger'd the running of his Ships upon the Sleep Rocks on the North side. From the first Narrow to the second is above 8 Ls. and the Reach betwixt them 7 Ls broad. He found a Bay on the North fide at the Point of the second Narrow, where one may ride in 8 Fathom Water in clear sandy Ground half a mite from the Shore. In the Channel of the second Narrow he found 38 Fathom Water, and several Bays and Cliffs with little Islands. He exchang'd several Trifles with the Natives for Bows and Arrows, and their Skin-Coats. They were of a middle Stature, well limb'd, with round Faces, low Foreheads, little Noses, small black Eyes and Ears, black flaggy Hair Of an indifferent length, their Teeth white, their Faces of an Olive-Colour, daub'd with Spots of white Clay and Streaks of Soot, their Bodies painted with red Earth and Grease, their Clothing of the Skins of Seals, Guianacoes and Otters, wrapt about them like the *Scotch* Highlanders. Plads. They had Caps of the Skins of Fowls with the Feathers on, and pieces of Skins on their feet to keep them from the ground. They are very active and nimble, and when about Business go quite naked; only the Women have a piece of Skin before them, and differ from the Men in Habit only by want of Caps, and having Bracelets of Shells about their Necks. They seem to have no manner of Government nor Religion, live by Hunting and Fishing, and are arm'd with Bows and Arrows; the latter 18 Inches long, and headed with Flint Stones. These People Sir *John* found in *Elizabeth-Isle* which lies near the second Narrow. In Port *Famine* Bay, S. Lat. 53. 35. he found good Wood and Water, and abundance of *Piemento* Trees. Their Language is guttural and flow. Sir *John* is of opinion, that the Mountains contain Gold or Copper. He computes the whole Length of the Straits at 116 Leagues. For the rest we refer to him.

I have insisted the longer on these Straits, partly because they are so much talk'd of, and partly to justify our going to the *South-Seas* by the way of Cape *Horne*, which is far more safe: so that in all probability the Straits of *Magellan* will be little frequented by Europeans in time to come.

The Land on the North side of the Straits is call'd *Patagonia*, and that on the South *Terra del Fuego*, because of the numerous Fires and the great Smoke which the first Discoverers saw upon it. It extends the whole Length of the Straits, and lies from East to West about 130 Leagues, according to *Ovalle*; and before the Discovery of the Straits of *St. Vincent*, otherwise call'd *Le Maire's* Straits, was suppos'd to join to some part of the *Terra Australis*. *Ovalle* says, that on the Continent of *Chili* near the Straits of *Magellan*, there's a People call'd *Cessares*, who are suppos'd to be descended from part of the *Spaniards* that were forc'd ashore in the Straits, when the Bishop of *Placentia* sent the Ships abovemention'd to discover the *Molucca* Islands. 'Tis suppos'd they contracted Marriages with some *Indian* Nation, where they have multiply'd, and taught them to build Cities and the Use of Bells. *Ovalle* says, that when he wrote the History of *Chili*, he receiv'd Letters and other Informations that there is such a Nation in those parts, and that one of the Missionaries had been in the Country with Captain *Navarro*, and found the People to be of a white Complexion with red in their Cheeks; by the Shape of their Bodies they seem'd to be Men of Courage and Activity, and by the Goodness of their Complexion 'twas probable they might be mix'd with a Race of *Flemmings*, who had been ship-wreck'd in those parts. But there being no farther Account of these People since *Ovalle's* Account of *Chili* in the Year 1646. we believe this Relation to be fabulous.

M. de *Beauchesne Gouin*, who is the last that attempted the Passage of the Straits of *Magellan*, that we have have heard of, came to an anchor at the *Virgins* Cape in the mouth of this Strait the 24th of *June* 1699. and the Wind being contrary, be lay at anchor betwixt the Continent and *Terra del Fuego*. He weigh'd again, the Winds being still contrary, and on the third of *July* anchor'd at Port *Famine* in the Straits, where the *Spaniards* had built a Garison, but were forc'd to quit it for want of Provisions. He observes, that from the Mouth of the Straits to this place, the Climate seem'd to be as temperate as in *France*, tho now the coldest Season of the Year in those parts. He found abundance of Wood for Firing, but the greatest Inconveniency he met with there, was from the great Storms of Snow, tho it did not lie long, being carry'd off by Rains which come from the West. He is of opinion that a Settlement might easily be made here, in a part of the Country extending above 20 Leagues; and that he was inform'd the Islands of *St. Elizabeth* in the Straits are proper enough for Corn and Cartel, if planted with them. He sent his Sloop ashore on *Terra del Fuego*, where he saw Fires, and found the savage Natives by 50 or 60 together in Companies, and some of them came aboard his Ship that lay 5 Ls. from the shore. They were very peaceable and friendly, but more miserable than our Beggars in *Europe* having no Clothes but a strait Coat of wild. Beasts Skins, that comes no lower than their knees, and pitiful Hutts made up of Poles cover'd with Skins of Beasts, and this is all the shelter they have against the Extremity of the Weather. They came in such multitudes to beg from him; as soon made him weary of their Company; so that he weigh'd again the 16th of *August*, and stopt at Port *Galand* to leave some Letters there for those who were to follow him from *France*, as had been agreed on, And here he observes, that both the. Climate and the Navigation of the Straits are very unequal; and that from this place to the Entrance of the *South-Sea* there's nothing but extraordinary high Mountains on each side, from whence come very impetuous and frightful Torrents, and Scarce any place for Anchorage to be sound, of one Day without either Rain or Snow. He adds, that he found an Island opposite to the Mouth of the Strait of *Sr. Jerem*, that is set down in none of our Maps. This Island, he says, has two good Harbours, which may be of great consequence to those who pass this way. He took possession of it, call'd it by the name of the Island *Louis le Grand*; the largest Harbour he nam'd Port *Dauphin*, and the lesser, which is very convenient, Port *Philippeaux*. After having given this Character of those Straits, he says one may be sure of a Passage thro them, provided it be in the proper Season, but 'tis very difficult in the Winter. He came out of those Straits into the *South-Sea* on the 21*st* of January, 1700. and went to view the Harbour of *San Domino*, which he says is the *Spanish* Frontier, and the only Place where a new Settlement can be made there, the rest being all possess'd already. He arriv'd there the 3d of *February*, 1700. and on the 5th anchor'd on the East of an Island call'd by different Names, but the latest Authors call it St. *Magdalen's* Island. He sent his first Lieutenant to view and take possession of it, who brought him word that it was a very pleasant place, and shew'd him some fine beautiful Shrubs and Pease-Blossoms that he sound upon the East side of it; from whence he conjectures that it may be a proper place to inhabit, tho he owns that the Climate is very moist, and they have frequent Rains and Mists, which he ascribes to the high Mountains. He made ready to discover four other islands, which lie in view of this Isle and the Main Land,

and founded as he went on, but durst not venture to go among 'em with so large a Ship, because there blew a strong North-West Wind, follow'd by a thick Mist, which made him lose fight of Land; so that to his great sorrow he could not compleat the Discovery of that Frontier. He adds, that 'tis full of high Mountains down to the very Sea; but was afterwards inform'd by a *Spaniard* who winter'd in those parts, that there's a very good Harbour for Ships to ride in, where they may be moor'd to tall Trees, and that there are very few Inhabitants on this Coast, but some wandring Savages, like those on the Straits of *Magellan*.

This and the other Journals convince me intirely that the best way to the *South-Sea* is round Cape *Horne*, the Route we pursu'd in our Voyage.

Besides what I said from my own Observation, to prove how extensive a Trade we might have in those Seas, I shall add the following Observations from M. *de Beauchesne*; who says, that tho he was look'd upon as a Free-Boater, and that the then *Spanish* Governours on those Coasts were forbid to trade or suffer the People to trade with any but their own Subjects in those Seas, and that at *Valdivia* and other places they fir'd at him when he approach'd their Harbour's and deny'd so much as to sell him any Provisions, or to suffer him to wood or water; yet at *Rika* some particular Persons traded with him to the Value of 50000 Crowns, and told him, That that place was not so proper for them to act so manifestly contrary to Law, but if he went to a place more retir'd, they would buy all he had, tho both his Ships were full of Goods. Accordingly, when he came to *Hilo*, a great number of Merchants bought all that he had of Value at good rates. He owns that the Cloth lie had on board was half rotten, that the Merchants were vex'd at their Disappointment, and express'd their Resentment that he should come to those parts so ill provided: but in other places the People bought all to the very Rags be bad on board, and brought him Provisions in abundance to sell, tho they were forbid doing so on pain of Death; and the Officers themselves conniv'd at it.

He return'd by the way of Cape *Horne* in 58 deg. 15 min. *January* 1701. and had as good a Passage and Season as could be desir'd, but few no Land on either side till the 19th of *January* 1701. when he discover'd a small Island about 3 or 4 Ls. round, in Lat. 52. odd min. not mark'd in our Maps, with Strong Currents near it; and on the 20th he came to the Isle of *Sebald de Wert*, which is a marshy Land with some rocky Mountains, no Trees, but abundance of Sea-Fowl.

It is proper here likewise to give an Account of the Straits of *Le Maire*, so call'd from *James Le Maire* an Amsterdam Merchant, their Discoverer in 1615. They lie in S. Lat. 55.36. and are form'd by the *Terra del Fuego* on the West, and an Island by the *Dutch* call'd *Staten-landt*, or the Country of the States, on the E. The Straits are 8 Leagues wide, with good Roads on each side, and plenty of Fish and Fowl. The Land on both sides is high and mountainous. The Discoverers saw very large Fowls bigger than Sea-Mews, and their Wings when extended above a Fathom long each. They were so tame that they flew into the Ships, and suffer'd the Sailors to handle them. In Lat. 57. they saw two barren Islands, which they call'd *Barnevelt*; and the South Cape of *Terra del Fuego*, which runs out in a Point to Lat. 57.48. they nam'd Cape *Horne*. Some compute this Strait to be only 5 Leagues in Length.

Ovalle says, that in 1619. the King of *Spain* being inform'd that *Le Maire* had discover'd these Straits, he sent two Vessels to make a further Discovery of 'em. These Ships came to the East side of the Straits of *Magellan*, where the Crew found a sort of Giants higher by the Head than any *Europeans*, who gave them Gold in exchange for Scissars and other Bawbles; but this can't be rely'd on. They went thro this Strait in less than a day's time, it being not above 7 Leagues in length,

Chapter VI

I return now to my Journal.

Jan. 16. Fresh Gales of Wind with cloudy Weather. These 24 hours we had extraordinary smooth Water, as if we were close under Land: Indifferent warm Weather. Wind from the W S W. to W by N.

January 20. Yesterday at three in the Afternoon we saw high Land bearing E by N- dist. about 10 Ls. being the Land about Port *St. Stephen's* on the Coast *or Patagonia* in the *South-Sea*, describ'd in the Draughts. S. Lat. 47.

Jan. 22. Fair Weather, with fresh Gales of Wind from W by S. to the W N W. Last night *George Cross* died; he was a Smith by Trade, and Armourer's Mate. We and the *Dutchess* have had a great many Men down with the Cold, and some with the Scurvey; the Distemper that this Man died of. The *Dutchess* bad always more sick Men than we, and have so now: They buried but one Man that died of Sickness, and tell us they hope the rest will recover. We have but one Man whose Life we doubt of, tho most want a Harbour. This day Capt. *Courtney* and Capt. *Cook* din'd with us. At two a clock we saw the Land on the Coast of Patagonia, being very high, distant about 14 Ls. Lat. 44. 9. S.

Jan. 26. Fresh Gales with Clouds and Rain, We spoke with our Consort this day, who complains their Men grow worse and worse, and want a Harbour to refresh 'em; several of ours are also very indifferent, and if we don't get ashore, and a small Refreshment, we doubt we shall both lose several Men. We are very uncertain of the Latitude and Longitude of *Juan Fernandez*, the Books laying 'em down so differently, that not one Chart agrees with another; and being but a small Island we are in some doubts of striking it, so design to hale in for the main Land to direct us.

Jan. 27. Fair Weather, smooth Water, pleasant Gales of Wind, veerable from the W. to the N. W, had a good Amplitude, found the Variation to be 10 deg. Eastward. This is an excellent Climate. Lat. 36. 36. S.

Jan. 28. We have had moderate Weather. At six a clock we saw the Land, the Easternmost appearing like an Island, which we agree to be the Island of *St. Mary* on the Coast of *Chili*: it bore E by N. dist. 9 or 10 Ls. Our Consort's Men are very ill; their want of Clothes, and being often wet in the cold Weather, has been the greatest cause of their being more sick than our Ships Company.

Jan. 31. These 24 hours we had the Wind between the S. and S W by W. At seven this morning we made the Island of *Juan Fernandez*; it bore W S W. dist, about 7 Ls. at Noon W by S. 6 Ls. We had a good Observ. Lat. 34. 10. S.

February 1. About two yesterday in the Afternoon we hoisted our Pinnace out; Capt. *Dover* with the Boats Crew went in her to go ashore, tho we could not be less than 4 Ls off. As soon as the Pinnace was gone, I went on board the *Dutchess*, who admir'd our Boat attempted going ashore at that distance from Land: 'twas against my Inclination, but to oblige Capt. *Dover* I consented to let her go. As soon as it was dark, we saw a Light ashore; our Boat was then about a League from the Island, and bore away for the Ships as soon as she saw the Rights. We put out Lights abroad for the Boat, tho some were of opinion the Lights we saw were our Boats Lights; but as Night came on, it appear'd too large for that. We fir'd one Quarter-Deck Gun and several

Muskets, showing Lights in our Mizen and Fore-Shrouds, that our Boat might find us, whilst we ply'd in the Lee of the Island. About two in the Morning our Boat came on board, having been two hours on board the *Dutchess*, that took 'em up a-stern of us: we were glad they got well off, because it begun to blow. We are all convinc'd the Light is on the shore, and design to make our Ships ready to engage, believing them to be *French* Ships at anchor, and we must either fight 'em or want Water, &c.

Febr. 2. We stood on the back side along the South end of the Island, in order to lay in with the first Southerly Wind, which Capt. *Dampier* told us generally blows there all day long. In the Morning, being past the Island, we tack'd to lay it in close aboard the Land; and about ten a clock open'd the South End of the Island, and ran close aboard the Land that begins to make the North-East side. The Flaws came heavy off shore, and we were forc'd to reef our Top-Sails when we open'd the middle Bay, where we expected to find our Enemy, but saw all clear, and no Ships in that nor the other Bay next the N W. End These two Bays are all that Ships ride in which recruit on this Island, but the middle Bay is by much the best. We guess'd there had been Ships there, but that they were gone on sight of us. We sent our Yall ashore about Noon, with Capt. *Dover*, Mr. *Frye*, and six Men, all arm'd; mean while we and the *Dutchess* kept turning to get in, and such heavy Flaws came off the Land, that we were forc'd to let fly our Topsail-Sheet, keeping all Hands to stand by our Sails, for fear of the Wind's carrying 'em away: but when the Flaws were gone, we had little or no Wind. These Flaws proceeded from the Land, which is very high in the middle of the Island. Our Boat did not return, so we sent our Pinnace with the Men arm'd, to see what was the occasion of the Yall's stay; for we were afraid that the *Spaniards* had a Garison there, and might have seiz'd 'em. We put out a Signal for our Boat, and the Dutchess show'd a *French* Ensign. Immediately our Pinnace return'd from the shore, and brought abundance of Craw-fish, with a Man cloth'd in Goat-Skins, who look'd wilder than the first Owners of them. He had been on the Island four Years and four Months, being left there by Capt' *Stradling* in the *Cinque-Ports*; his Name was *Alexander Selkirk* a *Scotch* Man, who had been Master of the *Cinque-Ports*, a Ship that came here last with Capt. *Dampier*, who told me that this was the best Man in her; so I immediately agreed with him to be a Mate on board our Ship. 'Twas he that made the Fire last night when he saw our Ships, which he judg'd to be *English*. During his stay here, he saw several Ships pass by, but only two came in to anchor. As he went to view them, he found 'em to be *Spaniards*, and retir'd from 'em; upon which they shot at him. Had they been *French*, he would have submitted; but chose to risque his dying alone on the Island, rather than fall into the hands of the *Spaniards* in these parts, because he apprehended they would murder him, or make a Slave of him in the Mines, for he fear'd they would spare no Stranger that might be capable of discovering the *South-Sea*. The *Spaniards* had landed, before he knew what they were, and they came so near him that he had much ado to escape; for they not only shot at him, but pursu'd him into the Woods, where he climb'd to the top of a Tree, at the foot of which they made water, and kill'd several Goats just by, but went off again without discovering him. He told us that he was born at Largo in the County of *Fise* in *Scotland*, and was bred a Sailor from his Youth. The reason of his being left here was a difference betwixt him and his Captain; which, together with the Ships being leaky, made him willing rather to stay here, than go along with him at first; and when he was at last willing, the Captain would not receive him. He had been in the Island before to wood and water, when two of the Ships Company were left upon it for six Months till the Ship return'd, being chas'd thence by two *French South-Sea* Ships.

He had with him his Clothes and Bedding; with a Firelock, some Powder, Bullets, and Tobacco, a Hatchet, a Knife, a Kettle, a Bible, some practical Pieces, and his Mathematical Instruments and Books. He diverted and provided for himself as well as he could; but for the first eight months had much ado to bear up against Melancholy, and the Terror of being left alone in such a desolate place. He built two Hutts with Piemento Trees, cover'd them with long Grass, and lin'd them with the Skins of Goats, which he kill'd with his Gun as he wanted, so long as his Powder lasted, which was but a pound; and that being near spent, he got fire by rubbing two sticks of Piemento Wood together upon his knee. In the lesser Hutt, at some distance from the other, he dress'd his Victuals, and in the larger he slept, and employ'd himself in reading, singing Psalms, and praying; so that he said he was a better Christian while in this Solitude than ever he was before, or than, he was afraid, he should ever be again. At first he never eat any thing till Hunger constrain'd him, partly for grief, and partly for want of Bread and Salt; nor did he go to bed till he could watch no longer: the Piemento Wood, which burnt very clear, serv'd him both for Firing and Candle, and refresh'd him with its fragrant Smell.

He might have had Fish enough, but could not eat 'em for want of Salt, because they occasion'd a Looseness; except Crawfish, which are there as large as our Lobsters, and very good: These he sometimes boil'd, and at other times broil'd, as he did his Goats Flesh, of which he made very good Broth, for they are not so rank as ours; he kept an Account of 500 that he kill'd while there, and caught as many more, which he mark'd on the Ear and let go. When his Powder fail'd, he took them by speed of foot; for his way of living and continual Exercise of walking and running, clear'd him of all gross Humours, so that he ran with wonderful Swiftness thro the Woods and up the Rocks and Hills, as we perceiv'd when we employ'd him to catch Goats for us. We had a Bull-Dog, which we sent with several of our nimblest Runners, to help him in catching Goats; but he distanc'd and tir'd both the Dog and the Men, catch'd the Goats, and brought 'em to us on his back. He told us that his Agility in pursuing a Goat had once like to have cost him his Life; he pursu'd it with so much Eagerness that he catch'd hold of it on the brink of a Precipice, of which he was not aware, the Bushes having hid it from him; so that he fell with, the Goat down the said Precipice a great height, and was so stun'd and bruis'd with the Fall, that he narrowly escap'd with his Life, and when he came to his Senses, found the Goat dead under him. He lay there about 24 hours, and was scarce able to crawl to his Hutt, which was about a mile distant, or to stir abroad again in ten days.

He came at last to relish his Meat well enough without Salt or Bread, and in the Season had plenty of good Turnips, which had been sow'd there by Capt. *Dampier's* Men, and have now overspread some Acres of Ground. He had enough of good Cabbage from the Cabbage-Trees, and season'd his Meat with the Fruit of the Piemento Trees, which is the same as the Jamaica Pepper, and smells deliciously. He found there also a black Pepper call'd *Malagita*, which was very good to expel Wind, and against Griping of the Guts.

He soon wore out all his Shoes and Clothes by running thro the Woods; and at last being forc'd to shift without them, his Feet became so hard, that he run every where without Annoyance: and it was some time before he could wear Shoes after we found him; for not being us'd to any so long, his Feet swell'd when he came first to wear 'em again.

After he had conquer'd his Melancholy, he diverted himself sometimes by cutting his Name on the Trees, and the Time of his being left and Continuance there. He was at first much pester'd with Cats and Rats, that had bred in great numbers from some of each Species which had got ashore from Ships that put in there to wood and water. The Rats gnaw'd his Feet and Clothes while asleep, which oblig'd him to cherish the Cats with his Goats-flesh; by which many of them became so tame, that they would lie about him in hundreds, and soon deliver'd him from the Rats. He likewise tam'd some Kids, and to divert himself would now and then sing and dance with them and his Cats: so that by the Care of Providence and Vigour of his Youth, being now but about 30 years old, he came at last to conquer all the In conveniences of his Solitude, and to be very easy. When his Clothes wore out, he made himself a Coat and Cap of Goat-Skins, which he stitch'd together with little Thongs of the same, that he cut with his Knife. He had no other Needle but a Nail; and when his Knife was wore to the back, he made others as well as he could of some Iron Hoops that were left ashore, which he beat thin and ground upon Stones. Having some Linen Cloth by him, he sow'd himself Shirts with a Nail, and stitch'd 'em with the Worsted of his old Stockings, which he pull'd out on purpose. He had his last Shirt on when we sound him in the island.

At his first coming on board us, he had so much forgot his Language for want of Use, that we could scarce understand him, for he seem'd to speak his words by halves. We offer'd him a Dram, but he would not touch it, having drank nothing but Water since his being there, and 'twas some time before he could relish our Victuals.

He could give us an account of no other Product of the Island than what we have mention'd, except small black Plums, which are very good, but hard to come at, the Trees which bear 'em growing on high Mountains and Rocks. Piemento Trees are plenty here, and we saw some of 60 foot high, and about two yards thick; and Cotton Trees higher, and near four fathom round in the Stock.

The Climate is so good, that the Trees and Grass are verdant all the Year. The Winter lasts no longer than *June* and *July*, and is not then severe, there being on a small Frost and a little Hail, but sometimes great Rains. The Heat of the Summer is equally moderate, and there's not much Thunder or tempestuous Weather of any fort. He saw no venomous or savage Creature on the Island, nor any other sort of Beast but Goats, etc. as above mention'd; the first of which had been put ashore here on purpose for a Breed by *Juan Fernando* a *Spaniard*, who settled there with some Families for a time, till the Continent of *Chili* began to submit to the *Spaniards*; which being more profitable, tempted them to quit this Island, which is capable of maintaining a good number of People, and of being made so strong that they could not be easily dislodg'd.

Ringrose in his Account of Capt. *Sharp's* Voyage and other Buccaneers, mentions one who had escap'd ashore here out of a Ship which was cast away with all the rest of the Company, and says he liv'd five years alone before he had the opportunity of another Ship to carry him off. Capt. *Damp-*

ier talks of a *Moskito Indian* that belong'd to Capt. *Watlin,* who being a hunting in the Woods when the Captain left the Island, liv'd here three years alone, and shifted much in the same manner as Mr. *Selkirk* did, till Capt. *Dampier* came hither in 1684, and carry'd him off. The first that went ashore was one of his Countrymen, and they saluted one another first by prostrating themselves by turns on the ground, and then embracing. But whatever there is in these Stories, this of Mr. *Selkirk* I know to be true; and his Behaviour afterwards gives me reason to believe the Account he gave me how he spent his time, and bore up under such an Affliction, in which nothing but the Divine Providence could have supported any Man. By this one may see that Solitude and Retirement from the World is not such an unsufferable State of Life as most Men imagine, especially when People are fairly call'd or thrown into it unavoidably, as this Man was; who in all probability must otherwise have perifh'd in the Seas, the Ship which left him being cast away not long after, and few of the Company escap'd. We may perceive by this Story the Truth of the Maxim, That Necessity is the Mother of Invention, since he found means to supply his Wants in a very natural manner, so as to maintain his Life, tho not so conveniently, yet as effectually as we are able to do with the help of all our Arts and Society. It may likewise instruct us, how much a plain and temperate way of living conduces to the Health of the Body and the Vigour of the Mind, both which we are apt to destroy by Excess and Plenty, especially of strong Liquor, and the Variety as well as the Nature of our Meat and Drink: for this Man, when he came to our ordinary Method of Diet and Life, tho he was sober enough, lost much of his Strength and Agility. But I must quit these Reflections, which are more proper for a Philosopher and Divine than a Mariner, and return to my own Subject.

We did not get to anchor till six at night, on *Febr.* 1. and then it fell calm: we row'd and tow'd into the Anchor-ground about a mile off shore, 45 fathom Water, clean Ground; the Current sets mostly along shore to the Southward. This Morning we clear'd up Ship, and bent our Sails, and got them ashore to mend, and make Tents for our sick Men. The Governour (tho we might as well have nam'd him the Absolute Monarch of the Island) for so we call'd Mr. *Selkirk,* caught us two Goats, which make excellent Broth, mix'd with Turnip-Tops and other Greens, for our sick Men, being 21 in all, bat not above two that we account dangerous; the *Dutchess* has more Men sick, and in a worse condition than ours.

Febr. 3. Yesterday in the Afternoon we got as many of our Men ashore as could be spar'd from clearing and sitting our Ship, to wood and water, Our Sail-makers are all mending our Sails, and I lent the *Dutchess* one to assist them. This Morning we got our Smiths Forge put up ashore, set our Coopers to work in another place, and made a little Tent for my self to have the Benefit of the Shore. The *Dutchess* has also a Tent for their sick Men; so that we have a little Town of our own here, and every body is employ'd. A few Men supply us all with Fish of several sorts, all very good; as Silver-fish, Rock-fish, Pollock, Cavallos, Oldwives, and Craw-fish in such abundance, that in a few hours we could take as many as would serve some hundreds of Men. There were Sea-Fowls in the Bay as large as Geese, but cat fishy. The Governour never fail'd of getting us two or three Coats a day for our sick Men, by which with the help of the Greens and the Goodness of the Air they recover'd very fast of the Scurvy, which was their general Distemper. 'Twas very pleasant ashore among the green Piemento Trees, which cast a refreshing Smell.

Our House was made by putting up a Sail round four of 'em, and covering it a-top with another Sail; so that Capt. *Dover* and I both thought it a very agreeable Seat, the Weather being neither too hot nor too cold.

We spent our time till the 10th in refitting our Ships, taking Wood on board, and laying up Water, that which we brought from *England* and *St. Vincent* being spoil'd by the Badness of the Casks. We likewise boil'd up about 80 Gallons of Sea-Lions Oil, as we might have done several Tuns, had we been provided with Vessels, etc. We resin'd and strain'd it for the use of our Lamps and to save our Candles, tho Sailors sometimes use it to fry their Meat, when straiten'd for want of Butter, etc. and say 'tis agreeable enough. The Men who work'd ashore on our Rigging eat young Seals, which they prefer'd to our Ships Victuals, and said was as good as *English* Lamb; tho for my own part I should have been glad of such an Exchange.

We made what haste we could to get all Necessaries on board, being willing to lose no time; for we were inform'd at the *Canaries* that five stout *French* Ships were coming together to these Seas.

Febr. 11. Yesterday in the Evening having little or nothing to do with the Pinnace, we sent her to the South End of the Island to get Goats. The Governour told us, that during his stay he could not get down to that end from the Mountains where he liv'd, they were so steep and rocky; but that there were abundance of Goats there, and that part of the Island was plainer. Capt. *Dampier*, Mr. *Glendal*, and the Governour, with ten Men, set out in company with the *Dutchess's* Boat and Crew, and surrounded a great parcel of Goats, which are of a larger sort, and not so wild as those on the higher part of the Island where the Governour liv'd; but not looking well to 'em, they escap'd over the Cliff: so that instead of catching above a hundred, as they might easily have done with a little precaution, they return'd this Morning with only 16 large ones, tho they saw above a thousand. If any Ships come again to this Island, the best way is to keep some Men and Dogs at that part of the Island, and sending a Boat to them once in 24 hours they may victual a good Body of Men; and no doubt but amongst those Goats they may find some hundreds with Mr. *Selkirk's* Ear-mark.

Febr. 12. This Morning we bent the remaining Sails, got the last Wood and Water aboard brought off our Men, and got every thing ready to depart. The Island of *Juan Fernandez* is nearest of a triangular form, about 12 Leagues round; the South-west side is much the longest, and has a small Island about a mile long lying near it, with a few visible Rocks close under the shore of the great Island, On this side begins a Ridge of high Mountains that run cross from the S W. to the N W. of the Island; and the Land that lies out in a narrow Point to the Westward, appears to be the only level Ground here. On the N E. side 'tis very high Land, and under it are the two Bays where Ships always put in to recruit. The best Bay is next the middle on this side the Island, which is to be known at a distance by the highest Table Mountain right over this Bay. You may anchor as near as you will to the shore, and the nearer the better. The best Road is on the Larboard side of the Bay, and nearest the Eastermost Shore: provided you get well in, you cannot mistake the Road. The other Bay is plain to be seen under the North end, but not so good for Wood, Water, or Landing, nor so safe for riding. In this Bay, where we rode, there's plenty of good Water and Wood: the best Water is in a small Cove about a good Musket-shot to the Eastward of the place I have describ'd. You may ride from a Mile to a Bow-shot off the Shore, being all deep Water and bold, without any danger round the Island, but what is visible and very near in. This Bay where we rode is open to near half the Compass; the Eastermost Land in sight bore E by S. dist, about a mile and a half, and the outermost Northwest Point of the Island lies something without our Bay, and bears N W by W. dist, a good League. We were about a mile off the Shore, and had 45 fathom Water, clean sandy Ground; we design'd to have ran farther in, and new moor'd, but Mr. *Selkirk* inform'd us, that this Month proves the fairest in the Year, and that during Winter and Summer, the whole time he was here, he seldom knew the Wind to blow off from the Sea, but only in small Breezes that never brought in a Sea, nor held two hours: but he warn'd us to be on our guard against the Wind off shore, which blew very strong sometimes. The Bay is all deep Water, and you may carry in Ships close to the Rocks, if occasion require. The Wind blows always over the Land, and at worst along shore, which makes no Sea: It's for the most part calm at night, only now and then a Flaw blows from the high Land over us. Near the Rocks there are very good Fish of several sorts, particularly large Craw-fish under the Rocks easy to be caught; also Cavallies, Gropers, and other good Fish in so great plenty any where near the Shore, that I never saw the like, but at the best fishing Season in *Newfoundland*. Piemento is the best Timber, and most plentiful on this side the Island, but very apt to split till a little dry'd: we cut the longest and cleanest to split for Fire-wood. The Cabbage-Trees abound about three miles in the Woods, and the Cabbage very good; most of 'em are on the tops of the nearest and lowest Mountains. In the first Plain we found Store of Turnip-Greens, and Water-Cresses in the Brooks, which mightily refresh'd our Men, and cleans'd 'em from the Scurvey: the Turnips, Mr. *Selkirk* told us, are good in our Summer Months, which is Winter here; but this being Autumn, they are all run to seed, so that we can't have the benefit of any thing but the Greens. The Soil is a loose black Earth, the Rocks very rotten, so that without great care it's dangerous to climb the Hills for Cabbages: besides, there are abundance of Holes dug in several places by a sort of Fowls like Puffins, which fall in at once, and endanger the wrenching or breaking of a Man's Leg. Mr. *Selkirk* tells me, in *July* he has seen snow and Ice here; but the Spring, which is in *September*, *October*, and *November*, is very pleasant, when there's abundance of good Herbs, as Parsly, Purslain, Sithes in great plenty, besides an Herb found by the water-side, which prov'd very useful to our Surgeons for Fomentations; 'tis not much unlike Feverfew, of a very grateful smell like Balm, but of a stronger and more cordial Scent: 'tis in great plenty near the Shore. We gather'd many large Bundles of it, dry'd 'em in the shade, and sent 'em on board, besides great quantities that we carry'd in every Morning to strow the Tents, which tended much to the Speedy Recovery of our sick Men, of whom none died but two belonging to the *Dutchess*, viz. *Edward Wilts* and *Christopher Williams*.

Mr. *Selkirk* tells me, that in *November* the Seals come ashore to whelp and ingender, when the Shore is so full of them for a stone's throw, that 'tis impossible to pass thro them; and they are so surly, that they'l not move out of the way, but like an angry Dog run at a Man, tho he have a good Stick to beat them: so that at this and their whelping Seasons 'tis dangerous to come near them, but at other times they'l make way for a Man; and if they did not, 'twould be impossible to get up from the Water-side: they lin'd the Shore very thick for above half a mile of ground all round the Bay. When we came in, they kept a continual noise day and night, some bleeting like Lambs, some howling like Dogs or Wolves, others making hideous noises of various sorts; so that we heard 'em aboard, tho a mile from the Shore. Their Fur is the finest that ever I saw of the kind, and exceeds that of our Otters.

Another strange Creature here is the Sea-Lion: The Governour tells me he has seen of them above 20 foot long and more in compass, which could not weigh less than two Tun weight. I saw several of these vast Creatures, but none of the abovemention'd Size; several of 'em were upward of 16 foot long, and more in bulk, so that they could not weigh less than a Tun weight. The Shape of their Body differs little from the Sea-Dogs or Seals, but have another fort of Skin, a Head much bigger in proportion, and very large Mouths, monstrous big Eyes, and a Face like that of a Lion, with very large Whiskers, the Hair of which is stiff enough to make Tooth-pickers. These Creatures come ashore to engender the latter end of *June*, and stay till the end of *September*; during all which time they lie on the Land, and are never observ'd to go to the Water, but lie in the same place above a Musket-shot from the Water-side, and have no manner of Sustenance all $_x$ that time that he could observe. I took notice of some that lay a week, without once offering to move out of the place whilst I was there, till they were disturb'd by us; but we saw few in comparison of what he informs us be did, and that the Shore was all crouded full of them a Musket-shot into the Land. I admire how these Monsters come to yield such a quantity of Oil. Their Hair is short and coarse, and their Skin thicker than the thickest Ox-Hide I ever saw. We found no Land-Bird on the Island, but a sort of Black-Bird with a red Breast, not unlike our English Black-Birds; and the Humming Bird of various Colours, and no bigger than a large Bumble Bee. Here is a small Tide which flows uncertain, and the Spring-Tide flows about seven foot.

I shall not trouble the Reader with the Descriptions of this Island given by others, wherein there are many Falshoods; but the Truth of this I can assert from my own knowledg. Nor shall I insert the Description of the Cabbage and Piemento Trees, being so well known and so frequently done, that, there's no manner of need for it. I have insisted the linger upon this Island, because it might be at first of great use to those who would carry on any Trade to the South-Sea.

Febr. 13. At a Committee held on board the *Dutchess* the 13th of February, 170 8/9. it was agreed as follows:

Resolv'd to steer from *Juan Fernandez*. N.E. by E. for the Land; and when come within six Leagues of the Shore, to keep that distance steering along Shore to the Northward.

The next Place we design'd to stop at, to build our Boats and land our Men, is the Island of *Lobos de la Mar*. In case of losing Company, to wait for each other 20 Leagues to the Northward of the place where we accounted we were when we separated.

Then to lie at six Leagues distance from the Shore the space of four days, and to proceed with an easy Sail for Lobos, in cafe of not meeting; taking special care of the Rocks call'd *Ormigos*, lying about that distance off from *Callo*, the Sea-port of the City of *Lima*.

In case of seeing one or more Sail, the Signal for chasing, if not out of call, is to clew up our Maintop-gallant Sheets, with the Yards aloft. And the general method we design to take in chasing, is, for the Ship that fails best, or is nearest the Chase, to chase directly after the Sail discover'd, and the other to keep to or from the Shore at a convenient distance, as occasion shall require, to prevent being known. And if the Ship that is nearest the Chase believes her to be too big for one Ship alone, then to make the same Signal, or any other plainer to be distinguish'd than the Signal for the Chafe: And if either Ship comes up with the Chafe, and have her in possession or under command, if in the day, to show a white Jack on the Maintop-Mast head; and if in the night, to make two false Fires, and carry as plain Lights as possible.

To leave off Chase, the Signal by night is one good Light at the Maintop-Mast head; and to fire no Gun, but in a Fog, or very thick Weather, either night or day, to prevent being discover'd.

To leave off Chase by day, the Signal is to haul down the Top-sails, keeping out our Maintop-gallant Stay-Sail; and in case of losing Company, we refer our selves to our weekly Signals to discover each other.

In case either Ship in Chase or otherways would run into any danger of Shoal-Water or other kind, then the Ship in such danger is to fire a Gun with a Shot, and to stand from it.

In case of a Separation, each Ship as they enter *Lobos* to carry an *English* Pennant at the Foretop-Mast head; and if the other happens to be there, she must show her *English* Colours. And if either Ship anchor short of the Road, she shall put out three Lights, *viz.* at the Maintop-Mast head, Poop, and Boltsprit end.

"Either Ship arriving at Lobos, and not finding his Consort there, he is immediately to set up two Crosses, one at the Landing-place nearest the farther end of the Starboard great Island going in, with a Glass-Bottle hid under ground 20 Yards directly North from each Cross, with Intelligence of what has happen'd since parting, and what their further Designs are. This to be done and in readiness, that if they give Chase, or beforc'd out by the Enemy, the miffing Ship may not want Intelligence from her Consort."

We began this Method at *Cork*, to secure the best place we could possible to rendevouz at; hoping by this means and our Signals always to keep Company, and know each other thro the whole Voyage. These Directions being something particular, made me insert them in the Journal.

Febr. 13. Yesterday in the Afternoon we sent our Yall a fishing, and got near 200 large Fish in a very little time, which we salted for our future landing. This Morning we concluded what we began last night, being the foregoing Agreement to direct our Affairs from this plate; and as all our success depends on a strict Secrecy, the Precautions may not be useless.

Febr. 14. Yesterday about three in the Afternoon we weigh'd, had a fair pleasant Gale at S S E. Mr. *Vanbrugh* came on board our Ship again, and exchang'd with Mr. Bath, I hope for the best. Course N. Lat. 32. 32. Long. W. from *London*, 83. 06.

Febr. 16. Had moderate Gales of Wind with Calms. This Morning I went on board the *Dutchess*, with Capt. *Dover* and Capt. *Dampier*, and din'd there. Wind at S.

Febr. 17. Most part of this 24 hours was calm, and cloudy Weather. About ten a clock we hoisted our Boat out, and fetch'd Capt. *Courtney* and Capt. *Cook* to dine with us: whilst they were on board, we settled and sign'd the following Instrument, one for each Ship, further to secure our Methods, and to regulate the Affair of Plunder, which if well follow'd will prevent the bad effects of so dangerous an Obstacle to our good Proceedings; which has prov'd too hard a Task for all others in our time that have gone out on the same account, so far from *Great Britain*: which I believe is chiefly owing either to want of Unity or good Measures. God be thank'd we have a good Concord between each Ships Company hitherto.

At a Committee held by the Officers of the *Duke* and *Dutchess*, 17 Febr. 1709.

Mr. George Underhill, Mr. Lanc. Appleby, Mr. David Wilson, Mr. Sam. Worden:

YOU being chosen by the Officers and Men on board, the Duke, to be Managers of the Plunder which we may take in our Cruising at Sea on the Coast of New Spain, 'tis our Order that Mr. Lane. Appleby and Mr. Samuel Worden do go and continue aboard the Dutchess, in the place of two other Men from them; who are to search all Persons that return from such Prize or Prizes that may be taken by either Ship: as also all Persons that the Captains of either Ship shall five leave, whose Advice you are continually to follow, and apply to them for Assistance, if occasion require; and immediately to inform of any Persons belonging to either Ship, that shall be perceived to use clandestine Methods to hide Plunder, or endeavour to avoid the searching them.

If the Ships Duke and Dutchess are separated when any Prize is taken, then one of you is to be on board the Prize, and the other to remain on board the Ship; and in each place be very strict, and keep an exact Account of what comes to your hands, and as soon as possible secure it in such manner as the Captain of either Ship shall direct: still observing the Command of the superior Officer on board the Prize, who is also to assist you to the utmost of his power.

If any Person nor concerned in this Order, nor employ'd in the same by Capt. Courtney, concerns himself with the Plunder, except the Commanding Officer, you are to forbid him; and if he disobeys, to give immediate Information of such Person or Persons.

You are not to incumber the Boats with Chests or Plunder out of any Prize at first coming aboard, but mind what you see. And the first thing you are to do, is to take account of what you find aboard that is Plunder, and remove nothing without the Captains of either Ship's Orders; or in case of their Absence, of the chief Officer or Officers of either Ship that shall be aboard the Prize, to avoid Trouble and Disturbance.

You are by no means to be rude in your Office, but to do every thing as quiet and easy as possible; and to demean your selves so towards those employed by Capt. Courtney, that we may have no manner of Disturbance or Complaint: still observing that you be not overaw'd, nor deceived of what is your Due, in the behalf of the Officers and Men.

The Persons appointed to be Managers by the Dutchess, were the underwritten,

John Connely, Simon Fleming, Simon Hatley, Barth. Rowe.

To whom the foregoing Orders were also given, and sign'd by the Committee.

Tho. Dover, President, Carleton Vanbrugh,
Woodes Rogers, John Bridge,
Stephen Courtney, William Stratton,
William Dampier, John Rogers,
Edward Cooke, John Connely,
Robert Frye, William Bath,
Charles Pope, Geo. Milbourne,
Tho. Glendall, John Ballet.

Febr. 17. Capt. *Courtney* and Capt. *Cooke* being aboard, we agreed that Mr. *Appleby* should appear for the Officers on board the *Dutchess*, and *Samuel Worden* for the Men: Mr. *Simon Hatley* and *Simon Fleming* were to have the like Charge on board of us, to manage the Plunder according to the foregoing Orders.

Febr. 18. About three Yesterday afternoon, we saw the Main dist. 9 Ls. it's very high Land, with several Islands.

Febr. 28. Yesterday afternoon we came within about 6 Ls. of very high Land. This Morning we put both Pinnaces in the Water, to try them under Sail, having fix'd them with each a Gun after the manner of a Patterero, and all things necessary for small Privateers; hoping they'l be serviceable to us in little Winds to take Vessels. Wind at S. and S by E.

March 1. Having little Wind and smooth Water, we heel'd both Ships and tallow'd.

Mar. 2. We are in sight of Land, dist. 12 or 14 Ls. Within the Country there's a vast high Ridge of Mountains, nam'd *Cordilleras*, all along this Course; some parts I believe are full as high, if not higher, than the Pico *Teneriff*, with Snow on the top. We had a good Observ. Lat. 17. 03. Longit. 80. 29. West from *London*.

Mar. 4. Fine pleasant Weather, with fresh Gales of Wind. This day we came to an Allowance of three Pints of Water a Man per day tho we had a good stock aboard. My reason for it was,, that we might keep at Sea some time and take some Prizes, and not be forc'd to discover our selves by watring, before we attempted any thing ashore; because an Enemy being once discover'd there's nothing of Value, as I'm inform'd, puts to Sea from one end of the Coast to the other. They have great Conveniences of giving notice by Expresses and strict Orders for all Officers on the Shore to keep Lookers-out upon every Head-Land.

Mar. 8. Fine pleasant Weather, a brisk Gale at S E. At three this Morning we lay by, and at six saw the Land dist, about 14 Ls. after which I made sail. The *Dutchess* had a Boy fell out of the Mizen-top down on the Deck, and broke his Leg; of which he is in a fair way to recover. Lat. 12. 31. Longit. 84. 58,

Mar. 9. Fair Weather, a moderate Gale at S E. We go under an easy Sail, in hopes of seeing rich Ships either going or coming out of *Lima*, being now near it. We keep about 7 Ls. from Shore, to prevent our being discover'd. We shall not lie long here, but design to go for *Lobos* to build our Boats, and get things ready to land at *Guiaquil*.

Mar. 10. Pleasant Weather, moderate Gales at S E. This Morning, perceiving white Rocks at a distance which look'd like Ships, we brought to, and sent our Boats under the shore, having kept, them ready a-stern four days, that if we saw a Sail near the Shore, they might take them, to prevent their discovering us to those on the Continent.

Mar. 13. Fair Weather, moderate Gales at S E. This Morning we ran near Land, and the *Dutchess* kept in the Offing, to see if we could meet any of the Traders; there being, as I am inform'd, Ships of good Value sometimes on. this Coast. Our Men begin to repine, that tho come so far, we have met with no Prize in these Seas.

Mar. 14. The Nights are very cold in comparison of the Days, which are warm enough, but not so hot as I expected in this Latitude. Here's never any Rain, but great Dews in the night, almost equivalent to it, tho the Air be generally serene. At eight last night we hal'd up N N W. for the Island *Lobos*.

Mar. 15. We saw Land yesterday, and supposing it was *Lobos*, stood off and on all night. In the Morning it prov'd very hazy till ten, when we saw it again right a-head; we stood nearer till we were convinc'd it was not *Lobos*, but the main Land of *Peru* within it: so we stood off at twelve, and had a good Observ, Lat. 6. 55.

Mar. 16. Yesterday afternoon we spy'd a Sail; our Consort being nearest, soon took her. She was a little Vessel of about 16 Tun belonging to *Payta*, and bound to *Cheripe* for Flower, with a small Sum of Mony aboard to purchase it. The Master's Name was *Antonio Heliagos*, a *Mustees*, begotten between an *Indian* and a *Spaniard*: his Company was eight Men, one of them a *Spaniard*, one a *Negro*, and the rest *Indians*. We ask'd them for News, and they assur'd us that all the *French* Ships, being seven in number, sail'd out of these Seas six months ago, and that no more were to return; adding, That the *Spaniards* had such an Aversion to them, that at *Callo* the Sea-Port for *Lima* they kill'd so many of the *French*, and quarrel'd so frequently with 'em, that none were suffer'd to come ashore there for some time before they sail'd from thence. After we had put Men aboard the Prize, we hal'd off close on a Wind for *Lobos*, having shot within it; and had we not been better inform'd by the Crew of the Prize, might have endanger'd our Ships, by running in farther, because there are Shoals between the Island and the Main. The Prisoners tell us there had been no Enemy in those parts since Capt. *Dampier*, which is above four Years ago. They likewise inform'd us that Capt. *Stradling*'s Ship the *Cinque-Ports*, who was *Dampier*'s Consort, founder'd on the Coast of *Barbacour*, where he with six or seven of his Men were only sav'd; and being taken in their Boat, had been four Years Prisoners at *Lima*, where they liv'd much worse than our Governour *Selkirk*, whom they left on the Island *Juan Fernandez*. This Morning we saw the Island *Lobos*, which bore South about 4 Ls. at Noon it bore S by W. dist. 6 miles. We sent our Pinnace thither mann'd and arm'd, to see if there were any Fishermen upon it and secure 'em, lest they should discover us to the People on the Main.

Mar. 17. Yesterday about five in the Evening, we got well into anchor, but found no body at the Island. We had 20 fathom Water, clean Ground in the Thorow-fair between the two Islands, above a Cable's length from each Shore. 'Tis a bold going in and a good Road, the Wind blowing constantly over Land. We resolv'd here to fit out our small Bark for a Privateer, she being well built for sailing; and this Morning we had her into a small round Cove in the Southermost Island, where we haul'd her up dry on the Land. The Carpenters also got the Timber ashore, to build our Boat for landing Men.

Mar. 18. In the Evening we launch'd our small Privateer, having clean'd her Bottom well, call'd her the *Beginning*, and appointed Capt. *Cooke* to command her. We got a small spare Mast out of our Ship, which made her a new Main-Mast, and our Mizen-top Sail was alter'd to make her a Main-Sail. The *Dutchess* heel'd, and clean'd their Ship. This Morning I got all our sick Men ashore, and built Tents for them: the *Dutchess* also landed hers. We agreed to stay the building of our Boat and sitting out the Privateer, while the *Dutchess* cruis'd about the Island, and in fight of the Main.

Mar. 19. Yesterday afternoon we sent the Yall a fishing, got the Bark rigg'd, and almost ready, with four Swivel-Guns and a Deck near finish'd. This Morning the Dutchess sail'd a cruising, and appointed to meet the Bark off the South-East End of the Island.

Mar. 20. The Bark being got ready, this Morning we victual'd her out of our Ship, and put 20 of ours, and 12 of our Consorts Men aboard her well arm'd. I saw her out of the Harbour with our Pinnace, she looks very pretty, and I believe will sail well in smooth Water, having all Masts, Sails, Rigging, and Materials, like one of the Half-Galleys fitted out for her Majesty's Service in *England*: They gave our Ship's Company three Huzza's, and we return'd them the like at parting. I told Capt. *Cooke*, if we should be forc'd out of the Road, or give Chase hence, we would leave a Glass-Bottle bury'd near a remarkable great Stone, that I show'd him, with Letters in it, to give an account how it was with us, of the occasion of our Departure, and where to meet again: I bid him acquaint Capt. *Courtney* with it.

Mar. 22. This Morning a *Spaniard* belonging to us, nam'd *Silvester Ramos*, died suddenly, and we buried him at night: Most of our Men are healthy, except two or three who are ill of the Scurvey.

Mar. 23. This Morning we began to scrub our Ship, and clear'd abundance of Barnacles off her Bottom, almost as large as Muscles. A Ship grows foul very fast in these Seas.

Mar. 25. We caught plenty of very good Fish. The Seals are numerous here, but not so many as at *Juan Fernandez*: A large one seiz'd a stout *Dutchman*, had like to have pull'd him into the Water, and bit him to the bone in several places, in one of his Arms and Legs.

Mar. 26. This Morning the *Dutchess* came in with a Prize call'd the *Santa Josepha*, bound from *Guiaquil* to *Truxillo*, Burden about 50 Tuns, full of Timber, with some Cocou, and Coco-Nuts, and Tobacco which we distributed among our Men: The *Dutchess* and *Beginning* took her between this Island and the Main; she had very little of Value on board.

Mar. 27. This Morning we gave our Ship a good heel, and tallow'd her low down. A *Dutchman* belonging to the *Dutchess* died of the Scurvy ashore, and was buried on the Island.

Mar. 30. Yesterday afternoon we got the second Prize (which we call'd the *Increase)* aboard us, and clean'd her. We brought all off shore, and launched our new Boat to tow at our stern, and at ten a clock came to fail, after we had put Mr. *Stratton* to command the *Beginning*, and all our sick Men and a Doctor of each Ship aboard the *Increase*, of which Mr. *Selkirk* our second Mate, was appointed Master.

By Observation we had here, this Island lies in Lat. 6. 50. S. the Variation 3. 30. Easterly; and I reckon it lies in the Longitude of 87. 35. West from *London*. The two largest Islands, call'd *Lobos de la Mar* (to distinguish them from others call'd *Lobos de la Terra*, within 2 Ls. of the Land) are about 16 Ls. from the Main, and 6 Miles in length. There's another small Island close by the Eastermost to Windward, not half a mile long, with some Rocks and Breakers near the Shore, all round and off of each side of the Entrance to the Road, which is bold and has no visible Danger. There's a Passage for Boats to Windward, to come into the Road, which is to the Leeward of these Islands in a Sound between them. 'Tis not half a mite broad, but above a mile deep has from 10 to 20 fathom Water, and good Anchor-ground: there's no coming in for Ships, but to Leeward of the Islands. We went in with a small Weather-Tide, tho I never perceiv'd it flow above 3 foot whilst we lay here. The Wind commonly blows Southerly, veering a little to the Eastward: on the Eastermost Island (which was on our Larboard side as we lay at anchor in the Sound) there is a round Hummock, and behind it a small Cove very smooth, deep, and convenient enough for a Ship to careen in; there we haul'd up, and sitted our little Frigat. The highest part of the Island appears in the Road not much higher than a large Ship's Top-Mast head. The Soil is a hungry white clayish Earth, mix'd with Sand and Rocks. There's no fresh Water, or green things on the Islands: Here's abundance of Vultures, *alias* Carrion-Crows, which look'd so like Turkeys, that one of our Officers at landing bless'd himself at the sight, and hop'd to fare deliciously here: He was so eager, that he would not stay till the Boat could put him ashore, but leap'd into the Water with his Gun, and getting near enough to a parcel, let fly at 'em; but when he came to take up his Game, it stunk insufferably, and made us merry at his Mistake. The other Birds here are Penguins, Pellicans, Boobys, Gulls, and a Sort of Fowls like Teal, that nestle in holes on the Land: Our Men got Loads of 'em, which they skin'd, and prais'd them for very good Meat. We found abundance of Bull-Rushes and empty Jars that the *Spanish* Fishermen had left ashore: All over this Coast they use Jars instead of Casks, for Oil, Wine, and all other Sorts of Liquids. Here's abundance of Seals and some Sea-Lions; the Seals are much larger than at *Juan Fernandez*, but the Fur not so fine. Our People kill'd several with a design to eat their Livers; but one of our Crew, a *Spaniard*, dying suddenly after eating 'em, I forbad the use of 'em. Our Prisoners told us, they accounted those old Seals very unwholesom. The Wind always blowing fresh over the Land, brought an ugly noisom Smell aboard from the Seals ashore; which gave me a violent Head-Ach, and every body else complain'd of this nauseous Smell: we found nothing so offensive at *Juan Fernandez*.

Our Prisoners tell us, they expect the Widow of the late Vice-Roy of *Peru* would shortly embark for *Aquapulco*, with her Family and Riches, and stop at *Payta* to refresh, or sail near in sight as customary, in one of the King's Ships of 36 Guns; and that about eight months ago there was a Ship with 200000 Pieces of Eight aboard, the rest of her Cargo Liquors and Flower, which had pass'd *Payta* for *Aquapulco*: she would have been a welcome Prize to us, but since she is gone, it's not worth while to follow her. Our Prisoners added, That they left Signior *Morel* in a stout Ship with dry Goods for *Lima*, recruiting at *Payta*, where he expected in few days a *French*-built Ship, belonging to the *Spaniards*, to come from *Panama* richly laden, with a Bishop aboard. *Payta* is a common Recruiting-place to those who go to or from *Lima*, or most Ports to Windward, in their Trade to *Panama*, or any part of the Coast of *Mexico*. Upon this Advice we agreed to spend as much time as possible cruising off of *Payta*, without discovering our selves, for fear of hindring our other Designs.

At these Islands Capt. *Dampier* in his last Voyage left his Ship the *St. George* at anchor, and went to the *East-Indies* in a *Spanish* Brigantine with about 25 Men: After he had plunder'd *Puna* in 1704. and water'd his small Bark near it, he endur'd many Hardships, and for want of his Commission to show (which he lost at *Puna)* he was imprison'd, and had all his Goods seiz'd in the *Indies* by the *Dutch*.

Before we came hither, we held a Committee, and publish'd an Order in both Ships, forbidding our Officers or Men on severe Penalties to bold any Correspondence, or talk any thing that in the least; concerns the Voyage, with our Prisoners; which was strictly observ'd, to prevent the Discovery of our Designs to the *Spaniards*.

April I. Small Gales, fair clear Weather. This Morning I went in our Yall on board the *Dutchess*, and afterwards spoke with the *Beginning*: We agreed how to act, in case we see more than one bail, at a time to chase.

April. 2. Yesterday in the Afternoon we were surpriz'd with the Colour of the Water, which look'd as red as Blood for several miles, occasion'd by the Spawn of Fish. This Morning at Daybreak we spy'd a sail about 2 LS. to Windward: We immediately hoisted out and mann'd our Pinnace, commanded by Mr. *Frye* my chief Lieutenant, who by eight in the Morning took the Ship; she was call'd the *Ascension*, built Galeon-fashion, very high with Galleries, Burden between 4 and 500 Tun, two Brothers being Commanders, *viz. Joseph* and *John Morel*. She was laden with dry Goods and Timber, had above 50 Negroes, and several Passengers bound from *Panama* to *Lima*.

April. 3. We immediately mann'd this Prize, took some of the *Spaniards* out of her, and put in Mr. *Frye* Commander. We sound a good stock of fresh Provisions on board. In the Evening we saw another Sail, which the *Beginning* took, and brought her to the rest this Morning: She was a Vessel of 35 Tuns, laden with Timber from Guia*quil* to *Chancay* near *Lima*; the Master's Name was *Juan Guastellos*, the Grew 11 white Men and 1 Negro. We agreed with the *Dutchess* and *Beginning* when and where to meet; and having all our Stations appointed, they left us. We were inform'd by the Prisoners, that the Bishop of *Chokeaqua*, a Place far up the Country in the South Parts of *Peru*, was to have come from Panama in this Vessel for *Lima*, in his way to the said *Bishoprick*; but the Ship Springing a Leak at *Panama*, he went onboard a *French*-built Ship belonging to the *Spaniards* that was following them for *Lima*, but would stop at *Payta* to recruit, as the *Morels* had done. Being near that place, we resolve to watch narrowly in order to catch the Ship with his Lordship.

April 4. About six in the Evening we parted With Mr. *Frye* in the great Prize, having order'd him with the two other Prizes to keep together, and ply about 8 Ls. off shore in fight of the Hummocks call'd the Saddle of *Payta*, because they appear in that shape with low Land betwixt 'em. We stood in for the Shore, and next Morning saw a Ship to Leeward, and gave chase; she made a Signal, by which we knew her to be the *Dutchess*; but being at a distance, and we not having kept out our Signal long enough, they did not see it. We kept on sail till we came near her, which made them clear their Ship in Order to sight: I did this to Surprize them, and at Noon went on board.

April 5. I kept the *Dutchess* company till the Evening; and whilst I was on board her, the *Beginning* came down to us. We agreed on an exact Station; the *Beginning* to keep close in with *Payta*, the *Dutchess* 8 Ls. to Leeward, and I to lie right off of *Payta* about 7 or 8 Ls. a little to Windward, Just as the Sun set I left them; they fancy'd they saw a Sail, and chas'd in great haste: but we saw nothing except the blowing of a Whale, of which there are abundance on this Coast. Wind from the S E by S. to the E S E.

April 6. We came up with our three Prizes about four a clock in the Afternoon, and found all in good order, Mr. *Frye* had sitted out the great Boat we built at *Lobos*, which we call a Launch, with Sails and Oars, ready to give chase if they saw any thing in little Winds, having Men enough for that end, in these peaceable Seas, where they are in no fear of an Enemy.

April 7, At eight this Morning the Saddle of *Payta* bore E N E. 7 Ls. at Noon N E. dist. 10 Ls. I went on board the Galeon to Mr. *Frye*, and station'd him again, leaving Signals for the other two, if he saw 'em; and after having din'd on a good Qarter of Mutton and Cabbage with him, which is a great Rarity to us here, I came on board, in order to leave him the second time.

Mr. *Vanbrugh* threatning to shoot one of our Men at *Lobos*, only for refusing to carry some Carrion-Crows that he shot, and having lately abus'd Capt. *Dover*, as he said; the latter desir'd a Committee might be call'd to examine into Mr. *Vanbrugh's* Conduct, and we came to the following Issue: *'That Mr. Vanbrugh had committed sundry Misdemeanours, and according to our Orders, we not believing him a fit Person to be one of the Committee, had chosen Mr. Samuel Hopkins in his stead.* Which was sign'd, and agreed to by all the Committee in both Ships.

At the same time, while we were together, we had a second Committee; which concluded as follows.

WE have examin'd and do approve of all the Proceedings and Transactions since our leaving the Island of Grande on the Coast of Brazile, both as to punishing Offenders, our Dispatch at Juan Fernandez, and staying at Lobos to build our Boat, and acting in all cases for the best of our intended Voyage to this time. In Testimony of which, we have set our Hands the Day and Year above-written.

Sign'd by all the chief Officers in both Ships.

April 11. Yesterday afternoon we all met aboard the *Duke*, to consult how to act; for beginning to grow short of Water, we can't keep the Sea much longer.

April 12. This Morning we came to a full Resolution to land and attempt *Guiaquil*. In order thereunto we fix'd two Barks, put Ammunition and Arms on board them, with our four Quarter-Deck Guns and Field-Carriages. And for the Management of this Expedition, we held a Committee, and resolv'd on the following Particulars.

At a Committee held on board the *Duke-Frigot.*

WE have consulted and examin'd sundry Pilots taken in Prizes, and had several Meetings on this Occasion, being proved with conve-

nient *Vessels to carry our Men, Guns, Arms, and other Necessaries to Guiaquil: We resolve to attempt it, having also consulted the most secret way of managing our Attempts on it without discovery. We do approve and appoint Capt. Tho. Dover, Capt. Woodes Rogers, and Capt. Stephen Courtney, to command the Men design'd to land in three equal Parties; except 21 Men with Capt. William Dampier and Mr. Tho. Glendall, who are to manage and take care of the Guns, Ammunition, Provisions, &c. which we agree to be lodg'd in a, convenient place, as near as possible to the best Landing-place nearest the Water-side, in order to take care and help ship off the Effects that we may take in the Town; who are also to serve either Commander, where most wanted.*

We leave the Management of this Expedition wholly to the prudent Conduct of the above Commanders, whom we heartily wish and desire to consult each other on all occasions, as the most promising Method to succeed and keep our Designs secret; which is the only way to prevent the Enemies removing their Wealth, or giving us a vigorous Reception. This is our Opinion; in witness whereof we have set our Hands, the 12th of April 1709.

Sign'd by all the chief Officers in both Ships.

Memorandum,

WE have consider'd the Opinion of the foregoing Committee sign'd this Day, and do jointly concur with them, and accordingly design to prosecute it with our Lives and Fortunes to the utmost of our Tower and Judgment. Witness our Hands, this 12th Day of April 1709.

Tho. Dover, Presid. Stephen Courtney. Woodes Rogers,

April 13. We appointed an Officer to every ten Men, to prevent Disorders, and stragling ashore.

Chapter VII

The Committee having agreed on our Method of Command, left it to us jointly and vigorously to attack the Enemy ashore; we knew that Misfortunes attend Sailors when out of their Element; and hearing that they began to murmur about the Encouragement they were to expect for Landing, which they alledg'd was a risque more than they were ship'd for; to prevent their Desertion, which we had reason to apprehend, since they were a mix'd Gang of most *European* Nations, we the Commanders agreed on the most plausible Methods we could then think of, to form a good Discipline among 'em, if possible, and to give 'em all needful Encouragement, that we might depend on their good Order and Bravery; and therefore came to the following Resolves.

WHERE AS it is agreed to land and take the Town of Guiaquil we fully resolve to do it with all manner of Privacy and Dispatch; and that we our selves and our Men may have full Encouragement to attempt it bravely and cheerfully, we publish the following Order.

Imprim. All manner of Bedding and Clothes without stripping, all manner of Necessaries, Gold Rings Buckles, Buttons, Liquors, and Provisions for our own expending and use with all sorts of Arms and Ammunition, except great Guns for Ships, is Plunder, and shall be divided equally amongst the Men of each Ship, with their Prizes, either aboard or ashore, according to the whole Shares.

2. It is also agreed, that any fort of wrought Silver or Gold Crucifixes, Gold and Silver Watches, or any other Movables found about the Prisoners, or wearing Apparel of any kind, shall likewise be Plunder: Provided always we make this Reserve, That Monty and Women Ear-Rings, with loose Diamonds, Pearls, and precious Stones be excepted. And if any thing is short and omitted in this Publication, we do hereby declare, that when this Expedition is over, every particular Man shall have a Hearing; or the Persons already appointed for the Company of both Ships, may come to us, and insist on what is or oug't to be deem'd Plunder, either more or less than what is here inserted; and that a general Committee of the Officers of both Ships shall immediately meet, and at once resolve if any mors is or ought to be Plunder. And that we shall give all manner of Encouragement, without Fraud to the Owners, or Prejudice to our selves, Officers, and Men, in the same manner as agreed on at the Island of St. Vincent on this head: Provided always that our Intent and Meaning for the Mens Encouragement be not made liable to a Construction prejudicial to the Owners, or Ships Companies Interest; and that under pretence of the aforesaid Movables allow'd to be Plunder, no Person whatsoever do seize on, or clandestinely hide any wrought or unwrought Gold or Silver, Pearls, Jewels, Diamonds, and other precious Stones, which are not found about the Prisoners, or their wearing Apparel; which shall be accounted a high Misdemeanour, and punish'd severely: And that no Person do presume to keep any Plunder, but immediately deliver it to his Officers publicity, and carry it directly to the Place appointed for Plunder.

In case this or any other Town, Fort, Ships, or the like, be taken in this Expedition by Storm, then the same Encouragement shall be allow'd each Man, as agreed on at St. Vincent, over and above the Gratuity promis'd by the Owners, to such as shall signalize themselves in time of Action, as by their Instrument appears. But if any Party of ours, or the whole, or any separate Body shall be engag'd with the Enemy on shore, and become Victors, then all Prisoners, the Mony, Arms, and Movables about 'em, are immediately on that place to be brought to the Officer or Officers of that Body or Party, and put into a general Stock, to be divided proportionable amongst those only of our Men that were engag'd in that Action, who are to enjoy the whole Reputation and Right of it to themselves.

And tho there has been nothing yet taken worth a Division of Plunder, we don't question but the effecting this good Enterprise will equally encourage us all, and that we shall gladly and expeditiously get the Wealth of the Town brought to the plates appointed on shore. There shall at the same time be several Places appointed, and Men to receive Plunder, and a sufficient time before we leave the Town allow'd to ship it off by it self, and Men appointed to take care and an account of it; which, with all other Plunder, shall be enter'd in publick Books: and when we come on board, we hope and design to divide it equally, to the Satisfaction of all concern'd.

And to prevent all manner of pernicious and mischievous Ill-Conduct that may accrue by Disorders on shore, we pressingly remind you, that any Officer or other that shall be so brutish as to be drunk ashore in an Enemy's Country, shall not only be severely punish'd, but lose all share of whatsoever is taken in this Expedition. The same Punishment shall be inflicted on any that disobeys Command, or runs from his Post, discourages our Men, or is cowardly in any Action, or presumes to burn or destroy any thing in the Town without our Order, or for mischief sake; or that shall be so sneakingly barbarous to debauch themselves with any Prisoners on shore, where we have more generous things to do, both for our own Benefit and the future Reputation of our selves and our Country. We shall always take care to keep Prisoners of the best Note, as Pledges for our Men that may be accidentally missing: for as soon as any Man is wanting, we shall engage the Spaniards to bring him to us, or give a satisfactory account of him. But we desire no Man to trust to this, or be a moment from his Officers and Post. And if all the foregoing Rules be strictly follow'd, we hope to exceed all other Attempts of this nature before us in these Parts; and not only to enrich and oblige our selves and Friends, but even to gain Reputation from our Enemies. Dated and sign'd on board the Duke, the 13th of April, 1709.

Tho. Dover, Pres. Stephen Courtney. Woodes Rogers.

April 14. This Morning we got all our Arms, Ammunition, and Provisions, with part of our Men, etc. aboard. Our Bark being the largest, we took in part of Capt. *Courtney's* Men; and his Bark carrying the rest, we stood into the great Bay of *Guiaquil* all night, designing to leave the Ships a good distance at Sea, for fear of being discover'd from the Town call'd *Tombes*, which lying on the Starboard side going in, would ruin our Design. Wind at South, but very little. Lat. 4. 23. 85. 42.

April 15. At Break of Day we saw a Ship between us and the Land: being calm, we sent off both our Pinnaces mann'd and arm'd. But our Men expecting no Resistance from that Ship, they hurry'd from us, left out their Swivel-Gun, and carry'd but a slender Stock of Arms with them. My Brother *John Rogers* being unfortunately aboard our Ship, to assist me in getting ready, because he was to be Lieutenant of my Company ashore, he stept into our Boat. I had before this oppos'd his landing, which he resented as a Slight; and this hinder'd me stopping him now, tho it was not his business, he being second Lieutenant of our Consort, and we having Officers enough of our own for that Service: but Mr. *Frye*, who commanded the Boat, being related to us, was the occasion of my Brother's Willingness to go as a Volunteer with him. The *Dutchess's* Pinnace was worse provided than ours, and had not Arms enough for their Men, as Capt. *Cooke* told me afterwards. About nine a clock our Boat came within shot of the Ship, which prov'd to be the *French*-built Ship belonging to *Lima*, the same we have been a cruising for. They hoisted their *Spanish* Ensign in its place, and a Flag at their Top-Mast-Head; which our Boats took to be the Bishop's Banner, because it was broad, made of white Sattin and fring'd, which was unusual Colours in Ships. They fir'd a Gun at our Boat, which lay still above half an hour before the *Dutchess* Pinnace came up, she not rowing so well as ours. When they came up, Capt. *Cooke*, Mr. *Frye*, and my Brother consulted how to begin the Attack with advantage: They agreed that our Boat should ply her under the Stern, and the other on the Bow, till they could get near enough to board at once. But when they came up, the *Spaniards* brought a Gun right aft, and upwards of twenty small Arms pointed into the Boats; so that the Fight began before they could reach the Station agreed on, and both were forc'd to engage the Enemy abaft, where they had five Guns mounted. Our People were constrain'd to fall a-stern twice, after the loss of one Man kill'd and three wounded. The Boats and Sails were much damag'd by the Enemies Partridge-shot, yet they again attempted to come up and board her. At this Attack my unfortunate Brother was shot thro the Head, and instantly died, to my unspeakable Sorrow: but as I began this Voyage with a Resolution to go thro it, and the greatest Misfortune or Obstacle shall not deter me, I'll as much as possible avoid being thoughtful and afflicting my self for what can't be re-call'd, but indefatigably pursue the Concerns of the Voyage, which has hitherto allow'd little Respite. Our Men, upon this Disaster, left engaging, and put all their spare Men and Arms into the *Dutchess's* Boat; who was to keep between the Enemy and the Shore, to prevent them from landing their Riches. Our Ships having little Wind, were yet at a distance; and our Boat came aboard after noon, with two dead and three wounded Men.

April 16. We got possession of the *Spanish* Ship about two yesterday in the afternoon. She had upwards of 50 *Spaniards* and above 100 Negroes, *Indians*, and Molattoes on board. They would not strike till within half-shot of our Ships: The *Dutchess* being somewhat nearest, fir'd two Shot over her, and then she struck, and bore down to us. But we miss'd the Bishop, who ten days before landed at Point *St. Hellena*, with his Attendants, Plate, etc. designing to stop at *Guiaquil*. This Morning we saw a small Sail under the shore; we sent our Pinnace and the *Beginning*, who brought her off to us: she prov'd a small Bark from *Payta* with Soap, Cassia, Fistula, and Leather. About twelve we read the Prayers for the Dead, and threw my dear Brother over-board, with one of our Sailors, another lying dangerously ill. We hoisted our Colours but half-mast up: We began first, and the rest follow'd, firing each some Volleys of small Arms. All our Officers express'd a great Concern for the Loss of my Brother, he being a very hopeful active young Man, a little above twenty Years of Age.

April 17. We made ready to go ashore, and read the Encouragement agreed on the 13th to the Men, who all express themselves well pleas'd with the Undertaking, and were so forward to land, that they make all the Interest possible to go ashore; not considering that we must secure a sate Retreat, by leaving a sufficient number on board our Ships to man 'em and guard our Prisoners: but it was a proof of their Courage, since the Advantage was alike, either to stay on board or go ashore. To prevent their stragling when landed, we gave each Man a Ticket, that he might remember what Company he belong'd to; and appointed the best and soberest Man we could pick to command every ten Men under the Captains. Capt. *Courtney* and I being willing to compliment our President Capt. *Dover*, agreed that he should have the Preference in Command at our Landing: being a considerable Owner in our Ship, he had an equal third part of the Men allotted to be under his Command whilst ashore; we were afterwards to take it in turns.

April 18. Yesterday Afternoon Capt. *Courtney* and I settl'd every thing on board our Ships and Prizes, and got all the Men design'd for Landing on board the Barks. We proportion'd the rest, and put Irons on board every Ship, because having many more Prisoners than we could leave Men to guard 'em, we must have 'em well secur'd. We agreed to leave on board the *Duke* 42 Men and Boys, sick and well, *Robert Fry* Commander, 37 aboard the *Dutchess*, *Edward Cook* Commander; 14 aboard the Galleon, *John Bridge* Master; 14 aboard the *Havre de Grace*, *Robert Knowlman* Master; and 4 aboard the *Beginning*, *Henry Duck* Master: The whole being in, and 201 were design'd for the Shore. The Prisoners on board are above 300, more than one half *Spaniards* and *Indians*, the rest *Negroes*. The Captain and 7 of the chief *Spaniards* taken in the last Prize I carried aboard a our Bark to go with us to the Town, fearing they might be dangerous Persons to leave behind us. Last Midnight we left the Ships, every thing being in good order aboard both Imbarkations. We were, when we parted, about 9 Leagues distant from the Island *Sancta Clara*, and not lets than 36 from *Guiaquil*. We order'd Capt. *Cook* and fry to keep at ea undiscover'd 48 Hours, and then to make the best of their way to Point *Arena*, and stay there at an Anchor till our Return, having engag'd Sen. *Merell* and another *Spaniard* to be their Pilots. About 12 this Day we pass'd by the island *Sancta Clara*, having little Wind, and the Weather very hot. This Island appears like a Corps extended, therefore the *Spaniards* call it *Mortho*; it's not above two Miles long: We left it on the Starboard-side, which is not the Ships Channel; for none enter that way but Barks, by reason of Shoals both on the Island and towards the Main, within it, to the Northward.

About 10 last Night we came to an Anchor in sight of Point *Arena*, with both Barks, not being able to stem the Tide. At 4 in the Morning we weigh'd, when Capt. *Courtney* and I, with out Boats and 40 Men, left the Barks, and order'd 'em to lie at *Puna* one Tide after us, that we might have time to surprize *Guiaquil* before they should appear in fight of it to alarm them; for we had notice, that they keep a Look-out a League below the Town. We reach'd about half way to *Puna*, and landed on the Island, where we staid during the Ebb Tide, and hid our Boats under the Mangrove Branches. This Island is not passable, being full of thick Mangroves and Swamps, that swarm with Mus-keto's.

April 20. Yesterday in the Evening we rowed and towed one another with the Flood, that if seen in the Night, we might look like Drift Timber. We had an excellent Indian Pilot, that advis'd us to come to a Graplin about II at Night, to lie in our Boats about a Mile short of the Town, and to surprize 'em by Break of Day. We took his Advice, but just as we got in by the Town, saw two Lights by the Water-side in Bark Logs which we secured with all the Canoes; but an *Indian* escaping, he alarm'd the People about the Church, who ran into the Woods before we could reach the Houses: However we secur'd the Lieutenant that governs here, with his Family, and about 20 oth-ers, who assur'd us there could be no body to give notice of us to *Guiaquil*, now we had secur'd them, and the rest being fled to the Woods. We sent some of our Men, who took the Look-outs at their Posts, and cut all their Canoes and Bark-Logs to pieces there, and also at the Town. The Day was hot, and two of our Men finding Liquors in the Houses, got drunk betimes. This Place has about 30 Houses, and a Small Chappel. We found a *Spanish* Paper here, that gave us some Uneasiness, it was directed to the Lieutenant, who had the chief Command here, and order'd, him to keep strict Watch, sig-nifying that they had notice of Capt. *Dampier's* coming Pilot to a Squadron into these Seas. The Copy of this Paper was sent from *Lima* to all inhabited Places on the Coast of *Peru*, signifying, that the *French* were on the first notice to fit out after us; and the Bark that came from *Paita* told us of two great Ships that lay in *Callo* Road, and one at *Pisco*, besides two in *Concep-tion*, a Port of *Chili*; being all *French* Frigats from 40 to 50 Guns and upwards, notwithstanding the Report of their not coming into these Seas any more. But to our great Satisfaction we are certain, that we were not dis-cover'd before this, and that it's next to impossible any sufficient Force can arm out from *Lima*, to be here in less than 24 Days, by which time we hope to finish, and be gone where they cannot find us. But since we perceive their Accounts of us imperfect, and that they believe a Squadron comes under Capt. *Dampier's* Pilotage, and he being known by the People, because he sur-prized this Village when last in these Seas; we agreed amongst our selves how to improve this *Spanish* Story of a Squadron, which I hope will not only hinder their fitting out from *Lima*, but even alarm them there. The Substance of this *Spanish* Advice Paper, in *English*, is as follows.

To the Lieutenant General Don Hieronimo Boza y Soliz, *Corregidore and Judge of the City of* St. Jago de Guiaquil, *under the Jurisdiction of the Captain General for his Majesty.*

I Have a Letter I received from his Excellency the Lord Marquis de *Cas-tel dos Reys*, Viceroy, Governour, and Captain General of these Kingdoms, with the Copy of another of the tenor following.

In the Packet with Letters from *Spain*, which I have received, there are Orders from his Majesty, giving an account of a Squadron of 7 Sail, getting ready at *London* by several Lords, from 44 to 74 Guns each, to sail to the *South Sea*, under the Conduct of an *English*-man nam'd *Dampier*: That they are first to sail for *Ireland* in *April* to victual there, and afterwards to possess themselves of an Island and Harbour in these Seas, and particularly the Island of *Juan Fernandes*. You are to give an account to all those Provinces where 'tis necessary, that they may take proper Measures to guard the Coasts and Harbors. Order *Don Hieronimo*, as soon as he receives this, to give notice of it to the People on all the Coasts under his Jurisdiction to withdraw their Cattle and Provisions, and that he don't neglect to put this in execution; that so the Enemies finding no Provision, may be oblig'd to retire from these Seas, whither they can't bring Provision enough to maintain them for so long a Voyage. And let the said *Don Hieronimo* place Guards on all the Coasts, and in all the Sea-ports where 'tis necessary, with Orders to be vigilant, and carefully to observe every Sail that comes into any Port, and give an account of their Numbers with the utmost dispatch to *Don Hieronimo* the Corregidore, that he may send the same from one Corregidore to another till it come to the Viceroy's hands, without sail, all along the Coasts belonging to *Don Hieronimo* and particularly that those he has given Orders to, do immediately dispatch 'em for the King's Service. This I trust he will do to all that can give notice of the Enemies Motions, that it may be impossible for 'em to get Provisions on the Coast, when tis well guarded, or in the Villages of his Jurisdiction; and I trust to his Activity and Zeal for the Royal Service in a Matter of such weight and consequence; and that he also give notice if there be on the Coasts or Ports in his Jurisdiction any *French* Ships, as we hear there is in these Seas, and give 'em warning of the Enemy's Squadron, take a Certificate that he gave 'em such notice, and send it to me, that they mayn't pretend to have been, surpriz'd, if the Enemy get any advantage of 'em. God preserve *Don Hieronimo*, &c.

 Lima, March *El. Marq. De Castel de los Reyos.* 20, 1709. *Don Hieronimo Boza de Solis, etc.*

 The like Orders are sent to the Lieutenant General, and the other Officers belonging to the Sea Coast, and the Lieutenant of *Puna, etc.*

 April 21. At 2 Yesterday Afternoon I left Cape. *Courtney* and Capt. *Dampier* at *Puna*, and went inquest of the Barks admiring they did not come in sight, they being now a Tide and half behind. I carried with me the Lieutenant *of Puna*, and went with the great Launch and our Pinnace, designing to join Capt. *Courtney* and Capt. *Dampier* again, who are to lie all Night in the River, to prevent being discover'd by any Advice going up before us to *Guiaquil*. I found the Barks about 4 a Clock 4 Leagues below Puna: They had been with us according to Appointment, but last Night were misinform'd by the Pilot aboard the *Dutchess's* Bark, who brought 'em to anchor with a fair Wind below that Place, thinking they had got the Length of it; our Bark's Pilot (who was the best) being with us in the Boats. We got other Pilots at *Puna*, and left him aboard the Bark, where I punish'd one that I brought aboard drunk from *Puna*, and had him severely whipt before the whole Company as a Terror to the rest. I was not aboard above half an hour before low Water, and had just time to imbark Capt. *Dover* and part of his Company in the Launch, and as many more as we could carry in our Pinnace to get before the Barks up the River. We rowed till 12 at Night, judg'd it High Water, and came to a Graplin: We saw Lights, which we took to be *Puna*. It blow'd fresh, was very dark, with a small rolling Sea, and the Boat being deep laden and cram'd with Men, I had rather be in a Storm at Sea than here; but in regard we are about a charming Undertaking, we think no Fatigue too hard. At Day-break we saw a Bark above us in the River; we thought it to be a Stranger, and sent our Pinnace to her: I was in the Launch behind a Shole, which we were forc'd to go round to get into the Channel where the Bark was. By 8 a Clock I was aboard her, and found it to be our Bark, which the honest Pilot had brought so high the last Tide. We have no fight of the *Dutch-*

ess's Bark since we left her last Night. About 10 we came up with Capt. *Courtney* and Capt. *Dampier*, who told us they had kept a good Look-out, and that nothing had pass'd them up the River. About Noon it was High-water; we lay with the Boats under the Mangroves all the Ebb, and the Bark off in the River. We were now about half way up to *Guiaquil* from *Puna*, and might have gone farther, but that there was a Plantation or Farm a little higher, which would have discover'd us, and alarm'd the Town, should we have gone higher before Night.

April 22. It was very hot Yesterday, and we were pester'd and Stung grievously by the Muskitoes, as we lay under the Mangroves. At 6 in the Evening the Bark and Boats made way up the River. By 12 at Night we were in sight of the Town with all the Boats, in which we had no Men. We saw a very great Fire on the top of an adjoining Hill, and Lights in the Town. In half an hour we were a-breast of it, and ready to land, but saw abundance of Lights appear at once coming down the Hill, and the Town full of 'em. We enquir'd of the *Indians*, our Pilots, whether it was any Saint's Day, or what might be the Occasion of it, and they answer'd us, that it must be an Alarm. It was very dark whilst we lay still driving on the River, being just High-water, we heard a *Spaniard* from the Shore, talking loudly that *Puna* was taken, and that the Enemy were coming up the River. This made us conclude it was an Alarm. Immediately after we heard their Bells making a confused Noise, and then a Volly of small Arms, and two Great Guns. Above an Hour was spent in Debate betwixt Capt. *Dover*, Capt. *Courtney*, and my self, whether we should land. I asked the Consent of the Lieutenants in all the Boats about Landing, telling 'em I suppos'd this to be the first Alarm, and that we had best laud during their Consternation; but they differ'd in opinion, and sew were for landing in the Night. I asked Capt. *Dampier* how the Buccaneers behav'd themselves in such Cases, and he told me they never attack'd any large Place after it was alarm'd. It drew near two in the Morning, and the Ebb run so strong, that the great Boat and Yall could not row up to Land; so that it being too late to attempt the Town, I advised to fall down the River out of Sight of it to meet our Barks, and land with the Morning Flood. Upon this all our Boats drove down with the Ebb about a League below the Town, where we lay till Day-break, and saw our Bark, Mr. *Glendall* Commander, brought by the honest *Indian* Pilot a Mile above us, for we had palled by him in the Night: We rowed back to him, and recruited our Men as well as we could. We found the Water fresh there, and drank of it, tho' yesterday it war, a little brackish. The Bark lay against a Wood of tall Trees close by the Shore, and we kept a File of Musketeers with their Arms pointing into the Wood, with Orders to fire if they saw any Men; and we kept firing a Musket now and then into the Woods, to prevent Ambuscades. About 3 our Yall and Launch came aboard, for they could not row back with us to the Bark, till the Tide slackened, and the Flood was coming. At 10 we saw the *Dutchess's* Bark come in sight; immediately I ordered the Anchor to be got up to fall on the Town, which was about two Miles from us; but Capt. *Dover* oppos'd it, press'd that we might have a Consultation with as many of the Officers as were present, and to lie in the Boat a-stern of the Bark, that what was debated might not be overheard by the rest of our Company. We immediately assembled there accordingly, and Capt. *Dover* insisted on the Difficulty of attempting the Enemy now they had been so long alarm'd; alledging we should but throw away our own and our Mens Lives, or else weaken our selves so much, as might occasion the Loss of the remaining part of the Voyage, that chiefly brought us from *England*, and was our greatest Dependance: That the Town appeared large, and consequently was much more able to hold out than we to attack it; and tho' the *Spaniards* in these Parts had no extraordinary fighting Character, yet if they armed the Mullatto's, as they generally did on the like Occasions, we might find the Attempt very desperate, with other Objections not fit to recite here. He concluded, that our best Method would be to send a Trumpeter with Proposals to the Enemy to trade with us for the Cargoes of Negroes and other Goods aboard our Prizes, that an immediate Meeting should be appointed, the Prices for the Negro's and Goods fix'd, and good Hostages given us for the Performance within a limited Time, and if they agreed to this, that we would not land. This Proposal I withstood by the best Arguments I could, and urged our landing immediately, least the Enemy gaining Time by our Delays, might send off their Wealth, and get leisure to strengthen themselves, so as to bid us defiance. This being put to the Vote, the Majority was for landing, and as an Obligation on Capt. *Dover*, who was a part Owner in our Ships, we agreed he should lead on the Attack as he requested, and if he took the Town, he should give the Watch-word that Night, and Capt. *Courtney* and I to take it in turns after him: But this Resolution did not hold; for Cape. *Dover* reflected on me, and said I should be answerable for all the Damage that might happen to us on our Landing. By these Reflexions, and some other Peoples Indifferency, I had reason to doubt, the Consequence of attempting the Enemy with Success since we were so divided amongst ourselves; therefore at length I yielded to send two of our Prisoners, instead of a Trumpeter, as Capt. *Dover* first propos'd, with the foregoing Proposals. The other Prisoners in our Bark oblig'd themselves for the Return of these two in less than an Hour; and this Method every one seem'd to be pleas'd with; so we put the Captain of the *French*-built Ship, and the Lieutenant of *Puna* ashore in our Boat, and charged them to return from the Shore in less than an Hour otherwise we would land. In the mean while we ran up with the other Bark, and lay against the Middle of the Town at an Anchor. As we sail'd up we saw 4 Barks put off from the Town to go higher up the River, and just as the limited Hour was past, we sent our Boats well mann'd and arm'd after them, who soon took and brought 'em to us. Mean while our Prisoners returned in a Boat from the Town, with the *Spanish* Master le Camp, who discoursed with us, and told us, that at his Return ashore the Corregidore or Governour, with another Gentleman, would come off and treat with us. We soon put him ashore again, and quickly after came off the Corregidore with another Gentleman. Cape. *Dover* and I met them in our Boat, with a Linguist, and carried them aboard one of the Barks that our Boats had taken as they endeavour'd to escape up the River.

April 23. We did nothing yesterday in the Afternoon, but secure the Barks, and treat with the Governour. Several of our Prisoners told us they did not doubt to find Credit here, and that they would also deal with us; so that we were in hopes of more Profit by felling our Cargo's and Negro's than if we had ransack'd the Town. The Corregidore and we had verbally agreed for the Goods by the Lump, at 140 Pieces of Eight per Bale, one fort with another, and talked of the Price for other things. We parted about Five in the Afternoon, he having desir'd to go ashore, that he might prevail with the other Gentlemen to agree with him, and promis'd to meet us three Commanders on board one of our Prizes at 8 in the Evening. We order'd our Linguist to get Candles lighted, and the best Entertainment we could provide for them; but the Time being elapsed, and they not appearing, it gave us great reason to suspect we were trick'd; therefore we sent our Boats again above the Town, and alarm'd them afresh in the Night. Our Centinels hail'd a Boat after Midnight, that came aboard us with a Gentleman, who told us he was sent from the Corregidore with a Present of 2 Bags of Flower, 2 Sheep and 2 Hogs ready kill'd, 2 Jars of Wine and 2 of Brandy; and to assure us the Governour had been with us according to Appointment, but that one of the chief Merchants concern'd was absent; yet he would come off in the Morning by 7 a Clock, on board one of the new Ships next the Shore, where he desir'd us to meet him, and requested us to believe he was a Man of Honour; for tho' he had been considerably reinforced since he left us, and that more Men were continually coming into the Town he resolved to discharge yesterday's Promise, and therefore hoped we would forbear offering any Hostilities above the Town because the Women and Children were there in Sanctuary, with little or no Wealth to prompt us to plunder them. We the 3 Commanders return'd our humble Service to the Corregidore, and our kind Thanks for his Present, being sorry we had nothing to oblige him with by way of Return; but desir'd he might be told from us, that we all admir'd at his not keeping his Word according to Appointment, and still depended that he would convince us he was a Man of Honour, by meeting us at 7 in the Morning where we agreed last Night, otherwise our Treaty was at an end. We were all uneasy till 7 in the Morning, when we saw a Flag of Truce aboard the new Ship, and supposing the Governour to be there, we mann'd our Pinnace, and sent our Linguist to give our Promise, that if the Corregidore came aboard the Bark our Prize, he should be at liberty to return: Upon this he with three more came aboard, and we order'd our 2 Frigats Barks to go close under the Shore next the best Part of the Town, and that every thing should be kept in readiness for Landing, left we should not agree with these Gentlemen. Nothing else was transacted this Morning, but our Conference with these Men: Our first Proposals were 50000 Pieces of Eight Contribution for the Town, and we would deliver them their 2 new Ships that lay near the Shore, and 6 Barks, provided they would oblige themselves to buy our two Prizes Cargoes of Goods and Negroes, and gave us sufficient Hostages for Payment within 9 Days. The latter they gave us some Hopes of complying with, if we would take their Words and two Hostages, which we thought too little; for tho' they came to our Price for the Goods, they would not give near that Sum for the Town and Ships, alledging they were not yet in our Power, and consequently not liable to so large Contributions; adding, that they had Men and Arms sufficient in the Town, and Ships to protect them. We all concluded by their dilatory Treaty, that they only design'd to trick us, and gain Time, upon which we gave 'em this Answer: That the Ships we could have in a Minute, or set them on fire; that we did not fear taking the Town at pleasure; that we look'd upon it as much our own, as is it was in our Possession, and must have the Money or good Hostages; otherwise before Night we would set it on fire. By Noon the Corregidore and the other Gentlemen agreed with us to buy both Cargoes, and to give Hostages for 40000 Pieces of Eight for the Town, 2 new Ships, and 6 Barks: But neither of us were to sign this Agreement till it was confirm'd by the chief Men of the Town ashore, which the Corregidore was to procure in an hours time.

April. 24. About One Yesterday Afternoon the Governour was put ashore in my Pinnace: Some insisted on our Slopping him, because not long before an *Indian* came in a Canoe from the Master le Camp, and the other Officers ashore, to know whether the Governour had agreed. Because our

Barks lay near the Shore the *Spaniards* kept to Arms, expecting we might fall on them suddenly; and said they wanted nothing but him, and if he could not come, his Orders when to begin the Fight with us, if we did not agree. This Message was deliver'd in our Hearing, and occasional Disputes among us about keeping him Prisoner; those who were for it urg'd, that if he went ashore the Enemy would certainly fight us, and that as he had broke with us last Night, we might break with him now; but I was utterly against it, since we had given him our Word of Honour to the contrary; and at last we agreed, and sent him ashore. The three Gentlemen staid with us as Hostages, upon request of the Corregidore, neither they nor we doubting but the Agreement would be ratified ashore. The Time allotted for Answer being past, a Messenger from the Town came to inform us, they could raise but 30,000 Pieces of Eight, and not a word of the Trade; so we sent our Linguist and a Prisoner with our final Answer, that if they did not in half an hour send us three more good Hostages for the 40,000 Pieces of Eight agreed on, we would take down our Flag of Truce, land, and give no Quarter, and fire the Town and Ships. In the mean time we saw the *Spaniards* quit the new Ships, and we took possession of them; our Messenger return'd, and in half an hour; Men more from the Town came to the Bank against our Barks, holding out a white Handkerchief to parley again: They told us their Resolution was to give us 32,000 Pieces of Eight, and no more; so we order'd our Linguist to tell 'em we had done treating, and bid the *Spaniards* ashore retire forthwith, and keep out of shot of us, if they design'd to save their Lives. We all at once hal'd down our White Flag of Truce, and let fly our English and Field Colours. I order'd 2 of our Guns of about 600 Weight each, mounted on Field Carriages, into the Great Launch to land before their Faces, and we fill'd our; Boats full of Men. I went in our Pinnace, Capt. *Dover* in the Launch, and Capt. *Courtney* in his Pinnace, the 3 Boats landing about 70 Men: We towed the Launch ashore, Mr. *Glendal*, 3d Lieutenant of our Ship, tarried aboard our Bark with 10 Men, to ply our Guns over our Heads into the Town as we landed. The Enemy drew up their Horse at the End of the Street which fronted our Men and Barks, and also lin'd the Houses with Men within half Musket-Shot of the Bank where we landed. They made a formidable Show in respect to our little Number that was to attack them. We landed, and fired every Man on his Knee at the Brink of the Bank, then loaded, and as we advanc'd, call'd to our Bark to forbear firing, for fear of hurting our Men. We who landed kept loading and firing very fast; but the Enemy made only one Discharge, and retired back to their Guns, where their Horse drew up a Second time; we got to the first Houses, and as we open'd the Streets, saw 4 Guns pointing at us before a spacious Church; but as our Men came in fight, firing, the Horse scower'd off. This encourag'd me to call to our Men to run and seize the Guns, and I immediately hasten'd towards 'em with 8 or 10 of our Men till within Pistol-Shot of the Guns, when we all fir'd, some at the Gunner, and others at the Men in Arms in the front of the Church, where they appear'd very numerous; but by the time we had loaded, and more of our Men came in fight, the Enemy began to run, and quitted the Guns, after they had fired them with round and Partridge Shot, one of the last was discharg'd at us very near, but Thanks to God did us no Hurt, and they had hot Time to relade them. We that were foremost raft into the Church, and seized about 10 or 12 Prisoners. By that time many of our Men were coming up, and Cape. *Courtney* and Capt. *Dover*, with the rest of their Company came all to the Church, where I staid to secure that Post with a few Men, the rest march'd with them to the other End of the

Town. From the Time we landed till we took their Guns, and Possession of the Church; (which lies above a Furlong from the Water-side) I believe was not much above half an hour: I posted Capt. *Dampier* and above 25 Men with the Guns, which we turned on the Enemy, who run clear out of the Town. By this time the remaining part of our Men were landed, and joined me at the Church; then I marched after Capt. *Courtney* and Capt. *Dover* with this latter Gang; for most of those chat got to the Church with me first I could not flop, after I had secur'd the Guns; so that 7 of them ran into the Valley and Woods adjoining to pursue the *Spaniards*, and having Cowards to deal with came well back; but being offended at their Boldness, I reprimanded them, and they promis'd never to be guilty of the like Folly again. All the Men in general behav'd themselves with great Courage, but like Sailors could be kept under no Command as soon as the first Piece Was fired; however it happen'd much better than we could expect, for now the Attack is over, they keep handsomly together, and forbear immoderate Drinking. I overtook Capt. *Dover* and Capt. *Courtney* at the other End of the Town, and left Capt *Dover* to keep guard at a.church there; as I march'd back with Capt, *Courtney*, I left him in the Middle of the Town at another Church, and I came to my first Post at the Church where the Guns were planted, and sent Capt. *Dampier* with his Men to reinforce Capt. *Courtney* and Capt. *Dover*. Thus we were in quiet possession of the Town by Sun-set, and ported our Guards, having had no Opposition after the Enemy quitted the great Church. In the Evening I went on board our Barks, settl'd a good Watch, and secur'd the *Spaniards* the Corregidore left behind him, then I return'd ashore to the Church. Capt. *Dover* set the Houses on fire that fronted the Church where he was posted, which burnt all Night and the next Day. There was a Hill near his Quarter, and thick Woods within half Shot of the Church; so that the Enemy were almost continually popping at him all Night. He told me that the next Day some Parties appear'd out of the Woods; but when he fired a Volley at 'em, they retir'd, our Quarters were quiet, and out of hearing all Night. The Enemy might have done him Mischief, had they been couragious, since we were not near enough to assist him in the Night. For the Town being long, we could not keep the whole without dividing at such a distance; but his firing the Houses covered the worst part of his Quarters that Night, which was of great service to him. Capt. *Courtney* relieved him at Day-break, and they both quitted Capt. *Dover's* Quarters, as being too much expos'd to the Enemy. An *Indian* that I had taken Prisoner told us, that he knew of much Money up the River in Bark-logs and Houses; upon which Capt *Courtney* and I last Night detached 21 Men four of our Companies, and lent 'em in his Boat up the River under the Command of his new second Lieutenant Mr. *Connely*: I would fain have sent both Pinnaces to make the best use of our time, and seize that Wealth, finding little or none in the Town; but the rest would by no means consent to it, left the Enemy might engage us next Morning, and then we should want our Boats and Men. When I could not possibly prevail for another Boat, and Men enough to mann both Pinnaces, I desired Capt. *Courtney's* Boat might go, because the largest, and she was mann'd out of both our Companies. In the Morning we began with Iron Crows and Mauls to break open the other two Churches, and all the Score-houses, Cellars, &c. which was soon done, for no body was left at home, nor much of Value to be found, but Flower, Peas, Beans, and Jars of Wine and Brandy in great Plenty. We began to carry it to the Water-side; but having sultry hot, wet and unhealthful Weather, and our Men being fatigued, they became so weak that they could not work very well at this new Imployment. They would fain have had the boarded Floor of the Church taken up to look amongst the Dead for Treasure, fancying the *Spaniards* might hide their Money there; but I would not suffer it, because of a contagious Distemper that had swept off a great Number of People here not long before; so that the Church Floor was full of Graves. We have yet found but two of the Enemy kill'd in the Town, and one Prisoner, who was slightly wounded in the Head; but this Day I heard if of 'em were kill'd and wounded, amongst whom was the chief Gunner, an *Irish*-man, that fired the last Gun at us, who had lived some Years amongst 'em. On our side we had but two Men wounded, one of 'em *Terrick Derrickson*, a *Dutch-* man, belonging to my Company, was shot thro' between the lower Part of his Neck and Shoulder, but I believe not mortal; and one *John Martin a Portuguese*, mortally wounded aboard the Bark, occasion'd by a Cohorn Shell, which split as soon as fired out of our Cohorn Mortar. The *Spaniards* Force being variously reported by our Prisoners, I'll not insert it till I am better inform'd. The Fatigue I have had since I left our Ships in this hot Weather has weakened and disorder'd me very much.

April 25. We kept our Colours flying on the Tower of the Church, Capt. *Dover* keeping Guard there all Day, whilst I and Capt. *Courtney* took care to get every thing we found useful carried to the to Water-side. Yesterday in the Afternoon we sent the Lieutenant of *Puna* and another Prisoner into the Country, with Proposals to ransom the Town, a great part of the Enemy being in the Woods about a League from us; they have but ordinary Quarters, because of the great Rain. Their Horses being in Parties; and continually in sight, alarm us several times in a day. The Prisoners return'd to us in the Evening with an ambiguous Answer; but desir'd they might go again in the Morning to prevent burning the Town. About 10 last Night the Boat returned that we had sent up the River, having been from us about 24 Hours; they were 7 Leagues up, and 16 of 'em landed at 6 several Places, the other 5 kept the Boat, having a Swivel Gun to defend themselves. At one place they separated, and Mr. *Connely* with 3 others rambled so far in the Woods to look for Wealth, that after hours Search they could not find the Way back to the rest, but by Accident met again, and got to the Boat. *William Davis*, one of my Men, was shot through the hinder part of the Neck by the Enemy, the Wound not dangerous, and none of the rest hurt; they chased 35 Horsemen well arm'd, that were coming to help those of *Guiaquil*. The Houses up the River were full of Women, and particularly at one place there were above a Dozen handsom genteel young Women well dress'd, where our Men got several Gold Chains and Ear-rings, but were otherwise so civil to them, that the Ladies offer'd to dress 'em Victuals, and brought 'em a Cask of good Liquor. Some of their largest Gold Chains were conceal'd, and wound about their Middles, Legs, and Thighs, *etc.* but the Gentlewomen in these hot Countries being very thin clad with Silk and fine Linnen, and their Hair dress'd with Ribbons very neatly, our Men by pressing felt the Chains, &c. with their Hands on the Out-side of the Lady's Apparel, and by their Linguist modestly desired the Gentlewomen to take 'em off and surrender 'em. This I mention as a Proof of our Sailors Modesty, and in rasped to Mr. *Connely* and Mr. *Selkirk* the late Governour of *Juan Fernandoes*, who commanded this Party: For being young Men, I was willing to do 'em this Justice, hoping the Fair Sex will make 'em a grateful Return when we arrive in *Great Britain*, on account of their civil Behaviour to these charming Prisoners. They call'd at this House for Provisions as they return'd down the River, and being so civil 'at first, they gave their fair Landladies, no Uneasiness nor Surprize at a 2*d* Visit: They took a large empty Bark, but left her up the River, and brought with 'em in Gold Chains, Ear-rings and Plate, I believe above 1000 *l.* Value, with a Negro that had been serviceable in discovering part of the hidden Treasure; but they all agree that the Want of another Boat lost much more than they got; for while they search'd and plunder'd one Side, the Canoes and Bark-logs did cross the River, and carry the People and Purchase out of their reach, for want of another Boat to prevent it. They also inform'd us, that in the Places where they had been above the Town, they saw more than 300 arm'd Horse and Foot in several Parties; so that we apprehended the Enemy design'd to gain Time by pretending to ransom, till with a vast Odds they might attack us, and reckoned themselves sure of Victory, but we for fear of being surprized, agreed to assemble in a Body at every Alarm, which was beat several times a day on the sight of large Parties, tho' it hinder'd our Business. We found 5 Jars of Powder, some Match and Shot, with a good Quantity of ordinary Arms, 3 Drums, with several Swords and Launces, in the Church, where I pick'd up the Corregidore's Gold-headed Cane, and another Captain's with a Silver Head; for among the *Spaniards* none carry a Cane but the chief Officers, and of those none under a Captain must wear a Cane with a Silver or Gold Head: So that those Gentlemen were much in haste to leave the Badges of their Office behind them. After Capt. *Dover* had quitted his Post yesterday Morning, one of our Men came to tell me, that the Enemy was coming down the Hill that way upon us: We beat an Alarm, and leaving part of our Men with the Guns, I march'd with the rest, and met Capt. *Courtney* and part of his Company on the Bridge retiring: He told me the Enemy was numerous and well arm'd in the North End of the Town; I desir'd him to join us, and we would visit them; he left his chief Lieutenant and the rest of his Men at Arms in his Quarters, and we went together with 70 Men to face the Enemy. As we march'd forward, they retir'd only now and then they shot at us out of the Woods. We look'd into the two Churches, and several Houses, but found no body. The Woods were very thick, and join'd to the Backs of the Houses, from whence we had several Shot all round us, which we return'd at a venture, but none of 'em touched us, which was a very great Providence, for it was really strange that they miss'd us. Capt. *Courtney* and I could nor agree to keep that End of the Town, so we march'd back again, took what we lik'd best into our Boats, and carried it aboard the Barks.

April 26. About one Yesterday in the Afternoon our Prisoners return'd with an Offer of 50000 Pieces of Eight for the Town, with their Ships and Barks, to be paid in 12 Days, which we don't approve of, nor should we stay so long for a greater Sum. By these Delays they design to gain Time, that if they don't fight us, they may draw their Forces from *Lima*; for we know an Express was dispatch'd thither immediately on our Arrival. The Morning we sent our final Answer, *viz.* that they should see the Town all on fire by 3 in the Afternoon, if they did not agree, and give us sufficient Hostages for the above-mention'd Sum, to be paid within 6 Days. During which time we would grant a Cessation of Arms between *Guiaquil* and *Puna*, where we expected they would meet is, and purchase our Cargoes. A *French*-man belonging to my Company, whom I sent with others, by request of Capt. *Courtney*, to strengthen his Quarters, being put Centinel last Night, shot *Hugh Tidcomb*, one of their Men, so that he died. The Accident happened by a too severe Order at their Quarters to shoot any in the Night that did not answer; and neither this Man nor the Centinel, as I am informed, understood how to ask or answer the Watch-word, by which Neglect a Man was unaccountably lost. Mr. *Gardner*, one of their Officers, and 9 Men more, yesterday in the Afternoon engag'd at the North-end of the Town with a Party of *Spaniards*, whom they chased into the Woods, but following 'em too far, were attack'd by others, and one of our Men shot through the Calf of his Leg, and another of them, while he stopt to relade his Piece, was shot against the Middle of the Pole-ax that hung at his Side, which made an Impression on the Iron, and bruised the Part under it, so that it prov'd a Piece of Armour well placed. The other Man who was wounded in the Leg, by his Irregularity and hard drinking fell into a Fever that carried him off. At the same time Mr. *Stratton*, Cape. *Courtney's* chief Lieutenant, having his Pistols hanging at his Side, one of them unluckily discharg'd it self against the Outside of the thickest part of his Leg, and left a Bullet in the Flesh; but there's little Danger of his Life: He being by this Accident disabled to make a quick Retreat, if occasion requir'd, his Captain immediately order'd him on board the Bark. Upon these Accidents, and perceiving the Enemy to increase and grow bolder, Capt. *Courtney* brought his Company to my Quarters. Last Night we all lay in the Church, round which we kept Centinels within a Musket-Shot; the Centinels, as customary, calling to each other every Quarter of an Hour, to prevent their Sleeping, and our being surprized in the Night. Every Man kept his Arms and Ammunition in exact Order by him, and was strictly charged to rise at the least Alarm. We unhung a small Church Bell, and sent it aboard for our Ships Use. We have done little this 24 Hours towards shipping off Goods, because the Enemy were continually popping at us from the Woods. The Weather was very wet, hot and faint, the Streets deep and slippery, and the Ways to the Water-side very bad, which mightily incommoded us.

April 27. Yesterday about 2 in the Afternoon Our Prisoners return'd with two Men on Horseback from the Enemy's sorry damp, and told us the Agreement was concluded as we last proposed, that if we suspected them, they would stay for Hostages, and that the Lieutenant of *Puna*, who as a Messenger forwarded the Treaty, with an old Gentleman already on board our Bark, were to be the other two. We contented our selves with the latter, and let the two Strangers return to their Camp with our Messenger, who was to bring back the Agreement sign'd but they sent another back to us, signifying that we had omitted to take notice that the Town was taken by Force of Arms, which we afterwards inserted both in the *Spanish* and *English* Paper. This Morning the *Spanish* Agreement was brought back sign'd by 'em, and we sent ours in *English* sign'd to them as follows;

Whereas the City of *Guiaquil*, lately in Subjection to *Philip* V. King of *Spain*, is now taken by Storm, and in the Possession of the Capts. *Thomas Dover*, *Woodes Rogers*, and *Stephen Courtney*, commanding a Body of Her Majesty of *Great Britain's* Subjects: We the underwritten are content to become Hostages for the said City, and to continue in the Custody of the said Capts. *Tho. Dover*, *Woodes Rogers*, and *Stephen Courtney*, till 50000 Pieces of Eight shall be paid to them for the Ransom of the said City, 2 new Ships, and 6 Barks; during which time no Hostility is to be committed on either side between this and *Puna*. The said Sum to be paid at *Puna* in six Days from the Date hereof, and then the Hostages to be discharg'd, and all the Prisoners to be deliver'd immediately, otherwise the said Hostages do agree to remain Prisoners till the said Sum is discharg'd in any other Part of the World. In witness whereof we have voluntarily set our Hands this 27th Day of *April*, Old Stile, and the 7*th* of *May*, S.N. in the Year of our Lord, 1709.

The two Hostages lay this Night at our Quarters, and we ship'd 'em off, with all we had got together, by II a Clock, and march'd towards our Barks with our Colours flying, while the *Spaniards* return'd to their Houses. I march'd on the Rear with a few Men, and pick'd up Pistols, Cutlasses and Pole-axes, which shew'd that our Men were grown very careless, weak, and weary of being Soldiers, and that 'twas time to be gone from hence. The hardest Work we had was to get the Guns down to the Water, the Earth being so soft, that they who help'd to carry them sunk half Leg deep. To make it as easy as I could, I contriv'd a Frame of Bamboe Canes, under which 60 Men could stand, and bear equal Weight on their Shoulders. Tho' they were large 4 Pounders, the Gun and the Frame did not exceed 15 *C*. Weight; but had not the Prisoners we took help'd us (tho' it had been an easy Task in a cold Country) I could hardly have pick'd Men enough of our own for the Work, *John Gabriel*, one of my Company, a *Dutch*-man was missing.

April 28. Yesterday in the Afternoon we settl'd every thing on board the Barks as well as we could, and separated our Men aboard the Prizes, where we had put most of our Town Goods and Plunder, being about 230 Bags of Flower, Beans, Peas and Rice, if Jars of Oil, about 160 Jars of other Liquors, some Cordage, Iron Ware, and small Nails, with about 4 half jars of Powder, about 3 Tun of Pitch and Tar, a Parcel of Clothing and Necessaries, and as I guess about 1200 *l.* in Plate, Ear-rings, *etc.* and 150 Bales of dry Goods, 4 Guns, and about 100 *Spanish* ordinary useless Arms and Musket Barrels, a few Packs of Indigo, Cocoa and Anotto, with about a Tun of Loas-Sugar. We left abundance of Goods in the Town, besides Liquors of most sorts, and Sea-Stores, with several Warehouses full of Cocoa, divers Ships on the Stocks, and 2 new Ships unrigg'd upwards of 400 Tun, which cost above 80000 Crowns, and then lay at Anchor before the Town. We are also to deliver 4 Barks ashore, and leave two here to bring down the Ransom. By this it appears the *Spaniards* had a good Bargain; but this Ransom was far better for us than to burn what we could not carry off. About 2 yesterday Afternoon our *Dutch*-man that was missing rose out of his Brandy-wine Fit, and came aboard; he was disturb'd by the honest Man of the House where he lay, who first called in his Neighbours, and cautiously seized his Arms, then gently rais'd him, and when his Eyes were open, told him there was his Arms again, and bid him hasten aboard to us. This is the only Man that I know of since we cook *Guiaquil*, who had so much transgressed our Orders by drinking beyond his bearing. This Morning about 8 we weighed, and sailed with all our Barks, and at parting made what Shew and Noise we could with our Drums, Trumpets and Guns, and thus took our Leave of the *Spaniards* very cheerfully, but not half so well pleased as we should have been, had we taken 'em by Surprize; For I was well assur'd from all hands, that at least we should then have got above 200,000 pieces of Eight in Money, wrought and unwrought, Gold and Silver, besides Jewels, and a greater Plenty of such Necessaries as we now found, tho' the Place has not been poorer these 40 Years, by reason that a sudden Fire about 18 Months ago had destroy'd the better half of the Town, which is now mostly rebuilt. Before I go any further, 'tis proper to describe the Town.

Chapter VIII

A Description of Guiaquil.

'Tis the Metropolis of its Province, about a Mile and half long, and divided into Old and New, joined by a wooden Bridge above half a Mile in Length, but passable only by People on foot. There are some Houses at a distance on each side the Bridge, and those of both Towns may be about 4 or 500 in the whole, besides 5 Churches, and the Inhabitants about 2000 in all. Their chief Church is that of St. *Jago* or St. *James* the Apostle, which has 7 Altars, and before it a handsom Square; the others are those of St. *Austin*, St. *Francis*, St. *Dominick*, and St. *Ignatius*. The latter belongs to the Jesuits. Before that of St. *Dominick*, which is not quite finished, there is also a Square, with a Half-moon, upon which they formerly planted Guns, but none were mounted there when we took it. Three of these Churches were very lofty, one of them of Stone, and alt adorn'd with Altars, carv'd Work, Pictures, *etc.* and there was an Organ in that of St. *Augustin*; but the Priests and their Scholars had carry'd off all the Plate belonging to those Churches, and retir'd with it into the Woods before we landed. Some of the Houses of the Town were very high, several built of Brick, but most of them of Timber, and the meaner sort of Bamboes. There is but one regular Street along the Side of the River to the Bridge, and from thence along the Old Town. The Situation is in a low boggy Soil, so dirty in Winter, that without the Bridge they could scarce go from one House to another. The Town is govern'd by a Corregidore, who is their chief Magistrate, and appointed by the King. His Name was *Don Jeronymo Bos*, a young Man of about 24 Years of Age, and a Native of the *Canaries*. The Town is well seated for Trade, and building of Ships, for which they have Sheds to cover the Workmen from the Sun. It lies 14 Leagues up from Point *Arena*, and 7 from *Puna*. The River is large, receives several others, has many Villages and Farm Houses on its Banks, with abundance of Mangroves and Sarsaparilla, which impregnates its Water, and makes it good against the *French* Pox but in the Time of Floods it is unwholesome, because of the poisonous Roots and Plants wash'd down from the Mountains. They have Plenty of Provisions, black Cattle, Sheep, Goats, Swine, Poultry, several sorts of Ducks unknown in *Europe*, and Store of Horses. The Water of the River is fresh at low Water, almost as far as *Puna*. An *Englishman* who had liv'd here some time, came over to us, inform'd us of many Particulars, and told us that in *December* last they had 3 Weeks Rejoycings for the Birth of the Prince of *Asturias*, when they muster'd 1100 Foot and 500 Horse in Arms, besides a much greater Number that had none; but most of those Troops came from the adjacent Country. During this Solemnity, they baited many Bulls to Death, after the manner of *Spain*, and run at the Ring, *&c.* which are their chief Diversions: He told us likewise that Ships are frequently built here for the King. The Hostages inform'd us, that during the Treaty, 80000 Dollars of the King's Money was sent out of the Town, besides their Plate, Jewels, and other Things of greatest Value: But they were robb'd of a great deal by the Blacks, to whom they had given it in the Hurry to carry off: We took several of 'em with stoln Goods, as we went the Rounds by Night; and therefore we made a Signal to the Inhabitants to return, as we march'd off that they might not suffer any more Loss by those Villains.

The *French*, by their Commerce in these Seas, as the *Spaniards* in general told us, damage their Trade so much, that their Sea-ports are sensibly impoverish'd and this Town was much richer 6 Years go than now. A mile below I took my Leave of the Barks, with the Pinnace double mann'd, designing to get before them to the Ships at Point *Arena*. The Day came on very hot, and we saw many Alligators in the River.

Apr. 29. Last Night I reached *Puna*, and met Mr. *Duck* and Mr. *Hatley* in the *Beginning* and an empty Park which the *Duke's* Yall had taken in our Absence; the *Spaniards* having run ashore and left her at Anchor off of Point *Arena*. Our People were concern'd at our being absent so long and hearing no News of us, the Scarcity of Water had made 'em give the Prisoners but a Pint a Day for some time; and they sunk the last small Prize we took coming from *Payta*, to prevent the Prisoners running away with her, for they had not Men to spare for manning her themselves. By Day-light I got aboard, where I sound all our People overjoyed at our Meeting again, after 12 Days Absence on an Undertaking subject to so many fatal Accidents, which we happily escaped. Captain *Cook* and *Frye* were very uneasie in our Absence, and had their full Share of Care and Fatigue. They usually gave the Prisoners Liberty by Day, but kept their Arms always ready, and the after Part of the Ships to themselves: At Night they shut 'em up in the Fore-Castle, or between Decks; but aboard the Prize, which was not so secure, they put them in Irons every Evening, and let 'em out in the Morning; but never suffer'd any Correspondence between the Prisoners in the several Ships, by which Means they neither knew their own Strength, nor our Weakness, any further than in the respective Ships they were confin'd to. *Roger Booth*, one of the *Dutchess's* Men, who was wounded through his Wind-pipe, in the Engagement with the *Havre de Grace*, died the 20th Instant. *William Essex*, a stout Sailor, one of our Quarter-Masters, being wounded in the Breast in the same Fight, died the 24th Instant: So that out of both Ships we lost 4 Good Men, including my dear Brother, by that Engagement. Mr. *James Stratton*, Quarter-Master belonging to the *Dutchess* that was wounded at the same time, by a Musket-Ball in his Thigh, is now out of Danger, The wound ed in these Parts, are more frequently attended with Fevers, and other dangerous Accidents, than in *Europe*.

Apr. 30. About 3 Yesterday Afternoon a Sail from under the Main appear'd in sight running up the Channel to *Guiaquil* Capt. *Cooke* sent the *Havre de Grace's* Boat in pursuit of her, but my Pinnace sailing better, followed and took her before Sun set: She was a Bark of above 30 Tuns, from *Sania*, call'd the *Francisco la Salma*, Senior *Jacomo de Brienas* Master with 6 Men on board: She was laden with about 270 Bags of Flour, Beans and Pease; near 200 Sugar-Loaves; several Frails of Quinces, Marmalet, Sugar-plumbs, and other Sweetmeats, with a good Quantity of large Pomegranates, Apples and Onions; a little of this Country Cheese, and dried Beef: They had been out 7 Days, and heard nothing of us 5 but confirm'd the Story of an *English* Squadron expected in these Seas, and that there were several stout *French* Ships in their Harbours, particularly two at *Lima*, and one at *Pisco*, besides others in the Harbours of *Chili*: That at *Chenipe*, whence they came, being the Sea-port to *Sania*, there was a strict Order lately sent from *Lima* to the chief Officer there, to be on his Guard, and keep continual Watch in the same Manner as I have before noted, in the Order we found directed to the Lieutenant or Governour of *Puna*. This Morning, at 7, the *Beginning* came to an Anchor by us, from *Puna*, with a few Jarrs of Water, which we mightily wanted.

Mr. *Goodall* and others told me, there were no other Barks coming down but what went up with his, from the Ships for Water, and that he did not know the Reason why the rest stay'd there: He told me, he had a Letter from Capt. *Courtney* to his Second, Capt. *Cook*, but no Message or Letter from him or Capt. *Dover* to me; adding, he heard one of them say that they expected this Bark would meet the Ships half way coming up to *Puna*, and that they looked for me hourly. This unexpected Story surpriz'd me, but I supposed they might now have some Hopes of disposing our Cargo to the *Spaniards* at *Guiaquil*, which occasioned their Staying, and Expectation of my Return. I discours'd it with Capt. *Cooke* and Mr. *Frye*, and saw Capt. *Courtney's* Letter, but not a Word of Advice to me: However, I resolved to hasten away the *Beginning*, with some Negroes (the most troublesome Goods we had) to dispose of, that they might be at *Puna* before me. I began to unmore the *Havre de Grace*, in order to go up with the Flood, hoping to sell her Cargo, or good Part of it, while our Ships took in Water, resolving to save as much Time as possible. Mean while the other Water Bark arriv'd, but without any manner of Advice to me when those above design'd to come down, or to send the Men that were so much wanting aboard, to put things in order for our going to Sea.

May 1. Yesterday, in the Afternoon, I took Sen. *Morell* for a Pilot, and weigh'd with the *Havre de Grace*, but having little Wind, and being neep Tides, I did not get one Third of the Way up to Puna, with that Flood: I was likewise but ill mann'd; because I was obliged to leave the Pinnace and Crew that came down with me for the Security of our Ship. We weigh'd again with the Morning Flood, and met the *Dutchess's* Bark coming down, but without the least Advice to me from the 2 Captains at *Puna*, which farther confirm'd me that they waited for my Company, and the Ship, to sell her Goods: I was pleas'd at the Thoughts of this, for I concluded, that had it been otherwise, one, or both of them, would have come down, or have sent all the Barks, except one to stay for the Ransom. We were forced to anchor again before high Water; and the Tide shot tis over towards the Island. There is a Shole Sand above half Way up to *Puna*, near mid Channel, over on that side, which 'tis difficult to avoid, unless we have a commanding Gale to keep in the Channel which is nearest the Main; 'tis the Starboard Shore as you go up, and there are gradual Soundings on both sides to the Shoal on the Larboard side, or the main Land on the Starboard side, keeping between 4 and 7 Fathom Water; the Coast clear of all is N. E. up the Channel, bearing about two large Leagues off Point *Arena*, where it's bold, and all athwart, till we get 2 Leagues higher than Point *Arena*; and as we come against, or a little above, the white Chalky Cliff, near the Point or upper End, and the highest part of the Island of *Puna*, we must hall over for the Island, and come to an Anchor before the Houses, that are plain to be seen, when we get above the high Point, which is easily known, because ill the Land on the Island is even with the Water, and elsewhere there's nothing to be seen but Trees, down to the River. We must keep nearest the Starboard Shore, going up, which is the only Channel for Ships; 'Tis above 8 Leagues from Point *Arena* to the Town of *Puna*; which lies on the upper End of the Island of that Name.

May 2. We got up to an Anchor before *Puna*, by 10 this Morning, where I found 4 of the Barks that came down from *Guiaquil*. Capt. *Dover* and *Courtney* came on Board, and contrary to Expectation told me, they had not heard one Word from the *Spaniards* since we left them. This being the last Day appointed for Payment, a Boat came and brought us upwards of 22000 Pieces of 8, in part of the Ransom, which we immediately receiv'd, and dispatch'd the Boat back, telling them, we designed to leave this Place in the Morning, and would carry off the Hostages, if they did not come time enough with the rest of the Mony to prevent it.

May 3. Yesterday in the Afternoon Capt. *Courtney* took Charge of the *Havre de Grace*, and I agreed to follow him in the Morning, to Point *Arena*, after I had ship'd off 7 live Black Cattel, some Sheep, Hogs and Fowls, with a good Quantity of Plantains, about 80 Jarrs and some Casks of Water, 24 Packs of Cocoa, 2 Sails, and 4 large Brass Patereroes. Two Barks sail'd about Midnight with the *Marquiss*. I began again early in the Morning, and by 9 got all aboard. We agreed to leave the Lieutenant of *Puna* here, giving him 4 old sick Negroes, and a damag'd Bail of Goods for what we had taken from him, being a Man we had some Respect for: We also parted very friendly with several of our Prisoners we took at Sea, particularly an old Padre that I had treated civilly at my own Table, ever since we took him, for which he was extremely thankful.

About a League before the Town I saw the *Havre de Grace* at Anchor, near the Edge of a Shoal and the *Dutchess's* Pinnace coming from her, with Captains *Courtney*, *Dover*, and *Dampier*, who had quitted the *Havre de Grace*, and desired to exchange with me, which I did.

May 5. I went aboard the *Havre de Grace* about 2 in the Afternoon, and got her out of Danger into the Channel; but came to an Anchor again, by the Advice of Senior *Morell* and the *Indian* Pilot: I encouraged 'em and the Men to assist me as much as possible to get her under Sail, because we were in haft to be gone, but there being little Wind, I could not make use of half the Ebb, before I was again in shole Water, and came to art Anchor, where for the want of Wind we lay for the rest of these 24 Hours

May 5. This Morning I got the Length of our Ships again, and soon after Day went aboard the *Duke*, being quite sick by my long Fatigue. Capt. *Courtney* came to me aboard, and we agreed to throw the Timber and great Boat between Decks in the Galeon overboard, to make room for the Flour and *Guiaquil* Goods which were yet in the Barks. We gave the flour Prize to the Prisoners whom we let go, to carry to the Inhabitants of *Guiaquil*, and took in as much Water as we could get. Most of it was fetch'd half Way above *Puna*, in the River towards *Guiaquil*, and tho' but very indifferent, we had not half enough for want of Time.

May 6. Our Hostages are very uneasy, fearing the Mony will not come in Time to redeem them, and it's worse than Death, they say, to be carried to *Great Britain*. We got all aboard last Night, by 7 a Clock, our People being fatigued, I was willing to rest my self and them one Night before we sailed; but Capt. *Courtney* was in too much haft, and my Second, Capt. *Dover*, and my Pilot *Dampier* forsook me to go along with him. They sailed at Midnight with the *Havre de Grace*, leaving me and the rest at Anchor. Mr. *Connely*, who went in the Bark for Water, did not return till the Morning, when we saw our Consort and Prize at Anchor; for the Weather falling calm, they did not get 2 Leagues from us that Ebb. At high Water, about 10 this Morning, all the rest of us came to sail. Our small Bower Cable was cut with the foul Ground, and we lost our Anchor.

I endeavour'd, but in vain, to convince the other Captains that we were not yet in any danger from the Enemy, because it was not possible that the *French* and *Spaniards* could have Notice of us, and arm out time enough from *Lima to* attack us.

May 7. Yesterday, about 4 in the Afternoon we came to an Anchor again, in 13 Fathom Water, about 4 Leagues below Point *Arena*. At 2 this Morning, with a very small Breeze, we came to sail: Sometime after Senior *Morell*, that went with us up to *Guiaquil* from *Puna*, and a Gentleman of that Town related to our Prisoners, brought us about 3500 Pieces of 8, in Plate, towards the Ransom: They came as far as Point *Arena* in a Boat, and thence followed in one of the 4 Barks that we left by Agreement.

May 8. Yesterday, in the Afternoon, we discharg'd all our Prisoners, except the *Morells*, a little *Dutchman*, and a Gentleman's Son of *Panama*, with our *Indian* Pilots, that I took aboard to amuse the People of *Guiaquil*, that we should return thither, and 2 more that desir'd to stay with us, besides the 3 Ransomers. The Gentleman that came from *Guiaquil* had a Gold Chain and some other Moveables, with which he purchased the *Beginning* of us, and we gave the Captain of the *Havre de Grace* 5 Negroe Women, and Senior *Morell*, and Senior *Ignatius*, one a piece, and to all of them good part of their waring Apparel: So that we parted very friendly. They told us, A Prisoner we put a-shore at *Puna*, call'd Senior Don *Pedro Sinfuegos*, as a Man of great Credit at *Guiaquil*; that he had got a good Sum together before they came thence in order to buy Goods of us, and that they expected him in less than 12 Hours; adding, that there were several others coming down to trade with us, but the Majority of our Officers would not believe 'em, being resolved to make the utmost Dispatch for the *Gallapagos* Islands: They press'd to know where they might meet us to trade, but every one was against informing them of the Place where we design'd to rendezvous, left they should discover it to the Enemies Ships of War. At 8 last Night we came to an Anchor in 16 Fathom Water. The Island *Santa Clara* bore N. E. by N. 5 Leagues. At 2 this Morning we weighed with the Flood, Wind at S. W. at 6 the Island bore N. by E. 4 Leagues distance.

A Description of the Province of Guiaquil.

The City or Town of *Guiaquil* is the Metropolis of a Province of that Name in *Peru*, govern'd by a President with 5 or 6 Oidores, which makes a Royal *Audiencia* or chief Court of Judicature, accountable only to the Viceroy in military Affairs. Every Province has a Government of the same Nature.

These Governors are commonly appointed, or, to speak more properly, purchase their Offices in Old *Spain*, for Life, or good Behaviour; and in case any die, or misbehave themselves, the Viceroy may name another during his Time, which ought to be but 5 Years; but sometimes he gets these Officers of his own placing confirm'd by an Order from *Spain*, which is a considerable Part of the Viceroy's unknown Profits. The late Viceroy continued 14 Years, several new ones having died by the Way. The King of *Spain* himself scarce lives in more Splendor than his Vice roy in the City of *Lima*, where the chief Courts of Judicature are kept, and Appeals are brought thither from all Courts and Provinces of this extensive Kingdom. I should not here mention the vast Wealth the late Vice-roy obtain'd during his Government; the Sum being so large that I thought, it fabulous, but that I was inform'd of it by lo many

Hands, who told me, that about 4 Years ago he died at least worth 8000000 Pieces of 8, and left it to his Widow and Children, but the greatest Part to his eldest Son, the *Conde de la Monclo*, besides vast Sums he gave away in Charity, during his Life-time, and the many Churches, Fryaries, and Nunneries that he built.

He left a better Character behind him than any Vice-roy had done for an Age past. The Conde, his eldest Son, waits here, expecting to succeed the present Vice-roy of *Peru* or *Mexico*, if the Government holds in Old *Spain*; but I and every *Englishman* ought earnestly to hope, that K. *Charles* III. will happily recover that Monarchy, and gratefully place a Vice-roy here that will shew himself as good a Friend to the *English* Trade, as the present Vice-roy does to the *French*; for he openly espouses their Interest, and encourages them; whereas the *Spaniards* say, he racks and heavily oppresses their own Countrymen.

The Corregidore that last died at *Guiaquil* tho' he had possess'd the Office but 5 Years, had rak'd together 300000 Pieces of 8, tho' his Post was not allow'd to exceed above 2000 Pieces of 8 *per Annum*; but all the Corregidores make vast Advantages by Seizures, and trading privately themselves.

The Trade to and from *Mexico* is forbid here, under the severest Penalty, especially transporting Quick-silver from *Peru* thither, because Quantities are brought from Old *Spain*, which is impos'd on the Refiners at great Rates. Here are many Ships employed coasting in this Kingdom; but a Trade is so severely prohibited between 'em and *Mexico*, that all the Commodities with Silver and Gold in Returns, may have little other Circulation in these vast Countries, but by the Flota and Galeons to and from Old *Spain*. Yet notwithstanding the Severity us'd against private Traders, by the Vice-roys and Corregidores, there are some that use it, who have no Mercy shew'd 'em if caught, all being seiz'd in the King's Name, tho' his Majesty has little or no Share of it; All such Seizures (as I am told) being divided amongst these Officers, and the poor Sufferer banish'd or confin'd to a Goal.

All *English* and *Dutch* Goods, except what comes by the Galeons, are prohibited here, so that the private Traders, after they have by stealth purchased 'em in the *North* Seas, must vend 'em in like manner all over *Peru*, and if the wholesale Merchants have not a good Certificate from the Commerce of *Sevilia*, that their Commodities came by the Flota or Galeons; whenever the Goods are question'd, they must disown them, for fear of a worse Punishment, unless they have a good Interest in the Vice-roy, which costs dear to purchase, and preserve; so that the Trader makes little Profit, but where the chief Officers have a feeling: yet tho' these mercenary Vice-roys are so severe on Others, they themselves employ the Corregidores to negotiate a Trade for them by a 3d Hand, which cannot be done to the Purpose, without being publickly known; so that Ships are constantly imployed on their Account, and carry Quick-silver and all manner of prohibited Goods to and from *Mexico* out of By-ports. Thus, being their own Judges, they get vast Estates, and stop all Complaints in Old *Spain*, by Bribes. The Goods they trade for have a free Passage and Sale through the Continent, whilst others, if they do but offer at it, are punish'd as above.

Their other Ways of getting Money unjustly are too many; but in short, in my Opinion, there's no Country naturally more rich, nor any People more terribly oppres'd.

The *Spaniards* say, and I believe, not without Reason, That a Vice-roy, after purchasing his Place with all that he has, and quitting Old *Spain* as poor as *Job*, comes here like a hungry Lion, to devour all that he can; and that every Officer under him in the Provinces (who are ten times more than are necessary) are his Jackals to procure Prey for him, that they may have a Share of it themselves.

To this we may add, the Burden of a numerous and luxurious Clergy, that indulge their Pride, Sloth, Effeminacy and Bigottry, more than in the *Romish* Countries of *Europe*: So that were this Country possess'd by an industrious and well govern'd People, we might have reason to fear, that Silver and Gold would become so plentiful, and by consequence of so little Value, that the World would be at a Loss to find a less troublesome and more acceptable Species to satisfy Avarice and Luxury.

The River of *Guiaquil*, from about 2 Leagues above *Puna* to Point *Arena*, is so broad, that a Man can scarce see cross the Channel; the Land down to the Water-side, is low and cover'd with Mangrove Trees; the Tide flows above; Fathom, and an East and West Moon, as near as I could guess, makes High-water at *Puna*. The Tide has a quick Current, much stronger than in the *Thames*, and I believe the Ebb is little inferior to that at Bristol, and the Water as thick, and as much discolour'd. Not being able to describe the Channel plain enough to direct Strangers, I shall give a View of it from a *Spanish* Draught; for I had not time enough to draw the Channel, or sound it all along. There's need of a good Pilot to carry a Vessel to the Town. The River is 14 Leagues navigable beyond it, and the Tide flows 20 Leagues above it, but Canoes and Bark-Logs go much higher.

The Province abounds with several sorts of good Timber, which makes it the chief Country of *Peru* for building and repairing Ships; there's seldom less than 6 or 7 at a time on the Stocks before the Town of *Guiaquil*. The chief Commodity this City and its Province afford is *Cocoa*, which is so plentiful, as to supply most Places on the *South Sea*; they say there's never less exported in a Year than 30,000 Cargaus, each Cargau 81 Pound Weight, and sometimes double the Quantity: It was purchas'd generally at half a Royal per Pound, but now much cheaper, so that the Cargau may be bought for 2 Pieces of Eight and a half. Their coasting Trade is for Salt and Salt Fish, from Point *Santa Helena*, and most vended at *Quito* and other distant Places within Land. A vast quantity of Timber is laden here for *Truxillo, Chancy, Lima*, and other Sea-ports, where 'tis scarce; it pays a great Freight, and is a profitable Trade: They export also from hence Rice, Cotton, and some dry'd Jerkt Beef. There are no Mines of Silver or Gold in this Province, but Plenty of all sorts of Cattle, and very cheap, especially on the Island *Puna*, where we supply'd.' our selves with what we, could stow conveniently. Here's no other Corn but *Indian*, so that all their Flower is brought from *Truxillo, Cheripe*, and other Places in the Windward Parts, it blows here always Southerly. They are also supplied with several sorts of Woollen Cloth, and very good strong Bays made at *Quito*; their Wine, Brandy, Oil, Olives and Sugar, etc. come from *Pisco, La Nasca*, and other Places to Windward. All sorts of *European* Goods come hither from *Panama*, whither they are brought over Land from *Portobello* out of the North Seas; so that the Number of Ships chat come and go from hence, without including the Coasters, are no less than 40 Sail every Year, which shows that the Port of *Guiaquil* is no mean Place of Trade in this

Part of the World. A Market is also kept on Bark-Logs and Boats in the River every day before the Town, with all that the Country affords in great plenty.

Having thus given an account of the Wealth and Trade of the Town and Province from my own Knowledge, or good Information, I shall now proceed to give a further Account of the Strength and Government of the Province. The Corregidore is Governour in all Civil and Military Affairs of the whole; the next is his Lieutenant, call'd by the *Spaniards* Lieutenant General, and all the chief Officers reside in or near *Guiaquil*.

Their Method of trying Civil and Criminal Causes being different from ours, I shall give as clear an Idea of it as I can. When any Court is held, or urgent Affair happens, the following Persons are summon'd to the Council in *Guiaquil*. First, the Corregidore, the Lieutenant General, 2 Alcaldes or Justices, who are generally Men vers'd in the Law, and serve in the nature of Majors and Justices by turns every Year; the next is the Algozil Major, with 8. Regidores or Common Council-men, who supply the room of the superior Officers, in case of Absence or Death, till the Viceroys Pleasure be known, and always give their Votes in publick Affairs; in Cases of Law they are a standing Jury, and the Corregidore is Judge, but generally follows the Advice of the Alcalds. The Plaintiff or Defendant may appeal after Trial to the Supream Court of *Lima*, which is encourag'd by the Gentlemen of the Law, who improve Suits to such a Degree, that tho' they are almost as numerous as the Clergy, yet they are a thriving Society, seldom want Imployrnent, and have large Fees. There are 2 Attorneys call'd Clerks of the Court, and 4 Algozils or Serjeants. All Lawyers are allow'd to paradise here, and have a Sallary from the King besides their Fees, and since Money abounds here, many of 'em don't scruple taking Fees on both Sides.

The Inquisition rages worse here than in Old *Spain*; their chief Court is at *Lima*, but 4 Officers from that Court are settl'd at *Guiaquil*, besides 24 Clergy belonging to the Town, who inform against any Person that they suspect of Opinions contrary to the *Roman* Church, and with a violent Zeal prosecute 'em almost without any Formality. The Offenders are speedily Tent to the chief Court at *Lima*, where nothing but a great deal of Money can save 'em, if found guilty in the least degree.

Their Military Men affect great Titles, and their Strength is as follows.

The Corregidore is General, *Don Hieronimo Boso,*

Master le Camp, *Don Christopher Ramadeo de Areano.*

Serjeant Major, *Don Francisco Gantes.*

Commissaria de la Cavalaria, *Don Antonio Calabria.*

They have 5 Dons all Captains of Infantry, and each of 'em a large Company: One Don is a Captain of near 200 Horsemen, and there are Lieutenants, Ensigns, Serjeants, Corporals and Drummers to each Company, as customary among the *Spaniards*. By the most reasonable Computation of their Force, they could in a few days bring together 900 armed Horse and Foot Militia; and I was inform'd by them they had not less than 500 of these in a Body before we landed, and beat 'em out of the Town, there being always that Number ready in the Towns and adjacent Parts upon an Alarm. These and many more form'd a sorry Camp within a League of us in the Woods, whilst with about 160 Men we kept the Town till they ransom'd it. An *English*-man that run over to us after the Fight, who had lived 2 Years in the Town, and saw their Force, told us there were many more than what the *Spaniards* acknowledge by the abovemention'd Account, and that he saw at one time, a few Months before, upwards of 1100 Horse and Foot drawn up and muster'd before the Town.

Their other Towns are govern'd by Lieutenants deputed by the Corregidore; above half of 'em border on the same River and its Branches, so that they can join those of the Capital in 2 Tides, tho' at several Leagues distance. These Towns and Lieutenancies are as follow.

A List of the Lieutenancy of this Province.

Leagues

Yaquasche, govern'd by a Lieutenant, distant from *Guiaquil* 7

Bava 12

Pemocho has 6 Brass Guns of 16 Pound Ball, both govern'd by the same Lieutenant 14

Puna, by the same Lieutenant 9

Narangbal, by the same Lieutenant 14

Machala, by the same Lieutenant 14

Daule, a Lieutenant 7

Point *St. Helena*, by the same Lieutenant 30

Colonche, by the same Lieutenant 20

Chongong by the same Lieutenant 7

Chandoe, by the same Lieutenant 10

Obeba, by the same Lieutenant 21

Babaoya, by the same Lieutenant 6

Chilintoam, by the same Lieutenant 14

Porto Vaco, by the same Lieutenant 34

Charapeto, by the same Lieutenant 34

Peco Assaa, by the same Lieutenant 25

Manta, by the same Lieutenant 40

Hepe Hapa, by the same Lieutenant 30

Porto Vaco was formerly the Metropolis of the Province, before the Government was removed to *Guiaquil*.

In the Towns and the whole Province the *Spaniards* compute at lead 10000 Inhabitants; but I believe there are many more. They are distinguish'd by themselves into II Classes or Sorts, which being particular, and worth remarking, I shall add a Description of them, for the Information of such as have 'not been in those Parts.

The first and chief is the original *Spaniards*, never yet mix'd with other People (at least as they pretend) and these are most respected.

2. The *Mustees*, begot by *Spaniards* on *Indian* Women.

4. *Fine Mustees*, their Children married again with the *Spaniards*.

4. *Terceroons de Indies* their Children again mix'd with the *Spaniards*.

5. *Quarteroons de Inases* their Posterity again mix'd with the *Spaniards*. These last are allowed to be Primitive *Spaniards* again.

6 *Mullattoes*, begot by a *Spaniard*, or any *European*, on a Negro Woman.

7. *Quarteroons de Negroes* again mixt with the *Spaniards*, and esteem'd nor better than *Mullattoes*.

8. *Terceroon de Negroes*, a third Mixture with the *Spaniards*, still call'd *Mullattoes*, because they will not allow 'em the Privilege or Title of *Spaniard* after once debas'd with the Negro Breed, tho' some of 'em are as white as themselves; but they can't get off the ugly Name of *Mullatto*, unless they hide their Descent, which is no hard Task, if they remove their Abode to another Place where they are not known, which is often practis'd and conniv'd at by the Fathers of the Church, to increase the Number pf good Catholick *Spaniards*.

9. The 9th Sort *Indians*, who are all of a dark Olive-tawny Colour; these (tho' the true and antient Proprietors of the Country) are placed a Class below the worth of the *Spanish* Descendants, which are generally begot without Marriage on their Servants and Slaves

10. *Negroes*.

11. All the Species and Breeds between the *Negroes and Indians* are call'd *Sambos* tho' by mixing their Breed as they do, they commonly differ little or nothing to the Eye from the *Spanish* mix'd Descendants.

These II are the common Sorts, tho' some of 'em seem not very regularly distinguish'd: But they have rung Changes so often in those Peals of Generation, that there is no End of their Distinctions. The *Spaniards* are the sewest by far of all the Inhabitants; and were it not for those Mixtures, which the Bathers of the Church keep united, the *Indians* might again take possession of their Country for the *Spaniards* would be top few to keep it, and much more uncapable of peopling it. Few of those Prisoners that fell into our hands were healthy and sound; near half of the *Spaniards* discover'd publickly to our Coders their Malady, in order to get Physick from them against the *French* Disease, which is so common here, that they reckon it no Scandal to be deep in the Powdering Tub; and the Heat of the Country facilitating the Cure, they make wry light of it, All the *Spaniards* I discoursed allow that this rich Country is not a tenth peopled, nor are half the *Indians* far within Land civilized, tho' they affirm their King has in the *West Indies* more Subjects of several Colours, than in all *Spain*, or the rest of his Dominions in *Europe* (which may be true) and I believe they are such Subjects as no Christian King can boast of; for the King of *Spain* is able to match the Skins of his *Americans* to any Colour, with more Variety and Exactness than a Draper can match his Cloth and Trimming.

The Account that the *French* Buccaneers, *alias* Pirates, gave of this Place, is so false, that there's not the least Truth in it; so that by their Description it would not appear to be the same Place, had they not left infamous Marks of their being here: For when they took the Town of *Guiaquil* about 22 Years ago, they discover'd little or no Bravery in the Attack (tho' they lost a great many Men) and committed a great deal of Brutishness and Murther after they had the Place in their Power, which was above a Month here and at *Puna*. The Seasons here are improperly call'd Winter and Summer; the Winter is reckon'd from the Beginning of *December* to the last of *May*, and all that Season is sultry hot, wet and unhealthy. From the latter End of *May* to *December* 'tis serene, dry and healthy, but not so violently hot as what they call Winter.

Their *Cocoa* is ripe, and mostly gather'd between *June* and *August* and of the other Fruits natural to these Climates, some are ripe and others green all the Year. But I return to my Journal, and the Account of our Voyage to the *Gallapagoes* Islands.

May II. A fresh Gale at S. S. W. We had upwards of 20 Men that fell ill within these 24 Hours, and our Consort near 50, of a malignant Fever, contracted as I suppose at *Guiaquil*, where I was informed, that about a Month or f Weeks before we took it, a contagious Disease which raged there swept off 10 or 12 Persons every Day for a considerable time; so that the Floors of all the Churches (which are their usual Burial Places) were fill'd so fast, that they were obliged to dig a large and deep Hole of about a Rod square, close by the great Church, where I kept Guard; and this Hole was almost fill'd with Corps half putrified. The Mortality was so very great, that many of the People had left the Town, and our lying so long in the Church surrounded with such unwholsom Scents, was enough to infect us too.

Capt. *Courtney* was taken ill, and Capt. *Dover* went on board the *Dutchess* to prescribe for him.

May 14. This Day we saw a great many Albacores in pursuit of Flying Fish, and a very large Albacore leap'd into one of our Boats. We have now about 50 Men down, and the *Dutchess* upwards of 70; but I hope the Sea Air (which is very fresh) will make the Climate more healthy.

May 15. At 6 last Night *Mr. Samuel Hopkins*, Dr. *Dover's* Kinsman and Assistant, died; he read Prayers once a Day ever since we pass'd the Equinox in the North Sea: He was a very good temper'd sober Man, and very well beloved by the whole Ship's Company.

May 17. This Morning we saw the Land bearing S.S.W. about 10 Leagues distanc. It seems a large Island, and high Land: We tack'd and flood E. by S. Wind at S. by E. to turn up to Windward for the Island. Our Men in both Ships continue very ill; we have near 60 sick, and the *Dutchess* upwards of 80. We had a good Observation, Lat. 00°. 37'.S.

May 18. At 6 last Night the End of the Island bore S. by E. distant about 5 Leagues. *Edward Downe* died at 12 at Night. When Day broke we were within 4 Leagues of 2 large Islands almost joining together, having passed the other that we law yesterday. We sent our Boat ashore to look for Water, and agreed with our Consort where to meet in case of Separation. They turn'd towards an Island we saw to Windward, and left us to try this Island for Water: All our Prizes were to stay near us under Sail by a remarkable Rock.

May 19. Yesterday in the Afternoon the Boat return'd with a melancholy Account, that no Water was to be found. The Prizes we expected would have lain to Windward for us by the Rock, about 2 Leagues off Shore; but Mr. *Hatley* in a Bark, and the *Havre de Grace*, turn'd to Wind ward after our Consort the *Dutchess*; so that only the Galleon and the Bark that Mr. *Selkirk* was in staid for us. We kept plying to Windward all Night with a Light out, which they follow'd. At 5 in the Morning we sent our Boat ashore again to make a further Search in this Island for Water. About 10 in the Morning *James Daniel* our Joiner died. We had a good Observation, Lat. 00° 32". S.

May 20. Yesterday in the Evening our Boat return'd, but found no Water, tho' they went 3 or 4 Miles up into the Country: They tell me the Island is nothing but loose Rocks, like Cynders, very rotten and heavy, and the Earth so parch'd, that it will not bear a Man, but breaks into Holes under his Feet, which makes me suppose there has been a Vulcano here; tho' there is much shrubby Wood, and some Greens on it, yet there's not the least Sign of Water, nor is it possible, that any can be contained on such a Surface. At 12 last Night we lost sight of our Galleon; so that we have only one Bark with us now.

May 21. Yesterday in the Afternoon came down the *Dutchess* and the *French* Prize. The *Dutchess's* Bark had caught several Turtle and Fish, and gave us a Part, which was very serviceable to the sick Men, our fresh Provisions that we got on the main Land being all spent. They were surpriz'd as much as we at the Galleon, and *Hatley's* Bark being out of Sight, thinking before they had been with us. We kept Lights at our Top-mast's Head, and fir'd Guns all Night, that they might either see or hear how to join us, but to no Purpose.

Cape. *Courtney* being not yet quite recover'd, I went on board the *Dutchess*, and agreed with him and his Officers, to stay here with the *Havre de Grace* and Bark, whilst I went in quest of the missing Prizes. At 6 in the Morning we parted, and flood on a Wind to the Eastward, judging they lost us that way. Here are very strange Currents amongst these Islands, and commonly run to the Leeward, except on the Full Moon I observed it ran very strong to Windward; I believe 'tis the same at Change.

May 22. Yesterday at 3 in the Afternoon we met with the Galleon under the East Island, but heard nothing of Mr. *Hatley's* Bark. At 9 last Night *Jacob Scronder* a *Dutch*-man, and very good Sailor, died. We kept on a Wind in the Morning to look under the Weather Island for Mr. *Hatley*, and fired a Gun for the Galleon to bear away for the Rendevouz Rock, which she did.

May 23. Yesterday at 3 in the Afternoon we saw the Weather Island near enough, and no Sail about it. We bore away in sight of the Rock, and saw none but our Galleon; we were in another Fright what became of our Consort, and the 2 Prizes we left behind; but by 5 we saw 'em come from under the Shore to the Leeward of the Rock. We spoke with 'em in the Evening; we all bewail'd Mr. *Hatley*, and were afraid he was lost: We fir'd Guns all Night, and kept Lights out, in hopes he might see or hear us, and resolved to leave these unfortunate Islands, after we had view'd two or three more to Leeward. We pity'd our 5 Men in the Bark that is missing, who if in being have a melancholy Life without Water, having no more but for 2 Days, when they parted from us. Some are afraid they run on Rocks, and were lost in the Night, others that the 2 Prisoners and 3 Negroes had murder'd 'em when asleep; but if otherwise, we had no Water, and our Men being still sick, we could stay little longer for them. Last Night died *Law. Carney* of a malignant Fever. There is hardly a Man in the Ship, who had been ashore at *Guiaquil* but has felt something of this Distemper, whereas not one of those that were not there have been sick yet. Finding that Punch did preserve my own Health, I prescribed it freely among such of the Ships Company as were well, to preserve theirs. Our Surgeons make heavy Complaints for want of sufficient Medicines, with which till now I thought we abounded, having a regular Physician, an Apothecary, and Surgeons enough, with all sorts of Medicines on board. Our Owners believed so too, and did often at home set forth the uncommon Advantage we had in being so carefully provided for this tedious Voyage; but now we found it otherwise, and had not sufficient Medicines to administer for the Recovery of our sick Men, which so many being sick in both Ships, makes it a melancholy Time with us.

May 21. Yesterday at y in the Afternoon we ran to the Northward, and made another Island, which bore N. W. by W. distant 5 Leagues; and this Morning we sent our Boat ashore, to see for the lost Bark, Water, Fish or Turtle. This Day *Tho. Hughes* a very good Sailor died, as did Mr. *George Underhill*, a good Proficient in most pares of the Mathematicks and other Learning, tho' not much above 21 Years old: He was of a very courteous Temper, and brave, was in the Fight where my Brother was kill'd, and served as Lieutenant in my Company at *Guiaquil.* About the same time another young Man, call'd *John English*, died aboard the *Haver de Grace*, and we have many still sick. If we had staid in the Harbour, we should in all probability have lost near half of our Men. We had a good Observation, Lat. 00°. 14?. N.

May 25. Yesterday at 6 in the Evening our Boat return'd from the Island without finding any Water, or seeing the Bark. About 4 in the Morning we stood to another Island, that bore about N. E. distant 4 Leagues, and that *Dutchess* went to view another to the S. W. of it. Last Night *Peter Marshal* a good Sailor died. This Morning our Boat with *Mr. Selkirk's* Bark went to another Island to view it. We had an Observation, Lat. 00°. 35?. N.

May 26. Last Night our Boat and Bark return'd, having rounded the Island, found no Water, but Plenty of Turtle and Fish. This Morning we join'd the *Dutchess*, who had found no Water. About 12 a Clock we compar'd our stocks of Water, found it absolutely necessary to make the best of our way to the Main for some, then to come off again; and so much the rather, because we expected that 2 *French* ships, one of 60, and another of 40 Guns, with some *Spanish* Men of War, would suddenly be in quest of us.

May 27. At 6 last Night the Body of the Eastermost Island bore S. E. by S. distant 4 Leagues, from whence we took our Departure for the Main. Last Night died *Paunceford Wall*, a Land-man. A fresh Gale at S. E. with cloudy Weather.

May 30. Fair Weather with moderate Gales from the S. S. E. to the S. by E. We are forced to water the Bark and Galleon every Day with our Yall: 'Tis a very great Trouble to hoist our Boat out daily; now that our Men are so very weak. Senior *Morell*, and the other Prisoners, tell us, that it frequently proves Calm between these Islands and the *Terra firma* at this time of the Year, which if it should now happen, but for a few Days, would very much incommode us for Want of Water. Had we supplied our selves well at Point *Arena*, we should, no doubt, have had time enough to find the Island *S. Maria del' Aquada*, reported to be one of the *Gallapagos*, where there is Plenty of good Water, Timber, Land and Sea Turtle, and a safe Road for Ships. This was the Place we intended for, and would have been very suitable to our Purpose, which was to lie some Time concealed. It's probable there is such an Island, because one Capt. *Davis*, an *Englishman*, who was a buckaneering in these Seas, above 20 Years ago, lay some Months and recruited here to Content: He says, that it had Trees fit for Masts; but these sort of Men, and others I have convers'd with, or whose Books I have read, have given very blind or false Relations of their Navigation, and Actions in these Parts, for supposing the Places too remote to have their Stories disprov'd, they imposed on the Credulous, amongst whom I was one, till now I too plainly see, that we cannot find any of their Relations to be relied on: Therefore I shall say no more of these Islands, since by what I saw of 'em, they don't at all answer the Description chat those Men have given us.

Nothing more remarkable happened till the 6th of *June*, but that *Thomas Morgan*, a *Welch* Land-man, died the 31st of *May*; *George Bishop*, another Land-man, the 4th *of June*; and that we had Advice from some of our Men on board the Galeon, that the Prisoners and Blacks there had form'd a Plot to murder the *English*, and run away with the Ship in the Night. We examined the S*paniards* who positively denied it; yet some of the Blacks own'd there had been such a Discourse betwixt some Negroes and *Indians*, but they did not believe they were in earnest: So we contented our selves to disperse those Prisoners into several ships, as the best Way to break the Cabal.

Chapter IX

June 6. Yesterday at 4 a Clock in the Afternoon we spied a Sail, and at the same time saw the Land, the *Dutchess* being a Mile a Head, gave chase first, we followed, and about 7 in the Evening the *Dutchess* took her; we immediately sent our Boat aboard, and took out some of the Prisoners. She was a Vessel of about 90 Tun, bound from *Panama* to *Guiaquil*, call'd the St. *Thomas de Villa* and St. *Demas, Juan Navarro Navaret* Commander. There were about 40 People aboard, including 11 Negro-Slaves, but little of *European* Goods, except some Iron and Cloth. Captain *Courtney* sent to tell me, the Prisoners he had knew nothing of our being in these Seas, and brought no News from *Europe*, but confirmed the Story that they expected the Arrival of a squadron from *England*, my Lord *Peterborough*, Admiral and General, by Sea and Land, which was dreaded every Day, and that they were inform'd he design'd to secure some Port in the North Sea, and send part of his Squadron to the South Sea. They had a Passenger of Note on board, call'd Don *Juan Cardoso*, he was going to be Governour of *Raldivia*, and said he had been taken not long before in the North Sea, by *Jamaica* Cruisers. We bore away by Agreement for the Island *Gorgona*. This Morning we saw *Gallo*, near the Shore, a small Island, and the Main to the North of it, which by the Shore is low Land. Our late Prize ran aboard the *Havre de Grace*, and lost her Main Top-mast, but did little Damage to the other Ship. The *Dutchess* took the Prize into a Tow. We had a good Observation. Lat.2°.00?. N.

June 7. Yesterday at 2 in the Afternoon we made the Island of *Gorgona*; about 4 the Body bore E. N. E. 5 Leagues.

June 8. Yesterday at 4 in the Afternoon we got to an Anchor, about a good Cable's Length from the Shore in 30 Fathom Water, on the East side of the Island the Southernmost point of it in sight bore S. E. about 3 Miles, and the Rocks off the North Point bore N. half W. a Mile and a half.

June 8. At 8 this Morning we spied a Sail to the Southward of the Island, between it and the Main; our Pinnace being ashore for Water, the *Dutchess's* Boat went first after her, ours followed on the other side of the Island, that if the Prize bore away, she might meet her on the West Side. In the mean time I took in Water from the Island.

June 9. Yesterday in the Afternoon our Boats return'd and brought the Prize with them, being a small Bark of about 35 Tuns, call'd the *Golden Sun*; she belong'd to a Creek within this Island, on the Main, and was bound for *Guiaquil, Andros Enriques.* Master, With 10 S*paniards* and *Indians*, and some *Negroes*; no Cargo but a very little Gold Dust, and a large Gold Chain, together about 500 *l*, value, which were secured aboard the *Dutchess*. The Prize design'd to purchase Salt and Brandy with 'em. The Prisoners said they had no Notice of us, so that News does not spread in this Country so fast as we believ'd, especially this Way; the Land being, as I am informed, full of Woods and Rivers, and bad for Travellers or Posts. About 6 in the Evening there was a Consultation on board the *Dutchess*, with some of my Officers, Cape. *Dover* and others; being discompos'd I was not with them, but resolved to act in consortship, according to their Agreement. After they had examin'd the Prisoners, they resolved to go to *Malaga*, an Island which had a Rode, where we design'd to leave our Ships, and with our Boats row up the River, for the rich Gold Mines of *Barbacore*, call'd also by the S*paniards*, the

Mines of St. *Juan*, from a Village about two Tides up the River of that Name; there we design'd to surprize Canoes, as fitter than our Boats to go against the Stream; for this Time of the Year being subject to great Rains, which makes a strong Fresh down the River, our Pilot, an old *Spaniard*, did not propose to get up to the Mines in less than 12 Days. I had often before suspected his Knowledge, but according to their Resolutions on board the *Dutchess* we came to sail about 12 a Clock at Night, and steer'd N. E. for the Place. In the Morning I discours'd Captain *Morrel*, as I had done several Times before, and all the rest of the Prisoners, who agreed that this Island, call'd *Malaga*, was an unfrequented Place, and not fit for Ships, that ever they heard of. I had also 2 Prisoners aboard, that were taken in the last Prize, who had been at the said Island very lately; I examin'd 'em separately, and they agreed, that a Ship could not be safe there, and the Place being so narrow, 'twas impossible to get in, but with the Tide, which ran very strong; that the Entrance was full of Shoals, and had not Water enough, but at spring Tides, for our Ships to get out or in; besides that if a Ship gets loose (as we must moar Head and Stern) she would turn all adrift, and very much endanger the whole; they added that the River was so narrow before we could get to the Mines, that the *Indians* and *Spaniards* might fell Trees across; and cut off our Retreat, there being thick Woods on the Banks of the River, from whence the *Indians* would gall us with their poison'd Arrows; for those about the Mines were in Amity with the *Spaniards*, and a bold and a very numerous People. Upon this Information I was surpriz'd that the Council had not inform'd themselves better before they resolved on going to this Place, and immediately sent Mr. *White* our Linguist with the two Prisoners, on board the *Dutchess*, to undeceive Capt. *Courtney* and his Officers, and to desire his Company with some of the rest without Loss of Time, that we might agree how to act for our Safety and Interest, and not to proceed farther on this hazardous Enterprize.

June 10. Yesterday Afternoon Capt. *Courtney* and Capt. *Cook* came aboard us. We immediately agreed to return to *Gorgona*, to refit our Prizes, and that there we would come to a final Resolution. We saw the Island at 6 in the Evening, bearing S. W. Distance about 8 Leagues. In the Night, we had much Rain with Lightning and Squalls of Wind, by which the *Havre de Grace* lost her main Top-mast. This Morning died *Jonathan Smyth*, a Smith by Trade, and Armourer's Mate of our Ship. I went on board the *Havre de Grace* and *Dutchess*, and lent them what was necessary for their Assistance. Our Men being very much fatigued, many of them sick, and several of our Good Sailors dead, we are so weak, that should we meet an Enemy in this Condition, we could make but a mean Defence. Every thing looks dull and discouraging, but it's in vain to look back or repine in these Parts.

June 11. We had good Soundings, but came no nearer the Shore than 36 Fathom Water, it being uncertain Soundings, and dangerous for Ships to venture within that Depch here.

June 12. Had rainy Weather, with little or no Wind. At 8 this Morning saw the Island of *Gorgona*; bore S. half W. distant about 9 Leagues. We impatiently long to be there again, at an Anchor, being in an ordinary Condition to keep the Sea, tho' when there, we are open to all Advantages against us, if the Enemy is out after us, which we expect, and that this is a Place they will search, but having no other Place so convenient, we must run the Risque of it.

June 13 About 4 in the Morning we came to an Anchor again at *Gorgona*, in 40 Fathom Water, and most of both Ships Officers having some Thoughts of Careening here. We held the following Committee:

Gorgona: 13 June, 1709. At a Committee held on Board the Duke.

We have agreed on Mr. Lancelot Appleby to succeed Mr. Samuel Hopkins, and Mr. Robert Knowlesman to succeed Mr. John Rogers, who being deceased, these we approve as the fittest Men to be Members of a Committee in their Places; and having at the same time consider'd the Necessity of cleaning our Ships, we do desire Capt. Courtney to use all manner of Dispatch to get ready for a Careen, and that the Men and Officers assist him as much as possible, and then he to assist the Duke, as soon as his Ship is completed, and off the Careen, because one Ship ought robe in a Readiness to protect the other whilst on a Careen, in case we be attack'd by the Enemy.

Tho. Dover, Pres Wm. Stratton,

Woodes Rogers, Cha. Pope,

Step. Courtney, Tho. Glendall,

Wm. Dampier, John Connely,

Ed w. Cooke, John Bridge.

Rob. Frye,

While we were together, we agreed to sit out the *Havre de Grace* with twenty Guns, and put Men out of each Ship aboard her, under Captain *Cook's* Command, resolving to carry her home with us, and to make a third Ship to cruise in our Company, whilst in these Seas.

June 14. I proposed before, we should careen at Port *a Penees*, because it was an unfrequented Place, and good Harbour, where we might lie sometime undiscover'd, and from thence go to the Bay of *Panama*, when ready; but considering our present Condition, every body seem'd most inclinable to stay here, which I the more readily agreed to, because it was pleasing to the rest, and that, if any Casualty happen'd, I might not be reflected on, if I had over-perswaded them to go elsewhere. We began, according to agreement, to careen the *Dutchess* first, and I to lye on the Guard the mean while, in case of being attack'd, which we had reason to fear, having been so long from *Guiaquil*. The *Dutchess* began to make ready for a Careen. Captain *Courtney* and I went a fishing together, and had pretty good Luck, Fish being plenty here.

June 15. We had indifferent fair Weather, but very sultry. We put all our sick Men, with our Consort's on board the Galeon, being about 70 in Number, besides sick Officers, whom we put on board the *Havre de Grace*.

June 16. We built a Tent ashore for the Armourer and Cooper; set several Men to cutting of Wood, and clearing a Place for the sick Mens Tents.

Nothing remarkable pass'd from the 16th, but that we had frequent Thunder, Lightning and Rain, which retarded our Careening the *Dutchess*, till the 21st that we finish'd her, and began upon our Ship: We were forc'd to carry most of our Stores ashore, for want of Barks, which are full of the *Dutchess* Provisions and Materials. We seldom miss catching good Fish daily, and keep a Boat and Men imploy'd for that purpose, there being very little Refreshment in the Island. We spent till the 25th in careening; the Sea swelling into the Road hinder'd us heaving our Keel wholly out; however we clean'd within less than 2 Streaks of the Keel; and being upright again,

June 28. We got our Provisions aboard, and mounted all our Guns; so that in 14 Days we had calk'd our Ships all round, careen'd, rigg'd and stow'd them again, both fit for the Sea; which was great Dispatch, considering what we had to do was in an open Place, with few Carpenters, and void of the usual Conveniencies for careening. The *Spaniards* our Prisoners being very dilatory Sailors, were amazed at our Expedition, and told us, they usually take 6 Weeks or 2 Months to careen one of the King's Ships at *Lima*, where they are well provided with all Necessaries, and account it good Dispatch. *June* 29. Yesterday in the Afternoon we built a Tent ashore for the sick, who are now much better than when we came to the Island, neither the Weather nor the Air here being half to bad as the *Spaniards* represented, which made us think 'twould be worse than we found it. This Morning we got-the sick Men into their Tents, and put the Doctors ashore with them: We unloaded the *Havre de Grace*, and chose a Place very easy to lay her ashore, to clean her Bottom. A clear Sand about a Mile and half from the Place where we rode, near the South End of the Island.

June 30. I went to her this Morning, and left Capts. *Courtney* and *Cooke*, with the Carpenters, etc. to grave her Bottom, whilst I took the most experienced Prisoners, and walked through the Island (which is every where full of Wood) to look out Masts for her. The *Spaniards* knew best what Wood was most fit for this Purpose here. We found one Tree proper to be a Fore mast, having before that cut down a great Tree big enough, but a wrong sort of Wood. All the Timber here is too heavy, but we must use it, her old Masts and Yards being unserviceable, her Sails rotten, and very little of her Cordage fit to be us'd; so that it's near equal to rigging out a-new. She is a very sharp Ship, but lies easy on soft red Sand, which is dry at little more than half Tide. The Worms had not much damag'd her Bottom, but her Rudder and Cutwater were eaten to pieces. It flows 15 Foot at spring Tides.

July 1. We have Men imploy'd in our Tents ashore, to prepare the Rigging as fast as possible; a Rope-maker at work to make twice-laid Cordage, and a Smith, Block-maker and Sail-maker at the same time; so that we want no Tradesmen to fit her out. Necessity makes us of all Trades on this occasion.

The Natives of Old *Spain* are accounted but ordinary Mariners, but here they are much worse; all the Prizes we took being rather cobled than fitted out for the Sea: So that had they such Weather as we often meet with in the *European* Seas in Winter, they could scarce ever reach a Pore again, as they are sitted, but they sail here hundreds of Leagues. The *French* us'd her as a Victualling Ship, and sold her at *Lima*, as they have done several others, for 4 times the Money they cost in *Europe*. 'Tis certainly a good Method they took at first trading hither, to bring a Victualling SHIP with no other Goods but Provisions and Stores along with 'em. Generally one of these small Ships comes out with two Traders, and since infix, nine, or 12 Months time, which they stay in these Seas, they expend their Provisions, and lessen their Men by Mortality or Desertion, they fell their Victualling Ship, and being recruited with Men and Provisions out of her, they return well victualled and mann'd to *France*. But now they put into *Chili*, where they fell the remaining Part of their Cargo, and salt up a new Stock of Provisions for their homeward bound Passage, so that they need bring no more Victuallers.

July 2. We had showers of Rain, with Thunder and Lightning last Night, and few Nights are without Rain, but 'tis pretty dry in the day-time. This day I got a fine Tree for the Main-mast; the Island is so cover'd with Trees, that we are forced to clear a Place for a Yard to work in. The Wood that we us'd for Masts and Yards is 3 sorts, but the best is *Maria* Wood, of the Colour and Grain of our English Oak, all of the Cedar Kind, good Timber, but very heavy. There are several other sorts fit for Masts, but Care must be taken not to use any that is short-grain'd, or soft and white when green.

July 3. The Prize Flower we took in Bags being much damag'd by the Rats, I order'd the Coopers to put it up in 36 Casks: The little *English* Bread we have lest is eaten as hollow as a Honeycomb, and so full of Worms, that it's hardly fit for Use. Last Night we met aboard our Ship to consult of the quickest Method for Dispatch, and the Officers agreed each to take his share of looking after the Ships, and forwarding the several Workmen: so that most of our little Commonwealth being ashore very busy, 'twas a Diversion for me to oversee the several Companies at work in our Yard, from Break of Day till Night, which otherwise in this hot Country would have been very burdensome to me.

We were imploy'd till the 9*th* in refitting the *Havre de Grace*, and when finish'd call'd her the *Marquis*. We saluted each of the other Ships with 3 Huzzas from on board her, distributed Liquor among the Company, drank her Majesty's and our Owners Healths, and to our own good Success. The Ship look'd well, so that we all rejoic'd in our new Consort to cruize with us. The next thing we did was to clear Mr. S*elkirk's* Bark to carry our Prisoners to the Main, who being 72 in Number, were very chargeable to maintain; but we could not discharge them sooner, left they should have allarm'd the Country, and inform'd the *French* and *Spanish* Men of War where to find us. But being now almost ready to depart, we call'd a Committee, and came to the following Resolutions.

At a Committee held on board the *Duke*, riding at Anchor in the Road of *Gorgona, July* 9. 1709.

> *We think it convenient to turn all our Prisoners ashore, in a Bark already provided for that purpose, and at the same time to Plunder the Settlements on the Main opposite to this Island, and do desire Capt. Thomas Dover, Mr. Robert Fry, and Mr. William Stratton to command the Bark and 45 Men on the same Expedition, and to make what Dispatch they can, and return bither with such Refreshments, &c. as they can get for our sick Men.*

Tho. Dover, Pres. William Stratton,

Woodes Rogers, Cha. Pope,

Stephen Courtney, John Connely,

William Dampier, John Ballett,

Edw. Cooke, John Bridge,

Robert Frye, Lan. Appleby.

After this we gave them the following Instructions.

Capt. Tho. Dover,

Mr. Robert Frye,

Mr. W. Stratton, Gorgona, 9 July, 1709.

Gentlemen,

We having agreed with you in a Committee, That you take a Bark under your Care, and transport our Prisoners to the Main, and having order'd about 45 Men under your Command to proceed with you, and attempt the Plundering where you judge most convenient: We only recommend the utmost Dispatch, and that you keep in mind, we hope to be ready in 8 Days, and shall earnestly expect you as much as possible within that Time. Of her things relating to this you'll know better how to act than we can here direct.

Should a powerful Enemy attempt us in your Absence, we'll be certain to leave a Glass Bottle buried at the Root of the Tree whence the Fore-mast was cut, to acquaint you, then Quibo is the Place we will wait for you at, if we are well, and you must leave a Glass Bottle at this Place in case we return hither again: But this we don't expect, if once chas'd away.

Woodes Rogers, Tho. Glendall, Stephen Courtney, John Connely, William Dampier, Geo. Milbourne, Edward Cooke, John Bridge, William Bath, John Ballett, Cha. Pope.

July 10. Early this Morning we put our 72 Prisoners aboard the Bark. We had several times discours'd our Prisoners, the two *Morells*, and *Don Antonio* about ransoming the Goods, and were in hopes of selling them to advantage, but deferr'd coming to Particulars, till now that we plainly saw, unless they could have the Cargoes under a quarter Value, they would not deal with us. I propos'd going to *Panama*, and to lie 6 Days as near it as they pleas'd, till they brought the Money we should agree for at a moderate Rate; provided they left a Hostage aboard us, whom on failure we would carry to *England*. To this they would have agreed, provided we would take 60000 Pieces of Eight for all the Prize Goods. Then I propos'd their ransoming the Galleon, and putting good part of the Goods aboard her, provided one of them three and another they could procure would be Hostages for the Sum. They answer'd. That neither of them would go Hostage to *England* for the World. Then I propos'd delivering the Galleon and Cargo to them here, provided 2 of them would be Ransomers to pay us the Money at any other Place but *Panama* or *Lima*, in Six Days, if they would give us 120000 Pieces of Eight, being the lowest Price we could take for all the Prizes and Goods, Negroes, &c. They told us that Trade with Strangers, especially the *English* and *Dutch*, was so strictly prohibited in those Seas, that they must give more than the prime Cost of the Goods in Bribes, to get a License to deal with us: So that they could not assure us of Payment, unless we fold the Goods very cheap; therefore not finding it worth our Time, and knowing the Danger we must run in treating with them, we desisted, and order'd them all ashore, still hoping that this would necessitate the *Morells* and *Navarre* to get Money for us, and prevent our burning the Ships, and what we can't carry away. Every one now wish'd we had kept some others of the topping Prisoners, to have try'd whether they had a better Foundation and Method to trade; the Goods being of little value to us here, and we must fill our Ships so full, that we fear 'twill spoil our failing.

July II. Yesterday our Bark and 2 Pinnaces sail'd with our chief Prisoners. *Don Antonio*, the *Fleming*, Sen. *Navarre*, and the *Morells*, who did not expect to part with us so suddenly, but by continuing with us, and knowing we could not carry away all the Prizes and Goods, they hop'd we should of course have freely given them what we could not keep. We apprehended that was the principal Reason of their hot closing with our Terms, which were advantageous to them. Besides, should we have been attack'd, they believ'd we must then put them in possession of their Ships, which were of no use for fighting. But to obviate all their Hopes of benefiting themselves at this easy Rate, without our participating of their Money, the Magnet that drew us hither, I made them sensible at parting, that as we had treated them courteously like generous Enemies, we would sell them good Bargains for whatever Money they could bring us in 10 Days time, but that we would burn what we did not so dispose of or carry away. They beg'd we would delay burning the Ships, and promised to raise what Money they could, and return within the time to satisfy us.

One of the chief Prisoners we now parted with was *Don Juan Cardoso*, design'd Governor of *Baldivia*, *a* brisk Man of about 35 Years of Age; he had serv'd as a Collonel in *Spain*, had the Misfortune to be taken in the North Seas by an *English* Privateer near *Portobello*, and carried to *Jamaica*, from whence he was sent back to *Portobello*: He complain'd heavily of the Usage he met with from the *Jamaica* Privateer; but we parted very good Friends, and he returned us his hearty Thanks, and a Stone Ring for a Present to one of the *Dutchess's* Lieutenants that had lent him his Cabbin while he was sick on board.

We allow'd Liberty of Conscience on board our floating Commonwealth to our Prisoners., for there being a Priest in each Ship, they had the Great Cabbin for their Mass, whilst we us'd the Church of *England* Service over them on the Quarter-deck, so that the Papists here were the Low Churchmen.

July 13. This Morning our Vessels return'd from landing our Prisoners, and brought off 7 small Black Cattle, about 12 Hogs, 6 Goats, some Limes and Plaintains, which were very welcome to us; they met with little else of Value in the Village they were at, and the others being far up the River, they did not think it worth while to visit them. The Country where they landed was so poor, that our Men gave the Prisoners 5 Negroes, some Bays, Nails, etc. to purchase themselves Subsistence. The Inhabitants ashore had notice of our taking *Guiaquil*, and were jealous of our being at this Island, because they heard our Guns, when we fired in order to scale them after careening. This Place bears S. E. about 7 Leagues from the Body of *Gorgona*, is low Land full of Mangrove Trees; but within the Country the Land is very high. The River is hard to be found without a Pilot, and has shole Water for above 2 Leagues from Shore. There are some poor Gold Mines near it, but the Inhabitants agree that those of *Barbacore* are very rich, tho' difficult to be attempted, as we were informed before.

July 16. Yesterday about Noon came aboard one *Michael Kendall*, a free Negro of *Jamaica*, who had been sold a Slave to the Village we plunder'd but not being there when our People were ashore, he follow'd them privately in a small Canoe; and the Account he gave of himself was, that when the last War was declared at *Jamaica*, he embark'd under the Command of one Capt. *Edward Roberts*, who was join'd in Commission from the Governour of *Jamaica* with Capts. *Rash*, *Golding* and *Pilkington*; they had 106 Men, and design'd to attempt the Mines of *Jaco* at the Bottom of the Gulph of *Darien*: There were more Commanders and Men came out with them, but did not join in this Design. They had been about 5 Months out, when they got near the Mines undiscover'd; they sail'd 15 Days up the River in Canoes, and travel'd 10 Days by Land afterwards. By this time the S*paniards* and *Indians* being alarm'd, laid Ambushes in the Woods, and shot many of them. The Enemy having assembled at least 500 Men, and the *English* being diminish'd to about 60, including the Wounded; the *Spaniards* sent them a Flag of Truce, and offer'd them their Lives after a small Skirmish, wherein the *English* lost 4, and the Enemy about 12 Men. The *English* being in want of Provisions, quite tir'd out, and not knowing their Way back, agreed to deliver their Arms, on condition to be us'd as Prisoners of War. Having thus yielded, the S*paniards* and *Indians* carried them in Canoes 3 Days up the River, that leads to the same Mines they design'd to attempt, treated them very well, and gave them the same Food that they eat themselves; but the 4th Day, when they came to a Town beyond the Mines, and thought all Danger had been past, an Order came from the chief *Spanish* Officer to cut them all off, which the *Indians* and *Spanish* Troops did, as those poor disarm'd Wretches sat at Victuals; so that in this barbarous manner they were all massacred in a few Minutes, except a *Scots*, a *French*, and an *English* Boy, with 12 free Negroes, which at the Intercession of a Priest they kept for Slaves. This Man being one of 'em, happen'd to be sold, first to the Mines, where he says he clear'd at least 3 Pieces of Eight a day for his Master, and from thence he was sold to this Place. By this we may see what a mighty Advantage the S*paniards* make of their Slaves to imploy at these Mines, which are accounted the richest in *New Spain*. The rest of the free Negroes being farther up the Country, could have no Opportunity to escape. This is enough to shew what merciless and cowardly Enemies we have to deal with in these Parts of the World. I have heard of many such Cruelties in the S*panish* Parts of *America*, to the eternal Scandal of those who encourage or connive at them.

July 17. About 10 this Morning, the two *Morells*, Mr. *Navarre*, and his Son in-law, our old Prisoners came in a large Canoe, with some Money to ransom what they could of us: We told them of the Barbarity of their Countrymen, and of the different Treatment they met with from us; and that we had reason to apprehend, that if we became Prisoners here, that few of us would ever return to our native Country.

July 18. A Negro belonging to the *Dutchess* was -bit by a small brown speckl'd Snake, and died within 12 Hours, notwithstanding the Doctor us'd his utmost Endeavours to save him. There's abundance of Snakes on this Island, and the *Spaniards* say some are as thick as the Middle of a Man's Thigh. I saw one as big as my Leg, and above 3 Yards long; their Bite proves generally mortal. Yesterday in the Afternoon we had a Confutation, and agreed that the small Bark we took belonging to the Main right against this Island, should be given the Lieutenant's Brother that we plunder'd, and who came over with our Bark; for being a Man in some Authority ashore, we hope this Favour will have some Influence on 'em to trade with us whilst we are here. This Morning Mr. *Morell* and *Navarre* went a second time in our Bark for Money. One of the same fort of Snakes that kill'd the Negro was found on our Forecastle this Morning, and kill'd by our Men; we suppose it came aboard on the Cable, they being often seen in the Water.

July 19. We continued discharging the Galleon, and lading the *Marquiss*, and put a Parr aboard of us and the *Dutchess*. We found in the *Marquiss* near 500 Bales of Pope's Bulls, 16 Reams in a Bale. This took up abundance of

Room in the Ship; we throw'd most of them overboard to make room for better Goods, except what we used to burn the Pitch of our Ships Bottoms when we careen'd 'em. These Bulls are imposed upon the People, and sold here by the Clergy from 3 Ryals to 50 Pieces of Eight a-piece, according to the Ability of the Purchaser. Once in two Years they are rated, and all the People obliged to buy them against Lent; they cannot be read, the Print looking worse than any of our old Ballads, yet the Vulgar are made believe it's a mortal Sin to eat Flesh in Lent, without being licensed by one of these Bulls, the Negro Slaves not being exempted. This is one of the greatest Branches of Income the King of S*pain* has in this Country, being a free Gift from the Pope to him, as the *Spaniards* and Natives told us. We should have made something of them, if we had taken the Bishop before mentioned; but now they are of no use to us.

July 20. At Noon *Navarre* return'd with a little more Money, some Limes, Fowls, etc. He told us he had left Mr. *Morell* to get more, and that he would be soon with us.

July 21. We sent aboard the *Marquiss* 2 of our Main Deck Guns, and the *Dutchess* did the like, which with 4 we took at *Guiaquil*, and 12 taken in the same Ship, make 20 good ones. The Carriages are all new, or very much repair'd, and as good and strong as if mounted in *England*. Another Canoe came with Limes, Guavas, and other Fruit, and brought a little Money to trade with us. The Main here is a poor Country, and I believe we might have pick'd up a good Quantity of Money any where else on this Coast, notwithstanding their severe Orders against trading with us.

July 22. Two of our Negroes, and three of the *Dutchess* ran into the Woods to hide themselves, and go to the S*paniards* after we are gone: We caught one of 'em to day, and punish'd him severely.

July 23. At 6 last Night our Stream Cable broke, and we lost our Anchor: The Ground here is a black Mud, which in all hot Countries rots Cables in a very little time. We have often Thunder, Rain and Lightning all the Night, tho' clear dry Days. This is accounted by the S*paniards* the worst part of all the Coast for wet dirty Weather. We have had enough of it, but God be thank'd are now pretty well, there not being above 30 Persons in all our Ships unhealthy.

July 24. We caught our Negroes that ran away, and one of the *Dutchess's*, Hunger having brought 'em out of the Woods.

July 25. I put 35 Men aboard the *Marquiss*, and Capt. *Courtney* 26, so that her Complement will be 61 White Men, and 20 Negroes. Captain *Edward Cooke* Commander, and our Second Lieutenant, Mr. *Charles Pope*, his Second. We design to agree, that the Captain with his Officers and Men shall have equal Wages with others in the like Posts, to encourage them.

July 26. Last Night the *Marquiss* sprung a Leak, and made 8 Inches Water in an Hour; but the Carpenters stopt it. A Canoe came from the Main, and bought some Negroes of us.

July 27 At 8 this Morning, the Canoe return'd, with Mr. *John Morell*, who desir'd he might go ashore to his Brother, and forward his getting of more Money to deal with us for Goods, since he saw that we were resolved to leave nothing of Value behind us.

July 28. Yesterday Afternoon, Mr. *John Morell* return'd, having met his Brother coming with what Money he could get; he told us the Country being alarm'd, he had much ado to get Leave to come to us; that the Governour of *Barbacore* was at the Water-side, with above 200 Men commanded by himself, to prevent our Landing, or that any thing should be brought to us; and that all the Shore was lined with Men for that End. We have took out of the Galleon 320 Bails of Linnen, Woolen, a little Silks, and molt sorts of Goods, usually in Bails, besides Boxes of Knives, Scizzars, Hatchets, etc. The *Dutchess* and *Marquiss* have also taken what they can; so that all our 3 Ships are full. We found aboard the Galeon a great Quantity of Bones in small Boxes, ticketed with the Names of *Romish* Saints, some of which had been dead 7 or 800 Years; with an infinite Number of Brass Medals, Crosses, Beads, and Crucifixes, religious Toys in Wax, Images of Saints made of all sorts of Wood, Stone, and other Materials, I believe in all near 30 Tun, with 150 Boxes of Books in *Spanish, Latin, &c.* which would take up much more Stowage than 50 Tuns of other Goods: All this came from Italy, and most from *Rome*, design'd for the Jesuits of Peru; but being of small Value to us, we contented our selves to take only a Sample of most Sorts to shew our Friends in *England*, and left the rest. A large wooden Effigies of the Virgin *Mary* being either dropt or thrown over board, from the Galeon, and drove ashore near the North Point of the Island, the *Indians* that came in the Canoes with Senior *Morell, &c.* from the main Land, being then a Fishing, took up the Image, and brought her in the Canoe to the Shore just over against our Ship, where we gave our Prisoners Liberty to walk that Day: As soon as they saw her, they cross'd and bless'd themselves, and fancied that this must be the Virgin *Mary* come by Water from *Lima* or *Panama*, to relieve them in their Necessity. They then set it up on the Shoar, and wip'd it dry with Cotton; and when they came aboard, told us, that tho' they had wip'd her again and again, the continued to sweat very much; and all but those employed in wiping her, stood around devoutly amaz'd, praying and telling over their Beads: They also shew'd the Cotton to our Linguist and the Ransomers, wet by the excessive sweat of the holy Virgin, as they fondly seem'd to believe, and kept it as a choice Relick. The *Morells* perceiving me laugh at the Story, they told me a much stranger, in order to convince me, *viz.* That a few Years ago, at a Procession in the Cathedral Church of *Lima*, which was at that time very richly furnished, and worth some Millions of, Pieces of 8 in Gold, Silver and Jewels; the Image of the Virgin was more richly adorn'd with Pearls, Diamonds and Gold, than the rest; and those Ornaments being left in the Church, according to Custom, till the Night after Procession, without any Guard, because the People concluded that none durst be so sacrilegiously impious as to rob the Church; an unfortunate Thief, resolving at once to enrich himself, got into the Church at Midnight, and made up to the Image; but whilst he was going to take off a rich String of Pearls from the Virgin's Wrists, she caught him fast by the Arm, and held him, till being found in that Posture he was apprehended and executed. This Story was confirm'd as an unquestionable Truth by all the other Prisoners, who assured us, That all the Fathers of the Church at *Lima* confidently affirm the same, as well as a considerable Number of Lay-Brethren, who (they say) were Eye-Witnesses of it; so that it passes amongst them as currant, as an Article of their Faith: By this we may see how the Belief of those false Miracles, by the Cunning of the *Romish* Clergy in these Parts, obtains Credit among those Men who are not so easily imposed on in their worldly Affairs. Thus I am ape to believe those

Gentlemen invented the Story of the sweating Miracle, out of Zeal to their Church, and thinking thereby to deter us from carrying away any more of the Relicks out of Senior *Morell's* Galeon. Before this, when I heard such Stories, I took 'em to have been invented meerly to ridicule the *Romanists*, but when I heard such silly Stories related by 8 grave Men, of a handsome Appearance and good Reputation amongst the S*paniards*, I was convinc'd of the Ignorance and Credulity of the Papists.

July 29. Having for a long time been importun'd by the Companys of each Ship, to divide what we was forc'd to agree to as Plunder, we resolved on a Committee to be called to morrow to settle that Affair, which we did in the following Manner.

At a Committee on board the *Duke*, the 29th Day of *July*, 1709. It's agreed, that the following Articles shall regulate Plunder, and be in part a Satisfaction allowed by the Committee of the *Duke* and *Duchess*, for past Services, more than each Man's Agreement with the Owners.

Impr. Gold Rings found in any Place, except in a Goldsmith's Shop is Plunder. All Arms, Sea Books and Instruments, all Cloathing and Moveables, usually worn about Prisoners, except Women's Earrings, unwrought Gold or Silver, loose Diamonds,, Pearls or Money; all Plate in use aboard Skips, but not on Shear, (unless about the Persons of Prisoners) is Plunder.

All manner of Clothes ready made, found on the upper Deck, and betwixt Decks, belonging to the Ships Company and Passengers is Plunder also, except what is above limited, and is in whole Bundles and Pieces, and not open'd in this Country s that appears not for the Persons use that owns the Chest, but design'd purposely for Merchandise, which only shall not be plunder. And for Encouragement, we shall allow to James Stratton 40 Rupees to buy him Liquor in India, in Part of Amends for his smart Money. To William Davis and Yerrick Derrickson 20 Rupees each, as smart Money, over and above their Shares. We also give the Boats Crews over and above their Shares, that were engage'd with the Marquiss, when taken, four Bails of Goods, to be sold when and where they think convenient; which Bails shall be 1 of Serges, 1 of Linnen, and 2 of Bays; and this over and above their respective Shares. Also a good Suit of Clothes to be made for each Man that went up the River above Guiaquil, the last time in the Duchess's Pinnace. In witness whereof, We have hereunto set out Hands the Day and Tear above-mentioned.

Tho. Dover, Pres. John Connely,

Woodes Rogers, William Bath,

Stephen Courtney, Tho. Glendal,

William Dampier, Geo. Milbourne,

Edw. Cooke, John Bridge,

Rob. Frye, John Ballett,

William Stretton, Lan. Appleby.

The Cause why we delay'd adjusting what should be Plunder so long, was the unreasonable Expectations of some among us: This made us wait till now we had a proper Opportunity, and could better insist on our Owner's

Interest: Besides, we were not willing that any Difference should arise about this knotty Affair, when the Prisoners were on board, nor till we had finish'd the Rigging of our Ships, left it should have put a full Stop to our Business, or at least have hinder'd our Proceeding cheerfully.

July 30. We over hall'd our Plunder-Chests, and what was judged to be Plunder, (by Men appointed with the Owners Agents) was carried aboard the Galeon, which was kept clear between Decks, in order to divide it. Mr. *Frye* and Mr. *Pope* were to be Appraisers for the *Duke*, and Mr. *Stratton* and Mr. *Connely for* the *Dutchess*, so I hope to get over a troublesome Job peaceably.

July 31. Mr. *Navarr's* Bark grew leaky, and *Benjamin Parsons*, one of our Midshipmen that had charge of her, ran her a-shore without Orders, at high Water, thinking to have stop'd her Leak at low Water, and got her off the next Tide; but contrary to his Expedition, the Vessel strain'd and sunk; so that we had much ado to get out what we had a-board her Time enough; and were forced to leave in her 10 Bails of damag'd Bays, and a great deal of Iron Work, which we gave Senior *Navarr*, in part of Payment for what we have received of him from the Settlement on the Main.

August 1. The Officers we appointed to praise the Plunder met on board the Galeon, and valued the Cloathing, in order to divide it amongst the Officers and Men of each Ship, according to their respective Shares.

August 2. We continued appraising the Plunder, and found it a very troublesome Task.

August 3. Capt. *Cooke* told me they had discover'd another Leak, and was troubled at so many Leaks in a Harbour; so that I began to dread that all our Labour and Time was lost on the *Marquiss*, but hop'd for the best.

August 4. Yesterday in the Afternoon they made an End of appraising the Clothes at a very low rate, amounting to upwards of 400 *l.* and the Silver-handled Swords, Buckles, Snuff-Boxes, Buttons, and Silver Plate in use aboard every Prize we took, and allow'd to be Plunder at 4 *s.* 6 *d. per* Piece of 8, amounted to 743 *l.* 15 s. besides;3 tb 12 2\3 of Gold, which was in Rings, Gold, Snuff-boxes, Earrings, and Gold Chains, taken about Prisoners. This I believe to be an exact Account.

This Morning we had like to have a Mutiny amongst our Men: The Steward told me, that several of them had last Night made a private Agreement, and that he heard some Ring-leaders by way of Encouragement, boast to the rest, that 60 Men had already signed the Paper. Not knowing what this Combination meant, or how far it was design'd, I sent for the chief Officers into the Cabin, where we arm'd our selves, secured two of the chief of those mutinous Fellows, and presently seized two others. The Fellow that wrote the Paper we put in Irons; by this time all Hands were upon Deck, and we had got their Agreement from those who were in the Cabin, the Purport of which was to oblige themselves, not to take their Plunder, nor to move from thence till they had Justice done them, as they term'd it. There being so many concern'd in this Design, Captains *Dover* and *Fry* desired I would discharge those in Confinement upon their asking Pardon, and faithfully promising never to be guilty of the like, or any other Combination again. The Reason we shewed 'em this Favour was, that there were too many guilty to punish them at once; And not knowing what was design'd a-board the *Dutchess and Marquiss*, we were of Opinion they had concerted to break the Ice first a-board the *Duke*, and the rest to stand by them. Upon this I us'd what Arguments I could offer, shew'd them the Danger and Folly of Combinations, and exhorted them to believe they would have Justice in *England*, should any thing seem uneasy to them now, or in the whole Course of the Voyage; adding that we had done all that we could for their good, and would continue our Endeavours, not doubting their good Intentions, provided they were not misled. With these and other healing Arguments, all appear'd easy and quiet, and every Man seem'd willing to stand to what had been done, provided the Gentlemen that were Officers, and not Sailors, amongst us, had not such large Shares, which they alledg'd was unreasonable, and that they could not possibly in a Privateer deserve what they were allow'd, in proportion to the rest of the Ships Company: This we did in part yield to, in order to appease those Malecontents, by making some Abatements on Mr. *White's*, Mr. *Bath's, and* Mr. *Vanbrugh's* Shares; so that we hoped this difficult. Work would, with less Danger than we dreaded, be brought to a good Conclusion: For Disputes about Plunder is the common Occasion of Privateers Quarrelling amongst themselves, and ruining their Voyages. Sailors usually exceed all Measures when left to themselves, and account it a Privilege in Privateers to do themselves Justice on these Occasion, tho' in every thing else I must own, they have been more obedient than any Ship's Crews engag'd in the like Undertaking that ever I heard of. Yet we have not wanted sufficient Tryal of our Patience and Industry in other things; so that if any Sea-Officer thinks himself endowed with these two Virtues, let him command in a Privateer, and discharge his Office well in a distant Voyage, and I'll engage he shall not want Opportunities to improve, if not to exhaust all his Stock. Had Capt. *Courtney* and I kept what is always allow'd to be Plunder in Privateers, and not voluntarily given our Parts amongst the Men, but for a greater and more generous Design in view, (*viz.* The Good of the Voyage) our Parts of the Plunder would have been above 10 times so much as now it is, because very little valuable Plunder was taken out of any Place but the Great Cabbins; and all this in every Prize is of right due to the Commander that takes it; but if we had acted thus, we foresaw the fatal Consequences that we must have suffer'd by it, for the Officers and Crews would plunder unaccountably, as is too often practis'd in Privateers to keep their Men together, tho' but meanly to their Duty; so that we (to preserve a good Discipline) gave an eminent Example to them, of preferring the common Interest before our own, to our particular Loss.

We have had lately almost a general Misunderstanding amongst our Chief Officers, and some great Abuses, which I suppose sprung at first from several unhappy Differences arising at and before our Attempt on *Guiaquil*. This made me so particularly relate all that pass'd material in that Attempt, so that I doubt not any ones contradicting this Journal to my Disadvantage; yet in Differences of this kind amongst the Sailors we all join and I hope agree: Tho' I long for a Reconciliation and good Harmony amongst Us, which is so essential to the Welfare of the Voyage; but not being willing to make the Reader a Party-taker or trouble his Patience to read over unreasonable Feuds, I have left 'em as much as possible out of my Journal.

Capt. *Morell*, that went for the Main to get Victuals, return'd. The Negro we caught first and punished, we kept in Irons, but this Night miss'd him. We suppose he got his Irons off, and swam ashore.

We held the following Committees, confirmed the Officers of the *Marquiss*, agreed to sell the Bark and her Cargo, got off all our Wood and Water, and made Preparation for sailing. We design to leave the Launch we built at *Lobos* with Sen. *Morells* and *Navarre*, being of no farther use to us, tho' hitherto she had done us very good Service. Here follows what we agreed on in Council.

At a Committee held on board the *Dutchess*, riding *at Gorgona, August* 6. 1709.

We whose Names are hereunto subscribed, appointed as a Committee on board the Ships Duke and Dutchess, do hereby impower and order Capt. Cooke to command the Marquiss, Mr. Charles Pope Lieutenant, Mr. Robert Knowlman Master, Mr. William Page Chief Mate, Joseph Parker Second Mate, Mr. John Ballet Doctor, Benjamin Long Boatswain, George Knight Gunner, Edward Gormand Carpenter, and other Officers as the Captain shall direct aboard the Marquiss: Each of the above Officers, or the others, on their good Behaviour, to have such Wages as those in the same Offices on board the Duke and Dutchess, and to cruise on this Coast in our Company, or where else Capt. Cooke shall think convenient, in his Return to Bristol, should he be unfortunately separated from us. Witness our Hands.

Tho. Dover, Pres. Tho. Glendall,

Woodes Rogers, John Connely,

Stephen Courtney, William Bath,

William Dampier, Geo. Milbourne,

Robert Frye, John Bridge,

William Stratton, Lan. Appleby.

Memorandum,

We have now done careening, fixing, and loading our Ships, with the Marquiss, and taken all manner of Goods out of our Prizes, as much as our Ships can carry, having received a valuable Consideration of Mr. Morell and Navarre, the Masters of our 2 Prizes we are all of opinion we bad best leave them in possession of their Ships, and what Negroes we cant carry hence; our present Circumstances and the Condition of the Prizes not allowing us to remove them from this Place, could we make ever So great advantage of 'em elsewhere. so judge it our present Interest to ply to Windward, to try for other Purchases and Sale of the Goods, and if possible to take or buy Provisions. We all agree to land one of the Guiaquil Hostages at Manta, in order to procure Money to pay for the Ransom of the Town, and a Bark we have fold the fame Man, laden with Prize Goods. Witness our Hands this 6th of August, 1709.

Tho. Dover, Pres. William Stratton,

Woodes Rogers, Tho. Glendall,

Stephen Courtney, John Connely,

William Dampier, William Bath,

Edw. Cooke, John Ballett,

Robert Frye, Lan. Appleby. Cha. Pope.

I drew up the following Agreement, to which we Officers swore on the Holy Evangelists, because I thought it the mod proper Method to prevent the

Confusions which were like to happen among us, because of the Jealousies that were entertain'd of one another, and came to such a height, that I fear'd a Separation.

We having made a solemn Agreement, do this Instant sign voluntarily, and give each other our Oaths on the Holy Bible; and as we hope for Forgiveness of Sins, and Salvation by the alone Merits and Intersession of our Blessed Lord Jesus Christ, to keep severely and strictly this serious concerted Memorandum. First we agree to keep company, and assist each other on all Occasions, and with all Necessaries, as far as our Abilities reach, and our common safety requires. Secondly, that in case we engage at any time with the Enemy, we design it in Consortship, and that each Commander and Second in each Ship, hereto subscribed, shall on all Occasions, without the least Reserve, and to the utmost of his Power, be forward and ready to assist, rescue or defend each other, with the utmost Dispatch, Bravery and Conduit, even to the apparent Hazard of his Ship and all that is dear to him: Well knowing all of us, that on whatever Occasion should either of our Ships be deserted by the other two, and taken or lost in these barbarous and remote Parts, it's very improbable ever the Men will get home, and the Survivors would be in as bad, if not in a worse Condition than the Dead.

On these and the like Confederations we do hereby solemnly agree never to desert each other in time of Need, if possibly we can avoid it, and to be to the utmost of our Tower and Knowledge alike brave in attacking or defending our selves against the Enemy to the last Extremity.

But if we are so unfortunate to see one Ship inevitably perish, then the two remaining (after they have us'd their utmost Endeavours for the distress'd Ship, and find all past Recovery) may then agree on the best Methods for their own Security. 'The like for one Ship if two are lost, but for no other Reason to desert this firm and solemn Agreement of Consortship; and to shew that none of us is so unbecoming a Man as to shrink back, or flight this Agreement in time of Action, we agree it shall not be altered without the Consent of all us three Commanders, and the major fart of the Officers hereto subscrib'd, and to a Duplicate in each Ship of the same Date in Gorgona, the sixth Day of August, 1709.

Tho. Dover, *Pres*, Woodes Rogers, Stephen Courtney, Edward Cooke, Rob. Fry, William Stretton, Charles Pope, John Connely, Tho. Glendale.

Another Paper was also drawn up for every Man to swear what Clothes, Goods, &c. he had received of the Agents, and to restore whatever he, had taken without the Agents Knowledge, in order to a just distributions of the Plunder and every one was to oblige himself in a Penalty of 20 s. for every Shilling Value that should be found about him conceal'd, besides the former Penalty agreed on of losing his Share of any Prize or Purchase for concealing above the Value of half a Piece of Eight; and for the Incouragement of Discoveries the Informer was to have half the Penalty, and the Protection of the Commanders. This Paper was objected against by several of the Officers, who insisted, that there ought to be a greater Latitude allowed them to advantage themselves, since they had ventured their Lives hither on so difficult an

Undertaking, which made us defer the signing it till a better Opportunity; for unless such Agreements as these had been constantly promoted, as occasion required, the Temptation of Interest wou'd have made us fall into irrecoverable Confusions a-broad, which generally end in a Separation, or worse.

Aug. 7. We gave Sen. *Morell* and *Navarre* their Ships, and all the Goods we could not carry away, for what Money our Agents received of 'em, tho' they expected to have had 'em at an easier Rate. We came to sail this Morning; the dividing the Plunder has took up more Time than we were willing to spare; but 'twas absolutely necessary to do it. We took Sen. *Navarre* with us before we came to sail: I went ashore, and shew'd Sen. *Morell* how we left things between his Ship and the other Prize. Mr. *Navarre* left his Son-in law in charge of this Vessel and Goods, then came with me on board our Ships, expecting to have the Bark betwixt him and our Ransomers, if they paid us at *Guiaquil*. Wind veerable in the South Weft Quarter, a Lee Current.

August 8. Yesterday at 6 in the Evening the Island of *Gorgona* bore S. by E. distant 6 Leagues. Just before Night we took our Men out of the Bark, and left her in possession of an old *Indian* Pilot, and some Negroes and *Indian* Prisoners, putting our ordinary Ransomers aboard to go in her, as we agreed on before we came out. I and Capt. *Dover* sign'd a Paper to protect them from being seiz'd by the S*paniards*, if they should lose Company with us; but order'd them not to stir from us. I also desir'd the S*paniards* aboard the *Duke*, who had agreed for her, strictly to charge the Crew in the Bark not to leave us willingly, which they did, because our Agreement was not in Writing,, but only Verbal, promising us 15000 Pieces of Eight for the Bark and her Cargo, including the Remainder of the Towns Ransom, we designing to have it under their hand in S*panish* and *English* to morrow, before we would wholly let go the Bark: But this Morning, to our surprize, the Bark was out of sight. The *Marquiss* is very crank, and sails heavy on a Wind. We held the following Committee to endeavour to help the *Marquiss* failing.

At a Committee-held on board the *Dutchess* at Sea, off the Island *Gorgona, August* 8*th*, 1709.

Memorandum,

THE Marquiss *not answering our Expectations, but proving crank and sailing heavy: We now advise Capt.* Cooke *to heave the* Dutchess's *two heavy Guns overboard, and* 20 *Boxes of Snuff, with two spare Top-masts, and bring his Ship more by the Stern, flowing every thing as low as possible in the Ship, to endeavour to make her stiffer, and if he finds any thing more necessary for the Benefit of the Ship, we desire him to do it. Witness our Hands.*

Signed by the Majority of our Council.

Amongst our Prisoners taken on board Sen. *Navarre's Ship* from *Panama*, there was a Gentlewoman and her Family, her eldest Daughter a pretty young Woman of about 18, was newly married, and had her Husband with her. We assign'd them the Great Cabin aboard the Galleon, and none were suffer'd to intrude amongst them, or to separate their Company, yet the Husband (I was told) shew'd evident Marks of Jealousy, the S*paniards* Epidemick Disease; but I hope he had not the least Reason for it amongst us, my third Lieutenant *Glendall* alone having charge of the Galleon and Prisoners: For being above 50 Years of Age, he appear'd to be the most secure Guardian to Females that had the least Charm, tho' all our young Men have hitherto appear'd modest beyond Example among Privateers; yet we thought it improper to expose them to Temptations. At this time Lieut. *Connely*, who behav'd himself so modestly to the Ladies of *Guiaquil*, was some days in possession of *Navarre's Ship* before we stopt here, to remove these Prisoners aboard the Galleon, where he gain'd their Thanks and publick Acknowledgments for his Civilities to these Ladies, and even the Husband extols him. We had notice these Ladies had some conceal'd Treasure about them, and order'd a Female Negro that we took, and who spoke *English*, to search them narrowly, and found some Gold Chains and other things cunningly hid under their Clothes. They had before deliver'd to Capt. *Courtney* Plate and other things of good Value, We gave them most of their wearing Apparel and Necessaries, with 3 Female Mullatto Slaves, and parted very friendly. They confess'd to our People, who put them ashore, that we had been much civiller than they did expect, or believe their own Countrymen would have been in the like case, and sent back the Husband with Gold to purchase some Goods and two slaves of us. I come next to the Description of *Gorgona*.

Chapter X

Gorgona is 3 Leagues in Length, N. E. and S. W. but narrow. It's about 6 Leagues from the Main, full of Wood and tall Trees, one of 'em call'd *Palma Maria*, of which the S*paniards* make Masts, and use a Balsam that flows from it for several Diseases. The Island appears at a distance indifferent high, and in 3 Hummocks. There is Riding for Ships all over against the North East side; but in some places foul Ground, and shoal'd near the Shore, particularly on the South East Side, and near the South Weft End, where there's a small Island almost joining, with shoal Ground, and Breakers near a Mile to the Eastward from that End. Capt, *Dampier* has been here several times, but never rode where we did, which is the best and only good Road in the Island. The S*paniards* told us of strange Storms and heavy Turnadoes of Wind about this Island; but we found it otherwise, and had only frequent showers and Thunder: But in the time of Breezes, which the S*paniards* call our Winter Months, and in Spring, till the Beginning of *May*, here are now and then Northerly strong Breezes of Wind, and then I believe the Road must be shifted to the other Side of the Island, which may be at that time the best Riding; but this we had no Time to try, neither do I think it half so bad as these puny Manners tell us. About this Island are several remarkable Rocks, at the South West End there's one looks like a Sail half a Mile off shore; at the North East End there are Several high ones, round and steep, near a Cable's Length off Shore, where the Sea-Fowls breed. The Beasts and Insects we saw in this Island are Monkeys, Guinea Pigs, Hares, Lizards, Lion Lizards, the latter change their Colours, and are fine Creatures to look at, several Species of great and small Snakes, and so numerous, that 'tis dangerous for a Man to walk the Island, for fear of treading on them. There's great Variety of Plants and Trees peculiar to these hot Climates, and little or nothing resembling what we have in *Great Britain*; but it being out of my Road to describe such things, I refer 'em to such whose Talents lie that way. Here are also several sorts of Fish unkown in our Seas, be-sides Mullets in great Plenty, but hard to be caught with Hook and Line, which I suppose is occasion'd by the Clearness of the Water, so that they easily see the Hook and avoid it. Here's also some white Coral, and abundance of Oysters, and as I am told by the Prisoners, good Pearls in them. We caught an ugly Creature here, which I suppose may be of the Monkey Kind, because it look'd like one of the middling sort, but with this difference; his Hair was thicker and longer, his Face, Eyes and Nose less, and more wrinkled and deformed; his Head of the same Shape, but his Ears not so large; his Teeth longer and sharper,, his hinder Parts more clumsey, and his Body thicker in proportion, with a very short Tail, and instead of 5 Claws like Fingers as a Monkey has, he had only 3 on each Paw, with the Claws longer and sharper. We let one of 'em go at the lower part of the Mizon Shrouds, and it was about 2 Hours getting to the Mast Head, which a Monkey would have performed in less than half a Minute; he mov'd as if he had walk'd by Art, keeping an equal and slow Pace, as if all his Movements had been directed by Clock-work, within him. The S*paniards* call it a *Sloth*, and not improperly; they say it feeds on the Leaves of a certain lofty Tree, and when it has clear'd one, before it can get down and walk a little Way to find and climb another, would grow lean and be almost starved.

I saw no Land Birds here; because I suppose the Monkeys destroy their Nests and Eggs: We shot many of them, and made Fricassees and Broth for our sick Men; none of our Officers would touch them, Provisions being not yet so scarce; but Capt. *Dampier*, who had been accustomed to such Food, says he never eat any thing in *London* that seemed more delicious to him than a Monkey or Baboon in these Parts.

August 9. I proposed sending the *Marquiss* to *India*, and thence to *Brazil*; and then we could add to our own Stock of Bread and salt Provisions, and if she got well to *Brazil*, would vend her Goods at an extraordinary Rate, to the Advantage of the Voyage, and we two should be strong enough to wait for the *Manila* Ship, but Capts. *Dover* and *Courtney* did not think it reasonable.

August 10. We got to wind-ward very slowly, here being a constant Current, which runs down to Leward into the Bay of *Panama*.

August 11. Yesterday Afternoon I went aboard the *Dutchess*, and carried with the Doctor *Dover*; we discoursed about parting with Capt. *Cooke*, and giving him only a Sailing Crew to go for *Brazil*, and sell his Cargo; but finding the Majority against my Proposition, I dropt it, tho' I fear we shall repent it, were there no other Reasons but to save Provisions. Capt. *Cooke* came to us a-board the *Dutchess*, to put in Execution the Order of the 8th instant, where we agreed as before to throw 2 of the heaviest Guns overboard he had out of the *Dutchess*, being less valuable than the Goods between Decks, and what Lumber they had besides, which he did, and we perceive his Ship much stiffer, and sails better; our Consort, Capt. *Courtney* and his Officers, with some of mine, are uneasie at parting with the Bark, so that if we come up with her, we must take to her again for Peace sake.

August 12. Yesterday Evening, the Island of *Gorgona* was in sight, and bore E. half S. about 13 Leagues. At 6 this Morning, we met with the Bark, and put Mr. *Selkirk* aboard her, with his Crew. At 9 this Morning, we sent our Boat for Capt. *Courtney* and Capt. *Cooke*, when we had a second Consultation, which again concluded with keeping the *Marquiss* and Bark: Tho' I was of Opinion, they'd be rather a Detriment than Furtherance to us in any thing, so long as the *Marquiss* sails so heavily, besides the Benefit of more Provisions that would have been left for us that must stay behind.

August 13. In the Evening last Night, we saw the Island of *Gallo*, bearing S. by E. distant 6 Leagues. We have a strong Current runs to Leward, so that we lost Ground, and at 8 this Morning was again in sight of *Gorgona*, bearing N. E. by E. distant about 12 Leagues; had rainy Weather all Night, with Thunder and Lightning, but indifferent fair in the Morning. Wind veerable in the S. W. Quarter. This Coast is more subject to hot Weather than any other Part of *Peru*.

August 15. We sounded several Times in the Night, and had Ground in about 50 Fathom Water, not above two Leagues off Shore.

August 16. This Day I muster'd our Negroes aboard the *Duke*, being about 35 lusty Fellows; I told them, That if we met the *Spaniards* or *French*, and they would fight, those that behav'd themselves well should be free Men; 32 of 'em immediately promis'd to stand to it, as long as the best *Englishman*, and desired they might be improv'd in the Use of Arms,, which some of them already understood; and that if I would allow 'em Arms and Powder, these would teach the rest. Upon this, I made *Michael Kendall*, the *Jamaica* free Negro, who deserted from the *Spaniards* to us at *Gorgona*, their Leader, and charged him to be continually exercising them, because I did not know how soon we might meet an Enemy: I took down the Names of those that had any, and such as wanted I bestow'd Names on them, and to confirm our Contract made them drink a Dram all round to our good Success; at the same time I gave 'em Bays for Clothes, and told them they must now look upon themselves as *Englishmen*, and no more as Negro Slaves to the S*paniards*, at which they express'd themselves highly pleas'd: I promise my self good Assistance from them, if need be, having this Proverb on their Side, that Those who know nothing of Danger fear none; and for our own Parts, we must not submit to be Prisoners, tho' forced to engage at the greatest Disadvantage, but every one resolv'd to stand to the last, for if taken we shall be worth than Slaves.

August 18. At 6 this Morning we saw a Sail, which bore W. N. W. of us; we and the *Dutchess* gave Chace, and took her in about an Hour. The *Dutchess* had kept her Company ever since 12 at Night, and thought her to be our Bark. She was a Vessel of about 70 Tun, bound from *Panama* to *Lima*, but was to slop at *Guiaquil*. They had very little aboard besides Passengers, for they knew of cur being in these Seas: The best of her Cargo was about 24 Negroes, Men and Women. I sent our Agent aboard, to examine the Prize.

August 19. After Dinner aboard the *Dutchess*, we examin'd the Prisoners; they could tell us little News from *Europe*, but said there came Advices by a Packet to *Portobell* from S*pain*, and by a *French* Ship from *France*, not long before they came out of *Panama*; that all was kept private, only they heard in *Panama*, that his Royal Highness Prince *George* of *Denmark* was dead, which we were not willing to believe, but drank his Health at Night, which can do him no Hurt if he is dead. We read several Letters from *Panama*, by which we understood, that when they heard of our taking *Guiaquil*, they kept their Gates shut Day and Night for above a Week, and that the Inhabitants kept Guard on their Walls, being afraid we should attack them next, and by what I can guess, we might have taken that Town as well as *Guiaquil*, had we but double our Number of Men. They had various Conjectures about us when at *Panama*, and were continually allarm'd, not knowing where to expert us.

August 20. At 10 in the Morning we bore down I to the *Dutchess*, who had S*panish* Colours flying, to make a sham Fight to exercise our Men and the Negroes in the Use of our great Guns and small Arms. Here I must not forget a *Welchman* that came to me, and told me, He took the Ship we were going to engage for the *Dutchess*, till he saw the S*panish* Colours, and that being over-joyed with the Hopes of a good Prize, he had loaded his Musket with shot, and design'd to fire amongst the thickest of 'em, which he would certainly have done, had he not been forbid. By this it appears, that blundering Fools may have Courage. During this sham Engagement, every one acted the same Part he ought to have done, if in earnest, firing with Ball excepted. Our Prisoners were secured in the Hold by the Surgeons, who had their Instruments in order, and to imitate Business for them, I order'd red Lead mixt with Water to be thrown upon two of our Fellows, and sent 'em down co the Surgeons, who, as well as the Prisoners in the Hold of the Ship, were very much surpriz'd, thinking they had been really wounded, and the Surgeons actually went about to dress them., but finding their Mistake, it was a very agreeable Diversion.

August 23. Yesterday, at one in the Afternoon, we tack'd and stood for the Shore, but at two we drew near discolour'd Water, and sounded, had but 8 Fathom, and very near an ugly Shoal, which the S*paniards* cell me runs off about 2 Leagues from the Shore, off a high white Cliff, 3 Leagues to the N. of *Tecames*. At 6 last Night, Cape St. *Francisco* bore S. by W. distant about 6 Leagues. We sounded again, and had 40 Fathom Water. We stood off at Night, and at 6 in the Morning tack'd for the Shore. The Wind is here always more Southerly, as we draw near the Equinox.

August 24. At 10 this Morning, I went with Captain *Dover* aboard the *Dutchess*, where we agreed to send the Bark into *Tecames*, being now under our Lee, and we to follow them. We order'd our Linguist to buy Provisions of the *Indians* there, and put several Men well arm'd a board, to keep the Bark till our Ship could arrive near enough to protect her, if occasion, in Case of an Attack.

August 25. About 2 Yesterday in the Afternoon we bore away for *Tecames*, after the Barks. I went aboard the *Dutchess*, and found our Pilot, and most of the S*paniards*, who are generally ignorant, uncertain whether it was the Port under our Lee, tho' I never saw more remarkable Land; this made us the more timorous, and me in particular, because Capt. *Dampier*, who was here last Voyage, and said he had pass'd near it very often, was full as dubious as our selves, that never saw it: This occasion'd me to hurry aboard our own Ship to secure her; for I doubted our being near Shoals, because the Water was very thick and white. Capt. *Courtney* sent his Pinnace a Head sounding, and we follow'd, he having then all the Pilots aboard. We kept the Lead sounding from 40 to 13 Fathom Water, very uneven Depths, till we came within 2 Leagues of the Anchoring place. We had every Cast about 14 Fathom Water, and saw the Houses by the Water-side; then I was easy and satisfied. Before we got in, the Barks were at Anchor, and our Linguist, Mr. *White*, without Orders, ventur'd a-shore with a *Spanish* Prisoner; we design'd that the Prisoner alone should discourse the *Indians*, and try to trade for a Refreshment: It was Night as they landed, just against the Houses, where the *Indians* lay in Ambush, with Fire-Arms, Bows, Arrows, and Lances, among the Trees, and fir'd several Times at our Boats, tho' they told the *Indians* in *Spanish*, that they were Friends, and call'd to them often to forbear firing. Our Men having the good Luck to escape being shot, they hid themselves all Night, whilst we feared they were either kill'd or taken; but at Day-light they call'd again to the *Indians*, and prevailed with them to trade for what we wanted, provided their Padre would give Consent, he lived about 6 Leagues off, and they promis'd to send and ask his Leave. Our Linguist told them we had a Padre aboard, whom we esteemed, and he would absolve them, if they traded with us: Upon this, they desired we would permit him to come a-shoar, which we granted.

August 26. The Padre aboard, who was zealous to conclude this Treaty with the *Indians* to our Content, went this Morning a-shore, and return'd a-board in the Evening, while he was a-shore, he writ a Letter to the Priest of the place in our Favour, earnestly recommending a Trade, and expressing the many Civilities we shewed to him and the other *Spanish* Prisoners, beyond their Espscta tion, adding that we were sensible of the smallest Favours, and would not sail of making very grateful Returns. He convinc'd the Inhabitants ashore, and also inform'd the Padre, how easily we could land, and burn the Church and Houses, and lay waste all the adjacent Parts; but that we were full of Charity, and very kind to those in our Power. This wrought so well on the People, that they promis'd faithfully they would only wait till to morrow, and if the Padre did not consent, would notwithstanding trade with us. They brought with them a naked *Indian*, who like a Savage view'd very narrowly every Part of our Ship; he was wonderfully taken with the Great Cabbin, where he lay on his Side, scarce satisfy'd after an Hour's gazing wildly about him, till giving him a Dram of Brandy, and a few Toys to be rid of this Visitant, I obligingly led the Gentleman out, and giving him old Bays for Clothing, our Yall carried him ashore, to influence the rest by our kind Usage of him. At the same time all the rest of our Boats full of Casks, with the Men well arm'd, went up the Creek between us and the Village, for fresh Water, where they accidentally met one of the chief *Indians* painted, and armed with Bows and Arrows: He came friendly, and advised them to go higher up the River, otherwise the Water would be brackish: They offer'd him a Dram out of a Quart Bottle of strong Brandy; he drank the major Part of it at once, and went away extreamly pleas'd, telling them we should be supply'd with what we wanted from the Village.

August 27. Last Night the Boats came from the Village laden with Water, and brought a Letter from the *Tecames* Padre, assuring us he would not obstruct our Trade. The Inhabitants also told us, that Cattle, Hogs and Plantains would be ready for us, and desir'd we should bring ashore Bays and other Goods to pay for 'em, which we did, and this Morning our Boats return'd with Black Cattle and Hogs, leaving Capt. *Navarre*, one of our chief Prisoners, and Mr. *White* our Linguist, to deal with the *Indians*. This Morning we began to heel and clean our Ships Bottoms, and sent several of our best Sailors, and two Carpenters, to assist the *Marquiss*. Ashore our Men keep one half at Arms, while the rest load the Boats, left the *Indian*, who are generally treacherous, should watch an Opportunity to fall on 'em. Our People that came off the Shore took particular notice, that the red Paint with which the *Indians* were at first daub'd, was a Declaration of War, and after we had amicably treated with them, they rub'd it off, but. still kept their Arms. We sent them 3 large Wooden *Spanish* Saints, that we had out of *Morell's* Ship, to adorn their Church, which they accounted a great Present; and I sent a feather'd Cap to the chief *Indians* Wife, which was likewise very well accepted, and I had a Present of Bows and Arrows in requital

August 28. Yesterday in the Afternoon we made an end of heeling and cleaning our Ship; our Boats brought from the Shore at several times Water, Plantains, and other Provisions, with Hogs, and 2 Black Cattle. Our Linguist and Prisoner manage their Business beyond Expectation, felling very ordinary Bays at 1 Piece of Eight and half *per* Yard, and other things in proportion, so that we have Provisions very cheap,

August 29. Capt. *Cooke* buried one *John. Edwards*, a Youth, who died of a Complication of Scurvey and the Pox, which he got from a loathsome Negro, whom we afterwards gave to the Prisoners, that she might do no further Mischief on board.

In the Afternoon we concluded how to proceed from this Place as follows.

At a Committee held on board the *Duke* the 29*th* of *August*, 1709. in *Tecames* Road.

We have consider'd our mean Stock of Provisions, and that our Time is far spent; therefore do think it for the good of the Voyage to part with federal Negroes, besides those taken in the last Prize, and to wake as good a Contract as we can with two or more of the substantial Prisoners, and to return their Produce to Alderman Batcheller and Company our Owners in Bristol, in the best manner we can, having no other Method to make an advantage of them; we now being design'd to cruise for the Manila Ship: But if any Accident parts us, then our Place of Rendevouz is in the Latitude of Cape Corientes in sight of Land. It is likewise agreed to sell the Hull of the last Prize, to carry the small Bark with us, and to turn one of the Guiaquil Prisoners ashore here, in order to save Provisions.

The. Dover, Pres. William Stratton,

Woodes Rogers, Tho. Glendall,

Stephen Courtney, John Connely,

William Dampier, John Bridge,

Edw. Cooke, John Ballett,

Robert Frye, Lan, Appleby. Cha. Pope,

Then we found it necessary to agree as follows.

August 29. 1709.

IN *consideration of the great Risque that Capt. Edward Cooke and Capt. Robert Frye ran in attacking the Marquiss, when in the Hands of the Spaniards, we do in behalf of the Owners agree to give Capt. Cooke the Black Boy Dublin, and Capt. Frye the Black Boy Emauel of Martineco, as a free Gift.*

Tho. Dover, Pres. Charles Pope,

Woodes Rogers, John Connely,

Stephen Courtney, John Bridge,

William Dampier, John Ballet,

William Stratton, Lan. Appleby.

*August.*30. Yesterday *Peter Harry* a *Frenchman*, and *Lazarus Luke* a *Portuguese*, both good Sailors, ran from our Yall ashore. This *Peter Harry* was he who shot a Centinel at *Guiaquil* as beforemention'd. We did not punish him, because he was a Foreigner, and did not well understand *English*, but suppose he was afraid of a Prosecution in *England*. Yesterday Evening at the abovemention'd Committees aboard our Ship, after a long dispute, some Measures were agreed on contrary to my Expectations. If we had not grown irresolute since we left *Gorgona*, but continued our Design to put our old Ransomer ashore at *Manta*, and part with our Clog the *Marquiss*, which I so earnestly press'd the 9*th* instant, by this time in; all human probability we should have made good our Bargain to the advantage of the Voyage, besides getting Provisions and Necessaries that we shall mightily want. The Goods that we might have vended there for ready Money, I fear will rot before we get the like Opportunity, Time being now so far spent, we must proceed as we agreed for the *Gallapagos* to get Turtle to lengthen our Provisions, and then for the Coast of *Mexico* to look for the *Manila* Ship bound for *Acapulca*. The 2 Negroes given to Capt. *Cooke* and Mr. *Frye* in the Committee yesterday, is not an equivalent Gratuity for the Risques they voluntarily ran when they attack'd the *Havre de Grace*, now call'd the *Marquiss*. Such Actions ought sometimes to be particularly rewarded among us, else we may lose great Opportunities of Advantage, for want of due Encouragement to personal Bravery, and in this Action where there was bur a few concerned, 'twas a fit and cheap way of encouraging the rest, without Offence to any. We put our young Padre ashore, and gave him, as he desir'd, the prettied young Female Negro we had in the Prize, with some Bays, Linnen, and other things, for his good Services in helping to promote our Trade for Provisions here. We sent also a Male Negro and Piece of Bays to the *Tecames* Padre, in acknowledgment of his Kindness. The young Padre parted with us extremely pleas'd, and leering under his Hood upon his black Female Angel, we doubt he will crack a Commandment with her, and wipe off the Sin with the Church's Indulgence. The *Indians* ashore promise to bring our Men to us, if they can find 'em, we having offer'd 'em a large Gratuity to do it.

August 31. Yesterday in the Afternoon we put ashore our useless Negroes, I having concluded with Sen. *Navarre*, and taken the best Methods we could to be paid at *Jamaica* for them, he had also 4 Bales of Bays, and one Piece of Camlet, and became obliged to our Owners for 3500 Peices of Eight, to be remitted by way of *Portobello*, with the *English* trading Sloops to *Jamaica*; which if he do, 'tis much better than to turn the Negroes ashore as Prisoners of War, as otherwise we must have done to save Provisions. Capt. *Courtney* took one Obligation, and I the other, he having sign'd a Duplicate to us. We had the best Opinion of this Man's Honesty and Ability, which made us trust him solely. In the Evening we clear'd our Prisoners, and put them all aboard the Prize, which we left in the Road with only one ordinary Anchor and Hawser, and no Rigging, except what belong'd to the Fore-sail and Fore-yard, which we left them to run the Vessel at High Water into the River. We turn'd ashore here our lead responsible Hostage for *Guiaquil*, resolving to keep but two, which must be carried home. According to the last Conclusion in a Committee of the 29*th* instant, we came to sail, at 6 this Morning. Capt. *Cook* lost, *Spanish* Negroes, which he supposed swam ashore from his Ship in the Night. A fresh Gale at S. S. W. At Noon Cape St. *Francisco* bore S. by W. ½ W. distant about 6 Leagues.

The Land to the Northward, which is the Limits of the Bay of *Tecames*, is a long bluff high Point, and looks white down to the Water. The next Land to the Southward of *Tecames* is also white Cliffs, but not so high. I saw no Land on any pare of the Shore, like those white Cliffs. Between them, which is about 3 Leagues, the Land is lower, full of Wood, and trimming inward makes a. small Bay, and the Village of *Tecames* lies in the Bottom, consisting of 7 Houses and a Church, all low built of split Bamboes, cover'd with Palmetto Leaves, and standing on Posts, with Hog-sties under them. These Houses have notch'd Pieces of Timber instead of Stairs to get up to 'em. The Village lies close by the Water-Side, and may be seen when the Bay is open above 4 Leagues. 'Tis supposed they had sent off their best Furniture on notice of oar Approach, for there was nothing of Worth in their Houses nor Church. The Women had only a Piece of Bays tied about their Middle. The Men are dextrous at hunting and fishing. There is a large Village about 4 Leagues off, where the Padre resides, and several *Indians* live between these Villages. The next River, 3 Leagues to the Northward, is very large, and call'd *Rio de las Esmeraldas*, but shoal'd; the Country about is thinly inhabited by *Indians*, Mullattoes and Samboes. By the Village of *Tecames* there's a River into which a Boat may enter at half Tide; it flows here above 3 Fathom Water, the Flood runs to the Northward, and the Ebb to the Southward; there is an infinite Number of Plantains for 3 Days Journey into the Country, the nearest are about a League from the Houses, and were brought to our Boats down this River in their Canoes. Here runs a great Surf on the Shore, so that were it not in these Parts of the World,, it would be but an ordinary Road. Ships generally come in from the Southward, or at least directly in with the Southernmost white Land, and then bear away, because (as we were inform'd) there is an ugly Shole runs off the Northermost white Land, about 2 Leagues into the Sea, being the Place where we had but 8 Fathom Water on the 23d instant, as I noted before. We now came in from abreast off Cape St. *Francisco*, Lac. I°. 00". N. and this lies in about E. N. E. near 6 Leagues from Cape S*t. Francisco.* We came no nearer than half a League of the Shore, because there is a small Shole off of a Point about half way between *Tecames* and the Cape, which is an indifferent high Promontory, and as we made it, falls down like Stairs to the Water. We had good clean Ground where we rode near half a League from the Shore, in 7 Fathom Watery, but a League into the Bottom of the Bay, where the Houses lie, there's not above 3 Fathom a good Musket-shot from the Shore. There is another River enters in by a single House between us and *Tecames* Village, where we fetch'd our Water about 2 Leagues up this River; and it's very narrow, and shoal'd all from the Entrance; we went in on half Flood. Here's Sea and Land Breezes, as well as on all this Coast near the Main Land;the Sea Breeze at W. and W. S. W. the Land Breeze at S. and S. by E. The Sea Breeze comes generally in the After-noon, and holds till Midnight, when comes the Land Breeze, which dies away calm towards the Middle of the Day. There's a Rock under Water at quarter Flood, and a Shoal above a Cable's Length off Shore, from the first Point as you go in for the narrow River where we water'd. A Ship ought not to come to an Anchor near the Shore, if High Water, in less than 6 Fathom, because at certain times, and out of course, as the *Indians* told us, the Tide ebbs exceed-ing low. It's dry Weather here, tho' showry to the Northward, being the Lim-its of the Rains at this time of the Year. From *June* to *December* 'tis always dry, and from the Beginning of *January* to the last of *May* there are Showers now and then.

The *Indians* about this Place are sometimes barbarous to the S*paniards*, as our Prisoners tell us. Our People saw here about 50 armed with Bows and Arrows, and some good Fire-Arms; they are worse to engage than double the Number of *Spaniards*, so that it would have been folly in us to land Men here, where there is so little to be got; and the *Indians* with poison'd Arrows and Fire-Arms would line the Bushes down to the Water-side, and no doubt we should have lost many of our Men, had we landed by force; so that we are all extremely obliged to Mr. *White* our Linguist, for negotiating a Trade in so peaceable a manner with these poor mischievous Wretches, which must injustice be ascrib'd to his good Management, he accomplishing it voluntar-ily with the Danger of his Life.

'Twas off this Cape that sir *Francis Drake* in 1578. took the rich Plate Prize; and sir *Richard Hawkins* was taken by the S*paniards* in this Bay off of *Tecames* in 1594 both in Queen *Elisabeth's* Time.

Sept. 1 At 6 this Morning Cape St. *Francisco* bore S. E. distant 10 Leagues, from whence we take our Departure. Had fair Weather, Wind at S.

W. by S. We saw many Water-snakes, one of 'em crawl'd up the Side of Capt. *Cooke's Ship*, but was beat off by his Men. The S*paniards* say their Bite is incurable.

Sept. 6. This day I had Capt. *Courtney*, Capt. *Cooke*, and Capt. *Dampier* aboard, who dined with us, Capt. *Cooke* complaint of his Ship being crank, and that we need not have tack'd so near the Shore, since we might easily fetch the *Gallapagos* without Tacking. All agree to this except our Pilot, who is very positive of seeing other Islands about 100 or 110 Leagues from the Main under the Equinox. He tells us he was at them formerly when he was a Buccaneer, and has describ'd 'em in one of the Volumes he calls his Voyages, and says that those Islands we were at lay to the Westward of them; but he must be mistaken, or we had seen them in the last Runs to and from these Islands.

Sept. 8. We are run over and beyond where our Pilot affirm'd the Islands were, and no sight of them; so we all agree that the Islands he was at when a buccaneering can be no other but those we were at, and are going to now; the nearest part of them lies 165 Leagues to the Westward of the Main Land.

Sept. 10. The 8*th* we made one of the *Gallapagos* Islands, and in the Morning hoisted out our Pinnace; Capt. *Dover* and Mr. *Glendall* went in her for the Shore. The *Dutchess's* Pinnace return'd very soon laden with Turtle.

Sept. II Yesterday we came to an Anchor in about 30 Fathom Water, about 2 Miles off Shore, being rocky at bottom. In letting go the Anchor the Bucy Rope was immediately cut off, and our Ship drove; so that we thought our Cable was also cut, but after driving about half a Mile the Ship rode very well. In the Evening our Boats that left us after we came to an Anchor, return'd laden with excellent good Turtle: We sent our Yawl and some Men ashore to turn those Creatures in the Night, but to no purpose, because we afterwards found they only came ashore in the Day I sent away our Pinnace, and Lieut. *Frye* to sound out a better anchoring Place, while we hove up the Anchor, and came to sail. Our Boat return'd, and by 10 a Clock we had our Ship again to an Anchor within less than a Mile off the Shore, right against a white sandy Bay. The outermost great Rock being near the Middle of the Island, bore N. by E. distant 6 Miles; the little Rock appearing like a Sail bore W. by S. about 4 Miles. Here we rode very smooth in good sandy Ground; the Wind amongst these Islands generally blows from the S. E. to the S. by W. I went ashore in the Pinnace, and carried Men to walk round the Sandy Bay to get Turtle. The Island is high like the rest, but some low Land on this side down to the Sea; it's very rocky, dry and barren, without Water, like those we have already seen.

Sept. 12. This Morning I sent to the *Dutchess*, who was at an Anchor a good distance from us, to know how they were stock'd with Turtle. At 10 the Boat return'd with an Account they had about 150 Land and Sea Turtle, but not generally so large as ours: We had no Land Turtle as yet, but about 150 Sea Turtle; the *Marquiss* had the worst Luck.

Sept. 13 The *Dutchess's* People having inform'd us where they got their Land Turtle, I sent our Pinnace, which at Night return'd with 37,and some Salt they found in a Pond; and the Yawl brought 20 Sea Turtle, so that we are very full of them. some of the largest of the Land Turtle are about 100 Pound Weight, and those of the Sea upwards of 400: The Land Turtle lay Eggs on our Deck; our Men brought some from the Shore about the bigness of a

Goose's Egg white, with a large thick Shell exactly round. These Creatures are the ugliest in Nature, the Shell not unlike the Top of an old Hackney Coach, as black as Jet, and so is the outside Skin, but shrivel'd and very rough; the Lees and Neck are long, and about the bigness of a Man's Wrist, and they have Club Feet as big as one's Fist shaped much like those of an Elephant, with 5 thick Nails on the Fore Feet, and but 4 behind; the Head little, and Visage small, like a Snake, and look very old and black; when at first surpriz'd, they shrink their Neck, Head and Legs under their Shell, Two of our Men, with Lieut. S*tratton, and* the Trumpeter of the *Dutchess*, affirm, they saw vast large ones of this sort about 4 Foot high; they mounted 2 Men on the Back of one of them, who with its usual flow Pace carried them, and never minded the Weight: They suppos'd this could hot weigh less than 700 Pound. I don't affect giving Relations of strange Creatures so frequently done by others already in print; but where an uncommon Creature falls in my way, I shall not omit it. The S*paniards* tell us they know of none elsewhere in these Seas. This Morning we began heeling our Ship, and found that abundance of Worms had enter'd the Sheathing; we scrub'd, clean'd, and tallow'd as low as we could.

Sept. 14. Yesterday Afternoon we sent a Boat ashore for Wood, they brought off the Rudder and Boltsprit of a small Bark; we fancy'd it might be Mr. *Hatley's* that we lost amongst these Islands when here before, but.on view perceiv'd it to be much older. We also found 2 Jars, and a Place where Fire had been made on the Shore, but nothing to give us farther Hopes of poor Mr. *Hattley*. Our Pinnace came aboard and brought about 18 Bushells of Salt, and 18 Land Turtle more; the Men commend them for excellent Food, especially the Land Turtle, which makes very good Broth, but the Flesh never boils tender: for my own part, I could eat neither sort yet. Having got as much Turtle on board, as we could eat while good, we agreed to make the best of our Way to the Coast *of Mexico*, and this Morning our Consort and the *Marquiss* were under Sail by 8 a Clock, but we lying farther in were becalm'd, and could not follow them. We caught a good quantity of Fish here, which we split and salted for our future Spending. About 12 a Clock, being calm, we weighed our Anchor, and with the Help of our Boats and Ships Oars got off the Shore.

Sept. 15. We had a fine Breeze, canoe up to the rest, and agreed to lye by with our Heads to the Eastward, till Mid-night, being in sight of the Island and Rock where we lost poor *Hattley*, when last here. In the Morning we stood to the Westward amongst the Islands.

Sept. 16. At 4 a Clock in the Afternoon we sent our Yawl for Capt. *Cooke* and Capt. *Courtney*, with whom we agreed to bear away, seeing so many Islands and Rocks to the Westward, we did not care to incumber our selves amongst them in the Night. By 6 we found the Remedy worse than the Disease, and at Mast-head could see all low Rocks almost joining from Island to Island, that we seem'd Land-lock'd for three Parts of the Compass, and no Way open but to the S. E. from whence we came., so we resolv'd to return that Way, and made short Trips all Night, keeping Continual sounding for fear of Shoals, and had from 40 to 60 Fathom Water. In the Morning we had got far enough to Windward to return. We could have no Observation by the Sun, being in our Zenith, tho' we find the Weather here much colder than in any Latitude within 10 Degrees of each Side the Equinox.

Sept. 17. Yesterday Afternoon I went a-board the *Marquiss*, being brought too between the two Islands, in sight of the rendezvous Rock I have so often mention'd: Mean while the *Dutchess* (not being so well provided with Turtle as we) sent her Boat; a-shore on another Island, where they got her Lading of excellent Turtle, leaving a vast Number a-shore that they could not bring away. We have as many a-board as we have Room for, being, as we suppose, enough to last us to the *Tres Marias*, if they live. At 7 we all join'd, and agreed to lie by, till 2 in the Morning, when we again jogg'd on 'with an easy sail till Day-break. We were a-breast of the Thorowfare, where WE tried for Water the last time. I order'd a Gun to be fir'd at a venture, to see if it were possible Mr. *Hattley* could be there alive, and then seeing or hearing us, might make a Smoak a-shore, as a Signal, but we had no such good Luck; so that our Hopes of him are all vanish'd, and we finally conclude, that we can do no more for him than we have done already.

The 18th and 19th we saw several more Islands, one of 'em a large one, which we suppos'd reach'd near the Equinoctial, and abundance of small Islands betwixt us; the 19th at Noon, we had an indifferent good Observation. Lat. 2°. 2". N.

The *Gallapagos* Islands need no further Description than I have at several Places given of them; only that I believe, as others before have observed, that the Turtle come a-shore in the sandy Bays of these Islands, all the Year round.

We saw in all (some that we searched and others that we viewed at a Distance, at both times) no less than 50, but none that had the least Appearance of fresh Water. The *Spanish* Reports agree that there is but one that has any; which lies about Lat. I°. 30". S. Sen. *Morell* tells me, that a *Spanish* Man of War employed to cruize for Pyrates, was once at an Island that lies by it self in the Lat. I°. 20 or 30". S. They call it *S. Maria de l'Aquada*, a pleasant Island and good Road, full of Wood, and plenty of Water and Turtle, of both sorts, with Fish, *&c.* lying about 140 *Spanish* Leagues West from the Island *Plata*, but I believe it's at least 30 Leagues more, and that it's no other but the same Island, where Cape. *Davis* the *English* Buccaneer recruited, and all the Light he has left to find it again is, that it lies to the Westward of those Islands he was at with the other Buccaneers, which as I have before examin'd, can be no other than these Islands we have been twice at. We had no occasion to look for this Island the second Trip, tho' I believe it's easy to find it without farther Directions. Here's most sorts of Sea Birds amongst these Islands and some Land Birds, particularly Hawks of several forts, and Turtle Doves, both so very tame that we often hit them down with Sticks. I saw no fort of Beasts; but there are Guanas in abundance, and Land Turtle almost on every Island: 'Tis strange how the latter got here, because they can't come of themselves, and none of that sort are to be found on the Main. Seals haunt some of these Islands, but not so numerous, nor their Fur so good as at *Juan Fernando's*. A very large one made at me 3 several times, and had I not happen'd to have a Pike-staff pointed with Iron in my Hand, I might have been kill'd by him; (one of our Men having narrowly escap'd the Day before.) I was on the level Sand when he came open mouth'd at me out of the Water, as quick and fierce as the most angry Dog let loose. I struck the Point into his Breast, and wounded him all the three times he made at me, which forc'd him at last to retire with an ugly Noise, snarling and shewing his long Teeth at me out of the Water: This amphibious Beast was as big as a large Bear.

Sept. 22. The *Marquiss* had sprung a large Leak, for want of good Caulking at first in *Gorgona*: I went aboard with our Carpenter, who assisted theirs, and with a Piece of Lead nail'd over the Leak (being in the Water's Edge) soon stopt it, and we made Sail again in a little time. Wind at S. by E. We had a good Observation. N. Lat. 6°. 9". Every Day as we leave the Equinoctial more distant the Heat encreases very much.

October I. Yesterday we made the main Land of *Mexico*; it bore N. E. distant about 10 Leagues. We hoisted out our Yawl, and fetch'd aboard Capt *Cooke*, and his Lieutenant Mr. *Pope*, Capt. *Courtney* and Capt. *Dampier*; the latter says he knows this high Land; but the Latt. directs us all to know it. Capt. *Dampier*, near this Place, five Years past, met the *Manila Ship* in the St. *George*, and had a Fight at a Distance, but he says for want of Men could not board her, and after a short Dispute, was forced to let her alone. We hall'd off the Shore, W. N. W. not caring to be near enough to be seen from the Land, to allarm the Coast too soon. We had often Showers of Rain, Wind at S. S. E.

Octob. 2. Most part of this 24 Hours we had Squalls and then little Wind at S. S. E. intermixt with sultry hot Weather. Our Men begin to be unhealthy again, two having lately dropt down on the Deck, but after bleeding came pretty well to themselves. We agreed with our Consort to lie by from 8 at Night till day break. At Noon it clear'd up, and we saw the Land, at least 8 Leagues off, tho' we seem'd just under it, it was so very high. We made Cape *Corientes* bearing N. E. about 8 League, by which we judge according to our Observation at Noon, that it lies in Lat. 20°. 10". N. We know it to be Cape *Corientes*, because we could see no Land to the Northward of it, and that it was a Head-land. Capt. *Dampier* has been here also, but it's a long Time ago. We all agreed it was the Cape, and that we had best hall off N. W. to look for the Islands *Tres Marias*, which are not far from this Gape, but we are not certain of their Situation.

Octob. 4. Yesterday Afternoon, at 4, the Cape bore E. N. E. about 10 Leagues. We kept on under an easy Sail all Night. In the Morning we saw 2 Islands, being very clear Weather, at least 14 Leagues distant, one bearing N. by W. and the other N. by E. At Noon we had a good Observation. Lat. 20°. 45". N.

Tho' our Men have their Fill of Land and Sea Turtle, which keeps them from the Scurvy, yet I find them weak, it being but a faintly Food, except they had sufficient Bread or Flower with it, they having but a Pound and a Quarter of Bread or Flower, for five Men a Day, to prolong our Stock of Bread against we come to live wholly on our salt Provisions, and then must be forced to allow more. *Octob.* 6. In the Morning we sent Lieutenant *Frye* in the Pinnace ashore on the Eastermost Island, to try whether there was any good Road or Convenience for us to recruit there. At 9 they return'd, and told me the Island had foul Ground near half a Mile from the Shore; bad Anchoring, worse Landing, and no fresh Water; but Wood enough. A melancholy Story, our Water growing short. We hall'd on a Wind, for the middle Island which Capt. *Dampier*, I do believe, can remember he was at, when he belong'd to Captain S*wann*, and found Water. Being little Wind we sent our Boat towards the Island, to view it before we could get thither with the Ship.

Octob. 7. The *Dutchess's* People, and our Pinnace had been ashore at several Places on the S. E. side of the Island, and found bitter Water at every

Place. Our Ship got soon to an Anchor near the *Dutchess*, in 11 Fathom Water and sandy Ground, about a Mile and a half off Shore.

Octob. **8.** Those that had been on the Island saw no Sign of Peoples being lately there, but found a human Skull above Ground, which we suppose to have been one of the two *Indians* Capt. *Dampier* tells us were left here by Capt. *Swann*, about 23 Years ago; for Victuals being scarce with these *Buccaneers*, they would not carry the poor *Indians* any farther, but, after they had served their Turns, left them to make a miserable End on a desolate Island. We kept a Light out all Night, and a great Fire in the Island, that if the *Marquiss* and Bark, who had left Company, saw it, and had a Gale, they might come into Anchor Ground. But having no sight of them at Day-break, I went on board our Consort, and proposed my going out to look after 'em; but they made Light of it and thought it needless, believing they would be in after us, without any Assistance. The Recruit of Cattle, Hogs, and Plantains, at *Tecames*, held to the *Gallapagos*, and we have fed on the Turtle we got there ever since, excepting these two last Days. This accidental Stock of fresh Food has been some Refreshment to our Men, and prolongs our Stock of *European* Provisions. Now Bread or Flower will be the first thing wanting. We had little Wind Northerly, and often calm.

Octob. **9.** Yesterday I sent Lieut. *Glendall* to view the other side of the Island, and he brought me back word it was much better than this, with sandy Bays, and signs of Turtle in the Sand, which he believed came ashore the last Night. I sent back the Boat and Men to try to get Turtle; and this Morning they came back with their Boat's Load of very good ones, and left another lading behind them ready turn'd; they also had found indifferent good Water on the N. E. side of the Island, which rejoiced us to be so unexpectedly supplied; for the other Water on this side the Island, had purg'd those that drank it aboard the *Dutchess* like Physick. We had no sight yet of the Bark or *Marquiss*. 'Tis very hot, with an Air of Wind Northerly, but almost calm. Our Consort has sent their Pinnace in quest of the missing Ships.

Octob. **10.** Lieut. *Connely* of the *Dutchess*, that went in quest of 'em return'd without any News. And we having begun trimming our Ship, and stripping the Rigging; the *Dutchess* desired to go and look for them, mean while we were to employ our People to cut Wood and get a Stock of Turtle against their Return. We found an excellent Run of Water on the other side of the Island, and sent our Pinnace to view the Westermost Island, to see if either of the missing Ships had got into Anchor here.

Capt. *Dover* being willing to remove aboard the *Dutchess*, I desired our Officers to make the following *Memorandum*.

Tres S. Maria Islands.

WE the under-written, appointed part of a Committee now present on board the Duke, *decertify, that Capt.* Dover *requested to go on board the* Dutchess; *and desired us to take notice it was his own Choice so to do. Witness our Hands, this* 10*th Day of* October, 1709.

Stephen Courtney, Robert Frye, Woodes Rogers, Thomas Glendall, William Dampier, Lanc. Appleby.

At the same time the following Agreement was made where to meet with the *Dutchess*, and they took a Copy with them.

In case we aboard tie Duke *don't see the* Dutchess *return in* 10 *Days, then to be ready to sail, and first look in the Latitude* 20°. N. *in sight of the Land*: *If not to be found there, to run off the Land farther into Sea, and then in sight again, but no nearer than within* 6 *Leagues of the Land, to prevent Discovery. We are to bring all full of Water and Turtle for a second Recruit, to keep a continual Look-out for them, and leave a Signal at the South End of this Island.*

Octob. II According to this Agreement Capt. *Dover* went himself, and sent his Servant with his Necessaries aboard the *Dutchess*. In the Evening they came to sail, and carry'd above 100 large Turtle that we brought to them in our Boats for victualling, to save Salt Provisions. We hope the Current, that has hitherto run to Leeward, will quickly shift, and facilitate their Return, that we may not be obliged to follow them. I order'd 6 Yards of red and white Bays to be join'd together, to spread it as a Signal on the Island for directing them to a Letter from me in a Bottle by it, should we unexpectedly quit the Place in her Absence.

Octob. 12. Last Night our Pinnace, which had been in quest of the missing Ships, return'd from the Westermost Island, and saw no Sign of the Ships. Our People tell us, they heard aboard the *Dutchess*, that the Bark had not 2 Days Water when they left them, which made me very uneasy left she should go to the Main after Water, which would discover us, and might prove the Occasion of losing her also.

Yesterday we put Negroes ashore to cut Wood for the absent Ships, and last Night our Boat came off, and brought but 3 out of 10, 7 having run away into the Woods: Immediately we dispatch'd several Men round the Island with Arms, to endeavour to catch 'em when they come down out of the Woods to get Food at the Sea-side. These Negroes had an Antipathy against *Michael Kendall* the *Jamaica* Negro, and design'd to have kill'd him, had not one of those that came aboard given him timely Notice of it. A Negro amongst the Runaways could write well, which made me get our Ransomers to write 3 *Spanish* Papers of Encouragement to incline the Fugitives upon sight of 'em to return, promising that Negro his Freedom, and every thing else he or the rest of them could reasonably desire. These Papers we nail'd up against Trees by the Brook-side, where they will be sure to see them. My Reason for so doing was to prevent these Fellows from giving notice of us on the Coast, if they reach'd the Main on Bark Logs, which they could make with the Hatchets they had to cut Wood for us. If this Method fails of Success, 'tis in vain to hope for finding them by searching the Island, every part of it being full of duck Woods and Prickles, which make it unpassable. On the sandy Shore we began to imploy our Rope-makers to spin Twine for the *Dutchess* and *Marquiss*, who complain their Stock is short. Our People found another Spring of excellent Water on the other side of the Island.

Octob. 13 Yesterday Afternoon the *Dutchess* came in sight, with the Bark in Tow, and soon after we saw *the Marquiss*. We kept a Light out, that they might the better find us. In the Morning we saw them at Anchor between the 2 Islands. I weigh'd in their sight, and put out our Ensign for 'em to follow us to the Watering Place on the other side of the Island, which they did accordingly. The Wind continues Northerly, with a Lee Current.

Octob. 14. Yesterday in the Afternoon we came to an Anchor in 16 Fathom Water off the N.E. Side of the Island. I went immediately in our Pinnace aboard the *Dutchess*, that was then under Sail with the Bark in Tow, 2 Leagues from us. About 4 they and the *Marquiss* came to an Anchor; I told them of our Negroes deserting us, which had prevented our getting a good Stock of Wood in their Absence, and we agreed to keep all our Negroes on board the Ships, and narrowly watch 'em to prevent their Desertion for the future.

Mr. *Duck*, who was Master of the Bark, told me the Day they lost sight of us their Water was expended, and two of the Bark's Crew in a very small Canoe lest her almost out of sight of Land, and being smooth calm Weather, fortunately got aboard the *Marquiss* to acquaint Capt. *Cooke* they had no Water, upon which he bore down to them, and took her in Towe. Had he not done this, the Bark must have run for the Main Land to get Water, which might have alarm'd the Enemy, and endanger'd the Loss of the Vessel and Men. They were not above 8 Leagues off the Island, but it being hazey Weather, and having little Wind, and a Lee Current, they could not get in, or see us.

Octob. 15. We could not get to the Watering Place near the N. W. Corner of the Island, till 7 last Night, when we anchor'd in 7 Fathom Water, clean sandy Ground, about half a Mile from the Shore; the Westermost Point bore W. by N. about 3 Miles and the Eastermost E. by S. 6 Miles. The Body of the Westermost Island bore N. W. distant 4 Leagues. This Morning we got our empty Casks ashore, and began filling Water, Had we not very fair Weather at this Season, and little Wind, this Place would be but an ordinary Road.

Octob. 16. Capt. *Courtney* sent me word, that the *Marquiss*, who has been again missing, was well moored at the S. E. Side of the Island, and could not easily turn it hither; so we agreed she should lie there, and we would water her from hence with our Boats.

0ctob. 18. Lieutenant *Fry* went in the Pinnace last Night to view the Weather Island, and he returned this Morning, and told me there was a Road, but not very good, and that he could find no Water.

Octob. 19. We hal'd the Sain, and caught some Fish. This Morning we found some Bail Goods damaged, which we believe they received before we had 'em; we unpack'd and dry'd 'em, and sold what was most damaged amongst the Ships Company, repacking and flowing a way the rest. Very hot Weather, and a little Air of Wind North.

Octob. 23. We began this Morning to take aboard Our Turtle, and the Remainder of our Wood and Watery designing, in the Evening to return, and anchor on the S. E. Side of the Island, to join the *Marquiss*, and agree on a Station to cruize for the *Manila* Ship. Our Mea shot a Snake ashore, and brought it aboard dead; I saw it measured 15 Inches round, and near 10 Foot long; some of 'em are much larger; this was of a hazle colour, and spotted, called by the S*paniards* here a Leopard Serpent.

Octob. 24. All the Officers met aboard the *Dutchess*, and sign'd a Duplicate of every Conclusion in all Committees since we have been in these Seas. Many of the Resolutions wrote on board this Ship were in my Custody, and others wrote aboard the *Dutchess* in Capt. *Courtney's*; but it was thought advisable that each of us should have all the Copies signed alike. While we were together, we agreed on a Station to lie for the *Manila* Ship; but I lately proposed parting, and to meet again at Cape *Corientes* or any other appointed Station, and for us in the *Duke* to cruize off the same Place where Capt.

Dampier met the *Manila* Ship in the *St. George*, or else the *Marquiss* and *Dutchess* to take that Station, and I would go to Cape *St. Lucas*; since by either Method we should have 2 Chances for the Prize, and get Provisions, which we begin to want very much. This Method might prove much better than to be at one Place, where we could not be supply'd with Provisions; but the Officers of the *Dutchess* and *Marquiss* seeming unwilling to part Companies, and the Majority thinking Cape *St. Lucas* the properest Place to lie for the *Manila* Ship bound for *Acapulco*, I drew up our Resolution, which was signed by the whole Council, who on this Occasion were altogether.

At a Committee held on board the Dutchess at the Islands Tres Marias, October 24, 1709.

We whose Names are hereunto subscribed, being Members of a Committee appointed to manage the Affairs of the Duke, Dutchess and Marquiss, having recruited our Ships at these Islands, and being in a readiness to put to Sea again; We have examin'd the Opinion of Capt. Dampier, appointed Pilot by the Owners of the Ships Duke and Dutchess in Bristol, and have been well informed from all the Intelligences we have frequently had from Prisoners since our being in the South Seas, and do now finally determine to cruize off Cape St. Lucas, the Southermost Cape of California, in such Methods, and with such Signals to each other, as shall be agreed on in our next Committee.

We resolve with the utmost Care and Diligence to wait here the coming of the Manila Ship belonging to the Spaniards, and bound for Acapulco; whose Wealth on beard her we hope will prompt every Man to use his utmost Conduct and Bravery to conquer. This is our Opinion the Day above.

Tho. Dover, Pres. John Connely, Woodes Rogers, William Bath,

Stephen Courtney, Tho. Glendall,

Edw. Cooke, Geo. Milbourne,

William Dampier, Robert Knowlman,

Robert Frye, John Bridge,

William Stratton, John Ballett,

Cha. Pope, Lan. Appleby.

Chapter XI

Being all supply'd with Wood, Water, and Turtle, we came to sail at Eleven this Forenoon, Wind at N. by W. a fine Gale; but e'er I proceed with my Journal, I will give a short Description of these Islands.

The Islands of *Tres Marias* lie N. W. in a Range at equal Distances from each other, about 4 Leagues asunder: The largest Island is the Westermost, appears to be high double Land, and about: 5 Leagues in Length; the middle Island about 3 Leagues the longest way, and the Eastermost scarce 2 Leagues; these are also middling high Lands, and full of Trees. Near the least Island arc 2 or 3 small broken white Islands, one of the outermost of these appeared so much like a Ship under Sail at a distance, that we gave the usual Signal for a Chase, but soon found our Mistake.

These Islands have abundance of different sorts of Parrots, Pigeons, Doves, and other Land Birds, of which we kill'd great Numbers, with excellent Hares, but much less then ours. We law abundance of Guanas, and some Raccoon; the latter bark'd and snarl'd at us like Dogs, but were easily beat off with Sticks.

I think the Water more worthy of Remark than any thing we saw here, because we found but two good Springs, which ran down in large Streams near others, that were very bitter and disagreeable, which I suppose might proceed from Shrubs and Roots that grow in the Water, or from some Mineral.

The Turtle here is very good, but of a different Shape from any I have seen; and tho' vulgarly there's reckon'd but 3 sorts of Turtle, we have seen 6 or 7 different sorts at several Times, and our People have eat of them all, except the very large hooping or logger-head Turtle (as they are call'd) found in *Brazil* in great plenty, and some of them above 500 *l.* Weight. We did not eat of that sort, because then our Provisions were plentiful, which made those Turtles to be slighted as coarse and ordinary Food. Those at the *Gallapagos* Islands, both He's and She's, I observed came ashore in the Day-time, and not in the Night, quite different from what I have seen or heard of the rest.

All that we caught in this Island was by turning 'em in the Night, and were She's, which came ashore to lay their Eggs, and bury them in the dry Sand: One of these had at least 800 Eggs in its Belly, 150 of which were skin'd, and ready for laying at once. I could not imagine that Turtle were 6 Weeks in hatching, as some Authors write, considering the Sun makes the Sand so very hot whereever these Eggs are found, and instead of a Shell they have nothing but a very thin Film. In order therefore to be better informed, I order'd some of our Men ashore to watch carefully for one, and suffer her to lay her Eggs without disturbance, and to take good notice of the Time and Place. Accordingly they did so, and assur'd me they found the Eggs addled in less than 12 Hours, and in about 12 more they had young ones in 'em, compleatly shap'd, and alive. Had we staid a little longer., I might have given my self and others a thorough Satisfaction in this quick Production of Nature. From hence I am inclinable to credit the Report of divers of our Sailors, who assert, that where they have found Eggs in the Sand, and look'd for 'em 3 Days after in the same place, they found nothing but Films; this shews that the young ones are hatch'd within that time. They assured me also, that they had observed oftner than once, that the young Brood run out of the Sand every day directly for the Sea in great Numbers and quicker than the old ones.

At this time here was little Fish about the Shores of this Island, and of the same sorts mention'd at other Places in these Seas; but the Plenty of Turtle at this time supplies that Defect. We the chief Officers sed deliciously here, being scarce ever without Hares, Turtle Doves, Pigeons, and Parrots of various Sizes and Colours, many had white or red Heads, with Tufts of Feathers on their Crowns. I wish 'twould hold, but 'tis in vain to tantalize our selves; for we must soon fare otherwise, and take to our old Food of almost decay'd Salt Pork and Beef, which we must prize, and heartily wish we had more on't. We found good Anchor Ground about this middle Island, and gradual Soundings from 20 to 4 Fathom Water close by the Shore. Between this and the least Island 'tis about the same Depth; where we were between them I found no Shole, but what was visible, as a Rock off the S. W. Point, and a Shole off the N. E. Point of the same, with another at a greater distance from that Point off the least Island, but neither runs above half a Mile from the Shore. I know no Danger about them, but what with Care might be easily avoided.

Where we rode we could see Spots of high Land, which I suppose was the Continent join'd by low Land between it; the Northermost bore N. by E. half E. about 16 Leagues distance: I take it to be the Starboard Entrance into the Gulph or Strait of *California*; the nearest Land to us bore E. N. E. about 12 Leagues, and the Southermost E. S. E. at least 17 Leagues, very high, which I believe is the next Head-land to the Northward, of Cape *Corientes*. I had but two Opportunities to see it just at Sun-rising, because 'twas very hazey during our Stay here, so that I might err in the Distance; but the best Directions for these Islands is thus: We account the nearest bears N. N. W. from. Cape *Corientes* 28 Leagues, and that it lies in the Lat. 21°. 15?. N; and Longit. in 111°. 40?. West from *London*, I return to my Journal.

Octob. 28. At 6 this Evening the Westermost Island bore E. N. E. 15 Leagues. The Wind has, been very little, and veerable, with a great Swell out of the N. W. I sent our Yawl with a Lieutenant aboard the *Dutchess* and *Marquiss*, with whom we agreed to spread as we ran to the Northward, that the *Acapulco* Ship might not pass us, if they should arrive sooner than we expected: We agreed to be to the Leeward, the *Marquiss* to Windward, and the *Dutchess* between us, and all to keep in sight of each other. I order'd our Surgeons and Mr. *Vanbrug* to see the Inside of the Physick Chest that Capt. *Dover* left us, and take an Inventory of what was in it. We saw no more of the Islands.

Octob. 29. Still easy Gales, and sometimes quite calm, and extream hot. We can hardly keep our Ground against the Current, that runs strong to the Southward. We are in the same Latitude, and I judge about the same Place we were 2 Days ago.

Octob. 30. This Morning one of our Negro Women cry'd out, and was deliver'd of a Girl of a tawny Colour; Mr. *Wasse* our chief Surgeon was forced to discharge the Office of a Midwife, in a close Cabbin provided for that Purpose; but what we most wanted was good Liquor, to keep up, or imitate the Womens laudable Custom of a refreshing Cup, on such an Occasion. I accidentally found a Bottle of thick strong *Peru* Wine, a good Part of which was given to the sick Woman, who desir'd more than we could spare her. She bad not been full 6 Months amongst us, so that the Child could belong to none of our Company. But to prevent the other she-Negro (call'd *Daphne)* from being debauch'd in our Ship, I gave her a strict Charge to be modest, with Threats of severe Punishment, if she was found otherwise. One of the *Dutchess's* black Nymphs having transgressed this Way, was lately whip'd at the Capston. This I mention to satisfy the censorious, that we don't countenance Lewdness, and that we took those Women aboard, only because they spoke *English*, and begg'd to be admitted for Laundresses, Cooks and Semstresses.

Nov. I. This Day we saw high Land, being the Point of *California.* By Noon the Westermost in sight bore W. by N. 8 Leagues, and the Northermost N. half W. about 10 Leagues. We had an Observation Lat. 22 °. 55". Long. 113°. 38". W. from *London.*

Nov. 2. The Westermost Land we set yesterday Noon, we make to be Cape Sr. *Lucas*, the Southermost Head-land of *California.* We agreed on Signals and Stations; and to spread S.W. into the See, off of this Cape that now bore N. by W. from us.

Nov. 3. Our Stations being concluded, I was to be the outermost Ship, the *Dutchess* in the middle, and the *Marquiss* next the Land; with the Bark to ply and carry Advice from Ship to Ship: The nearest Ship to be 6 Leagues at least, and 9 at most from the Land: By this Agreement, we could spread 15 Leagues, and see any thing that might pass us in the Day, within 20 Leagues of the Shore, And to prevent the Ships passing in the Night, we were to ply to Windward all Day, and drive at Night. Whilst we were together, we at last settled the Form of our Agreement for each Ship; that all the Ships Companies might sign it, for every one to give an Account of all Plunder he has received, that he may be charged with what's more than his Share; and those (now or for the future suspected or accus'd of Concealment) when demanded shall give their Oaths before the Commanders, to the Truth of their Accounts, and if any one was found to conceal above the Value of half a Piece of 8. he is to be severely punished, and fined 20 Times its Value: This we did to deter every one from fraudulent Practices, which if we should happily take this Ship, might also prevent Disorders.

Nov. 4. I order'd a Sailor into Irons, for threatning the Cooper; and one *Peter Clark*, an ill abusive Fellow, I order'd to have the like Punishment, because he had wished himself aboard a Pirate, and said he should be glad that an Enemy, who could over-power us, was a-long-side of us.

Nov. 5. Yesterday in the Afternoon the *Dutchess* being near, I sent our Yawl aboard with Lieut. *Glendall*, to agree more exactly on some remarkable Land, that each of us knowing the same Land Mark, might the better keep our Stations. We agreed also, that the *Marquiss* should now be in the middle, and the *Dutchess* next the Shore, as being the properest Stations. This Morning we put all manner of Lumber and Chests down, designing to keep all as clear as possible, that we might not be in a Hurry if near the *Acapulco* Ship.

Nov. 6. This Day ended our Stock of Turtle we had at the *Marias*; being all Shes, with Eggs in them, they would not keep so long as those we had at the *Gallapagos* Islands: We have for some Days thrown more dead Turtle over-board than we kill'd for eating.

Nov. 7. Yesterday I went aboard the *Marquiss*, grid desir'd them to tell Capt. *Courtney*, when he came off the Shore, that we would take the inner

Birth, and exchange again for the same Number of Days, that we might have equal Chances for seeing the *Manila* Ship; because I now think the inner Birth the likeliest. Sir *Thomas Cavendish*, in Queen *Elizabeth's* Time, took the *Manila* Ship in this Place on the 4th of November.

Nov. 12. Yesterday Afternoon, all our Ships Company sign'd the before-mention'd Agreement, finally to settle Plunder. At the same time we sign'd another Agreement, to prevent gaming and wagering: some of our Crews having already lost most of their Clothes, and what else they could make away with. To prevent those loose and dissolute Courses, we sign'd both Agreements as follows.

> *We the Officers, Seamen and Landmen belonging to the Ship Duke, having made several former Agreements concerning the equal sharing of Plunder, do now desire and agree, That each Man give an exact Account of all Clothes, Goods of Value, or Necessaries of any kind he has over and above his Dividend deliver'd him at Gorgona, or has purchased of others since, to be rightly charged to him in his Account of Plunder, by the Agents appointed; and to restore whatever he has taken without the Agents Knowledge, and to prevent any Persons detaining and concealing any Goods or Riches of any kind, now or for the future, more than their respective Shares, in order to aright Distribution of Plunder, except Arms, Chests, Knives, Roman Relickts Scizzars, Tobacco, loose Books, Pictures, and worthless Tools and Toys, and Bedding in use, which are not included in this Agreement; and those that haw already only things of this kind, are not liable to a Penalty: We do voluntarily sign this, and offer our selves to be obliged firmly by these Presents, to be under the Penalty of 20 Shillings for every Shilling value taken hid or conceal'd by any of us, or removed out of any Prize without written Orders from the Commanders publickly; and that none but the Agents already named, or to be named here after, shall detain in Possession any Plunder; but whatever is found conceal'd shall be valued, and the Persons that hid it to be find as aforesaid, which Penalty we acknowledge to be laid on us by cur own Desire, Consent, and Approbation, over and above the former Penalty agreed on, That any Person shall loose his share of every Prize or Purchase taken, whether Cargo or Plunder, that conceals of either the Value of half a Piece of 8. and this to remain in Force, to the End of the Voyage.*

> *And to encourage Discoveries of such Concealments, whatever Person discovers the Fraud of any, who shall be so imprudent as to detain more than his due, in any Goods that has not been shar'd before as Plunder, or purchas'd of the Owners Agent or Commanders; the Informer of such Fraud shall haw one Half given him gratis, cut the Offenders Shares and Wages; the other Half for the Use of the Ships Company as Plunder; which Information shall be encouraged by the Commanders of each Ship, in order to prevent Frauds, as long as this Voyage holds; and that ever hereafter Accounts shall be made up, and the Plunder immediately adjudg'd to prevent Confusion.*

> *We likewise agree, That if any of us hereafter shall without farther Proof be accus'd of concealing Plunder or Goods of Value, belonging to any Prize, he shall, on request, before a Committee of all or either*

of the Ships Commanders and chief Officers, voluntarily make Affidavit to answer fully and satisfactorily to such Questions as shall then and there be demanded of him, in order to prevent fraudulent Concealments, and on his Refusal, agrees to be punish'd or degraded, and to be subject to such Penalty as a general Committee shall think fit to inflict on him or them. Every one hereunto subscribed is within 3 Days from the Date hereof to settle his Account of Plunder; after which time, this Instrument is in full Force and not before.

Sign'd by the Officers and Men of each Ship.

The Agreement to prevent Gaming was as follows.

WE the Ship's Company belonging to the Ship Duke now in the South Seas, being Adventurers so far to improve our Fortunes in a private Man of War, under the Command of Capt. Woodes Rogers, who has a lawful Commission from his Royal Highness Prince George of Denmark, and considering the apparent Hazard of our Lives in these remote Parts; do mutually agree to prevent the growing Evil now arising amongst us, occasion'd by frequent Gaming, Wagering, and abetting at others Gaming, so that some by chance might thus too slightly get Possession of what his Fellow-Adventurers have dangerously and painfully earn'd. To prevent this intolerable Abuse, we shall forbear and utterly detest all Practices of this kind for the future during the whole Voyage, till our safe Arrival in Great Britain, where good Laws of this kind take place, and designing effectually to confirm this our Desire and Agreement, We do jointly remit all sorts of Notes of Hand, Contracts, Bills, or Obligations of any kind whatsoever, that shall any ways pass, directly or indirectly, sign'd by either of us after the Date hereof, provided the Sum in each Note be for Gaming, Wagering, or Abetting any way whatsoever by any of us; and to prevent our being misled for the future, all manner of Obligations of this kind, and for this Confederation, shall be wholly invalid, and unlawful here, and in Great Britain or Ireland; And thoroughly to secure this Method, we farther jointly agree, that no Debt from this Time forward shall be lawfully contracted from Man to Man amongst us, unless by the Commanders Attestation, and enter'd on the Ship's Book, it shall appear done publickly and justly to prevent each others Frauds being conniv'd amongst us; And that none of us may fraudulently do ill things of this kind for the future, and make a Pretence to Ignorance, We haw all publickly and voluntarily set our Hands, desiring the true Intent and Meaning hereof may take place without the least Evasion, it being (as we very well know) for our common Interest and publick good, that not one of us employ'd on this dangerous and remote Undertaking, might be so unhappy to arrive at his wish'd for Country and Habitation poor and dejected: And being throughly sensible of the Necessity of this Agreement, we haw set our Hands.

Sign'd by all the Officers and Men in each Ship in sight of *California*, Nov. n. 1709.

*Nov.*13. The Water being discolour'd, and we near the Shore, we hove the Lead but found no Ground.

Nov. 17. Yesterday we sent the Bark to look for Water on the Main, and this Morning they return'd, having seen wild *Indians* who padled to them on

Bark-Logs; they were fearful of coming near our People at first, but were soon prevail'd with to accept of a Knife or two and some Bays, for which they return'd 2 Bladders of Water, a Couple of live Foxes, and a dear Skin. Till now we thought the *Spaniards* had Missionaries among those People, but they being quite naked, having no sign of *European* Commodities, nor the least Word of *Spanish*; we conclude they are quite savage. We dispatch'd the Bark and Boat a second Time with odd Trifles, in hopes to get some Refreshment from 'em.

Nov. 19. Before Sun set last Night we could perceive our Bark under the Shore; and having little Wind she drove most part of the Night, that she a might be near us in the Morning. We sent our Pinnace, and brought the Men aboard, who told us, that their new Acquaintance were grown very familiar,, but were the poorest Wretches in Nature, and had no manner of Refreshment for us. They came freely aboard to eat some of our Victuals; and by Signs invited our Men ashore; the *Indians* swama-shore in the Water to guide the Bark Logs, that our Men were on, there being top much Sea to land out of our Boat: After they got safe on Shore the *Indians* led each of our Men betwixt two of 'em, up the Bank; where there was an old naked Gentleman with a Deer-skin spread on the Ground, on which they kneeled before bur People, who did the like, and wip'd the Water off their Faces, without a Cloth; those that led them from the Water-side, took the same Care of 'em for a quarter of a Mile, and led them very slowly thro' a narrow Path to their Hutts, where they found a dull Musician rubbing two jagged Sticks a-cross each other, and humming to it, to divert and welcome their new Guests. After the Ceremonies were over, our People sat on the Ground with them, eat broil'd Fish, and were attended back in the same manner, with the *Indian* Musick. The Savages brought a Sample of every thing they had except their Women, Children, and Arms, which we find are not common to Strangers: Their Knives made of Sharks Teeth, and a few other of their Curiosities, our People brought aboard to me, which I have preserved to shew what Shifts may be made.

*Nov.*21. Last Night we saw a Fire ashore, which we interpreted to be a Signal from the Inhabitants, that they had got something extraordinary for us; and we wanting Refreshments, sent our Bark and Boat this Morning with one of our Musicians, to shew that we could at least equal them in Musick.

Nov. 22. Our Boat return'd and brought an Account, that they had found a very good Bay, with a fresh Water River, and that they saw near 500 *Indians*, who lived there in small Hutts, but had no Recruit for us, besides a little Fish. They met them as customary, and pilotted the Bark to that Place, which we suppose was the same that Sir *Thomas Cavendish* recruited at in Queen *Elizabeth's* Time, *Anno* 1588.

Nov. 23 Our main Top-Gallant-Mast being broke, we got up another, but the Rope breaking the Mast fell down upon the Deck, amongst the Men, but by God's Providence hurt no body. At 8 last Night our Ship sprung a Leak; so that we were forced to keep one Pump a going.

Nov. 25. Capt. *Courtney* came aboard in his Yawl, and complain'd his Stock of Water was almost spent; I agreed with him to send in our Pinnace, and a Bark, to supply them with Water.

Nov. 26. This Morning our Pinnace return'd from Shore, brought 3 Barrels of Water, and 2 very large Fish from the *Indians*, which serv'd most of the Ships Company. Those that came from the Shore observed the *Indians* were not so friendly to our Men as customary.

Nov. 27 They refus'd to let them come a-shore after it was Night, which could not be to prevent their thieving, because the miserable Wretches had nothing to lose; yet they are jealous to keep what they have; and though they make no Use of their Land, might be afraid of Rivals.

Nov. 28. Yesterday in the Afternoon we heard the *Marquiss* fire a Gun, which was answer'd by the *Dutchess*, who had the middle Birth. We tackt immediately, and made all possible Sail, supposing they had seen a Stranger; the *Marquiss* stood to us towards the Shore, and we soon met her; by 4 a Clock I was aboard them, and enquiring into the Cause of the Alarm, was surpriz'd to hear they took us for the *Manila* Ship, and the Gun they fired was to alarm the *Dutchess* to give chase, as she had done all the day, tho 'not regarded by us, who knew the *Marquiss*, and admir'd they could mistake the *Duke*. Immediately each Ship return'd to his Station; soon after our Main-tye gave way, and our Main-yard came down at once, but did no other Damage. This Morning we saw the Bark coming off Shore, where she had been becalm'd; being longer wanting than usual, we were afraid they were cut off by the *Indians*. We got our Bale Goods up from abaft to see for the Leak, but all to no propose; we found some of the Bales that had receiv'd old Damages, which we dry'd and repack'd, and sold what was damaged among the Ship's Company.

Nov. 29. Last Night our Lazareto Door being broke open, and losing Bread and Sugar, this Morning I order'd a Search, and found the Thief; I blam'd the Steward for his Remissness; he told me he lay next the Door, with the Key fastned to his Privy parts, because he had it once stoln out of his Pocket, I suppose by the same Thief, who was so dextrous to get it now without disturbing him; but not being ingenious enough to fasten it to the same, Place, he was discover'd: His Mess-mart was also guilty, but knowing his Friends in *Bristol*, I am unwilling to punish him, tho Provisions being scarce, it makes the Crime the greater, for we expect no Recruit till we get to the *East Indies*. I order'd the first to be severely whipt at the Geers, and the other and a *Dutchman* to be afterwards left with him in Irons.

Dec. 9. Mr. *Duck* the Master of the Bark came aboard, and presented me with some Dolphins he had from the *Indians*. I order'd our Master to go with him, and endeavour, if possible, to discover the Shore along to the North-ward, to find out a better Harbour than that where the *Indians* lived, and if they met with the *Dutchess*, to tell Capt. *Courtney*, I thought it convenient for one of the Ships to go into the Bay we had already discover'd, and there to take in Water and Wood, &c. so to sit our Ships by turns to save time, and consequently Provisions, which begin to grow short with us. We were now something dubious of seeing the *Manila* Ship, because it's near a Month after the time they generally fall in with this Coast.

Dec. 14. Yesterday I went aboard the *Dutchess*, where 'twas agreed the *Marquiss* should go into the Harbour and refit with all manner of Dispatch. In the mean time we to keep the outer Birth, and the *Dutchess* to be betwixt us and the Shore, and to cruize but 8 Days longer, without we had a Prospect of the *Manila* Ship, because our Provisions grow short.

Dec. 20. Having compared our Stock of Bread, and of what would serve to prolong it, we agreed that a Committee should be held, and that every one should give his Opinion in Writing, whether we should attempt taking a Town to victual us, and so continue the Cruize for some time longer; or to make all possible Dispatch to refit, and sail hence for the Island *Guam*, one of the *Ladrones*, and there if possible to get a fresh Recruit. My Opinion was as follows.

On board the Ship *Duce*, cruising off Cape *St*. Lucas *in* California, this 19*th* of *December*, 1709.

> *Eight Days ago I was with Capts. Courtney and Cooke, and computed what Bread there might be left aboard the 3 Ships; and we all agreed there might be 64 Days Bread of all sorts for each Ship, when equally divided.*
>
> *Since which Time there is 8 Days spent, so that there should be left no more than 56 Days Bread*
>
> *But on a Rumage of both Ships Duke and Dutchess, and strictly computing every thing that will help prolong our Bread, we hope to make 14 Days more Bread*
>
> *Which may be in all 70 Days Bread to come.*
>
> *We must expect before we can get sitted hence to spend at least 9 Days, and add to that our Passage to Guam, which we can't think will be less than 50 Days, is 59 Days Bread*
>
> *By this Account, which is the utmost,- 11 Days Bread will be left when we come to Guam.*
>
> *I am of opinion now we have search'd each others Ships to prevent Frauds, that there can be no more than 11 Days Bread left when we come to Guam, as above, except we shorten our Allowance very much, which we can't do till driven to the last Extremity, our Allowance being very small already; but if we should have an unexpected long Passage from hence to Guam, it will go bard with us at the present Allowance, besides we are not certain of a Recruit at Guam.*
>
> *By the foregoing Account it's plain what Flower and Bread-kind we have left, and the risque we must now run to get to the East-Indies, with so mean a Stock. This I doubt not will be full Satisfaction to our Imployers, that we have prolonged our Cruize to the utmost Extent, in hopes to meet the Rich Manila Ship: But since Fortune has not favour'd us, we must think of other Methods to promote our Safety and Interest. Except we resolve to take a town here to victual us, 'tis evident we can't cruize, and 'tis my Opinion, that now our Time is so far spent, we ought to attempt nothing more in these Seas, left our too long Stay might be the Loss of all, because the Worm has already entred our Sheathing. For these and other Reasons, I think it highly necessary, that from this Instant we make all manner of Dispatch to fit, and sail hence for the Island of Guam, one of the Ladrones Islands, and there, if possible, to get a fresh Recruit, and consult how father to proceed for the Interest of our Imployers, and our own Advantage and Reputation. This I give as my Opinion aboard the Dutchess, this 20th of December, 1709.*
>
> *Woodes Rogers.*

This my Opinion being perused with the rest. we came to the following Resolve.

WE the Officers present in a Committee on board the Dutchess, having farther considered our short Store of Bread and Bread-kind, and finding it too little to continue our Cruize longer here for the Manila Ship, do therefore now agree to get a Harbour and. there to recruit with the utmost dispatch, and sail for the Island of Guam, or any other Place where we can revictual. We design to consult father of our next Proceedings, when in Harbour. This is our present Opinion. Witness our Hands this 20th of December, 1709.

Signed by the Officers of the Committee.

At signing this in the Committee we all looked very melancholy and dispirited, because so low in Provision, that if we should not reach *Guam* in the limited Time, or accidentally miss it, we shall not have enough till we arrive at any other Place.

Necessity forces us to design from hence to GUAM, and thence to the *East Indies* for; if we had Provisions to go back round Cape *Horne*, arid to stop in *Brazil*, and there to sell OUR *Europe* Prize Goods, it might be much more for our Advantage, and be sooner at *Great Britain*.

Dec. 21. Pursuant to Yesterday's Agreement we made the best of our Way into the Harbour call'd by Sir *Tho. Cavendish* Port *Segura*, where the *Marquiss* was refitting; but having Calms most part of the Afternoon, and a Current setting to Leeward we rather lost than got ground. Towards Morning there Sprung up a Gale, and we found our selves to Leeward of the Port, tho' we took all Advantages of the Wind: But to our great and joyful Surprize about 9 a Clock the Man at Mast-head cry'd out be saw a Sail besides the *Dutchess* and Bark, bearing West half South of us, distant about 7 Leagues. We immediately hoisted our Ensign, and bore away after her, the *Dutchess* soon did the same; but it falling calm, I order'd the Pinnace to be mann'd and arm'd, and sent her away to make what she was: Some were of opinion 'twas the *Marquiss* come out of the Harbour, and to confirm this, said they could discern the Sail to have no Fore-top mast; so the Boat being not out of call, return'd back, and we put a Gap in her for the *Marquiss*, then sent her away again, by which time it was Noon. The Cape then bore N. N. E. of us, distant about 5 Leagues.

Dec. 22. We had very little Wind all Yesterday Afternoon; so that we near'd the Ship very slowly, and the Boat not returning kept us in a languishing Condition, and occasion'd several Wagers, whether 'twas the *Marquiss* or the *Acapulco* Ship. We kept sight of our Boat, and could not perceive her to go aboard the Ship, but made towards the *Dutchess* Pinnace who was rowing to them; they lay together some time, then the *Dutchess's* Boat went back to their Ship again, and ours kept dogging the Stranger, tho' at a good distance, which gave us great hopes that 'twas the *Manila* Ship. I sent Mr. *Frye* aboard the *Dutchess* in our Yawl, to know what News, and if the Ship was not the *Marquiss*, to agree how to engage her. We then hoisted a *French* Ensign, and fired a Gun, which the Stranger answer'd. Mr. *Frye* return'd with the joyful News that it was the Ship we had so impatiently waited for, and despair'd of seeing her. We agreed the 2 Pinnaces should tend her all Night, and keep showing false Fires, that we might know whereabouts they and the Chase was; and if we were so fortunate to come up with her together, agreed to board her at once. We made a clear Ship before Night, had every thing in a Readiness to engage her at Day-break, and kept a very good Look-out all

Night for the Boat's false Fires, which we law and answer'd frequently. At Day-break we saw the Chase upon our Weather-Bow, about a League from us, the *Dutchess* a-head of her to Leeward near about half as far. Towards 6 our Boat came aboard, having kept very near the Chase, all Night, and receiv'd no Damage, but told us the *Dutchess* pass'd by her in the Night, and she fired 2 Shot at them, but they return'd none. We had no Wind, but got out 8 of our Ships Oars, and rowed above an Hour; then there sprung up a small Breeze. I order'd a large Kettle of Chocolate to be made for our Ship's Company (having no spiritous Liquor to give them;) then we went to Prayers, and before we had concluded were disturb'd by the Enemy's firing at us. They had Barrels hanging at each Yard-Arm, that look'd like Powder Barrels, to deter us from boarding 'em. About 8 a Clock we began to engage her by our selves, for the *Dutchess* being to Leeward, and having little Wind, did not come up. The Enemy fired her Stern Chase upon us first, which we return'd with our Fore Chase several times, till we came nearer, and when close aboard each other, we gave her several Broad-sides, plying our small Arms very briskly, which they return'd as thick a while, but did not ply their great Guns half so fast as WE. After some time we shot a little a head of them, lay thwart her Hawse close aboard, and plyed them so warmly, that she soon Struck her Colours two thirds down. By this time the *Dutchess* came up, and fired about 5 Guns, with a Volley of small Shot, but the Enemy having submitted, made no Return. We sent our Pinnace aboard, and brought the Captain with the Officers away, and having examin'd 'em, found there was another Ship came out of *Manila* with them, of a bigger Burthen, having about 40 Brass Guns mounted, and as many Patereroes; but they told us they lost her Company 3 Months ago, and reckon'd she was got to *Acapulco* before this time, she sailing better than this Ship. This Prize was call'd by the long Name of *Nostra Seniora de la Inearnacion Disenganio*, Sir *John Pichberty* Commander; she had 20 Guns, 20 Patereroes, and 193 Men aboard, whereof 9 were kill'd, 10 wounded, and several blown up and burnt with Powder. We engag'd 'em about 3 Glasses, in which time we had only my self and another Man wounded. I was shot thro' the Left Cheek, the Bullet struck away great pare of my upper Jaw, and several of my Teeth, part of which dropt down upon the Deck, where I fell; the other, *Will. Powell*, an *Irish* Land-man, was slightly wounded in the Buttock. They did us no great Damage in our Rigging, but a shot disabled our Mizen Mast. I was forced to write what I would say, to prevent the Loss of Blood, and because of the Pain I suffer'd by Speaking.

Dec. 23. After we had put our Ships to rights again, we stood in for the Harbour, which bore N. E. of us distant about 7 Leagues. Our Surgeons went aboard the Prize to dress the wounded Men.

Dec. 24. About 4 Yesterday Afternoon we got to an Anchor in Port *Segura* in 25 Fathom Water, found the *Marquiss* in a sailing Posture, and all the Company much overjoy'd at our unexpected good Fortune. In the Night I felt something clog my Throat, which I swallow'd with much Pain, and suppose it's a part of my Jaw Bone, or the Shot, which we can't yet give an account of, I soon recover'd my self; but my Throat and Head being very much swell'd, have much ado to swallow any sort of Liquids for Sustenance. At 8 the Committee met aboard us, and agreed that the *Dutchess* and *Marquiss* should immediately go out, and cruize 8 Days for the other Ship, being in hopes she had not pass'd us; in the mean time we and the Prize to stay and refit, and dispatch the Prisoners away in the Bark, and if we could get Security from the *Guiaquil* Hostages for the Payment of the Remainder of the Ransom, to let 'em go likewise. We lie land-lockt from the E. by N. to the S.S.E. distant from the Eastermost Point about 4 Mile, from the Southermost Rock about half a Mile, and near the same Distance off Shore. The Committee we held resolv'd as follows.

> *On board the Duke riding in Port Segura on the Coast of California, Dec. 24. 1709.*
>
> *Hawing Information from the Prisoners taken on board the Prize the 22d instant, bound from Manila to Acapulco that they came out in company with another Ship bound for the fame Port, from which they parted in Lat. 39. N. It is resolved that Capt. Courtney in the Dutchess, and Capt. Cooke in the Marquiss, do forthwith go out upon a Cruise for 8 Days, to look after the said Ship.*
>
> *Signed by the Majority of the Council.*

Capt. *Courtney, Cooke*, and their Officers of the Council, would not agree that the *Duke* and *Dutchess* should go out as I desir'd, with most of the Men belonging to the *Marquiss* divided between them, in order to cruise for the biggest *Acapulco* Ship, which we were in hopes had not passed us; and by being thus well mann'd, might if they meet her carry her by boarding at once, and that in the mean time the *Marquiss* with a very small number of Men might be sufficient to stay in the Port, and send off the Bark with the Prisoners.

But there having been some Reflections amongst the Sailors because the *Dutchess* did not engage this Prize before the *Duke* came up, it made them obstinate to cruize for her without us and the Officers of our Consorts being agreed, made the Majority of our Council; so that according to the foregoing Committee we were obliged to stay in the Harbour against our Will.

Dec. 25. Last Night the *Dutchess* and *Marquiss* went out; We put 10 good Hands aboard the *Dutchess*, that if they should be so fortunate as to see the Great Ship, they might be the better able to attack her. In the Morning we began to put part of the Goods aboard the park into the Prize, in order to Tend the Prisoners away. Capt. *Dover* and Mr. *Stretton*, who were aboard the Prize, came to me, and we all agreed to send off the *Guiaquil* Hostages, the Captain of the *Manila* Ship (who was a *French* Chevalier) having given us 5 Bills of Exchange for the same, payable in London for 6000 Dollars, being 2000 more than the Ransom Money, for which we allow'd him the Benefit of the Bark and Cargo, the Captain and Hostages giving us Certificates, that it was a Bargain concluded at their own Requests, and very much to their advantage. Sir *John Pichberty* being, we hope, a Man of Honour, will not suffer his Bills to be protested, since we have so generously trusted him, tho' a Prisoners, without a Hostage, which is always demanded for less Sums.

Dec 25. We plac'd two Gentries to keep a good Look-out upon the Top of a Hill, with Orders if they saw 3 Sail in the Offing, to make 3 Waffs with their Colours.

Dec. 36. Yesterday Afternoon the Centrys made 3 Waffs, and we immediately sent the Yawl to them for better Satisfaction, and found there were 3 Sail out at Sea; upon which we immediately put all the Prisoners aboard the Bark, taking away her Sails, and fetch'd our Men aboard, leaving only 22 Hands belonging to us, aboard the Prize, to help refit and look after her. The

Prisoners, who were about 170, being secur'd aboard our Bark, without Arms, Rudder, Sails, or a Boat, and moar'd near a Mile from our Prize, a few more of our Men than was sufficient, to give them Victuals and Drink, might have guarded them very lately; yet for the more Security, we left a Lieutenant of each Ship, and the above Men well arm'd Aboard our Prize, and immediately weigh'd in order to go and assist our Consorts to attack the great Ship, which then came in sight. Capt. *Dover* thought fit to go on board the Prize, and exchange Posts with one of the Lieutenants that guarded the Prisoners, and sent him to us in his stead. I was in so weak a Condition, and my Head and Throat so much swell'd, that I yet spoke in great Pain, and hot loud enough to be heard at any distance; so that all the rest of the chief Officers, and our Surgeons, would have perswaded me to stay in the Harbour in Safety aboard our Prize. We weigh'd our Anchors, and got under Sail by 7 a Clock: We saw Lights several times in the Night, which we took to be our Consorts Boats making false Fires. In the Morning at Day-break we saw 5 Sail to Windward of us; but were so far distant, that we could not make which were our Consorts, and which the Chase, till about 9 a Clock, when we saw the *Dutchess* and Chase near together, and the *Marquiss* standing to them with all the Sail she could crowd. We made what Sail we could, but were to Leeward of them 3 or 4 Leagues, and having a scant Wind, made little Way. At Noon they bore S. E. of us, being right to Windward about 3 Leagues.

In the Afternoon we saw the *Marquiss* come up with the Chase, and engage her pretty briskly; but soon fell to Leeward out of Cannon-shot, and lay a considerable Time, which made us think she was some way or other disabled. I order'd the Pinnace to be mann'd, and sent her away to her, that if what we suspected prov'd true, and we had not Wind to get up with them before Night, our Boat might dog the Chase with Signals till the Morning, that she might not escape us and the other Ships; but before the Boat could get up with them, the *Marquiss* made sail and came up with the Chase, and both went to it again briskly for 4 Glasses and upwards: Then the Ship which we took to be the *Dutchess* stretch'd a-head to Windward of the Enemy, I suppose to fix her Rigging, or stop her Leaks; mean while the other kept her in play till she bore down again, and each firing a Broad-side or two, left off, because 'twas dark: They then bore South of us, which was right in the Wind's Eye, distant about 2 Leagues. By Midnight we were pretty well up with them, and our Boat came aboard, having made false Fires, which we answer'd: They had been on board the *Dutchess* and *Marquiss*, and told me the former had her Foremast much disabled, and the Ring of an Anchor shot away, with several Men wounded, and one kill'd, having receiv'd a shot in their Powder Room, and several in their upper Works, but all stopt. They engag'd the Ship by themselves the Night before, which was what we took to be the Boats Lights, being out of the hearing of the Guns, At that time they could perceive the Enemy was in disorder, her Guns hot being all mounted, and consequently their Netting-deck and Close-Quarters unprovided; so that had it been my good Fortune in the *Duke* to accompany the *Dutchess*, as I desired, we all believe we might then have carried this great Ship; or if they in the *Dutchess* had thought of taking most of the Men out of the *Marquiss*, who did not sail well and enough to come up to their Assistance at first, they alone might very probably have taken her by Boarding at once, before the *Spaniards* had experienc'd our Strength, being afterwards so well provided, as encouraged them to lie driving, and give us all Opportunity to board them when we pleas'd. Capt. *Cooke* sent me word, that the *Marquiss* had fired near all her shot and Powder, but had escap'd very well both in Masts, Rigging and Men. I sent our Boat with 3 Barrels of Powder, and Shot in proportion, and Lieut. *Frye*, to consult our Consorts how to engage the Enemy to the best advantage at Break of Day. The Chase had made Signals to our Ship all the Day and Night, because she took us for her Consort, which we had in possession, and after 'twas dark had edg'd away to us, else I should not have been up with her, having very little Wind, and that against us. In the Morning as soon as 'twas Day, the Wind veering at once, put our Ship about, and the Chase fired first upon the *Dutchess*, who by means of the Wind's veering was nearest the Enemy; she returned it smartly: we stood as near as possible, firing as our Guns came to bear; but the *Dutchess* being by this time thwart the S*paniards* Hawse, and firing very fast, those shot that miss'd the Enemy flew from the *Dutchess* over us, and betwixt our Masts, so that we ran the risque of receiving more Damage from them than from the Enemy, if we had lain on her Quarters and cross her Stern, as I design'd, while the Enemy lay driving. This forced us to lie along side, close aboard her, where we kept firing round Shot, and did not load with any Bar or Partridge, because the Ship's Sides were too thick to receive any Damage by it, and no Men appearing in sight, it would only have been a Clog to the Force of our Round Shot, We kept close aboard her, and drove as she did as near as possible. The Enemy kept to their close Quarters, so that we did not fire our Small Arms till we saw a Man appear, or a Port open; then we fired as quick as possible. Thus we continued for 4 Glasses, about which time we received a Shot in the Main Mast, which much disabled it; soon after that the *Dutchess* and we firing together, we came both close under the Enemy, and had like to have been all aboard her, so that we could make little use of our Guns. Then we fell a-stern in our Birth along side, where the Enemy threw a Fire-ball out of one of her Tops, which lighting upon our Quarter-deck, blew up a Chest of Arms and Cartouch Boxes all loaded, and several Cartridges of Powder in the Steerage, by which means Mr. *Vanbrugh*, our Agent, and a *Dutchman*, were very much burnt; it might have done more Damage, had it not been quench'd as soon as possible. After we got clear of each other, the *Dutchess* flood in for the Shore, where she lay brac'd to, mending her Rigging, &c. The *Marquiss* fired several Shot, but to little purpose, her Guns being small. We were close aboard several times afterwards, till at last we receiv'd a second Shot in the Main Mast not far from the other, which rent it miserably, and the Mast settl'd to it, so that we were afraid it would drop by the board, and having our Rigging shatter'd very much, we sheer'd off, and brought to, making a Signal to our Consorts to consult what to do; in the interim we got ordinary Fishes for a port to the Main-mast, and fasten'd it as well as we could to secure it at present. Capt. *Courtney* and Cape. *Cooke* came aboard with other Officers, where we consider'd the Condition the 3 Ships were in, their Masts and Rigging being much damified in a Place where we could not get no Recruit, that if we engag'd her again, we could propose to do no more than what we had already done, which was evident did her no great Hurt, because we could perceive few of our Shot enter'd her Sides to any purpose, and our Small Arms avail'd less, there being not a Man to be seen above-board; that the least thing in the World would bring our Main-mast, and likewise the *Dutchess* Fore-mast by the board, either of which by its Fall might carry away another Mast, and then we should lie a Battery for the Enemy, having nothing to command our Ships with, so that by his heavy Guns he might either sink or take us: That if we went to board her, we should run a greater hazard in losing a great many

Men with little Hopes of Success, they having above treble the Number aboard to oppose us, and there being now in all our 3 Ships not above 120 good Men fit for boarding, and those but weak, having been very short of Provisions a long time; besides we had the Disadvantage of a Netting-deck to enter upon, and a Ship every other way well provided; so that if we had boarded her, and been forc'd off, or left any of our Men behind, the Enemy by that means might have known our Strength, and then gone into the Harbour and took possession of the Prize in spight of all we could do to prevent it: Besides, our Ammunition was very short, having only enough to engage a few Glasses longer. All this being seriously consider'd, and knowing the Difficulty we should have to get Masts, and the Time and Provisions we must spend before we could get 'em sitted, 'twas resolved to forbear attempting her further, since our battering her signify'd little, and we had not Strength enough to board her: Therefore we agreed to keep her company till Night, then to lose her, and make the best of our way into the Harbour to secure the Prize we had already took. We engag'd first and last about fix or seven Hours, during all which time we had aboard the *Duke* but eleven Men wounded, 3 of whom were scorch'd with Gun powder. I was again unfortunately wounded in the Left Foot with a Splinter just before we blew up on the Quarter-deck so that I could not stand, but lay on my Back in a great deal of Misery part of my Heel-bone being struck out, and all wider my Ankle cut above half thro', which bled very much, and weaken'd me, before it could be dressed and stopt. The *Dutchess* had about 30 Men killed and wounded, 3 of the latter and one of the former were my Men. The *Marquiss* had none kill'd or wounded, but 2 scorch'd with Powder. Thee Enemy's was a brave lofty now Ship, the Admiral of *Manila*, and this the first Voyage she had made; she was call'd the *Begonia*, of about 900 Tuns, and could carry 60 Guns, about 40 of which were mounted, with as many Patereroes, all Brass; her Complement of Men on board, as we were inform'd, was above 450, besides Passengers. They added, that 150 of the Men on board this great Ship were *European*, several of whom had been formerly Pirates, and having now got all their Wealth aboard, were resolved to defend it to the last. The Gunner, who had a good Post in *Manila*, was an expert Man, and had provided the Ship extraordinary well for Defence, which made them sight so desperately; they had filled up all between the Guns with Bales to Secure the Men. She kept a *Spanish* Flag at her Main-top-mast Head all the time she fought us; we shatter'd her Sails and Rigging very much, shot her Mizon-yard, kill'd two Men out of her Tops, which was all the Damage we could see we did 'em; tho' we could not place less than 500 Shot (6 Pounders) in her Hull. These large Ships are bulk at *Manila* with excellent Timber, that will not splinter; they have very thick Sides, much stronger than we build in *Europe*. Whilst the Officers were aboard us, Capt. *Courtney* and others desir'd that what we had agreed upon might be put in Writing, and sign'd by as many as were present, to prevent false Reflections hereafter, which was done as follows.

At a Committee held on board the Duke, after we had engaged the bigger *Manila* Ship, *December* 27. 1709.

WE having consider'd the Condition of all our 3 Ships, and that our Masts are much damnified in engaging the Manila Ship, do think it for the Interest of the whole to forbear any further Attempts upon her having no Probability of taking her, but to do our endeavours to secure the Prize we have already took, which will be much more for the Honour and Interest of OUR selves and Country. This is our Opinion, in witness whereof we have set our Hands, the Day and Year above-written.

> *Woodes Rogers, Lan. Appleby,*
> *Stephen Courtney, Charles Pope,*
> *William Dampier, Henry Oliphant,*
> *Edw. Cooke, Alex. Selkirk,*
> *Rob. Frye, John Kingston,*
> *Tho. Glendall, Nath. Scotch,*
> *John Connely, John Piller. John Bridge,*

Thus ended our Attempt on the biggest *Manila* Ship, which I have heard related so many ways at home, that I thought it necessary to set down every particular Circumstance of it, as it stood in my Journal. Had we been together at first, and boarded her, we might probably have taken this great Prize; but after the Enemy had fixed her Netting-deck and close Quarters, they valued us very little. I believe also we might have burnt her with one of our Ships, but that was objected against by all the Officers, because we had Goods of Value on board all our 3 Ships. The Enemy was the better provided for us, because they heard at *Manila* from our *English* Settlements in *India*, that there were 2 small Ships fitted from *Bristol*, that design'd to attempt them in the *South Seas*. This was told us by the Prisoners we took on board the other Ship.

When I proposed parting Companies at the *Tres Marias*, and to cruise for the *Acapulco* Ship from *Manila* with our Ship and Bark at one Station, and the *Dutchess* and *Marquiss* at another, we then expected but one Ship from *Manila*, and she not so well provided as the least Ship now was; tho' as we have found it, we might probably have been better asunder, for then I make little question but we should have got some Recruit of Provisions, and consequently our Men had been stronger and better in heart to have boarded this great Ship at once, before they had been so well provided; but since Providence or Fate will have it as it is, we must be content.

Dec. 28. The Enemy lay braced to all the time the Council held, and run out 4 Guns of her lower Teer, expecting we would have the other Brush with her; but when we made sail, she fil'd and made away, W. N. W. and we betwixt the S. S. E. and the S. close upon a Wind. At 6 a Clock we sent the Pinnace with some Men into the Harbour to secure the Prize, not knowing what might happen before we could get in with our Ships. We unrigg'd the Main-top-gallant Mast, and got it down, securing our Main-mast with Runners and Tackles every way we could contrive, had little Wind all the Afternoon and Night, but this Morning a fresh Breeze sprung up at E. S. E. and soon after we saw nothing more of the great Ship.

Jan. I After we arriv'd again at Port *Segura*, we dispatch'd the Prisoners away in the Bark, and likewise the *Guiaquil* Hostages: having got Security for the Money as aforesaid, we supplied them with Water and Provisions enough to carry 'em to *Acapulco*; and gave Capt. *Pichberty* and his chief Officers, with a Padre, their Clothes, Instruments, Books, &c. So that they parted very friendly, and acknowledged we had been very civil to 'em, of which they desired me to accept the following Testimony;

We, whose Names are hereto subscrib'd, do acknowledge, that ever since we have been in the Hands of Capt. Woodes Rogers, and Capt. Stephen Courtney, Commanders of the Duke and Dutchess, two British private Men of War, we have keen by them very civilly treated; and whatsoever we have transacted or done, has been voluntary, and by our Consent, and particularly in passing Bills, and Obligations, thro' the Hands of Sir John Pichberty, for the Ransom of the Town of Guiaquil, and other valuable Considerations. Witness our Hands on the Coast of California. Jan. 1. 1709.

Don John Pichberty, Manuel de Punta. Don Antonio Guttera, Manuel Hemanes.

I wrote a Letter to my Owners, to acquaint 'em with our good Success, but could not be so full as I would, because I sent it by the Hand of an Enemy. We spent our Time till the 7th, in refitting, wooding, and watering; and were very glad to find as much Bread on board the Prize as we hop'd might, with what we had left of our old Store, make enough to subsist us in our next long Run. Capt. *Courtney* and his Officers, with those on board the *Marquiss*, are too willing to comple ment Capt. *Dover* with the chief Command of the Prize; which till now I thought he would not have accepted, his Posts already being above a Commander of any of our Prizes; but I and my Officers are against it; because we believe Capt. *Frye* or others, are sitter Persons to take Charge of her, which we insisted on; and Capts. Country and *Cooke* came to me, where they agreed to a Paper that was drawn up while we were all together, in such a Manner as I thought would have satisfied every one. Capt. *Courtney* carried this Agreement to Capt. *Dover* to sign it, not doubting but all would be content with what we had concluded; yet to our Surprize, they spent the Remainder of the Day, and instead of making Capt. *Dover* comply with it, undid all, and brought a Paper which impower'd him to be sole Commander, without the least Restraint, of not molesting those that should navigate the Ship, but to order every thing as he should think fit.

Jan. 9. We fetch'd our 3 wounded Men from on board the *Dutchess*; one of 'em was *Tho Young,* a *Welchman,* who lost one of his Legs; the other *Tho. Evans, a Welchman* whose Face was miserably torn; the third, *John Gold,* wounded in the Thigh; and one died of his Wounds, *viz. Emanuel Gonsalves,* a *Portuguese*: So that out of ten that went, only 6 return'd safe. I sent a Letter to Capt. *Courtney* this Morning, to know what Measures were going forward; having heard nothing from him since the 7th Instant, and desired that there might be no loss of time, but that the Committee might meet once more, to try if they would make use of their unbyass'd Reason. They were then all aboard the *Marquiss,* where I heard they had, ever since our last Meeting, concerted how to frame a Protest against me, and my Officers of the Committee, which was immediately answer'd by a Protest from us, both which are as follows.

KNOW all Men, by these Presents, That We, the Commanders of the Ships Dutchess and Marquiss, and other Officers, being the major Part of a Committee appointed by the Owners, for the regulating the Affairs of the Ships Duke and Dutchess, private Men of War, till their Return to Great Britain, as more largely Appears in their Orders and Instructions. Now, whereas we have lately taken a rich Prize bound from Manila to Acapulco, and the said Ship being safe at Anchor in a Bay near Cape St. Luke, on California. We held a general Committee on board the Duke the 6th Day of January, 1709-10. for appointing a Commander and other Officers for the said Prize, call'd by the Spaniards, when in their Possession, Nostra Seniora del Incarnation de Singano, but now named by us The Batchelor Frigate, wherein it was carried by Majority of Votes for Capt. Thomas Dover, who came out second Captain of the Duke, and President of this Committee, and Owner of a very considerable Part of both Ships Duke and Dutchess, to command the said Prize, we thinking him the most proper Person for the Interest of the Owners and Company; we likewise proposing to put two of the best of our Officers on board, to command under him, and manage the navigating Part of the said Ship during the Voyage, with other substantial Officers and Men, sufficient to work the Ship and take Care of her.

NOW whereas Capt. Woodes Rogers, Commander of the Duke, and several of his Officers, Members of this Committee, did refuse to sign to the Agreement of the said Committee (the likenever having been refused by any before, when carried by Majority of Voices) to acknowledge the said Capt. Thomas Dover Commander of the Ship Batchelor Frigate; we do hereby, in the behalf of the Owners of the Ships Duke and Dutchess, our selves and Company, Protest against the unadvised. Proceedings an I Practice of the said Capt. Woodes Rogers, and the rest of the Officers of the Committee, that refused to sign and agree to the same, it being directly contrary to the Owners Orders and Instruction, (Reference being had thereto) and the Union and Peace of the Ships Companies (by them likewise recommended). And whatever Damage may ensue, either by Loss of Time, Want of Provisions, or Men sufficient to manage the said Ship, or any Mutiny or Disagreement that may arise from hence between the Ships Companies, or any other Disaster whatsoever, &c. we do likewise Protest against, in the behalf of the Owners, ourselves, and Company, as aforesaid; expecting from the said Captain Woodes Rogers, and Officers of the Committee aforesaid, full Satisfaction and Reparation of all Losses and Damages whatsoever, that may happen to the said Ship during her Voyage to Great Britain.

IN witness whereof, we the Commanders and Officers, being the major Part of the Committee have set our Hands, this 9th Day of January, 1709-10. on board the Marquiss, at Anchor near Cape St. Luke, on California.

Sign'd by the Officers of the Dutchess and Marquiss.

Which Protest was answer'd by another from our Ship.

WE the chief Officers in behalf of ourselves, and the rest of the Ship's Company of the Duke, having taken a rich Spanish Prize, in Consortship with the Dutchess and Marquiss, call'd Nostra Seniora del Incarnation de ingano, and did design to use the securest Methods to carry her to Great Britain, both for our Employers Interest and our own Advantage. But being in a remote part of the World, we offer'd and desired our Consorts to put one or more able Officers in the principal charge of the aforesaid Prize, if being so valuable that a Retali-

ation for all our Risques and Hardships is in her Riches, which highly behoves us to be very careful in preserving. But against all our Ships Companys Consent, (tho' we are so nearly concern'd) our said Consorts Officers, Capt. Stephen Courtney, Capt. Edward Cooke, Capt. William Dampier, Mr. William Stretton, Mr. Charles Pope, Mr. John Connely, Mr. George Milbourne, Mr. Rob. Knowlman, and Mr. John Ballett, have sign'd an Instrument, and combin'd together, to put Capt. T. Dover in Command of the said Ship. We therefore (being inclin'd to Peace and Quietness aboard, and not to use any Violence to remove the said. Captain Dover out of the aforesaid forc'd Command, although he is utterly uncapable of the Office) do hereby publickly Protest against the aforesaid Commander, and every one of those that have already, or shall hereafter combine to place him in. The Ship now being in safety, we declare against all Damages that may arise or accrue to the said Ship, or Cargo under his Command; and that the aforesaid Combiners, who have put the Care of the said Ship under an uncapable Command, we expect are accountable and liable to us for all Damages that may happen. This is our publick Protest. Witness our Hands, aboard the said Ship Duke, riding at Anchor in a Port of California, the 9th of January, 1709-10.

Sign'd by the Officers of the Duke.

'Twas our great Unhappiness, after taking a rich Prize, to have a Paper-War amongst our selves. I am sorry to trouble the Reader with these Disputes, which continued for two Days about a proper Commander for this Prize; because it highly concern'd us to take the utmost Precautions for her Safety, having a long Run through dangerous unknown Passages, into the *East Indies*, and most of the Recompence for our great Risques and Hardships lay in her Riches, I had always desired that Capt. *Dover* might be aboard her, for being a considerable Owner, we all agreed he was a very proper Person to take Care of her Cargo, and to have all the Freedom and Accommodation that could to made for him in that Ship, which was of such vast Consequence to us and our Employers, that in their Intrusions to me, they strictly charged me to use the securest Methods to bring her safe home, in case we should be so fortunate as we now are, to take one of the *Acapulco* Ships: So that after the Protests were over on both sides, I desired they might assemble together, and finally determine what the Majority would agree on, that no Time might beloft. So all the Council met again on board the *Batchelor*, to endeavour an Accommodation. I being very weak, and in much Pain, was not able to stir, therefore sent my Opinion in Writing, as follows.

My Opinion is, That 'tis not for the Safety of the risk Spanish Prize, that Capt. Dover command her, because his Temper is so violent, that capable Men cannot well act under him, and himself is incapable Our Owners directed me to use the securest Method to bring the Ship home, if we should have the good Fortune to take her; and 'tis not so, if an ignorant Person have the Command: And tho' it may be pretended that fall not command the sailing Part, there are other Parts necessary for a Commander; so that whosoever has the Charge of one, ought to act wholly in the rest, or else Confusion follows a mix'd Command, that would be very pernicious in this Case; and which it highly concerns us to beware of. I am content, and desire Capt. Dover may be aboard, and have Power to take Care of the

Cargo and all the Liberty and Freedom in her, he can in reason other-wise desire, and that none may have the like Power on board the Prize but himself. This is my Opinion. Jan. 9. 1709-10.

Woodes Rogers.

This Dispute is against my Desire already put in Print, from the publick Notes of the Voyage, otherwise I had left it wholly out of my Journal, as I had done several other of our Differences, being unwilling to trouble the Reader with the Contests that too often happen'd in the Government of our sailing Common-wealth.

After a long Debate, they voted Mr. *Frye* and Mr. *Stretton*, both to act in equal Posts, to take Charge of the navigating the Ship, tho' under Capt. *Dover*, but they were to be no ways molested, hinder'd nor contradicted in their Business by him, whose Duty 'twas to see that nothing should be done contrary to the Interest of the Owners, and Ships Companies, in the Nature of an Agent, almost in the same Manner I proposed at first, only he had the Title of Chief Captain in that Ship, which was so small a Difference, where Titles are so common, that we all consented to it; and at the same time they chose Officers, agreeing that we should put 30 Men aboard her, the *Dutchess's* 25, and the *Marquiss* 13, which with 36 *Manila Indians*, call'd *Las-Carrs*, and other Prisoners we have left, her Complement will be about 110 Men. The Majority keeping to their first Agreement I was obliged to corns into it according to my Instructions from our Owners; so that all our Differences about this Affair were at an end, and we drank to our safe Arrival in *Great Britain.*

The Council agreed as follows.

At a Council held on board the Batchelor Frigate, at Anchor in Port Segura, on California, Jan. 10. 1709-10

IT is agreed, by the Majority of this Council, that Capt. Robert Frye and Capt. William Stretton, shall both act in equal Posts in the sole Navigating, Sailing and Ingaging, if Occasion should be, under Capt. The. Dover, on board the Batchelor Frigate, and that the said Capt. Tho. Dover shall not molest, binder or contradict 'em in their Business; and we do appoint Alexander Selkirk Master, Joseph Smith chief Mate, Benj. Parsons second Mate, Charles May Surgeon, John Jones Carpenter, Rob. Hollinsby Boatswain, Rich. Beakhouse Gunner, Peirce Bray Cooper, James Stretton and Richard Hickman Midshipmen, Denis Reading Steward, and all other inferior Officers, as the Commanders shall think fit.

Sign'd by the Majority of our Council.

In the Morning we put 35 good Hands aboard her. The *Dutchess* and *Marquiss* put no more than their Share. Mean while Capts. *Courtney* and *Cooke*, and 2 or 3 more of the Committee came to me, where we signed a Paper for Capt. *Dover* and the two Commanders, recommending Peace and Tranquility amongst them. And that in case of Separation, the Place of Rendezvous was to be *Guam*, one of the *Ladrones* Islands, where we design'd to touch at, God willing, to get Provisions; Every thing being thus Settled, and all in a Readiness to sail; before I proceed with the Relation of our Voyage from hence, I shall give an Account of *California.*

Chapter XII

California *described.*

IT is not yet certainly known whether it be an Island, or joins to the Continent, nor did either our Time or Circumstances allow us to attempt the Discovery. I heard from the *Spaniards,* that some of their Nation had sail'd as far up betwixt *California* and the Main, as Lat. 42 N. where meeting with Shoal Water, and abundance of Islands, they darst not venture any further: So that if this be true, in all Probability it joins to the Continent, a little further to the Northward; for Shoal Water and Islands is a general Sign of being near some main Land: but the *Spaniards* having more Territories in this Part of the World than they know how to manage, they are not curious of further Discoveries. The *Manila* Ships bound to *Acapulco* often make this Coast in the Latitude of 40 North, and I never heard of any that discover'd it farther to the Northward. Some old Draughts make it to join to the Land of *Jesso,* but all this being yet undetermin'd, I shall not take upon me to affirm whether it's an Island, or joins to the Continent. The *Dutch* say, they formerly took a *Spanish* Vessel in those Seas, which had sail'd round *California,* and found it to be an Island; but this Account can't be depended on, and I choose to believe it joins to the Continent. There is no certain Account of its Shape or Bigness, and having seen so little of it, I shall refer the Reader to our common Draughts for its Scituation. What I can say of it from my own Knowledge is, That the Land where we were is for the most part mountainous, barren and sandy, and had nothing but a few Shrubs and Bushes, which produce Fruit and Berries of several Sorts. Our Men who went in our Bark to view the Country about 15 Leagues to the Northward, say it was there cover'd with tall Trees. The *Spaniards* tell us of several good Harbours in this Country, but we found none of them near this Cape. We frequently saw Smoak in several Places, which makes us believe the Inhabitants are pretty numerous. The Bay where we rode had but very indifferent Anchoring Ground., in deep Water, and is the worst recruiting Place we met with since I came out. The Wind at this Time of the Year generally blowing over Land, makes it good Riding on the Starboard Side of the Bay, where you ride on a Bank that has from 10 to 25 Fathom Water; but the rest of that Bay is very deep, and near the Rocks on the Larboard-side going in there's no Ground.

During the Time of our Stay the Air was serene, pleasant, and healthful, and we had no strong Gales of Wind, very little Rain, but great Dews fell by Night, when 'twas very cool.

The Natives we saw here were about 300, they had large Limbs, were straight, tall, and of a much blacker Complexion than any other People that I had seen in the South Seas. Their Hair long, black, and straight, which hung down to their Thighs. The Men stark naked, and the Women had a Covering of Leaves over their Privities, or little Clouts made of Silk Grass, or the Skins of Birds and Beasts. All of them that we saw were old, and miserably wrinkled. We suppose they were afraid to let any of their young ones come near us, but needed not; for besides the good Order we kept among our Men in that respect; if we may judge by what we saw, they could not be very tempting; The Language of the Native was as unpleasant to us as their Aspect, for it was very harsh and broad, and they pronounc'd it so much in the Throat, as if their words had been ready to choak them. I design'd to have brought two of 'em away with me, in order to have had some Account of the Country, when they had learn'd so much of our Language as to enable them to give it; but being Short of Provisions, I durst not venture it. Some of them wear Pearl about their Arms and Necks, having first notch'd it round, and fasten'd with a String of Silk Grass; for I suppose they knew not how to bore them. The Pearls were mix'd with little red Berries, Sticks, and Bits of Shell, which they look'd upon to be so fine an Ornament, that tho' we had Glast Beads of several Colours, and other Toys, they would accept none of them. They coveted nothing we had but Knives, and other cutting Instruments, and were so honest, that they did not meddle with our Coopers or Carpenters Tools, so that whatever was left ashore at Night, we found it untouch'd in the Morning.

We saw nothing like *European* Furniture or Utensils among 'em. Their Huts were very low, and made of Blanches of Trees and Reeds, but not sufficiently cover'd to keep out Rain. They had nothing like Gardens or Provisions about them. They subsisted chiefly on Fish while we were here, which with the Miserableness of their Huts, that seem'd only to be made for a rime, made us conclude they had no fix'd Habitation here, whatever they may have elsewhere and that this was their Fishing Season. We saw no Nets or Hooks, but wooden Instruments, with which they strike the Fish very dexterously, and dive to admiration. Some of our Sailors told me they saw one of 'em dive with his Instrument, and whilst he was under Water put up his Striker with a Fish on the Point of it, which was taken off by another that watch'd by him on a Bark Log. The Reader may believe of this what he pleases, but I give it the more credit, because I my self threw some rusty Knives overboard, on purpose to try those Divers, who seldom miss'd catching a Knife before it could sink above 3 or 4 Fathom, which I took to be an extraordinary Proof of their Agility.

Instead of Bread they us'd a little black Seed, which they ground with Stones, and eat it by Handfuls; some of our Men thicken'd their Broth with it, and say it tastes somewhat like Coffee. They have some Roots that eat like Yams, a sort of Seeds that grow in Cobs, and taste like green Pease, a Berry which resembles those of Ivy, and being dry'd at the Fire, eats like parch'd Pease. They have another like a large Currant, with a white tartish Pulp, a Stone and a Kernel; this sort of Fruit they seem to value much. They have also a Fruit which grows on the prickle Pear-tree, tastes like Gooseberries, and makes good Sawce. They have many other Seeds and Plants unknown to us, but I was not in a condition to view or describe them.

They seem to have a Season of Hunting by the Skins of Deer, &c. we saw among them: They paid a sort of Respect to one Man, whose Head was adorn'd with Feathers made up in the Form of a Cap in other respects they seem'd to have all things in common; for when they exchang'd Fish with us for old Knives, of which we had plenty, they gave the Knives to any that stood next, and after they had enough, we could get no Fish from them. They appear'd to be very idle, and seem to look after no more than a present Subsistence. They stood and look'd upon our Men very attentively, while they cut Wood and fill'd Water; but did not care to lend us a Hand at either, or indeed to do any thing that requir'd hard Labour. Their Arms are Bows and Arrows, with which they can shoot Birds flying. Their Bows are about 7 Foot long, and of a tough pliant Wood unknown to us, with Strings of Silk Grass; their Arrows about 4 Foot and a half, made of Cane, and pointed with Fish Bones that they shape for the purpose. Most of their Knives and other cutting Instruments are made of Sharks Teeth. I saw 2 or 3 large Pearl in their Necklaces and Bracelets, and the *Spaniards* told me they had Store of them from the inner part of the Gulph of *California*, where they have Missionaries planted among them. Our Men told me they saw heavy shining Stones ashore, which look'd as if they came from some Mineral, but they did not inform me of this till we were at Sea, other-wise I would have brought some of 'em to have try'd what Mettal could be extracted out of 'em. The *Spaniards* likewise inform'd me, that the Country in general within on the main Land of *Mexico*, is pleasant and fruitful, and abounds with Cattle and Provisions of all sorts. The Natives grew very familiar with us, and came frequently aboard to view our Ships, which they mightily admir'd. We saw no Boats or Canoes among them, nor any other Sailing Craft, but Bark-Logs, which they steer'd with Paddles at each End. We gave one of the Natives a Shirt, but he soon tore it in pieces, and gave it to the rest of his Company to put the Seeds in which they us'd for Bread. We saw no Utensils for Cookery about them, nor do I suppose they have any; for they bury their Fish in a Heap of Sand, and make a Fire over it, till they think it fit for eating. There were all the Fishes usual in those Seas to be found in the Bay. The fresh Water here is good, and they have abundance of Samphire. They make a Fire in the middle of their Huts, which are very low and smoaky. We saw no extraordinary Birds here. I am told by our People that have been ashore, that they get Fire by rubbing two dry Sticks against each other, as customary among the wild *Indians*.

The Entrance into the Harbour may be known by sour high Rocks, which look like the Needles at the Isle of *Wight*, as you come from the Westward; the two Westermost in form of Sugar-loaves. The innermost has an Arch like a Bridge, through which the Sea makes its way. You must leave the outermost Rock about a Cable's Length on the Larboard side, and steer into the deepest part of the Bay, being all bold, where you may anchor from 10 Fathom to 20 or 25 Fathom Water. Here you ride land-lockt from E. by N. back to the S. E. by S. yet it is but an ordinary Road, if the Wind should come strong out of the Sea, which it never did while we lay there.

Mexico *descrid'd.*

I Shall next give a brief Account of *Mexico* from the best Information and Authors. This Country lies betwixt Lat. 8. and 50 or 55 North, but it is little known or inhabited by die *Spaniards* to the Northward of 35. 'Tis divided into Old and New, and the former is also called *New Spain*. The Country in general includes all the West Side of Northern *America*, as far as 'tis known. 'Tis divided into the *Audiences*, or Jurisdictions of St. *Domingo*, *Mexico* properly so call'd, *Guadalajara* or *New Gallicia*, and *Guatimala*, and these again are subdivided into several Provinces, with which I shall not trouble the Reader, since that is the Business of a Geographer, and not of a Sailor. That part of it call'd *New Spain* is the best and most famous Part of all *North America*, and the Name is sometimes extended by the *Spaniards* to the whole; The Air in general is mild, temperate and healthful, and the Soil so fertile, that in some places it produces 100 for one of Corn, and of Maiz 200; but the great Rains in Summer hinder their having good Oil and Wine. Their most remarkable Plant is that call'd *Maguey*, which abounds in this Country, and some of it we found in the *Maria Islands*; of the Juice the *Spaniards* and Natives make a small Wine, Vinegar, and Honey, and of the Leaves and other Parts they make Cordage, Thread, and Cloth for Sacks and Shirts. They have great and small Cattle, and Fowl in such plenty, that they frequently kill them only for the Skins and Feathers. They have also excellent Horses of the best *Spanish* Breed. There are few Gold Mines in this Country, but abundance of Silver, and tho' not so rich as those of *Peru*, are much easier to be work'd, with less Expence of Money, and far less Danger of Mens Lives. Their other chief Commodities are Iron, Steel, Copper, but none of 'em much wrought, Hides, Wool, Cotton, Sugar, Silk, Cochineal, Scarlet-Dy, Feathers, Honey, Wax, Balm, Amber, Ambergris, Salt, abundance of Medicinal Drugs, Cocoa, Cassia, Gold in the Sands of their Rivers, Figs, Oranges, Citrons, and other Fruit peculiar to the Climate, besides all those common in *Europe*; wild Beasts, and Fowl of all sorts Chrystal, Turquoises, Emeralds, Marcasites, Bezoar Stones, and Pepper. This must be understood of *Mexico* in general; for all those Commodities are not in one Province, but some have one Sort and some another. Nor is the Temper of the Climate every where the same, for those Places towards the *South Sea* are warm, but in and about the Mountains 'tis cold; and in some places they have continued Rains almost for 8 or 9 Months in a Year, and are much infected with Serpents, Moskitto's, and other Insects, especially near the Torrid Zone.

I shall not swell my Book with the fabulous Accounts of the Origin of the antient *Mexicans*, which are (hocking to common Sense, nor pretend to give the Reader the History of their Kings, because 'tis not my Business; besides 'twould puzzle the ablest Critick to distinguish betwixt Truth and Falshood in those pretended Histories, preserv'd by fanciful Hieroglyphics, which will bear what Sense any Author pleases to impose upon them. Therefore I shall only say in general, that the *Spanish* Authors who write of thole Countrys say the Kings of *Mexico* were very potent, that they had 25 or 50 petty Kings their Tributaries, that their ordinary Guards did usually consist of 2 or 3000 Men, and that on occasion they could raise 2 or 300,000; that their Palaces were magnificent, their Temples Sumptuous, and their Worship barbarous, it being ordinary for them to farcifice their Enemies, and sometimes their own Subjects. The Natives of Old *Mexico* say they are not of that Race of People, but that their Ancestors came from divers Nations, who inhabited the Northern parts of the Continent, and particularly that call'd New *Mexico*; and by the Account their Historians give of their Travels to settle here, 'twould seem those who compos'd the Story had heard something of the Travels of the Children of *Israel* in the Wilderness, and design'd to write something like it; and by Calling their Leader *Mexi*, they would make his Name resemble that of *Moses*. 'Twas a long time before they united into one Monarchy; for *Montezuma*, who reign'd when *Fernando Cortex*, invaded them, was only the 9*th* in their Catalogue. The Divisions among the Natives, and the Hatred which the Neighbouring Princes bore to their Kings, made the Conquest of *Mexico* much easier to the *Spaniards* than they expected; so that in the Bishoprick of *Los Angeles*, &c. there are many thousands of *Indians* exempted from extraordinary Taxes, because their Ancestors assisted the *Spaniards* in the Conquest of the Country. The Natives of *Mexico*, properly so call'd, are the most civiliz'd, industrious and ingenious; they are noted for admirable Colours in their Paintings, tho' their Figures are not proportionable; they draw 'em with the Feathers of their *Cincons*, a small Bird, which they say lives only upon Dew. They make use of certain Characters instead of the Letters of the Alphabet, by which they have preserv'd some Fragments of their History. The *Spanish* Governour of *Mexico*, our Author says, with much difficulty got it out of the Hands of the Natives, with an Explanation in their own Language, and had translated into *Spanish*. The Ship in which 'twas sent to the Emperor *Charles* V. being taken by a *French* Ship, the Manuscript fell into the Hands of *Andrew Thevet* at *Paris*, from whose Heirs our *Hackluyt*, being then Almoner to the *English* Ambassador, purchased it. Sir *Walter Raleigh* got it translated into *English*, and the Learned Sir Henry *Spelman* prevail'd with *Purchas* to get the Figures engraven. They represent Princes and others in several Postures, and bring down their History from the Year 1324. to the Beginning or Middle of the 16*th* Century, or thereabouts. This History is divided into 3 Parts; the first contains little but an Account of the Names and Conquests of their Princes, with a Summary of their Vices and Virtues, so that it is not worth infixing upon. The second has an Account of the Tributes paid by the People, which were Proportions of the Product of the Country for Provisions, Cloches, Arms, warlike Habits and Ornaments, Paper and Houshold Furniture. The third gives an account of the Economy, Customs and Discipline of the *Mexicans*, which because they are odd enough, I shall give a short Account of the most remarkable.

Four Days after a Child was born, the Midwife carried it to the Yard of the House, laid it upon Rushes, and after washing it, desir'd 3 Boys, who were there at a Sort of Feast, to name it how they pleas'd. If it was a Boy, she put into its Hand the Tools belonging to its Father's Imployment; and if a Soldier, his Arms. If 'twas a Girl, she put a Distaff or other Utensils of Women by it. If the Boy was design'd for the Church, they carried it to a Temple with Presents, when of a sufficient Age, and left it with the High Priest to be educated; and if design'd for War, they carried him co an Officer to reach him the Use of Arms. The Parents corrected them by Blows, or pricking them with Needles made of the Maguey Tree: The Father prick'd the Boys, if unlucky, all over their Body, and the Mother prick'd her Daughters only in the Fists. When Boys were pretty well grown, they ty'd 'em Hand and Foot, and laid 'em in muddy Water naked a whole Day, and then their Mothers took 'em out and clean'd 'em at Night, When a Maid was to be married, the Marriage-maker carried her on his Back to the Bridegroom's House, 4 Women bearing Torches before her; the Bridegroom's Friends receiv'd her in the Yard or Court, carried her to a Room, and set her down by him on a Mat, and ty'd the Skirts of their Garments together, offer'd Incense to their Idols, and had 4 old Men and Women to be Witnesses; after a Feast the Witnesses exhorted 'em to live well together, and so the Ceremony concluded.

The Priests train'd up their Novices in sweeping the Temples, carrying Branches, *etc.* to adorn them, to make Seats of Cane, to bring Needles or Thorns of Maguey to draw Blood for Sacrifices, and Shrubs to keep a perpetual Fire; and if they fail'd in their Duty, return'd to their Parents, or were catch'd with Women, they prick'd 'em with those Needles. One of the chief Priests went by Night to a Mountain, where he did Penance, carried Fire and Perfume to sacrifice to the Devil, and was always attended by a Novice; others of the Priests play'd on Musical Instruments by Night, and some of 'em observ'd the Stars, and told the Hours. The Novices arriv'd to the chief Dignities of the Priesthood by degrees, and some of 'em always attended the Armies to encourage the Men, and perform their Rite

Those who train'd to Youth to War, punish'd their Scholars by throwing burning Coals on their Heads, pricking them with Sticks of Pine sharpen'd at one End, or by burning off their Hair. Their Kings rewarded the Soldiers according to the Number of Prisoners they took, with Military Habits of several Colours, or Posts in the Army, till they came to the highest. Their Chief Priests were also Men of Arms, and capable of all Military Preferments.

Their capital Punishments were Strangling or Stoning to Death. If a Caicque or petty Prince rebell'd, all his Subjects shar'd in his Punishment, except they found some Method to appease the King. They punish'd Drunkenness in young Men by Death, but allow'd it in old Men and old Women of 70. Highway-men and Adulterers they ston'd to Death. They had Assemblies for publick Affairs, wherein the Great Master of the Emperor or King's Houshold exhorted the Youth to avoid Idleness, Gaming, Drunkenness, and other Vices.

This is the Sum of what that Hieroglyphically History says of the antient *Mexicans*.

As to the present Natives, most of 'em are subject to the *Spaniards*; but in some of the Mountains and Northern Pares they are not reduc'd; so that they frequently attack the *Spaniards*, when they meet with a favourable Opportunity.

In that call'd *New Mexico* some of the Natives am very barbarous, and much given to Arms, the Men wear nothing but Skins, and the Women scarce any other Covering than their Hair; they live for the most part on raw Flesh, and go together in Troops, changing their Habitation as the Season requires, or for the Conveniency of Pasturage. Their Oxen and Cows are large, with small Horns, their Hair almost like Wooll, long before, and shore behind, with a Bunch on their Backs, great Beards like Goats, and their Fore Legs shore; they are et an ugly Aspect, but very strong; they are the principal Riches of the Natives, their Flesh serves them for Diet, their Skins for Clothes and Coverings to their Huts, they make Thred of their Hair, Bowstrings of their Nerves, Utensils of their Bones, Trumpets of their Horns, keep their Drink in their Bladders, and use their Dung for Firing, because they are scarce of Wood. They have Sheep as large as our Asses, and Dogs so strong, that they make 'em carry their Baggage. This Country is inhabited by People of different, Languages and Manners; some of them live in Cities, of which 'tis said there are several that contain from 30 to 50,000 Inhabitants; others wander about in Herds like the *Arabs* or *Tartars*; but in short, this Country is so little known, and Travellers differ so much in their Accounts of it, that there's not much to be depended upon.

I think it proper here to say something of the peopling of it. There are many Opinions about the peopling of *America*, but the most reasonable to me is, that it was peopled from *Tartary* by way of the North Pole, where they suppose it to join with some part *Asia*. This I think very probable, because the *Spaniards*, who come yearly hither from *Manila* or *Luconia*, one of the *Philipine* Islands in the *East Indies*, are forced to keep in a high Latitude for the Benefit of Westerly Winds, and have often founded, finding Ground in Lat. 42, N. in several Places of the Ocean betwixt the *East Indies* and *America*, which makes me conclude that there most be more Land, tho' none of 'em as I have heard of, ever saw any Continent till they fall in with *California*, in about 38 or 39°. N. Lat. I have often admir'd that no considerable Discoveries have yet been made in South Latitude from *America* to the *East Indies*: I never heard the South Ocean has been run over by above three or Sour Navigators, who varied little in their Runs from their Course, and by consequence could not discover much. I give this Hint to encourage our *South Sea Com-*

pany, or others, to go upon some Discovery that way, where for ought we know they may find a better Country than any yet discover'd, there being a vast Surface of the Sea from the Equinox to the South Pole, of at least 2000 Leagues in Longitude that has hitherto been little regarded tho' it be agreeable to Reason, that there must be a Body of Land about the South Pole, to counterpoise those vast Countries about the North Pole. This I suppose to be the Reason why our antient Geographers mention'd a *Terra Australis Incognita*, tho' very little of it has been seen by any body. The Land near the North Pole in the *South Sea*, from *California* to *Japan*, is wholly unknown, altho' the old Maps describe the Streights of *Anian*, and a large Continent, it is but imaginary; for the *Dutch* themselves, that now trade to *Japan*, say they do not yet know whether it be an Island, or joins to the Continent.

Gemelli having, been in this Country in 1697, who is the latest Traveller that has publish'd any thing about it, and his Accounts being in the main confirmed to me by our *Spanish* Prisoners, I shall give a brief Hint of what he says, especially of what relates to Trade and Provisions.

Their best Product is Gold and Silver, Pearl, Emeralds, and other precious Stone: He saw the Silver Mines of *Pachma*, 11 Leagues from the City of *Mexico*: One of 'em he says is 225 *English* Yards deep, the other 195: He adds, that in the Space of 6 Leagues there are about 1000 Mines, some laid aside, others still in use. There are many thousands of People imploy'd to dig 'em, from some the Metal and the Water is brought up by Engines, and from others the Metal is brought up on Mens Backs to the great Danger of their Lives, besides Numbers that are lost by the falling in of the Earth, and pestilential Damps; They go down to them by notch'd Potes, which being' wet and slippery, the poor *Indian* Slaves many times fall, and break their Necks. Our Author says he was in danger of doing the like when he went to see them. He adds, that the Work-men inform'd him, that from one of the Veins, where near 1000 Men work'd *per diem* they had m 10 Years Dug 40 Millions of Sliver, that 2 Millions had been laid out in Timber-work to support it, and that it became so dangerous as the Owner stop'd it up, I refer to him for the Manner of separating the Metal from the Oar. Every Discoverer of a Mine must pay the 5*th* of the Product to the King, who allows him only 60 S*panish* Yards round from the Mouth, or all on one side, if he pleases. *Gemelli* says there's 2 Millions of Marks, of 8 Ounces each, entred at *Mexico* in a Year from those Mines, besides what is stole, and 700,000 Marks of it are coin'd annually into Pieces of Eight there, for which the King has a Royal *per* Mark. There being Gold mix'd with the Silver, they make use of *Aqua Portis* to separate them. The Officers of the Mint have very profitable Places, but I can't insist upon their Sallaries.

'Tis needless to see particular in describing the Birds and Beasts of this Country; they having been to often done by others, I shall only lay, they have enough for Provisions, and many of both sorts unknown to us. Tis the like as to their Fruits and Plants, which serve them for Food and Physick; but I have not room to be particular.

Mexico is the Capital City of this vast rich Country and lies in N. Lat. 19. 40. in the Middle of a Valley, which is 14 *Spanish* Leagues long, and 7 broad, encompass'd by a Ridge of Mountains. The City is surrounded by a Lake, and is square; with long, wide, and well pav'd Streets, cross one another. 'Tis 2 Leagues round, and the Diameter half a League. There are 5 Causeys or Banks through the Lake into the City, which vies with the best in

Italy for noble Structures and beautiful Women, who prefer *Europeans* to their own Country-men; this occasions irreconcilable Prejudices betwixt cherry so that an *European* can scarce pass the Streets without being insulted. The Inhabitants are about 100000, the major part Blacks, and Mulatto's, because of the vast Number of Slaves carried thither. *Europeans* seldom marry there, because finding no way to get real Estates, they generally become Clergymen, which takes up most of those that come from *Old Spain*. There are 22 Nunneries and 29 Friaries of several Orders within the City, and all richer than they ought to be, says *Gemelli*. The Cathedral is exceeding rich, maintains 10 Canons, 5 dignify'd Priests, 6 Demi-Canons, 6 half Demi-Canons, 1 Chief Sacristain, 4 Curates, 12 Royal Chaplains, and 8 others chosen by the Chapter, besides many others nam'd by the King. The Revenue of the Cathedral is 300000 Pieces of Eight *per Annum*. The Climate here is uncertain, as through all the Country, being for most pare both cold and hot at the same time, *viz.* cold in the Shade, and hot in the Sun, but is never excessive either way; yet the Inhabitants complain of the Cold in the Mornings, and of the Heat form *March* till *July*; from thence to *September* the Rains cool the Air, and from tint time *till March* the Rains are but small. The *Indians* reckon those Nights cold, but the *Europeans* like the Climate well enough. Their Water is very cool. Tin neighbouring Country produces 3 Harvests *per Ann.* one in *June*, the 2d in October, and the 3d uncertain, as the Weather proves. Maiz, or *Indian* Corn is their chief Grain, the earliest being sow'd in *March*, the latest in *May*. It yield a wonderful Increase, and other Provisions being plentiful, one may live well here for half a Piece of Eight *per* Day, and all the Year round there's Fruit and Flowers in the Market. There's no Brass Money here, and the least Piece of Silver is Three-pence; so that they buy Herbs and small Fruit with Cocoa Nuts, 60 or 70 of which, as the Time goes, are valu'd at 6*d*. I cannot insist on the particular Description of the Churches and Monasteries. The Archbishop has 11 Suffragans under him, whose Revenues in all amount to 5160000 Pieces of Eight. The Cathedral founded by *Fernando Cortez*, who conquer'd this Country, was not finish'd in 1697. 'tis carried on at the King's Charge. They have admirable Conveyances to let the Water run out of the Lake by Canals, to prevent its overflowing the City, as sometimes it has done. The Expence of these Canals is so prodigious, that it seems incredible; the Curious may find it in *Gemelli*, as also an Account of the Royal Palace and other Structures. I say nothing of the fabulous Accounts which the Natives give of the Foundation of this City.

The present Habit generally wore by the Natives of this Country is a short Doublet and wide Breeches, a Cloak of several Colours on their Shoulders, which they cross under the Right Arm, and tye on the Left Shoulder by the 2 Ends in a great Knot: some wear Sandals, the rest go bare footed and bare-legg'd, and all Wear their Hair long, which they will by no means part with. The Women wear a fine white Cotton Cloth, and under it a thing like a Sack; they wear another upon their Backs, with which they cover their Heads when abroad or in Church. The Natives adorn their narrow Coats with Figures of Beasts, Birds and Feathers. Both Sexes are of a dark Colour, but endeavour to make themselves fair with pounded Herbs. They daub their Heads with thin Clay, to refresh them, and make their Hair black. The Mestizzo, Mulatto, and black Women, are most in Number, but not being allow'd to wear Veils, or the *Spanish* Habit, and despising the *Indian* Garb, they wear a thing like a Petticoat a-cross their Shoulders, or on their Heads, which makes 'em look like so many Devils. The Blacks and Mullattoes are very insolent, and so much increas'd, that if it ben't prevented, they may at one time or other endanger the Country. The Indians of most Parts of *Mexico* are nothing so industrious as formerly, and the *Spaniards* say they are cowardly, cruel, Thieves, Cheats, and so beastly, that they use Women in common, without regard to the nearest Relations, lie on the bare Ground, and are nasty in their Way of living, which perhaps may proceed from the Slavery they are kept under, being worse treated than those in the Mines. He adds that there's Scarce one fair dealing Man to be found among 100 Mullattoes.

Acapulco lies in Lat. 17. bating some few Minutes, he says it is rather like a poor Village of Fishermen, than fit to be the chief Man of the *South Sea*, and Port for *China*. The Houses are mean, built of Wood, Mud and Straw, it is cover'd by high Mountains on the East side, and very Subject to Distempers from *November* till the End of *May*, during which time they have no Rain, or very little. 'Tis as hot here in *January*, as in our Dog-days, they are much pester'd with Gnats and Earthquakes. He observes that it never rains in *New Spain* in a Morning. This Town is dirty, and ill furnish'd with Provisions, so that a Man can scarce live for a Piece of Eight *per* Day. Most of the Inhabitants are Blacks and Mullattoes, for the *Spanish* Merchants are gone as soon as their Business is over at the Fair, for Goods brought hither from *China* and *Peru*. It has nothing good but the Harbour, which is surrounded with High Mountains, and the Ships are moar'd to Trees that grow on the shore. It has two Mouths, the small one at N. W. and the great at S. E. The Mouth is defended by 42 Brass Cannon. The Castellan, who is chief Magistrate during the Fair, has 20000 Pieces of 8, from the Duties paid in the Harbour, and the Comptroller and other Officers as much; the Curate has 14000 *per Ann.* Tho' the King allows him but 180, but he exacts terribly on Baptisms and Burials, so that he will scarce bury a rich Merchant under 1000; The Trade of this Place being for many Millions, every one, in his Profession gets a great deal in a short time; for a Black will scarce work for less than a Piece of 8 *per diem*, All the Dependance of the Inhabitants is on the Fort, which also maintains the Hospitals, Monasteries and Missionaries.

During the Fair, this Town resembles a populous City, because of the great Concourse of Merchants: from *Peru* and *Mexico*; then the miserable Huts in which there was nothing before but a few nasty Mullattoes, are fill'd with gay *Spaniards*, and rich Merchants, and the very Porters do generally earn 3 Pieces of 8 *per Diem* by loading and unloading of Goods, &c. but when this Trade is over, the Porters make a sort of a Funeral, carry one of their Dumber about upon a Bier, and pretend to bewail his Death, because their Harvest for Gain is then at an End, till the next Year.

I shall not here say any thing further of the Seaports of *Mexico*, because the Reader will find them in the Appendix, which gives a full Account of all the noted Harbours in the South Sea, but shall add, that the Trade of *Mexico*, on this Coast, is very little, compar'd with that of Peru, because those of the former have their Goods brought to their chief Ports in the N, Sea, directly from *Europe*; so that except when the two Ships come yearly from *Manila* to *Acapulco*, they have little Commers in this Seas I must here observe, that the Ships which come from *Manila* use to be much richer than our Prize; for she waited a long time for the *Chinese* Junks to bring Silk, which not arriving she came away with a Cargo mix'd with abundance of coarse Goods. The Prisoners told me, that the *Manila* Ship did often return from *Acapulco*, with 10 Millions of Dollars, and that the Officers never clear'd less than from 20 to

30000 Dollars each in a Voyage; and the Captain whom they call General, seldom got less than 150 or 200,000 pieces of '8; so that it would have been an extraordinary Prize, could we have met with them at the Time.

I think k proper to observe here, because it belongs to the Subject, that when we arrived at the *Texel* in *Holland* there were two *Spanish* Ships there, bound for *Cadiz* and on board of one of 'em a Sailor, who told us he was aboard the large *Spanish* Ship from *Manila*, when she arriv'd at *Acapulco*, very much disabled by the Engagement she had with us off of *California*; that 'twas the Gunner who made them engage us so resolutely at first, and forced them to continue the Fight by keeping in the Powder-Room himself, and having taken the Sacrament to blow up the Ship in case, we had boarded and over-power'd her. I was the more apt to believe this Man had seen the Ship, and this Story might be true because he related almost every Passage of the Fight, as I have given it before in my Journal.

I shall also take Notice here that Capt. *Stradling*, who was taken Prisoner in *America*, when his Ship stranded, and came off Prisoner in a *French* Ship, some Months after we left the South Seas, inform'd me, that the Corregidore of *Guiaquil* sent an Express to *Lima*, upon the first Notice of our being in those Parts, that they then apprehended us to be part of a Squadron of Men of War, and therefore lay still until they had certain Advice of our Strength, and in about 3 Weeks after we took the Town, they sitted out 3 Spanish Men of War, which was all their South Sea Strength, against us; the biggest carried not above 32 Guns, but they were join'd by 2 *French* Ships, one of so, and the other of 36 Guns, and all well Mann'd. They stop'd at *Payta*, till Mr. *Hatley* and his 4 Men, who lost Company with us at the *Gallapagos* Islands, being in want of Provisions, and having had no Water for 14 Days, stood in for the Main, and landed near Cape *Passao*, almost under the Equinox, among a barbarous sort of People, who are a mix'd Breed of *Negroes* and *Indians*, They voluntarily surrendred themselves, being in a starving Condition, yet those *Brutish* People, instead of giving them Food, tied their Hands, then whipp'd them and hang'd them up, so that they must unavoidably have lost their Lives, had not a Padre, who liv'd in the Neighbourhood, came time enough by good Providence, to cut 'em down, and save them. There are several Letters come from Mr. *Hatley* since, which signify that he is a Prisoner at *Lima*. Capt. *Stradling* likewise told me that the *French* Ship, which brought him to *Europe*, was the very Ship that we chas'd in sight of *Falkland* Island, before we passed Cape *Horn*. She had before attempt ed to sail round Cape *Horn*, to the South Sea; but it being the wrong Season, she met with bad Weather, and was forc'd to bear away to recruit at the River of *La Plata*, and there wait for a more proper Season to go round *Terra del Fuego*, into the South Sea. When we chas'd her, she had not above 100 healthful Men on board, so that had we been able to come up with her, she must certainly have been our Prize.

Capt. *Straying* told me they ran their Ship on an Island, and afterwards surrendred Prisoners to the *Spaniards*, to save their Lives, she being ready to sink; so that the Report I formerly mention'd, that part of their Crew was drown'd in the Ship, proves a Mistake.

In *Mexico* the Prisoners who are employ'd in cutting Log-wood, have no way to escape the, Cruelty of the *Spaniards*, but to turn Papists, and be baptized after their Manner; then they have the Liberty to chuse a Godfather, who is generally a Man of Note, and they serve him its Livery-men, *etc*. One

Boyse, who fled to us at *Guiaquil*, was baptized thus by an Abbot, in the Cathedral of *Mexico*, had Salt put in his Mouth, and Oil poured upon his Head, arid small parcells of Cotton, which rub'd it off, were distributed as precious Relicks among the Penitents, because taken off the Head of a converted Heretick, as they call them. The native *Spaniards* enjoy all the Posts in the Church and Monasteries, and admit no *Indians*, nor any mix'd Breed, to those Preferments; which they think a necessary Piece of Policy, that they may the better keep the Country in Subjection to *Spain*. Some of these Prisoners who are forced to be pretended Converts, do now and then make their Escape, tho' it be dangerous to attempt it, for if taken they are generally confin'd to the Workhouses for Life. There are several *Englishmen* who were Prisoners in this Country, that, by Compliance, have obtained their Liberty, with die Loss of their Religion in exchange for Riches; particularly one *Thomas Bull*, who was born in *Dover*, and taken in *Campeche*; he is a Clockmaker, has been 18 Years there, is about 45 Years old, lives in the Province of *Tabasco*, and grown very rich. One Capt. *James Thompson*, born in the Isle of *Wight*, has been there about 20 Years, is about 50 Years old, grown rich, and commanded the Mullattoes who took Capt. *Packe*, at the Beginning of the War. The Person who told me this was a Comb-maker, and endeavour'd to escape from *La Vera Crux*, but was taken, and sent Prisoner to *Mexico*, where he came off to *Peru*, after he had his Liberty, by pretending he went to buy Ivory to make Combs; he gave me a long Account of his Ramble amongst the *Indians*, and says, he was at the Mouth of the River *Missisippi* which falls into the Gulph of *Mexico*, but could not pass it: He adds, That the *Indians*, on the Bay of *Pillachi*, have murder'd several of the Padres, out of an Aversion to the *Spaniards*, but show a great Inclination to trade with the *English*. There are other *Englishmen* who now live near the Bay of *Campeche*, as I was inform'd; one of 'em is *Tho. Falkner*, he was born at the Hen and Chickens in *Pall-man*, where his Friends kept an Alehouse. He is married to an *Indian* Woman. Such of them as won't comply to turn Papists are kept in miserable Slavery, either in the Mines or Workhouses at *Mexico*, which City he says, is about as large as *Bristol*. Those that are put in Workhouses are chain'd and imploy'd in carding Wool, rasping Logwood, &c. They have more Manufactures of Woollen and Linnen in *Mexico* than in *Peru*. Abundance of raw Silk is brought from *China*, and of late Years worked up into rich Brocades equal to any made in *Europe*.

The *Mullattoes* and *Indians*, on light Occasions are put into the Workhouses, and kept there, till they pay their Debts or Tribute; but no *Spaniards*, except for the worst of Crimes: There are many *Englishmen*, who were taken cutting Logwood in the Bay of *Campeche*, in several of these Workhouses, kept at hard Labour, and will end their Days in Slavery, unless their Liberty be demanded by her Majesty at the general Peace.

There's abundance of Sheep in this Country, which yield excellent Wooll, of which, I am inform'd, the *English* Prisoners have taught them to make Cloth, worth about 15 *s.* a Yard in *England*, which there yields 8 Pieces of 8; They have also taught them to make Bays and other coarse Woollen.

At *Chopa* in *Mexico*, about Lat. 12 N. there's a great River which sinks into the Earth at once, runs under the Mountains, and rises bigger about if Leagues from the Place where it sunk. 'Tis twice as large as the *Thames*. This River afterwards joins that of *Tabasco*, and falls into the North Sea, as most of the great Rivers of this vast Continent do, he told me, about this Place.

There are high Mountains, with Plains on the Top, where the Air is very temperate, and all our *European* Fruits grow; whereas at the Bottom of these Mountains they have none but the Fruits of hot Climates, tho' 'tis not above 5 Leagues asunder.

There are also Woods of Pines, *etc.* on those Mountains, among which there are Flocks of harmonious Birds, which sing together in an agreeable Consort, that resembles a fine Organ, so that Strangers are amaz'd to hear such Musick strike up of a sudden in the Woods. There's also a Strange Creature in those Woods, call'd by the *Spaniards* an Ounce, much of the Form and Size of a Woolf-dog, but it has Talons, and the Head is more like that of a Tyger: It kills Men and Beasts, which makes travelling through the Woods dangerous; 'tis said to eat nothing but the Heart of its Prey.

I had many more Relations from this Man, who had been 7 Years a Prisoner in this Country; but they being too tedious, I shall add nothing more concerning *Mexico*, but that the Worm is larger, and eats the Bottoms of the Ships more on its Sea-Coasts, than any other Place where we were. All the Coast from *Guiaquil* in *Peru* to the Northward as far as the Latitude of 20 in *Mexico*, 'tis: reckon'd unhealthful, but the contrary from *Guiaquil* to the Southward.

Peru *Described.*

I Shall not trouble the Reader with the History of its Conquest by the *Spaniards*, nor the fabulous Stories of its *Incas* or Princes, the Curious may find them in the *Spanish* Writers, and for the Natives, they are much the same as those I have described in other Pares.

PERU, properly so called, is about 1000 Leagues long, but the Breadth various, from 100 to 300 Leagues. The best known Part of it lies on the *South Sea*, and is divided into the 3 Audiences of *Quito* in the North, *Lima* in the Middle, and *La Plata* in the South. The Air of *Quito* is temperate enough, tho' under the Line; the Soil is fruitful, abounds with Cattle and Corn, and they have Mines of Gold, Silver, Quick-silver and Copper; they have also Emeralds and Medicinal Drugs. The Audience of *Lima* is most noted, because of its Capital of the same Name, being the Residence of the Viceroy of *Peru*. This Country abounds with Mines of Gold, Silver, Quicksilver, Vermilion, and Salt. The Audience of *La Plata* I have already described in my Account of that River. I shall only add, that tho' the Silver Mines of *Potosi* be much decay'd, yet some say the King of *Spain* has annually about 2 Millions of Crowns *per Annum* for his Fifth; and that those of *La Plata* and *Porco*, in the same Province, which were, upon discovery of the Mines of *Potosi*, less used, may probably be open d again to advantage, now Goods are sold so cheap by the continual Supplies from *France*, that the *Indians*, who were imploy'd in the Manufactures, must again work at the Mines, their own coarse Goods being brought thither cheaper than they can make 'em.

The *Spanish* Writers in general say, that for 500 Leagues in Length, from *Tumbez*, to *Chili*, it never thunders, lightens nor rains, which agrees with the Informations that I had from our Prisoners, *viz.* that from Cape *Blanco* in S. Lat. 4. to *Coquimbo*, Lat. 30. it never rains, but the Want of this is supply'd by great Dews, so that they have as good Corn and Fruit, particularly Wheat, about *Truxillo*, as any in *Europe*. In the Vallies near the Sea the Climate is hot, but temper'd with Breezes from the Ocean and Mountains. In the Hilly part, far into the Country, 'tis Winter, and very rainy, when 'tis Summer in the

Plains, though in the same Latitude. The Product, Beasts and Birds, being much the same with other Parts of the *South Sea* Coast, I shall not insist upon 'em.

They have their Cordage, Cotton, Cloth, Pitch and Tar from *Chili* and *Rio Lezo* in *Mexico*, and tho' the Country abounds with Provision, 'tis always dear near the Mines, because there Husbandry is neglected. The Cordage they use is made of coarse Silk Grass, which is very tough, draws small when strain'd, but grows twice as big when slack'd.

Capt. *Stradling* told me he travel'd the great Road from *Quito* towards *Cusco*, in his way to *Lima*, which has Piles of Stone on each side for some hundreds of Miles. When he and his Men were brought Prisoners to *Lima*, the *Spaniards* put them in a close Dungeon, used them very barbarously, and threatened to send them to the Mines, because he attempted his Escape, and sail'd in a Canoe from *Lima* towards *Panama*, near 400 Leagues, intending to cross the Isthmus, and to get to *Jamaica* by some of our trading Sloops, but was taken and brought back to *Lima*. Before he came thence he saw several of the *Spaniards* who had been our Prisoners, and said, they all own'd we had treated them very civilly, which has in part taken off the bad Impression they had conceiv'd of the *English* in those Parts; for not being used to War, they account all alike that come to cruize, because of the unheard of Cruelties and Debaucheries which were committed about 25 Years ago by the Buccaneers in those Parts, which their Priests did improve to give them an ill Idea of all those they think fit to call Hereticks, not considering that most of those Disorders were committed by *French* Buccaneers of their own Religion.

Having said so much of *Peru* in several Parts of my Journal, and given an account of its chief Harbours in my Appendix, I need not enlarge upon it here; the *Spaniards* extend it from *Panama* to *Coquimbo*, which is above 800 Leagues but the Breadth various. The Gold Mines are most of 'em in the North Parts, betwixt *Panama* and the Equinox.

Before the *French* traded hither round Cape *Horne*, there was a considerable Commerce from *Panama* to all the Ports of the *South Sea*, as I noted before; but now they have supplied the Country so much with *European* Goods, and so cheap, that this Trade is in a manner sunk; so that from hence forward there will be little sent over Land from *Panama* to the North Sea, but the King's Revenue. The *Spaniards* have a great many Ships and small Vessels belonging to the several Ports of *Peru*, which are chiefly imploy'd in carrying Timber, Salt, Salt-fish, Wine, Brandy, Oil, and other Commodities, from one part of the Coast to another, without which they could not well subsist; for this Country is laid to be more populous and better inhabited than *Mexico*. They make Woollen Cloth here of several sorts. I have seen some made at *Quito* worth about 8 *s. per* Yard, that is sold here for 5 Dollars. The *Indians* do likewise make a coarse fort of Cotton Cloth; but since the *French* furnish them better and cheaper, those Manufactures will come to nothing, and the People must betake themselves to digging of Mines, or what other Imployment they can get.

The *Spanish* Settlements in this Country, as well as in *Mexico* and *Chili* are not so full of *Indians* as formerly; for many of 'em are gone to remote Parts, and live in Colonies by themselves, to avoid the Slavery and Taxes impos'd on them by the *Spaniards*, for they were oblig'd to pay from 8 to 14 Dollars *per Ann. per* Head to the King, which had it been duly collected and faithfully paid, would have amounted to the greatest Poll Tax in the World; but 'tis now lessen'd by the removal of so many Natives as abovemention'd, and the Impoverishment of the rest, who are sensible enough of their Oppression, but are so dispirited, that they can do nothing to assert their Liberty, and they are besides kept under by the Artifices of the Priests.

The *Spaniards* here are very profuse in their Clothing and Equipage, and affect to wear the most corny things that can be purchas'd; so that those who trade hither with such Commodities as they want, may be sure to have the greatest Share of their Wealth.

Chili *describ'd.*

I Come next to the Kingdom *of Chili*, which lies nearest to those who shall think fit to attempt a Trade from *England* into the *South Sea*. Father *Ovalle*, a Native of this Country, and Procurator for it at *Rome*, agrees with our Maps, that it lies farthest South of any part of America on that call'd the *South* or *Pacifick Sea*. He bounds it *with Peru* on the North, the Straits of *Magellan* on the South, *Paraguay*, *Tucuman*, and *Patagonia* on the East, and the *South Sea on* the West. He begins it at S. Latitude 25, and extends it to Lat. 59, which is near 500 Leagues. The Breadth of it varies, and the broadest Place from East to West he makes about 150 Leagues, tho' *Chili* properly so call'd is not above 20 or 50 Leagues broad, from the Chain of Mountains named *Cordillera* to the South Sea; but when the King of *Spain* divided *America* into particular Governments, he added to *Chili* the vast Plains of *Cuio*, which are of an equal Length, and twice as broad as *Chili* it self. The Country in general *Ovalle* places in the 3*d*, 4*th* and 5*th* Climates; the longest Day in the 3*d* is 13 Hours, and in the 5*th* above 14.

The first *European* who took possession of it was *Don Diego d'Almagro*, a *Spaniard*, in 1535. He is said to march hither from *Peru* by Order of the King of *Spain*, with a Body of *Spanish* Troops and 15000 *Indians* and Blacks commanded by *some Indian* Princes, who had submitted to the *Spaniards*. I shall not trouble the Reader with the particular History of the *Spanish* Conquests till they reduced this Country, which they may find at large in *Ovalle*, *Herrera*, and others; but mall only say in general, that it was not totally in subjection to the *Spaniards* till the Year 1640, when the Inhabitants submitted to the Crown of *Spain*, on Condition that they should not be given in Property as Slaves. The *Spaniards*, who sufficiently experienc'd the Valour of this People, treat them with more Civility than they do the rest of the *Americans*, on purpose to keep them in Obedience, and for the most part they have submitted to the Church of *Rome*.

The Sansons say that *Chili*, in the Language of the Country, signifies Cold, which is so excessive in the Mountains call'd *Sierra Nevada*, a pare of the *Cordillera*, that it freezes Men and Cattle to Death, and keeps their Corps from Putrefaction; so that *Almagro* lost a great many of his Men and Horses as he past those Mountains. But the Vallies toward the Sea are very healthful, the Climate temperate, and the Soil excellent and fruitful, tho' with some difference, according as it lies nearer or further from the Equator; but the Coasts are subject to strong Gales of Wind.

The Country is divided into 3 Quarters, and those 3 into 13 Jurisdictions. The Quarter of *Chili* proper extends from the River *Copiapo* to that of *Maule*, and is hotter than *Spain*. The 2*d* Quarter call'd Imperial, reaches from the River *Maule* to that of *Gallegos*, and much resembles the Climate of *Spain*.

The Proximity of the Mountains on one side, and of the Sea on the other, makes it colder than otherwise it would be; but it has Warmth enough, to make it one of the best Countries in *America*. The Valley of *Copiapo* is so fruitful, that it frequently yields 300 for one single Measure, those of *Guasco* and *Coquimbo* fall very little short of it, and that of *Chili* proper is so excellent, that it gives Name to the whole Country by way of Eminence.

I come now to give a brief View of what *Ovalle*, a Native, says to it in general.

He tells us, that in *Chili*, properly so call'd, *viz.* the Country betwixt the Mountains and the Sea, the Soil and Climate, exceed those of any part of Europe in Goodness by the Concession of the *Europeans* themselves: He says it is like the best part of *Europe* in every thing, except the Opposition of the Seasons, it being Spring and Summer in the one, when it is Autumn and Winter in the other; but in the Vallies the Heat and Cold are not so excessive as; in Europe especially from Lat 36, or thereabouts, to Lat, 45, so that neither thereat of the Bay nor the Cold of the Night can be complain'd of, from whence it is that the Inhabitants make no difference between the Summer and Winter in their Bedding and Clothes. He adds, that they are not troubled here with Lightning, and seldom hear Thunder, except at a great distance. They have no Storms of Hail in the Spring, and seldom above 2 or 3 rainy Days together in the Winter, after which the Sky is serene without the least Cloud. The North Winds bring the Clouds and Rain, and the South Winds speedily make all clear. They have no poisonous or ravenous Creatures, except a small sort of Lions, which sometimes prey on their Flocks, but always fly from Men; nor are these Lions numerous, there being only a few of them in the Woods and Desarts. He observes as a peculiar Property of the Air of *Chili*, that no Bugs will live in it, tho' they swarm in *Cuio* on the other side of the Mountains. From the whole he infers, that there is no Country in *America* so agreeable to *European* Constitutions as *Chili*, the Air and Provisions are so like their own, but rather better.

The Spring begins about the Middle of our *August*, and lasts till the Middle of *November*; then the Summer holds to the Middle of *February*, the Autumn continues to the Middle of *May*, and the Winter from thence to the Middle of *August*. During this Season the Trees are deprived of their Leaves, and the Ground is cover'd with white Frosts, which are dissolved about 2 hours after the Sun rises. The Snow falls seldom in the Vallies, but in great Quantity in the Mountains, from whence it is melted in the Summer, and fructifies the Vallies and Plains with Rivulets. In the Spring the Fields are adorn'd with beautiful Flowers of all Colours and sorts, and of an admirable Scent, from whence they distil a fine Liquid called Angels Water, which makes a noble Perfume. The choicest Flowers and Plants that we cultivate grow wild there; they have Groves of Mustard Trees higher than a Man on Horseback, and the Birds build their Nests in them. They have many Physical Plants and Herbs, with which their *Indian* Physicians perform wonderful Cures, when the Patients are despair'd of by our *European* Doctors, but they are very shy of communicating those Secrets. Fruits and Seeds brought hither from *Europe* thrive very well, but those of *Mexico* and *Peru* don't. They have all our Sorts of Fruit in such abundance, that every one may cake what they please; so that none is sold, except a sort of extraordinary large Strawberries, which they cultivate. They have Oats, Wheat and Maiz in such plenty, that they are seldom troubled with Want of Grain. Their Pastures are so rich, and their Cattle of all sorts so numerous, that they don't value the Flesh, but salt the Tongues and Loins, and send 'em to *Peru* with the Hides and Tallow, which is a great Branch of their Trade. They have Store of noble and generous Wines, both white and red; their Vines are larger, and their Clusters of Grapes much bigger than any in *Europe*. They have also plenty of Olives, Groves of Cocoa Trees of several Leagues long, Almond-trees, and such Score of Silk grass, which they use instead of Hemp, that they furnish all the Coasts of the *South Sea* with Cordage for their Ships; they have also great Quantities of Annise and Cumminseed, Salt, Flax, Wool, Leather, Timber, Pitch, Amber, &c. So that, according to *Ovalle*, Merchants may trade from hence to other Parts in the *South Sea*, and specially *to Lima*, from 100 to 300 *per* Cent. Profit, of which I have also been informed by our Prisoners. Though they have abundance of Mulberry-trees, they breed no Silk-worms; so that the Ladies, who are extravagant in their Apparel, impoverish the Country by purchasing the richest Silks, tho' they might easily have enough of their own. They have plenty of Bees, yet have their Wax from *Europe*, for want of Industry to improve their own, and they have Pepper and other Spice from the *East Indies*, tho' they have a kind of Spice of their own, which might very well supply them. He adds, that the Herbage, Fishing, Hunting, Wood for Fuel and Timber, and Salt Mines, are here in common, so that every one may take what they please. They make little use of their Mines of Lead and Quick-Silver for *Peru* has enough of the latter to purify their Silver. *Ovalle* says the Gold Mines are so many that from the Confines of *Peru* to the Straits of Magellan there is no part of the Country without 'em; but they are not so much followed as in *Peru*, and they don't so much apply themselves to the Silver Mine's, because those of Gold are wrought with less charge; their Silver is dug from hard Rocks, ground to Powder in their Mills, and then resin'd with Quick-silver, which is, laborious as well as expensive; whereas they have NO other trouble with the Gold than to; wash the Earth from it; yet sometimes they follow the Veins of Gold through Rocks, when they have hopes that they will grow larger, as they frequently do, and one of these Veins is often enough to enrich the Discoverers. Gold is not dug here in such Plenty, since the War betwixt the *Spaniards* and *Araucarias* but the Natives wait for the Winter Rains, which wash it down from the Mountains, into Rivers, Ponds, *etc.* When the Women go into the Water, seel out the Grains with their Toes, and make up us much as supplys their present Necessaries, as our Author says, but to me this appears a very odd Way to get Gold. He tells us that he sent one of those Grains to *Seville*, where being couch'd, it was sound to be 23 Carats fine, without any manner of Purification. Most of the Bells and great Guns us'd in *Peru*, are made of the Copper of this Country.

He comes next to give an Account of the Chain of Mountains, named *Cordillera*, from his own Observation, and what he has read in Authors: He says they run from N. to S. from the Province of *Quito* to the Straits of *Magellan*, which is above a Thousand Leagues, and accounts them the highest Mountains in the World; they are generally 40 Leagues broadband intermixed with Abundance of habitable Valleys: These Mountains form 2 Ridges, the lowermost is cover'd with Woods and Groves, but the higher barren, because of the excessive Cold and Snow on them. The most remarkable Animals in these Mountains are, 1. that Species of Hogs which have their Navels on their Backs, call'd Pecarys, these go in great Herds, with each their Leader, and till he be kill'd, 'tis not safe for Hunters to attack them, but when he falls, they immediately disperse. 2. Wild Goats, whose Hair is as soft as Silk, and much us'd for fine Hats. 4. Their Sheep call'd Guanacos, shap'd like Camels, but of a far less Size, with Wool so fine that it is preferr'd to Silk for Softness and Colour. He adds, that the ancient *Incas*, or Princes, cut two Roads through those Mountains, and if we may believe *Herrera*, one of them was pav'd for 900 Leagues from *Cusco* to *Chili*, 'twas 25 Foot broad, and at every 4 Leagues, there was a noble Structure, and at each half League Couriers to relieve one another, in carrying Messages from the State. He says, there are still a sort of Inns on this Road, where Travellers find all Necessaries; but the Paths into the Mountains are so narrow, that a single Mule can scarce pass them. The Ascent begins at the very Shore of the Sea, but that which is properly call'd the Mountains, requires three or four Days Journey to the Top of them, where the Air is so very piercing and cold, that he found difficulty to breath, when he pass'd them, so that he and his fellow Travellers were obliged to breath quicker and stronger than ordinary, and to apply their Handkerchiefs to their Mouths, to break the extreme Coldness of the Air. *Herrera* says, That those who pass them from *Peru* are troubled with Reachings and Vomitings. *Ovalle* adds, That there are Meteors upon those Mountains sometimes so high in the Air, that they resemble Stars, and at other times so low, that they frighten the Mules and buz about their Ears and Feet. He says, on the Top of those Mountains they can't see the Country below for Clouds, tho' the Sky over their Heads is clear and bright, and the Sun shines with admirable Beauty. When he pass'd the highest Part of that which is properly call'd the *Cordillera*, he found no Snow, tho' in the beginning of Winter, whereas, in the lower Parts, 'twas so deep, that the Mules cou'd scarce travel. He supposes the Reason why there was no Snow on the Top is, that it reaches above the middle Region of the Air. There are 16 Vulcanos in this Chain of Mountains, which sometimes break out with dreadful Effects, cleave the Rocks, and issue great Quantities of Fire, with a Noise resembling Thunder. I refer to our Author for the particular Names and Places of those Vulcanos. He doubts not but there are many rich Mines among those Mountains tho' the Natives industriously conceal them, and make it Death to discover them, which has defeated several Attempts of that Nature by the *Spaniards*. The Natives have no occasion for those Mines themselves, because they have Plenty of Provisions, which is all they desire, and they are afraid that such Discoveries will occasion the *Spaniards* to dispossess them or to make them work in the Mines as Slaves. He concludes this Head with an Account that very rich Mines were discover'd at the Foot of those Mountains on the side of *Cuio*.

Those Mountains of the *Cordillera* are passable only in Summer, or in the Beginning of the Winter. There are frightful Precipices, and deep Rivers, at the sides of the narrow Passes, which frequently occasions the Loss of Mules and Travellers. The Streams run with such Violence, and so far below the Roads, that to look at them turns ones Head. The Ascents and Descents are so steep, that they are difficult to pass on Foot, but the Irksomeness of the Way is alleviated by the beautiful Cascades which the Water naturally forms as it falls from the Rocks and Mountains; and in some of the Valleys the Water Springs up to a great Height, like Fountains made by Art, amongst odoriferous Plants and Flowers, which make an Agreeable Prospect. All these Streams and Springs are so very cool, that a Man can't drink above 2 or 3 Sips at once, nor hold his Hand in them above a Minute. In some Places there are hot Springs, good against many Distempers, and leave a green Tincture in the Channels thro' which they run. One of those Rivers, call'd *Men-*

dosa, has a natural Bridge of Rock over it, from the Vault of which there hangs several Pieces of Stone, resembling Salt, which congeal like Icecles, as the Water drops from the Rock, and are form'd into several Shapes and Colours. This Bridge is broad enough for 3 or 4 Carts to pass a-breast. There's another Bridge near this, call'd the *Incas*, laid over by Art, betwixt 2 Rocks, as some say, but our Author thinks it is the Work of Nature: It is so very high from the River, that he could not hear the Stream, which runs with great Rapidity, and though it be a large River, it appear'd like a Brook when he look'd down from the Bridge, which he could not do without being struck with Horror.

He comes next to describe the particular Rivers which run from these Mountains; but I shall only mention the chief of them; and tho' most of them don't run above 30 Leagues, yet some of them, towards their Mouths, are navigable by Ships of the greatest Burthen. The first is that which rises in the Confines of *Peru*, about S. Lat. 25. 'tis call'd the River of Salt, because 'tis so salt that it can't be drank, and petrifies what's thrown into it. 2. *Copiapo*, which rises in Lat. 26. runs 20 Leagues from E. to W. and forms a Bay and a Harbour, at its Entrance into the Sea. 3. *Guasco* rises in Lat. 28. and forms likewise a Bay and Harbour. 4. The River of *Coquimbo*, which rises in Lat. 30. forms a noble Bay and a Port, with beautiful Myrtles, and other Trees on the Bank, that make a noble and a pleasant Grove. 5. *Aconcagua*, a large deep River that rises about Lat. 33, runs thro' several fruitful Valleys. 6. *Maypo* rises about Lat. 33 and a half. It is so rapid, that it admits no Bridge but one made of Cables; it enters the Sea with so much Force, that its Waters form a Circle, and are distinguished a great Way. It is brackish, noted for excellent Trouts, and the Sheep which feed on its Banks, afford Mutton of a curious Relish. There are several other Rivers which fall into it; the first is, that of St. *Jago*, alias *Mapocho*; 'tis divided into several Streams, to water the District of St. *Jago*, which sometimes it over-flows: Not far from the City it sinks under Ground, and rises again in a Grove, about 2 or 3 Leagues distant. 2. The River *Poangue*, its Water is extraordinary clear and sweet, and flowing thro' Veins of Metal, very much helps Digestion. It runs for several Leagues under Ground, fructifies the Valley which lies over it, and produces excellent Corn and Melons. The Banks of this River are adorn'd with beautiful Trees. 3. The Rivers *Decollina* and *Lampa*, which unite together within 10 or 12 Leagues off their Rise, and form the noted Lake of *Cudagues*. It is so deep, that great Vessels may sail in it, is about 2 Leagues long, and its Banks cover'd with Trees that are verdant all the Year. It abounds with excellent Trouts and Smelts, which are a great Conveniency to the City of St. *Jago*. 7. *Rapel* is nothing inferior to *Maypo*, enters the Sea about Lat. 34. and a half, and receives several other rapid Streams. The adjacent Country has excellent Pastures for fattening of Cattle. 8. *Delora* rises in Lat. 34 three quarters, and is exactly like the former. 9. *Maul*, a great River, which rises in Lat. 35". and bounds the Jurisdiction of St. *Jago*. The Natives call all the Country betwixt those Rivers, *Promocaes*, *i.e.* a Place of Dancing and Delight, which our Author says is very just, for he never saw a more pleasant Country, nor one better furnish'd with Provisions of all sorts. The *Spaniards* have many noble Farms in these Parts. Near the Mouth of this River, there's a Dock for building of Ships, and a Ferry belonging to the King for the Conveniency of Passengers. 10. *Itata*; 'tis 3 times as large and deep as the *Maul*, and enters the Sea about Lat. 36 In most Places they pass it on Rafts, and in some it is fordable. 11. *Andalien*, a River which runs slow, and enters the spacious and pleasant Bay of *Conception*, at Lat. 36 three quarters. There's another small River, which runs through the middle of the City of *Conception*, a little above which it falls from a high Rock, and gives the Inhabitants an Opportunity to form all sorts of Water-works from it, among pleasant Groves of Lawrels, Myrtles, and other odoriferous Plants. 12. *Biobio*, a famous River, which enters the Sea, in Lat. 37. 'tis the largest in *Chili*, and is from 2 to 3 Mile broad at its Mouth. Our Author says its Waters run thro' Veins of Gold, and Fields of Sarsaparilla, which make them very wholesom, and good against several Distempers. This River is the Boundary betwixt the *Indians* who are Friends to the *Spaniards*, and those who are their Enemies, and make frequent Incursions upon them. This obliges the *Spaniards* to keep many Garrisons in those Parts, but the Natives trust to their Mountains. This River swells so much in the Winter, that it becomes impassable, and occasions a Cessation of Arms on both sides. These People, says *Ovalle*, have given the *Spaniards* more trouble than all the other Natives of *America*; so that they are forced to maintain 12 Forts, well provided with Men and Cannon, besides the City of *Conception* and *Chillam*, to over-aw the Natives. 13. *Imperial*, a pleasant River, which fells into the Sea, about Lat. 39. after having receiv'd many other Rivers, and among 'em two which run into the famous Lake of *Buren*, where the *Indians* have an impregnable Fortress. 24. *Tolten*, about 30 Miles from the River *Imperial*, is deep enough for great Ships, where it enters the Sea. 15. About 8 Leagues farther, the River *Quenale* enters the Sea, and is capable of small Barks. 16. *Valdivia*, so called from Pedro *de Valdivia*, one of the Conquerors and Governors of *Chili*, who built a Port and City, near the Mouth of it, where great Ships may come up about 3 Leagues from the Sea. This River opens to the North, and over-against the City lies the pleasant Island of *Constantine*, with two others; the River is navigable on both sides of the Island, but deepest on the South side. 17. *Chilo*, which rises from a Lake at the Foot of the *Cordillera*, where there are Baths good against the Leprosy and other Distempers. Our Author says so little of the Rivers on the East side of the *Cordillera*, that we pass them over.

Ovalle gives an Account of many remarkable Fountains, both hot and cold, good against mod Distempers; but I shall not insist on them. He says, they have many Sea Lakes or Bays, which bring great Profit to the Owners, because their Fisheries are more certain than those of the Sea; and furnish most part of the Lenten Fair to the Inhabitants, and in the hot Season abundance of Salt.

He adds, that in the Valley of *Lampa*, near St. *Jago*, there's an Herb, about a Foot high, resembling Sweet *Basil*. In Summer it is cover'd with Grains of Salt, like Pearl, which is more savoury, and has a finer Flavour than any other Salt. Our Author comes next to treat of the Fertility of the Coast, which, he says, among other Fish produces Shell-Fish in greater Quantities, larger than any where else, and I. Oisters, valuable both for their Meat and Pearls. 2. Chores, a fine Sort of Shell-fish, which also breed Pearl. 3. Manegues, which have 2 round Shells, the inside of which resembles Mother of Pearl. In short, he says, the Sea throws up Shell-fish, in such Quantities, upon some Parts of the Coast, that Ships may be loaded with them, and their Shells are of such Variety of Colours and Shapes, that our *European* Virtuosos might from hence have a curious Collection, where as the *Indians* only burn them for Chalk. There are other Sorts of Fish on these Coasts, some of which they call Sea-Stars, others Suns and Moons, because they referable those Planets, as they are usually painted, which are common elsewhere, but not SO large as here. These Fish reduc'd into Powder, and drank in Wine, are an infallible Remedy against Drunkenness, and frequently us'd for that end, because it creates an Abhorrence of Wine in those who drink it, says our Author. He adds, that great Quantities of Amber are found on this Coast, particularly, the grey fort, which is the best. They have all other sorts of Fish, common to us in *Europe*, besides others, peculiar to themselves.

He comes next to their Birds, and besides those which are common in *Europe*, there are I. Flamencos, bigger than Turkeys, their Feathers of a white and scarlet Colour, of which the Natives make Ornaments, and their Legs are so long that they walk thro' Lakes and Ponds. 2. The Child Bird, so call'd, because they look like a swadled Child, with its Arms at Liberty: They are very good Meat. 3. Airones, so much valued for their Feathers, to make Tufts, that formerly, they say, every Feather upon their Heads cost 2 Reals. These Birds are rare. There are others call'd Garcolos, whose Feathers are generally us'd by Soldiers. 4. Voycas, from whose Notes the *Indians* pretend to foretel Death, Sickness, or other Misfortunes; the Feathers on their Breasts are of a deep scarier Colour, and the rest brown. 5. Pinguedas, their Body is of the size of an Almond; they feed upon Flowers, and shine like polish'd Gold, mix'd with green; the Males have a lively Orange Colour, like Fire on their Heads, and the Tails of those Birds are a Foot long, and 2 Inches broad. 6. Condores, which are white as Ermin, their Skins are extreme soft and warm, and therefore us'd as Gloves. They have abundance of Ostriches, and Variety of Hawks in this Country. *Ovalle* comes next to treat of their Beasts. He says, they had no Cows, Horses, Sheep, Hogs, House-Cats, nor common Dogs of any sort, Goats, Asses, or Rabbits, till they were brought hither by the *Spaniards*, but now all these are increased to a wonderful Degree by the Richness of their Country and Pasture, so that one Cow frequently yields 150 tb Weight of Tallow. *Herrera* says, that when the *Spaniards* came first hither, a Horse was commonly sold for 1000 Crowns, but now they are so plenty that they send them yearly to *Peru*. The most remarkable Animals, which are not common with us, are, I. Their Sheep, mention'd before, shap'd like Camels, tho' not so large: The Natives us'd them for Ploughing and Carriage, before they had *European* Cattle: Their upper Lips are slit, with which they spit at those who vex them, and whereever their Spittle falls, it causes a Scab. They govern'd them by a kind of Bridle put thro' their Ears, and they would kneel like Camels, to take on their Burden. 2. Wild Goats, which very much resemble those Sheep, but are all of a red clear Colour, so very swift that they out-run Horses, and are never to be tamed. They feed in great Herds, and are hunted by Dogs, which easily catch the young ones, that are excellent Meat. The Flesh of the old ones, dried and smoaked, is reckon'd the best of its kind. These Creatures, especially the oldest, have Bezoar Stones, in a Bag under their Belly. Our Author says, he brought one of those Stones to *Italy*, which weigh'd 32 Ounces, and was as perfect an Oval as if it had been form'd by a Turner; he gave the *Indian* who found it 70 Pieces of 8 for it.

Their most remarkable Trees, besides what are common to *Europe*, are, I. The Cinnamon Tree, so call'd, because the Bark resembles Cinnamon, in such Plenty, that they cover their Houses with them: They keep their Leaves all the Year, and resemble the *Italian* Lawrel Royal. 2. The Guyac Tree grows in the *Cordillera*, is as hard and heavy as Iron: The Decoction is good against many Diseases. 3. The Sandal Tree, that is very odoriferous, a Preservative against infectious Distempers, and therefore us'd by the Priests when they visit the Sick. 4. The Maguey, whose Leaves are admirable against Burnings; the Fruit is like Myrtle-Berries, and of an excellent Relish. 5. The Quelu, of whose Fruit they make a very sweet Drink. 7. Iluigan, the *Spaniards* call it *Molde*, 'tis of the Shape and Colour of Pepper: It grows on a small Tree, and makes an agreeable Liquor, coveted by those of Quality. 8. The Myrtilla which grows on the Mountains, from Lat. 37. and upwards: *Herrera* says, its Fruit is a common Food to the Natives, not unlike a Grape, and of this they make a Wine that exceeds all other Liquors. 'Tis of a bright gold Colour, will bear more Water than any other Wine, chears the Heart, and never offends the Stomach, but increases Appetite. The Vinegar made of it exceeds all other sorts. Our Author adds, that their Cypress, Cedar and Oak Trees are extraordinary good.

He comes next to the Islands of *Chili*. The first are those of *Juan Fernandez*, already describ'd. The second are the Islands of *Chiloe*, which lie about Lat. 43. and form an Archipelago of 40 Islands. He says the Nature of the Climate is such, that it rains almost all the Year, so that only Maiz on such other Grain can ripen here, as need little Sun The chief Diet of the Inhabitants is the Root *Papas*, which is larger here than any where else. They have excellent Shell fish, very good Poultry and Hogs, some Beeves and Sheep. The Capital of this Country is the City of *Castro*, which lies in the chief Island, and is garrison'd by the *Spaniards*. Here they have great Store of Honey and Wax, and some Gold Mines on the Coast. Their chief Manufacture is Clothing for the *Indians*, and they have vast Woods of Cedar Trees of a prodigious size, with the Planks of which they drive a great Trade to *Chili* and *Peru*. 3. The Islands of *Chonos*, in Lat. 45. but of little Use, because of the excessive Plains which drown the Soil. 4. The Fine Island, which lies almost in the same Latitude with *Val Paraiso* and St. *Jago*: It has a safe Harbour for Ships, where they may ride in 20 or 30 Fathom Water. The *Spaniards* say 'tis a very beautiful Island, abounds with Trees, wild Boars, and other Game, and excellent Water; and there's Plenty of Fish on the Coast. 5. The Island of *Mocha*, where the *Dutch*, under *Spilberg*, found a very generous Reception by the Natives, who furnish'd them with Plenty of Sheep, and other Provisions, in exchange for Clothes, Axes, &c. The North side of it is plain and low, but the South side rocky. 6. The Island of St. *Maria*, 13 Leagues S. W. from the City of *Conception*, and 3 from *Arauco*: It is very fruitful and temperate, lies about Lat. 37, and is well inhabited. 7. The Islands of *Pedro de Sarmiento*, so call'd, because he discover'd them, when in Pursuit of Sir *Francis Drake*. They are about 80 in Number, and lie about Lat. 50. so that we suppose them to be those now call'd *The Duke of York's Islands*, which lie a little to the Northward of the Straits of *Magillan*.

Our Author comes next to *Cuio*, the third Quarter of *Chili*, which lies on the other side of the *Cordillera* towards the East. 'Tis divided into several Provinces, and quite differs in Temperature from *Chili*. The Summer is excessive hot, and the Inhabitants so annoy'd with Bugs and Muskettos, that they lie abroad in their Gardens and Yards. They have almost perpetual Thunders and Lightnings and are mightily infested with poisonous Infects: These are the bad Qualities of the Country, to compensate which, the Soil, in many places, if possible, exceeds that of *Chili* in Fruitfulness; the Crops are richer, the Fruits larger, and of a better Taste, because of the greater Heats. They have Store of Corn, Wine, Flesh, and all the Fruits, Roots, and Herbs of

Europe, with large Plantations of Olives and Almonds. The Cold is not so sharp in Winter as that of *Chili*, and the Air much clearer, so that the Season is then very temperate: they have great Quantities of large excellent Trouts, and other River Fish. Their peculiar Fruits are, I. Algaroba, of which they make a Bread so sweet, that Strangers can't eat it. They supply *Tucuman* and *Paraguay* with Figs, Pomgranates, Apples, dry'd Peaches and Grapes, and excellent Wine and Oil. *Ovalle* says, That in his time there were rich Mines of Gold and Silver discover'd here, which were reckon'd to be better than those of *Potosi*, and that in short it had all Necessaries for Life in as great abundance as any other Country, and in general is very healthful. The Provinces *of Tucuman* and *Paraguay*, which bound this Counry we have already describ'd.

Chapter XIII

Jan. 10. I now go on with my Journal, being on our Departure from *California*, and returning to *Great Britain.* I shall not trouble the Reader with every Day's particular Transactions in this long and tedious Passage, but only take notice of such Occurrences as are worth remark, and to satisfy the Curious, shall subjoin a particular Table of each Day's Run, with the Latitude, Longitude and Variation betwixt Cape St. *Lucas* on *California,* and *Guam,* one of the *Ladrones* Islands. We re solved to keep an exact Account of the Distance and Variation not being certainly known to us from any former Voyagers.

Jan. 11. We weigh'd from Port *Segura* last Night, but were becalm'd under the Shore till the 12*th* in the Afternoon, when there sprung up a Breeze, which soon run us out of sight of the Land. We took our Departure from Cape *St. Lucas,* which bore N. by E. at 12 a Clock, distant about 15 Leagues. We were forc'd to go away with little or no Refreshment, having but 3 or 4 Fowls, and a very slender Stock of Liquor, which we got out of the *Batchelor.* Several of our Men were in a weak Condition, besides my self, Mr. *Vanbrugh,* and the rest that were wounded. We were forc'd to allow but I Pound and half of Flower, and I small Piece off Meat to 5 in a Mess, with 3 Pints of Water a Man for 24 Hours, for Drink and Drafting their Victuals. We struck down 10 of our Guns into the Hold, to ease the Ship; for being out of the way of Enemies, they are altogether useless betwixt this and the *East Indies.* On the 16*th* the *Batchelor* made a Signal to give us some Bread, they having found a good Quantity of Bread and Sweet-meats aboard her, but little of Flesh-kind: We had 1000 Weight of Bread for our Share, the *Dutchess* as much, and the *Marquiss* 500 Weight; in lieu of which we sent back to the Prize 2 Casks of Flower, one of *English* Beef, and one of Pork, they having but 45 Days Provision aboard in Flesh. This Morning *Thomas Conner,* a Boy, fell overboard, but the Launch being a-stern, we cur her Moarings, and cook him up just as he was tired with Swimming, and ready to sink.

On the 26*th* in the Morning the Water was very much discolour'd, at which being surprized, we immediately founded, but found no Ground. We spoke with the *Dutchess,* and agreed to go away W. S. W. till we got into the Lat. of 13°. because our *Spanish* Pilot told us it was dangerous going in 14, by reason of Islands and Shoals, where a *Spanish* Vessel was lost some time ago, ever since which the *Manila* Ship, in her Return from *Acapulco,* runs in. Lat. 13. and keeps that Parallel till they make the Island of *Guam.*

On the 28*th* the Steward missing some Pieces of Pork, we immediately search'd, and found the Thieves, one of 'em had been guilty before, and forgiven, on promise of Amendment, but was punish'd now, left Forbearance should encourage the rest to follow this bad Practice; Provisions being so short, and our Run so long, may prove of ill consequence. I order'd 'em to the Main Jeers, and every Man of the Watch to give 'em a Blow with a Cat of Nine-tails, and their Mess-mates being privy to the Theft, were put in Irons.

Feb. I. We buried one *Boyce,* betwixt 40 and 50 Years of Age, whom we brought from *Guiaquil,* where and in other Parts of *New Spain* he had been a Prisoner above 7 Years, since he was taken in the Bay of *Camprachy.*

On the 5*th* a Negro we named *Deptford* died, who being very much addicted to stealing of Provisions, his Room was more acceptable than his

Company at this time. On the 6*th* we spoke with the *Dutchess*; I was for augmenting the Mens Allowance in Meat, since we had such a favourable Gale, which was like to continue; but Capt. *Courtney* objected against it, alledging that if we miss'd *Guam*, we should all be starved; so we deferr'd it a Week longer. We have had very bad luck in fishing hitherto, having took only one Albicore since we came from Cape St. *Lucas*.

On the II*th* I agreed with Capt. *Courtney* to continue a W, by S. Course till we get clear of the Rocks call'd the *Bartholomews*, which are laid down in 13°. and a half; but the Distance of them being variously computed, makes us the more cautious, and keep a constant good Look-out. On the 13*th* the *Spanish* Pilot we took in the *Batchelor* died; we kept him, thinking he might be of use to us, if he recover'd of his Wounds; but he was shot in the Throat with a Musket-ball, which lodg'd so deep, the Doctors could not come at it. On the 14*th* we agreed with Capt. *Courtney* to give half a Pound of Flower or Bread more to a Mess. That same Day, in Commemoration of the antient Custom in *England* of chusing Valentines, I drew up a List of the fair Ladies in *Bristol*, that were any ways related to or concerned in the Ships, and sent for my Officers into the Cabbin, where every one drew, and drank the Lady's Health in a Cup of Punch, and to a happy Sight of 'em all; this I did to put 'em in mind of Home. On the 17*th* I was troubled with a Swelling in my Throat, which incommoded me very much, till this Morning I got out a Piece of my Jaw Bone that lodg'd there since I was wounded. Our Ship began to make more Water, so we clapt on a new Bonnet where we took the old one off; but after many fruitless Attempts, were forc'd to keep one Pump continually going, every two Men in the Watch taking their Posts once an Hour; which Labour, with the want of sufficient Food, make our People look miserably.

On the 18*th* we threw a Negro overboard, who died of a Consumption and Want together. Our Men began to be very much out of order, and what adds to their Weakness is our continual Pumping, nor can we pretend to make any further Addition to their Allowance.

On the 25*th Tho. Williams*, a *Welch* Taylor, died; he was shot in the Leg at engaging the 2*d Manila* Ship, and being of a weak Constitution, fell into a Dysentery, which kill'd him. On the 26*th* we Caught a Couple of fine Dolphins, which were very acceptable to us, having had but very indifferent Luck of Fish in this long Passage.

On *March* the 3*d* we buried a Negro call'd *Augustine*, who died of the Scurvy and Dropsy. We agree to give 6 Negroes the same Allowance as five of our own Men, which will but just keep those that are in health alive.

On the 10*th* we made Land, being the Island *Serpana*, which bore N. W. distant about 8 Leagues, The *Dutchess* made another Island to the Westward, which bore W. by S. distant about 10 Leagues; the latter they took to be the Island *Guam*, so we clapt upon a Wind, and stood for it.

March II. This Morning we had sight of both Islands, the Northermost bearing N. N. W. distant about 7 Leagues, and the Body of the Westermost W. S. W. 5 Leagues, The S*paniards* say there is a great Shoal between these Islands, but nearest to S*erpana*. We ran along the Shore, being satisfied it was the Island of *Guam*, from whence there came several flying Prows to look at the Ships; they run by us very swift, but none would venture aboard. At Noon the Westermost part of the Island bore West, and at the same time we made a small low Island joining to *Guam*, with a Shoal between it and *Guam*; the Island appear'd green and very pleasant, off of it there runs a Spit of Sand to the Southward, but keeping it a good Birth from you as you near it, there s no Danger, being gradual Soundings to the Shoal. After we were clear of it we sprung our Luff, and stood in for the Harbour, which lies mid-way betwixt this and the North part of the Island. There came heavy Flaws of Wind off Shore, sometimes for us, and at other times against us; but we got to an Anchor in the Afternoon in 12 Fathom Water, about half a Mile off Shore, where there was a little Village. The small Island to the Southward bore South of us, distant about 3 Leagues, and another small one to the Northward bore N. N. W. about 2 Leagues. The Necessity of our stopping at these Islands to get a Refreshment of Provisions, was very great, our Sea Store being almost exhausted, and what we had left was very ordinary, especially our Bread and Flower, which was not enough for 14 Days at the shortest Allowance. In order to recruit quietly, we endeavour'd to get some of the Natives aboard that were in the Prows, to keep 'em as Hostages in case of sending any of our Men to the Governour: One of 'em, as we were turning into the Harbour with S*panish* Colours, came under our Stern. There were 2 S*paniards* in the Boat, who asked what we were, and from whence we came? Being answer'd in *Spanish*, that we were Friends, and came from *New Spain*, they willingly came aboard, and ask'd if we had any Letter to the Governour ? We had one ready, but before we could get it signed by all the Commanders, there came a Messenger from the Governour, who demanded the same Account of us. We immediately sent him away with 2 of our Linguists, detaining one of the S*paniards* till they return'd. The Letter was thus:

SIR,

We being Servants to Her Majesty of Great Britain, and stopping at these Islands in our Way to the East Indies, will not molest the Set-tlement, provided you deal friendly by us. We will pay for whatever Provisions and Refreshments you have to spare, in such manner as best agrees with your Conveniency, either in Money, or any Neces-saries you want. But if after this civil Request you deny us, and do not act like a Man of Honour, you may immediately expect such Military Treatment, as we are with ease able to give you. This we thought fit to confirm under our Hands, recommending to you our Friendship and kind Treatment, which we hope you'll esteem, and assure your self we then shall be with the strictest Honour,

Your Friends and humble Servants,

To the Honourable Governour W..Rogers.

of the Island of Guam, March S. *Courtney.*

23. 1709. E. Cooke.

March II. In the Morning we and the *Dutchess* mann'd our Pinnace, and sent her ashore with a Flag of Truce, where they were entertain'd courteously by the Natives, who promis'd to supply us with such Provisions as they could spare, provided the Governour would give 'em leave. About Noon our Lin-guist returned and brought with him 3 *Spanish* Gentlemen from the Gover-nour, who in answer to our Letter sent another, expressing all Readiness imaginable to accommodate us with what the Island afforded, and that he had sent those Gentlemen to treat with us. I immediately sent for Capt. *Dover*,

Courtney, and *Cooke*, &c. being not able to stir out of the Ship, and desir'd they would come and consult with me how to act.

March 13. This Morning we had 4 Bullocks, 1 for each Ship, with some Limes, Oranges, and Cocoa Nuts. Our Misunderstandings at *California* have been very much augmented since by our Want of Provisions, one Ship's Company being jealous the other had most and best; but now being arriv'd at a Place of Plenty, we are all indifferently well reconciled, and an Entertainment was provided aboard the *Batchelor* for the *Spanish* Gentlemen, where most of our Officers appointed to meet. I being not able to move my self, was hoisted in a Chair out of the Ship, and also out of the Boat into the *Batchelor*; there we had a good Entertainment, and agreed, that on Thursday next a Representative for each Ship should wait upon the Governour, and make him a handsome Present for his Civility and Readiness to supply us.

March 15. This Morning we had another Entertainment aboard the *Marquiss*, where I likewise went in the same manner as before.

March 16. This Morning our Pinnace went with several of our Officers to accept of the Governour's Invitation ashore, who receiv'd them with all imaginable Friendship and Respect, having near 200 Men drawn up in Arms at their Landing, and the Officers and Clergy of the Island to conduct them to the Governour's House, which was a very handsome seat, considering where we are: They entertain'd them with at least sixty Dishes of several sorts, the best could be got on the Island, and when they took their Leaves, each fired a Volley of Small Arms. They presented the Governour, according as we had agreed, with 2 Negro Boys dress'd in Liveries, 20 Yards of Scarlet Cloth-Serge, and 6 Pieces of Cambrick, which he seem'd wonderfully pleas'd with, and promis'd to assist us in whatever lay in his Power.

March 17. This Day we got our Dividend, being about 60 Hogs, 99 Fowls, 24 Baskets of *Indias* Corn, and 14 Bags of Rice, 44 Baskets of Yams, and 800 Cocoa Nuts.

March 18. There was an Entertainment aboard us to day, where we had most of our Officers, and 4 *Spanish* Gentlemen from the Governour. I made 'em as welcome as Time and Place would afford, diverting 'em with Musick, and our Sailors Dancing till Night, when we parted very friendly. We got some more Bullocks on board, being small lean Cattle, but what we gladly accepted of; each Ship had 14 in all.

March 20. This Morning each Ship had 2 Cows and Calves more, being the last we are like to get. We had a Meeting on board the *Marquiss*, where 'twas agreed to make a handsome Present to the Governour's Deputy, who had the Fatigue to get our Provisions together, wherein he us'd all possible dispatch. We gave him and the rest of the Gentlemen what they esteem'd double the Value of what we received of them, which they certify'd under their Hands, and that we had been very civil to them. We also gave them the like Certificate, sign'd by all our Officers, to shew to any *English* that might have occasion to recruit there, and parted very friendly. Having finish'd that Affair, it was agreed, that we should steer from hence a West and by South Course to go clear of some Islands that lie in our way, and then thought it proper to steer directly for the South East part of *Mindanao*, and from thence the clearest Way to *Ternate*. It was also agreed, that our Ship being very leaky, I should deliver to Capt. *Courtney* one Chest of Plate and Money, to be put on board the *Dutchess*.

March 21. At Break of Day we hoisted our Colours, and fired a Gun for our Consorts to unmoar. In the mean time, with the Consent of the other Officers I put an old *Spaniard* ashore, call'd *Ant. Gomes Figuero,* whom we took in the 1*st* Bark in the S*outh Seas,* and design'd to carry him to *Great Britain,* to condemn all our Prizes took there; but he being now in all appearance not likely to live, we agreed to dismiss him, he giving us a Certificate that he saw us attack and take several Prizes, all Subjects to *Philip* V. King of *Spain,* &c. I gave him some Clothes and other odd things to help him in his Sickness, than put him ashore to the Deputy Governour, and the rest of the S*panish* Officers, who gave us a Certificate, that they receiv'd such a Person.

I shall here give a Description of the Isle of GUAM.

The Island of Guam *Describ'd.*

This Island is about 40 Leagues round; the Anchoring Place is on the W. Side, and about the Middle there's a large Cove, with several Houses built after the S*panish* Mode, with Accommodations for the Officers and Crew of the *Acapulco* Ship, the Settlement being made here on purpose for that Ship to recruit at, in her Way to *Manila.* There are about 300 S*paniards* on this and the Neighbouring Islands; most of the Natives are their Converts. They told us they have 8 Fathers, 6 of whom teach School, besides performing their Offices as Clergymen. They have also Schools taught by *Mullattoes* and *Indians,* who have learn'd the Language, so that most of the Natives understand *Spanish.* The S*paniards* inform me, that there's a Range of Islands from hence to *Japan.* Among which there are several abound with Gold, and they were now building a small Vessel to discover them, in order to get a Trade.

The Island of *Guam* it self abounds with Oranges, Lemons, Citrons, Musk and Water Melons, which were brought hither by the S*paniards.* The Orange Trees thrive very well here. The Island is full of Hills and Dales, and Streams of good Water. They have Plenty of Cattle, but small, poor, and generally white. The *Indico* Plant grows wild in such Abundance, that were they industrious, and had Coppers to boil it up, they might have great Quantities of that Commodity; but being so remote and out of the Way of Trade, they make no Use of it, nor do they improve any thing but what contributes to their present Subsistence; and having that, they are easie. Money is of so little Use, and so scarce among them, that they could not raise 1000 Dollars in the whole Island to purchase Commodities from us, which they would gladly have done. Here are about 200 Soldiers, who receive their Pay from *Manila* by a small Ship once *per Ann.* This Ship brings them Cloaths, Sugar, Rice, and Liquor, for which she carries back most of the Money again. This has made them of late sow Rice in their Valleys, and make other Improvements. They abound with Hogs, which are the best Pork in the World, because they feed altogether on Cocoa-Nutts, and Bread-Fruit, which are plentiful here; and were not the S*paniards* slothful, they might have most Necessaries of their own Growth for the Maintenance of Life.

Their Bread Fruit I thought the most remarkable Thing on the Island. I saw some of it which was as large as Orangey and much resembled them. They tell me, that when ripe they are three Times as large, and grow in many other Places near the Equinox in the *East Indies.* The Leaves are almost as large as those of Figs, something like them, but of a brown Colour. The Tree is large, arid they have such Plenty of this Fruit in the Season, that they fatten their Hogs with them. The Fruit has no Stone, and by the Account they gave, the Inside resembles a dry Potato or Yam, with which they likewise abound. The Wind blows constantly a S. E. Trade here, except during the Westerly Monsoons, which last from the Middle of *June* to the Middle of *August*. The Governour lives on the N. Side of the Island, where there's a small Village, and a Convent, being the chief Habitation of the S*paniards*. They marry with the Natives, and had not above four *Spanish* Women on the Island. The *Indians* are tall and strong, of a dark olive Colour, go all naked, except a Clout about their Posteriors, and the Women have little Petticoats. The Men are dextrous at slinging of Stones, which they make of Clay, of an oval Form, burning them, till as hard as Marble, and are so good Marks-men, that the S*paniards* say, they seldom miss hitting any Mark, and throw it with such a Force, as to kill a Man at a considerable Distance. I heard of no other Weapons that they used, but a Stick or Lance made of the heaviest Wood in the Island.

The Governour presented us with one of their flying Prows, which I shall describe here because of the Odness of it. The S*paniards* told me 'twould run 20 Leagues *per* Hour, which I think too large; but by what I saw, I verily believe, they may run 20 Miles or more in the Time, for when they viewed our Ships, they passed by us like a Bird flying. These Prows are about 30 Foot long, not above 2 broad, and about 3 deep; they have but one Mast which stands in the Middle, with a Mat Sail, made in the Form of a Ship's Mizen. The Yard is flung in the Middle, and a Man sits at each End with a Paddle to steer her, so that when they so about, they don't turn the Boat as we do to ring the Wind on the other side, but only change the Sail, so that the Jack and Sheet of the Sail are used alike, and the Boat's Head and Stern are the same, only they change them, as Occasion requires, to sail either Way; for they are so narrow that they could not bear any Sail, were it not for Booms, that run out from the Windward Side, fasten'd to a large Log shap'd like a Boat, and near half as long, which becomes contiguous to the Boat On these Booms a Stage is made above the Water, on a Level with the Side of the Boat, upon which they carry Goods or Passengers, The greatest Inconveniency in sailing these Boats is before the Wind, for by the Out-layer, which is built out on one Side, if the Wind presses any thing heaver on the contrary Side, the Boat is over-see, which often happens; having brought one of these Boats to *London*, it might be worth sitting up to put in the Canal in St. *James's* Park for a Curiosity, since we have none like it in this Part of the World.

As soon as the Boat return'd from landing Senior *Figuro*, we put under Sail, having a find Breeze of Wind at E. N. E. We had generally fair Weather here in the Day Time, and Showers commonly in the Night, but very sultry. The Wind always off Shoar betwixt the E. and N. E. Our Decks are filled with Cattle and Provender.

According to Promise, I have here inserted my Run from *California* to *Guam*. (see table next page)

At 3 a Clock in the Afternoon the Island of Guam bore W. by S. distant 10 Leagues.

March 22. At 6 last Night, the Body of the Island *Guam* bore E. N. E. Dist. 8 Leagues, from whence we took our Departure, designing for *Ternate*, one of the *Molucca* Islands belonging to the *Dutch*, and distant from *Guam* about 400 Leagues. We had a fresh Gale of Wind at N. E. and N. E. by E. with fair Weather, but very sultry. Lat 12. 45. Var. 5. 3°. E

April 11. Nothing remarkable has occurr'd worth noting, but that we have generally had a strong Current setting to the Northward. At Two Yesterday Afternoon we made Land, bearing S. E. distant about 5 Leagues, being a low flat Island, all green, and full of Trees. Lat. 2. 54. N. This Island is not laid down in any Sea Chart; our Ship continues very leaky.

April 14. Yesterday in the Afternoon we saw Land, bearing W. S. W. 12 Leagues, being very high. The Current has set to the Northward this 24 Hours very strong. Lat. I. 54.

April 15. Yesterday in the Afternoon we made other Land, which bore W. N. W. distant about 10 Leagues, and suppos'd it to be the N. E. Part of *Celebes*. We saw 3 Water-Spouts; one of which had like to have broke on the *Marquiss*, but the *Dutchess* by firing two Shot, broke it before it reach'd her. We saw a very large Tree a-float, with a Multitude of Fish about it; and 2 large Islands, the Southermost bearing S. W. distant about 8 Leagues, and the Northermost W. N. W. 7 Leagues, both being the same Land we saw Yesterday; and the latter we now suppose to be the S. E. Part of *Moratay*, and the other the N. Part of *Gilolo*. At Noon the Southermost Land bore S. W, by S. 10 Leagues, and the Westermost 5 Leagues. N. Lat. 02. 13.

April 17. We having a Westerly Gale, and the Current setting against us, we gained little Ground in turning to get about *Moratay*. We had indifferent fair Weather all Night and Morning, but standing pretty much to the Southward, lost Sight of the Land, a strong Current setting to the Northward.

April 23. We had very stormy Weather for most Part since the 17*th*, the *Marquiss* and we suffer'd both in our Rigging. So that we begin to despair of getting to Windward of this Island *Moratay*, to reach *Ternate*, which is now near us; but we are obliged to keep Company with the *Marquiss* and *Batchelor*, who sail but very indifferent upon a Wind; and it's the hardest upon our Ship's Company, who are wearied almost to Death with continual Pumping, the Leak having encreas'd upon US since we came out of *Guam*, so that it is as much as 4 Men are able to keep her free Half an Hour, all the Watch being oblig'd to come to it once in 4 Hours.

April 29. We got 292 *Lib.* Weight of Bread from the *Batchelor* Yesterday Afternoon, in Exchange for Meat we sent 'em, which with what we had before, will last us about 20 Days, and not much longer. We begin to be very much disheartned, because Captain *Dampier*, who has been twice here, tells us, that if we can't get *Ternate*, or find the Island *Tula*, we can reach no Port or Place to recruit at, and that it will be impossible to get Provisions for us on the Coast of *New Guinea*, should we be forc'd to go thither; upon which I sent my Opinion aboard of our Consorts, and desir'd they would call a Committee, and agree how to proceed next; which they did as follows.

At a Committee held on Board the *Batchelor* Frigat, *April* 29. 1710.

It is agreed to make the best of our Way to the Island of Tula, where we are in Expectation of supplying our selves with Woody Water and Provisions, to cruize 10 or 12 Days for this Island, being uncertain of its Scituation; and in Case the Wind should present sooner, that we can fetch Ternate, then, to make the best of our Way for it; but if the Wind should not present for Ternate, nor the Island Tula, then, if we see Occasion, to make the best of our Way to some

Port in Mindanao. And for all Opportunities in going about and car-rying a Light, we leave it to Captain Courtney in the Dutchess.

May 2. We shaped our Course for *Ternate* a second Time, being in all Probability to the Westward of *Gillolo*, having made by our Reckoning 3 Degrees of Longitude to the Westward of *Moratay.*

May 3. About 8 this Morning we made Land, which we took to be some of the Islands lying off the N. East Part of *Celebes.* It bore W. S. W. of us, distant about 15 Leagues.

May 7. Fair Weather till 4 this Morning, when there came up a violent Shower, with great Flashes of Lightning. At Break of Day we saw Land trending from S. E. by S. to S. S. W. which at first appear'd like 5 Islands, but after it clear'd up, we plainly perceiv'd it was one continued Land; we also saw other Lands to the Westward of that, which bore W. by S. distant about 10 Leagues, and were of Opinion, that we were got to the Eastward of *Gillolo* a second Time. We were the more inclinable to believe this, because whenever we try'd the Current, we generally found it set to the Eastward very strong, tho' we little thought it could have driven us so far back.

May 9. Yesterday in the Afternoon all the Officers met aboard us to consult about the Land, and what Course to take; but being divided in Opinions, we defer'd coming to a Resolution, till such Time as we were better satisfy'd. We try'd the Current at 4 a Clock, when it set N. N. W. after the Rate of 20 Miles in 14 Hours. We made no other Land all Day than that we first saw, so stood on and off all Night, expecting Gale to run in with it in the Morning, but having Calms for the most Part, and a Current setting against us; we still lost Ground, and made another round high Hummock about Moon, which bore S. E. by E. distant 8 Leagues; the Southermost Land bearing at the same Time S. by E. 7 Leagues, and the Westermost W. by S. 8 Leagues.

May 10. I sent the Pinnace aboard *the Marquiss* with 12 Hogsheads and a Barrel of Water, their Stock being almost spent, and in their Way order'd 'em to speak with the *Batchelor* and *Dutchess*, to be satisfy'd what Allowance of *Pady* (being Rice in the Husk) their Men were at; because ours had a Notion they had more, than we, I having order'd 'em but a Pound and a Quarter for 5 Men, whereas before they had two Pound. Upon Enquiry I found the Ship's Companies far'd all alike; but to make 'em easie, agreed with Capt. *Courtney* and the rest to make it 2 Pound again; at which Allowance we have not above 12 Days at most, being all the Bread Kind we have in the Ship.

May 12. We were satisfied that the many Islands and Land that we saw for these several Days was the Straights of *New Guinea*; we spoke with the *Dutchess*, who had been near that Land where we perceived the greatest Opening, and they told us the Reason of their keeping in with the Shore was with a Design to have anchored, but meeting with irregular Soundings, did not think fit to adventure it. They sent their Boat ashore to the Eastermost small Island, to see what they could meet with. We stood within a Mile and half of the Shore, when the Water began to discolor. We founded and had 30 Fathom Watery and presently after but 6; so we went about, and stood off till the *Dutchess's* Boat return'd, who gave us an account that they had seen the Tracks of Turtle, and Mens Feet, with Fire-places lately made. These Islands are in the same Climate with the spice Islands, and no doubt would produce Spice, if planted, I went on board the *Dutchess*, and agreed with Capt. *Court-*

ney to send the Pinnace ashore, standing on and off with our Ships all Night. Lat, 00. 24. S. Long. 236. 25. West from *London.*

May 13. We kept turning to Windward this 24 Hours, betwixt the Southermost long Track of Land we made first of all, and the Islands to the Eastward of it, where we expected to find the Passage betwixt *Gillolo* and *New Guinea.*

May 15. We being jealous of each other, who had the most Provisions, we this Day met aboard the *Batchelor,* and carried an Account with us of what each Ship had left, and on making a strict Rummage there, we found more Rice than we expected; so that with the shortest Allowance we may subsist at Sea above 3 Weeks longer. Each Ship's Proportion of the Provisions we had left being weigh'd, we then return'd to our Ships in a better State than we expected.

May 18. We have passed several Islands, and are now in sight of what we account the Point or Cape of *New Guinea,* and the South End of *Gillolo,* which Appears about 8 Leagues asunder, with some Islands near each side; we have commonly little Wind, and very verable. This being the Time that the S. East Monsoon begins, which made the Weather and Wind very uncertain. Lat. 2. S.

May 20. The *Dutchess* generally kept a-head in the Night, with her Pinnace a-head of her, because the Currents are so very uncertain, and being in an unknown Track, we cannot be too carefull in the Night. We are still in sight of the High Lands of *New Guinea,* and several Islands to the Northward, which we find laid down in no Draught, so we noted them as we past by. This Way into *India* would not be half so dangerous as it is imagined, were it well known. While we had any Breeze of Wind, in the Day we towed our Prize. We made another long high Island trending from S. by E. to W.S.W. distant about 12 Leagues, and crowded along Shore to make what it was, judging it to be the Island *Ceram.* We likewise made another Island to the Northward, which bore N. by W. distant about 7 Leagues. S. Lat. 03.

May 21. Being close under it, I sent the Pinnace aboard the *Dutchess* yesterday Afternoon to know what they made of the Land, and what they design'd to do; their Boat met ours, and told 'em Capt. *Dampier* was of the same Opinion with us, that it is the Island *Ceram.*

May 22. Had an ugly Gale of Wind, which drove us clear off the Island we took to be *Ceram.* Since the 18*th* that we past the Streights of *New Guinea,* we have had a Westerly Current, but before the Current generally set to the Eastward. We have now dark gloomy Weather, with a strong Gale of Wind at S. E. and S. E. by E. runs us out of sight of all the Land. Our Ship is still very leaky, and we begin to be in the utmost want of all manner of Refreshments and Necessaries, and doubtful where to harbour or refit, the Land being unknown to us for want of good Drafts, or an experienc'd Pilot. Lat. 3. 40. S. Long. 237. 21. W. from *London.*

May 24. We were in expectation of making Land this Morning, being in the Latitude of the Island *Bouro,* which is about 20 Leagues to the S. W. of *Ceram,* and near the same Distance in a parallel with *Amboyna*; the latter of which we design'd to have touch'd at, had the Wind been favourable; but the S. E. Monsoon being now set in, we are almost out of hopes of fetching it, and still doubtful what Islands we pass'd by last, not agreeing whether it was *Ceram* or *Bouro.* We found by our Observation at Noon, that we were in the

Latitude of the Southermost part of *Bouro*, and the Reason of our not seeing of it we impute to the Current's setting us to the Westward of it. S. Lat. 04. 30. Long. 237. 29. West from *Lond.*

May 25. I spared the *Dutchess* a But of Water, they having little or none but what they catch when it rains. We came to a Resolution to spend no more Time in search of *Bouro*, nor to wait for a Wind to carry us to *Amboyna*, but to make the best of our way for the Straights of *Bouton*, where if we arrived safe, we might get Provisions enough to carry us to *Batavia*; pursuant to which Agreement we hall'd away S. W. by S. for 'em, having a fresh Gale of Wind at East; but by 2 in the Morning we fell in with a parcel of Islands to the Eastward of *Bouton*, and had infallibly been ashore upon one of 'em, had not the Weather cleared up at once. We made a Shift, and wore the Ships, then stood off N. E. from the Land till Day-break, when we saw it trenting from S. by E. to S. W. by S. about 6 Leagues distant, which made like a fine large Bay, but as we stood in perceived an Opening, and that there were 2 Islands, with 3 lying thwart the Out-let to the Southward of both. We hoisted out our Pinnace, and sent her ashore, the *Dutchess* did the same; from whence they brought off some Cocoa Nuts, which were very plentiful here, and told us there were *Malayan* Inhabitants, who seem'd to be very friendly. We kept turning in with our Ships, and our Boats founding a-head, designing to anchor, if we could find any Ground, but found none with 60 and 80 Fathom Line. We saw Land to the N. W. of us, which we took to be the Island *Bouton*, being pretty high, and distant 8 or 10 Leagues. S. Lat. 05. 00. Long. 237. 51.

May 26. We could get no Anchor Ground all Yesterday Afternoon, tho' we run our Boltsprit almost ashore, and having the Current setting against us, made it a tiresome Piece of work to fetch within the reach of the Houses. At last some of the Inhabitants came off in a Canoe to our Boats, as they were founding a-head; they brought 'em aboard, and by Signs we understood there was plenty of Provisions ashore. So I sent the Pinnace and Yawl to see what they could meet with. In the mean time came several Canoes full of *Malayans*, with Cocoa Nuts, Pumpkins, *Indian* Corn, Fowls, &c, to truck with our People. Ashore they had Sheep and Black Cattle in plenty. The Officers I sent were admitted into the Presence of their King and Nobles, who were all bare-foot, and most naked, save a Clout about their Posteriors; they seem'd to be very courteous, and ready to supply us with what we wanted. We lay by and drove till Morning (having little Wind) that we might be nearer the other Ships, and resolve what to do. We found no Anchor-ground, but too near the Shore, and the Current setting strong to the S. W. and driving us out; which together with our having no Anchor-ground, if the Wind should take us out of the Sea, made us desist to attempt any farther here. We agreed to stand over for the Land to the Westward of us, the Northermost part of which bore W. N. W. distant 9 Leagues., and the Westermost W. by S. 10 Leagues. The Inhabit-ants call'd the Eastermost of these Islands *Vanseat*, the other next to it *Capota*, and the Westermost *Cambaver*. S. Lat. 05. 13. Long. 238. II. W.

May 27. We stood from these Islands to the Westward, and ran along shore as near as we durst, to weather the Westermost Point of Land, where we expected to find a Harbour, but as we near'd it, found a long Tract of High Land, trending to the Southward, as far as S. W. by S. We agreed in Opinion that 'twas the Island *Bouton*, but that we had over-shot the Straights. We made Sail to see if we could discover any Land further to the Southward; but finding none, we jogg'd on, keeping the Wind as near as possible, because of the Current, which sets strong to the S. W. By 2 a Clock in the Morning we were hors'd near a small Island, that bore S. S. W. of us about 2 Leagues; but having clear Weather, we stood from it till Day-break, there being no other Land near it that we saw, except that we came from, which we had open'd 5 Points farther to the Westward. I was unwilling to act any farther without the Consent of the Committee; so the major part of us met aboard the *Dutchess*, where we agreed to stand back and make the Land plain, so as to be fully satisfied what it was, and withal to find a Recruit of Water and Wood before we proceed any farther, being in want of every thing. S. Lat, 05. 50. Long. W. from *London*, 238. 38.

May 28. According to Agreement we stood back, and having a fresh Breeze of Wind at East, came up with the Land, which trended from N. E. by E. to N. We stood away with the Northermost, and by 6 a Clock brought it to bear E. by N. distant about 2 Leagues, having open'd Land farther to the Northward, which made like a Bay, and trimming to the Westward as far as W. N. W. distant about 10 Leagues. We made little or no Sail all Night, because the *Batchelor* and *Marquiss* were a-stern, and we were not willing to run too far in with the Land in the Night. In the Morning 'twas calm, and being clear Weather, we made all the Land very plain from W. S. W. to the E. S. E. making high double Land, with Islands under it. Most of it look'd as if it was inhabited, being pretty thick of Wood, and promised fair for other Refreshments, but we could find no Anchor-ground hitherto.

May 29. A Breeze sprung up, and we ran farther in, keeping nearest the Southern Shore, where we open'd a sandy Spit, off which we could perceive blue Water like Shold ground running across the Bay near half a League. A little to the Westward of this we got Ground in betwixt 30 and 40 Fathom Water, with good gradual Soundings, where we let go our Anchor. The *Dutchess* and the rest standing over to the other side of the Bay, could meet with no Ground, so they came back, and anchored by us. S. Lat.05. 41. Long. 238. 34. W. from *London*. A little before this, our Boat we had sent returned from the Shore, having by Presents engag'd a Canoe with some *Malayans* to come aboard with them, but for want of a Linguist we were little the better. I sent to the *Batchelor*, who had one, but Capt. *Dover* refus'd to let him come to me, altho' he had no use for him; then I sent a second time, that I might know the best anchoring Place for our Ships, and treated the People (who were impatient to be gone) with Sweet-meats and other things they fancy'd, but could not keep 'em, or send them aboard the *Batchelor* to Secure her, seeing white Shole Water near us. But they pass'd by us in danger of running on the Sholes, not knowing the best anchoring Place, for want of the Linguist I so earnestly desir'd, to understand the *Malayans* that had now left us. At parting they made Signs, and pointed to the Land to the Northward, which they call'd *Bootoo*. Our Pilot, Capt. *Dampier* says he has been formerly thro' the Streights, and in his Book tells us of a Town near the South part of 'em, where the King resided, but he knew nothing of it now, except the bare Story. Upon this we agreed to send one of the Pinnaces along with him and the Linguist to find out the Town, being willing to venture him to wait on his Majesty the King of *Bouton* to solicit for a Supply of Provisions, which we would gladly pay for; and to make the better Appearance, we sent Mr. *Vanbrugh* and Mr. *Connely* along with him. The Water flows here above 15 Foot; there are Places near to the Town which lie to the Northward about 6 Leagues, from whence we rode where a Ship might, on Occasion, be laid a-shoar to refit; and we should have carry'd the *Duke* there to stop her Leak, but were not willing to loose Time, since we found it did not encrease more than one Pump could vent, which we had Men enough to keep continually going. The King of *Bouton* has several Galleys built after a peculiar Form, and other small Imbarkations, on which they say, he can imbark eight Thousand Men on any Expedition; our People that were upon the Island tell me, all their Towns are built on Precipices, and hard to get at, and that the Chief City was built on the Top of a Hill, to which there was only one Passage very steep. We found a watering Place from a Spring put of the Rocks, but difficult to fill out of, because of its Ebbing and Flowing here, almost 3 Fathom, which dries the Rock near the Shoar.

May 30. This Morning a Messenger came from the King, with a Letter from our Officers that went to wait upon him, who were receiv'd very courteously, and promised a Supply of Provisions, in Case we could come to an Agreement. We show'd the Gentlemen Samples of what we had to dispose of, which they seem'd very well pleas'd with, and having made 'em a Present of some odd Things, and entertain'd 'em as well as we could, we dispatch'd 'em with a Letter of Directions to our Officers what to do, and at their going off saluted 'em with 5 Guns and 3 Huzza's from each Ship. We made a Present to the King of a Bishop's Cap, being of little or no Value to us, but what he highly esteem'd and gratefully accepted of. The Inhabitants began to come off fast enough with *Indian* Corn, Cocoa-Nutts, Pumpkins, Fowles, &c. to truck with our People, but they were very dear, compar'd with the other Islands we had been at.

June 1. We supply'd our selves indifferent well with Wood and Water, and our Pinnace return'd from the Town, with a mysterious Account of their Proceedings, and presently after Captain *Dampier* came with a small Quantity of Provisions, as a Present to the Commanders, having left our other two Officers to dispatch away what they could agree for.

June 2. This Morning there came 3 or 4 of the better Sort from the Town, with a *Portuguese* Linguist that belong'd to *Batavia*, under Pretence of looking upon Goods, and carrying Samples of 'em to their King, but by their Trifling, we are afraid we shall get nothing of 'em at last. We made much of the *Portuguese*, and gave him a small Present, hoping he would influence the People to dispatch our Business. We sent the *Dutchess* Pinnace with a Letter to our Officers, to hurry away as fast as possible with what Provisions they had got, and to agree if they could with the *Portuguese* Linguist for a Pilot, if they should give him 10 or 20 Dollars or more for a Present.

June 3 and 4. Our Ships have done Watering and Wooding, and the Country People have brought off much Provisions: so we conclude we are pretty well supplied for a Fortnight or Three Weeks; which, with what we had before, may carry us to *Batavia*, without any further Recruit from the Town; so that if we had our Boat and Men, it would be much more for our Interest to be gone, than to lie here, and spend time to no Purpose. An Officer aboard our Ship, and other Officers and Men aboard Capt. *Courtney*, began to be mutinous, and form a Conspiracy against us; but we prevented it, by chastising their Leaders, whom we put in Irons, on board different Ships, to break the Knot, which might otherwise have ruin'd the Voyage.

June 5. The *Dutchess's* Pinnace return'd with Mr. *Connely*, who acquainted us with the dilatory Proceedings of the King of *Bouton*, who having got a Quantity of Provisions together, would have oblig'd us to take it at an extravagant Price; and detain'd Mr. *Vanbrugh*, till such time as the Money was paid. In the Morning, there came some of his Mobility, with about 4 Last of Rice, which (for Dispatch-sake) we immediately agreed for, and a Cask of Rack, and after we had entertain'd 'em as well as Time and Place would afford, we sent 'em off in our Pinnace. This Morning, the *Portugueze* Linguist came with some Provisions of his own to sell, without any News from our People, which made us suspect they had some ill Design upon us, therefore we design'd to keep him till the Boat return'd, but he got out of the Ship, before we were aware, (he being jealous by his cold Reception, that we were uneasy) and rowed away as fast as possible. I sent the Yawl after him which overtaking his Canoe, the Men all jumpt over board, but the *Dutchess* Pinnace took 'em up, and our Boat brought the *Portugueze* Linguist aboard us, where seeing he was likely to be confin'd, he sent the Boat with the Men up to the Town, to desire our People might be dismiss'd as soon as possible.

June 7. This Morning our Pinnace return'd with Mr. *Vanbrugh*, and all our Men, having parted very friendly with his Majesty, but could not get a Pilot for Money; however we resolv'd to stay no longer, and to trust wholly to Almighty Providence for our future Preservation. We dismiss'd the *Portuguese* Linguist and began to unmoor our Ships.

We weigh'd on the 8th, about 4 in the Afternoon, and by six a Clock the Westermost Land in sight bore W. N. W. 9 Leagues, and the Southermost S. W. by S. distant 5 Leagues.

Bouton *Describ'd.*

The Island of *Bouton* is in Lat. 05. 20. S. and near about 30 Leagues long; the King, they say, can raise fifty Thousand Men, and has all the adjacent Islands under him; they boast of not valuing the *Dutch*, but I am satisfied, their Poverty is their greatest Security; they Speak the *Malayan* Language, which is universal amongst all the Islands of *India*. They are a well-set People, of a middle Stature, or rather small, of a dark Olive Colour, with the most indifferent Features of any People, that ever I saw; they profess the *Mahometan* Religion, but know little of it, save Bathing; a few other Ceremonies, as Forbearance of Hogs Flesh, keeping many Wives, *etc.* Here were several *Mahometan* Missionaries that came from *Arabia* and *Persia* to propagate their Doctrine; the *Dutch* have no Settlement here, but trade for Slaves and a little Gold, the Climate being near the same with the *Dutch* Spice Islands, I admire, they don't raise Quantities of Spice, but no Soft of it grows here, save a few Nutmegs.

June 9. In the Morning we made Land, from S, W. to N. W. by W. distant about 8 Leagues, which we cook to be the islands of *Zalayer*, S. Lat. S. 45. Long. W. from *Lond.* 240°. 21?. We likewise saw a Sail to Windward of us, and taking it to be a *Dutch* Vessel, we hall'd nearer the Wind, till 8 a Clock, then the *Dutchess* and we made Sail at once, to speak with her, but the Wind abating soon after, and she making the best of her Way from us, we mann'd our Pinnace, and sent it after her. We made 3 Islands to the Northward of *Zalayer*, and the Looming of other Land to the Westward of all, which we took to be the Southermost part of *Celebes*.

June 10. Our Pinnaces came up with this small Vessel, who told them they were bound for *Macassarts, a Dutch* Factory on the South Part of *Celebes*; The Pinnace took the Master of her aboard, (being a *Malayan*) who promis'd to pilot us not only through the Streights of *Zalayer*, but to *Batavia*, if we would keep it Secret, for fear of the *Dutch*. He sent his Vessel to lie in the narrow Passage, between the Islands, till such Time as our Ships came up. About 4 a Clock we enter'd the Streight, and came betwixt the Islands that are next to *Zalayer*. And another little one to the Northward of that being the middlemost of the three; where we found a good Passage, 3 Leagues over, all deep Water, steering through N. W. by W. to give the Larboard Islands a good Birth; then we made the Southermost Part of *Celebes*.

June 11. The Pilot promis'd to carry us thro' the Channel the great *Dutch* Ships generally went for *Batavia*, and by that Means avoid the Shoals call'd the *Brill* and *Bunker* Ground; the *Brill* has very uneven Soundings, and in many Places but 3 Fathom Water and less so we hall'd away to tho Northward, keeping the Islands *Celebes* aboard, the S. W. Part of which trents away in low Land, with high Mountains at the back of it; and off the Point their lies al Rock pretty high and remarkable; at 4 o Clock we came into Soundings, and had 10 Fathom the first Cast; the Rock off the S. W. Point bore then N. distant about 6 Leagues, and we had an Island a head of us, from N. W. by W. to N. N. W. being low and level, about 3 Leagues long, and near the same Distance from the main as we enter'd betwixt 'em, it grew narrower. We stem'd with the North Part of the Island, till we came within a League and half of it, then steer'd North a little to weather a Spit of Sand, lying off the Island, by which Means we open'd 3 small Keys; after we were clear of the Shoal, we hall'd up N. W. about 7, and came to an Anchor under the Island, behind the Spit of Sand, in 10 Fathom Water, very good clean Ground. The Rock of Celebes then bore N. E. by N. 4 Leagues; the Northermost of the Keys, W. 2 Leagues; and the Middlemost W. S. W. 3 Leagues: The other being shut in with the long Island. We kept the Lead going all the way constantly through, and had never less than 6 Fathom, nor more than 10. As soon as it was Day we weigh'd, and went betwixt the two small Keys, keeping nearest the Northernmost, founding all the Way, and had no more than 10 Fathom. The Water still deepning, being clear of them, we hall'd away West, and then S. W. having a fresh Gale of Wind at S. E. and S. E. by E. no Land in sight at Noon but Part of the high Land of *Celebes*, which bore East, distant about 12 Leagues. It is well for us, that we met with this Pilot, for having no good Charts nor any one acquainted with those Seas, we had run greater Hazards.

June 13. We made Land a second time, which bore S. W. by W. distant 6 Leagues.

June 14. We ran by the Island *Madura*, which is about 40 Leagues long, lying East and West, on the N. Side of *Java*, the Land we made in the Morning, being the N. E. part of it, which agreeing with the Pilot's Knowledge made us the more certain.

June 15. In the Morning we fell in with the Coast of *Java*, near the high Land of *Japara*, which bore W. by S. distant about 5 Leagues, We had Soundings betwixt 10 and 20 Fathom good easy Ground, and saw abundance of Fishing boats, but all kept at a Distance. We got our Guns out of the Hold, and scal'd them, in order to be in a Readiness against we come to *Batavia*, where in all Probability we shall get in 2 or 3 Days more, it being not above

90 Leagues from this Place: By Noon we brought the Land of *Japara* to bear S. by E. distant 4 Leagues, having open'd a large deep Bay, with other high Land, further to the Westward, which bore W. N. W. distant 9 Leagues, Lat. 6° 19". S. Long. 248 °. 47 ". W. from *London*.

June 16. We made a small high Hummock to the West ward of the high Land we set yesterday Noon, which, at 6 a Clock bore W. by S. distant 5 Leagues. We hall'd off N. W. by W. and W. N. W. and in the Morning made the Islands of *Caraman Java*, which bore N. E. by N. distant 3 Leagues, as also a ragged Island to the Eastward of it, bearing E. N. E. 5 Leagues, and 5 small Keys to the Westward, which are all call'd *Caraman Java*. We had Soundings most part of this 24 Hours, betwixt 20 and 30 Fathom ouzy Ground, Lat. 6. 7. S. Long. 250. 14. W. from *London*.

June 17. We made the high Land of *Cheribon*, which bore S. W. In the Morning we saw a great Ship right a head, and being very eager to hear News, I sent our Pinnace aboard to know what she was. She prov'd a *Dutch* Ship, about 600 Tuns, and 50 Guns, belonging to *Batavia*, and was plying to some of the *Dutch* Factories for Timber. They told us of Prince *George's* Death, which we heard of in the *South Seas*, but gave no Credit to it then: That the Wars continued in *Europe*; and that we had good Success in *Flanders*, and but little else where. They likewise told us, that 'twas about 30 *Dutch* Leagues from hence to *Batavia*; but no Danger. We borrowed a large Draft, which was very useful to us, and left 'em at Anchor. Towards Noon we made the Land, being very low, but had gradual Soundings, by which we was satisfied in the Night how to sail by the Sand.

June 20. In the Afternoon we saw the Ships in the Road of *Batavia*, betwixt 30 and 40 Sail, great and small, and got happily to Anchor just after Sunset, betwixt 6 and 7 Fathom Water, at the long desired Port of *Batavia*. Lat. 6. 10. S. Long. 252. 51. W. from *London*. By our Reckoning here, we alter'd our Account of Time, having, as customary, lost almost one Day in running West so far round the Globe.

June 22. We waited on his Excellency the Governour-General, whom we acquainted with the Necessity we lay under to refit our Ships. He was pleased to see and approve of our Commissions, as Private Men of War, and promis'd he would meet the Council, and soon resolve us how far he could afford such Assistance as we desired.

June. 30. I am still very weak and thin, but I hope to get Time and Leisure to recover my Health. During these 10 Days, I was nor able to go much on board, and whenever I went, found, that till then I was a Stranger to the Humours of our Ship's Company. Some of them were hugging each other, others blessing themselves that they were come to such a glorious Place for Punch, where they could have Arack for 8 Pence per Gallon, and Sugar for 1 Peny a Pound; others quarrelling who should make the next Bowl, for now the Labour was worth mere than the Liquor, whereas a few Weeks past, a Bowl of Punch to them was worth half the Voyage. 8 Days ago the Doctor cut a large Musket Shot out of my Mouth, which had been there near 8 Months, ever since I was first wounded; we reckon'd it a Piece of my Jaw-bone, the upper and lower Jaw being much broken, and almost closed together, so that the Doctor had much ado to come at the Shot, to get it out. I had also several Pieces of my Foot and Heel-bone taken out, but God be thanked, am now in a fair way to have the Use of my Foot, and to recover my Health. The Hole the

Shot made in my Face is now scarce discernable. I propos'd the calling of a Committee to regulate our Affairs,wherein we agreed as follows.

At a Committee, held on board the *Batchelor* Frigat, *June* 30. 1710. in the Road of *Batavia.*

Impr. I Tis agreed to pack and repack all Goods that appear damag'd, and to let other Bails, that are not, nor have not hen apparently damag'd, to be only new cover'd with Wax-cloth, or Tarpaulins, if necessary, in every Ship, and that Mr. Vanbrugh and Mr. Goodall be at every Place, and the rest of the Agents be accountable to 'em', and thy to leave a Duplicate of the whole with the other two, and be always ready to give an Account to a general Committee.

2dly, That Capt. Courtney do provide the Ships with all manner of Necessaries, as fast as wanting; and as soon as Captain Rogers is in Health, that be assist in it, and that every one give a List to 'em of what they want from time to time; that Mr. Charles Pope do continue a-shore, and send off Provisions for all the Ships, and keep a Book of the whole. Let every Ship take their daily turn to divide the Meat, and send off as early a possible, in a Country Boat, and near as be can no more nor less than 350 tb weight, every other Day, or as often as be can conveniently. Let him send off Greens, Carrots, Eggs, or any other small Refreshment, more than the common Allowance, to be equally divided with the Meat. 3dly, That a suitable Quantity of Rack and Sugar be sent aboard each Ship, to give a Quart a Mess to the Ships Companies, but whilst on the career, the Allowance may be enlarg'd as the Commanding Officers think convenient.

4thly, If any thing not included is necessary. to the Dispatch-and Out-set of our Ships, considering the Trouble and Loss of Time, to meet in a whole Committee, we to prevent dilatory Proceedings, unanimously leave such things to Capt. Thomas Dover, Capt. Woodes Rogers, Capt. Stephen Courtney, and Capt. Edward Cooke, who are to agree on a Time and Place to meet, and have the same Power in this Affair as a whole Committee. That if any thing requires such Dispatch that the four cannot be prefect at a time, then any three of them together, agreeing and signing what they have done for the Satisfaction of the rest shall be sufficient; but otherwise we desire them to act in conjunction.

5thly, We agree to continue Mr. Carleton Vanbrugh Agent of the Duke, Mr. James Goodall Agent of the Dutchess to make Mr. John Viger Agent of the Batchelor and Mr. Joseph Parker Agent of the Marquiss, to keep a strict Account of what they can in each Ship, and to preserve and take Care of the general Interest; to the utmost of their Power.

6thly, We likewise agree to divide the Plunder on board the Batchelor, and in order thereto, we appoint Capt. William Dampier, and Mr. Thomas Glendall, to. be Judges what ought to be divided as Plunder, who are to govern themselves as near as possible by our Resolutions, in a Committee of the 9th of July, 1709. And in order to dispatch Matters quietly without loss of time, we appoint Mr. John Ballett, Mr. Lancelot: Appleby, Mr. Alexander Selkirk, and Mr. Joseph Smith, to act for the Officers, in apprising and dividing the said Plunder, and we allow the Sailors to agree on a Man from each Ship, who is to act in conjunction with them, and in the whole to promote the general Good with

the utmost Sincerity and Dispatch. We also appoint Mr. Carleton Vanbrugh, and Mr. James Goodall to be in the Place when the Plunder is open'd or divided, and to receive what belongs to the Cargo.

7thly, It's farther resolved for our general Safety that all trading be prohibited by any of us with the Inhabitants of this City of Batavia, or this Island of Java, or any part of India. And to the End that no Person may plead Ignorance, a Protect shall be drawn up and published at the Mast of each Ship, prohibiting the aforesaid Commerce, and protesting against all Damages arising through the same, and the Person found guilty of it.

8thly, It is also agreed, That a Reward of 100 Rix-Dollars shall be given to the Pilot we made use of from the Straights of Zelaya to this Port.

9thly, It is further agreed, That the Marquiss shall go first upon the careen; and then to be next followed by the Duke; the Dutchess to be the last.

10thly, We have consider'd the Charge and Method of our Outsett, and do agree, in order to promote Dispatch, that 10000 Pieces of 8 be delivered to Capts. Dover, Rogers, Courtney, and Cooke, to-morrow being the 1st of July, 1710.

Sign'd by the Majority of our Council.

The Committee did likewise resolve on a Supply of Money to the Officers, as follows.

At a Committee held in *Batavia* Road, *July* I. 1710.

WE have resolved to supply these Officers of the Duke, Dutchess, Marquiss, and Batchelor, with the following Sums, to provide themselves with Necessaries in our long Passage to Europe. Pieces of Eight.

To Captain Thomas Dover 2000

Captain Rogers, and Captain Courtney, for

their present Expences 400

Total 2400

Brought over Pieces of Eight 2400

Captain Cook 800

Mr. Fry and Mr. Stretton 1000

Captain Dampier 200

Mr. Pope 350

Mr. Glendall, and Mr. Connely 700

Mr. Vanbrugh 250

Mr. Tho. Bridge, and Mr. Milbourne 100

Mr. Knowlman and Mr. Selkirk 80

To the Three Doctors of the Duke, Dutchess,

and Marquiss 90
To the Doctor of the Batchelor-20
To Mr. Goodall, and Mr. Appleby 80
Total 6070
All these Sums we order'd Mr. Vanbrugh and Mr. Goodall to dis-
charge out of the Money on Board the Duke or Dutchess, as either
Commanders shall think convenient, whenever the above-mentioned
Officers shall demand it, and the Receipts to Mr. Vanbrugh and Mr.
Goodall, so far as is here order'd, shall be sufficient, Witness our
Hands, July 1. 1710.
Signed by the Majority of our Council.

July 2. From the 22*d* of the last Month we lay leaky, and in a very ordinary Condition, not knowing when and how the General would please to
order us Assistance according to our present Necessities, which were then
laid open to him; and this Day, to shew that we could sufficiently vindicate
and justifie all our Proceedings like honest Men, we gave in an Abstract of
our Voyage, from the Day we set sail out of *King* Road, to the Day we arrived
in *Batavia*, which they desir'd to see, before they would assist us; so we gave
it 'em as short as possible.

July 7. To Day our Men finished appraising and dividing the Plunder-
Cloth in the *Batchelor*; which being tolerable good, amounts to about 400 *l.*
Sterling.

July 8. This-Day, after a great many dilatory Answers, we were at last
permitted to make Preparations for careening at *Horn* Island, which is about
2 or 3 Leagues to the Northward of the Road, (but were by no Means suffer'd
to go to the Island *Unrest*, where all the *Dutch* Ships are clean'd) being only
allow'd 8 or 10 *Malayan* Caulkers and small Vessels to put our Goods in. The
Marquiss began to careen aboard her; but the Carpenters having view'd her
betwixt Wind and Water, finding her very bad, and that she had but a single
Bottom, eat to a Honey-comb by the Worms, they judg'd her altogether unfit
to go to *Europe*; whereupon I desir'd the Committee to meet and agree to dispose of her, as follows.

It is agreed, that having now discharged the Marquiss of her Car-
goe brought from the South Sea, and finding great Part thereof per-
ish'd thro' the Weakness of the Ship, and Damage of the Worms,
which has eaten thro' her Bends, and good Part of her Bottom like a
perfect Honey-Comb; we have consider'd our present Condition, with
the great Charge and Loss of Time to repair her here, and judging our
3 Ships sufficient, and capable to carry the remaining Part of her
Cargoe: We, according to the best of our Judgment and Information
from a View made by the Carpenters, do believe it for our Safety and
Benefit for the Concern'd, to sell the said Ship the Marquiss here, as
soon as possible, for the most she will yield; and we do appoint Capt.
Woodes Rogers, Capt. Steph. Courtney, Capt. Edw. Cock, and Capt.

Tho. Dover, to treat of and conclude the Sale, letting the Pur-
chaser have sufficient Power (as far as we are capable) to condemn
her.
Sign'd by the Officers of the Committee.

July 20. The *Marquiss* being condemned to Sale, we had the Caulkers aboard us to make all Manner of Dispatch for careening. Our Ship being very leaky, we thought it high Time to wait on the Governour with the following Representation, which we got put into *Dutch*, but could not get the *Sabandar* to introduce us, as the Custom is here, therefore we went our selves, and gave Presents to the *Dutch* Guards to let us in to see the General; after an Hours waiting we were admitted, and deliver'd him a Copy of our Commissions, and were promis'd Assistance, but find it's no more than what he can't have a Pretence to deny us.

Our Memorial was as follows.

To His Excellency the Governour-General and Council of the *Dutch East-India* Company.

> *About four Weeks ago we arrived here, and waited upon your Excellency, acquainting you with our Circumstances, which according to your Order we delivered the same Day in Writing to your Sabandar, and have daily waited upon him for your Resolution thereupon. He has since visited our several Ships, and we question not but all Things appeared to him agreeable to our Representation.*

> *We have lain some time ready with leaky Ships to go to the Place appointed us to careen at, only waiting for a careening Vessel to heave down by. Which we humbly crave you will be pleas'd to order us.*

> *Delays are very prejudicial to our Ships, that have been long without the Benefit of a Friend's Port. Which we earnestly request, you'll please to consider.*

> *We have deferr'd troubling you, in daily Hopes of an Order for our Assistance by the proper Officer, till we can no longer account for our Loss of Time, without a direct Application.*

> *We hope for a Continuance of the common Benefits and Refreshments, and on our Parts shall persevere to behave our selves with all due Regard and Respect to the Government and Customs of this City.*

> *Batavia, July 20. 1710.*

> *Woodes Rogers. Steph. Courtney.*

The Governour immediately order'd us a Vessel to careen, and we took our Leaves.

July 23. We went over to *Horn* Island, having a Pilot to direct us, and a *Sampan* ready to heave down by, and take in our Guns, Carriages, &c. anchor'd on the South side of the Island, in 5 Fathom Water, about a Stone's Cast off Shore, where we careen'd.

We continued refitting our Ships, and re-packing our Goods, with a great deal of difficulty, till the 13*th* of *September,* during which Time nothing remarkable happen'd, but that, after I had refitted. as well as I could on *Horn* Island, I return'd to the Road of *Batavia*. Many of our Men fell ill of Fevers and Fluxes, occasion'd, as I was inform'd, by their drinking the Water upon the Island. We buried here *John Bridge* our Master, as also the Gunner of the *Dutchess*, with another of her Crew, and one belonging to the *Batchelor*. The Season being so far spent, and the Wind blowing fresh on *Horn* Island, I could not go again thither to careen my Ship, tho' she needed it much; therefore we try'd to get an Order to careen at *Unrest*, where the *Dutch* careen their own, as we might have done ours, in a few Days, and with little Trouble. I wrote from hence on the 21*st* of *August* to my Owners by the *Nathanael*, an *English E. India* Ship bound directly for *England*, to let them know of our safe Arrival here with our Effects, and that we hoped to be with them in a very short time.

On the 15*th* we called a Committee, and came to the following Resolutions.

Batavia, Sept. 15. 1710.

At a Committee held then, it is agreed to divide the Money received for a Quantity of Plate sold amongst the federal Ships Company, being what had been adjudged Plunder. Also that we should make out a Request, and deliver it the first Opportunity to the General, to the following Purpose, viz. to gain Leave, if possible, to careen the Duke at Unrest, &c. Also for Leave to set up the Marquiss for Sale here, and for a Supply of 10 Hogsheads of Dutch Beef and Pork, with a Permission to buy and carry aboard same Rack and Sugar for the 3 Ships Stores for our Company, &c.

It is also agreed to allow the following Particulars for tie use of the Officers in the Great Cabbin of each Ship, viz.

To each Ship as followeth.

Two Firkins of Butter.

Two Gallons of sweet Oil.

400 Cask of Bread or Rusk.

100 Pound Weight of Flower.

400 Pound Weight of Tamarinds.

Half a Leaguer of Spelman's Neep, or the best sort of Arrack.

3 Cheeses.

The Third part of a Leaquor of Gape Wine.

3 Peckel of fine Sugar.

Also 60 Dollars of Spanish Money to buy small Necessaries

Signed,

Tho. Dover, Pres. William Dampier, Woodes Rogers, Cha. Pope, Steph. Courtney, William Stretton, Edw. Cooke, John Connely.

Rummaging to day in the Powder-room, we found a Leak 3 or 4 Foot under Water, which we did our best to stop.

All *English* Ships are allowed by the Government here half a Leaguer of Arrack a Man for the Ships Use, and 'tis counted as part of the Provisions, but our Boats are not suffer'd to bring the least thing off Shore, without being first severely searched. This, tho we pay more, will likewise hinder all manner of Traffick with any one here. Our chief Officers have also prevented it aboard, and narrowly watch our Crews; so that I doubt they'll want several Necessaries that this Place affords. This we do to avoid giving the *India* Company in *England* any Pretence to clamour against us at home, on account of our trading here without their Permission. We requested the Governour to have Liberty to fell the *Marquiss* by Inventory to the highest Bidder at a publick Sale; but the Sabandar, or chief Customhouse Officer for Foreigners, told us it was the Governour and Council's Resolution to publish at the Sale, that if any *Dutch* Freeman should purchase the Ship, they must either rip her up or burn her. This we thought another great Hardship, that we could not get *Dutch* Carpenters a Liberty to careen and refit her at *Unrest*, nor get Freedom of Sale; so we drew up a Request, and got it put in *Dutch*, resolving to wait on the General, to set forth the Hardships we were under; and likewise requested to careen the *Duke* at *Unrest*, where we might have *Dutch* Carpenters, that being the only fit Place; how the Weather and Wind was changeable, and we could not do it at any other Island: But when Capt. *Courtney* and I came to the Castle, to wait on the General, the Guards told us, They had Orders, that no *Englishman* should see admitted without the *Sabandar*, and that they durst carry no Paper or Message from us to the Governour-General. We waited till past the middle of the Day, and then address'd our selves to one of the Rads of *India*, who us'd to listen to the *English*, when any was impos'd on: He treated us very handsomly, with our Linguists, Mr. *Vanbrugh* and Mr. *Swart*, at his House, and said, He believed we had not Justice done us; but the *Sabandar* being the General's near Relation, he should make Enemies, if he appear'd in our Affair, and could advise us no better than to try what we could do again with the *Sabandar*, who we knew was inflexible; so we were forced to be silent and let this drop, that we might dispatch for the Cape of *Good Hope*, as fast as possible; the best Season for our Passage being now at hand.

nJuly 30. The Plunder-Money was shar'd on the 24th Instant, which amounted to 26 *Shillings* ashare, being what was adjudg'd as Plunder, when at the Island *Gorgona*, to which I refer.

Octob. 7. This Week we made all Preparation for sailing, having got most of our Stores aboard, and discharged the *Marquiss*, which was so leaky that we sold her to Cape. *John Opey*, Commander of the *Oley* Frigate, lately arriv'd from London, for 575 *Dutch* Dollars, being an extraordinary Bargain; we had been offer'd much more before by another Person, but then I could not prevail with the Majority of our Council to consent to the Sale.

Octob. 12. At Day-break this Morning, we, our Consort and Prize, weigh'd out of the Road, taking the first of the Land Breeze: About Noon came too again, in 11 Fathom Water, about a Mile to the Northward of *Horn* Island. We had several *English* Gentlemen aboard our Ships, who favour'd us with their Company out of the Road, there being several that arriv'd during our Stay here.

English *Ships that arrived and sail'd hence during our Stay.*

Frederick, Capt. *Phrip*, arriv'd *June* 23. sail'd *July* 29. from *Bencouli*, bound to *ditto*. Rochester, Capt. *Stains*, arrived *July* 6. sail'd the 21*st*, from *England*, bound to *China*. Nathanael, Capt. *Neagers*, arriv'd *July* 27. sail'd *Aug.* 27. from *Bencouli*, bound to *England*, Stringer, Capt. *Pill* arriv'd *Aug.* 30. from *England*, bound to c *China*. We left her there, she having lost her Passage for *China*.

Oley, Capt. *Opie*, arriv'd *Sept.* 9. from *England*,

left there behind us.

Here follows,

A Description of Batavia.

Altho' this Place is well known, and has been so frequently describ'd, yet being such a noble Settlement, and a Proof of the Industry of the *Dutch* in these Parts; I can't omit giving the following Account of it. The Town lies on the N. W. side of the Island of *Java*, Lat. 5°. 50". S. The Time we were here it was not very healthy. The East and West Winds blow all the Year along the Shore, besides the ordinary Land and Sea Winds, which qualifie the Air, and makes it pleasant, otherwise it would be excessive hot. Their Summer begins in *May*, with continual Breezes from the East, and a very clear Sky till the latter End of *October*, or Beginning of *November*, when the Winter begins with hard Rains, which holds sometimes 3 or 4 Days without Intermission. In *December* the West Winds blow very violently, so that then there's little Trade on the Coast of *Java*. In *February* 'tis changeable Weather, with sudden Thunder-storms. In *March* they begin to sow: *June* is their pleasantest Month; in *September* they gather in their Sugar and Rice; and in *October* they have Plenty of Fruit and Flowers, Plants and Herbs of most Sorts: There's a large fenny plain Country before the City, but it's well improv'd by the *Dutch*, and to the Eastward, 'tis very full of Woods and Morasses. The City is four square, with a River running through it, and fortified by a Stone Wall and 22 Bastions. About 10 Years past there was an Earthquake, which broke down part of the Mountains, in the Country, and alter'd the Course of the River, so that the Canals in and about *Batavia*, are not near so commodious as they have been, nor the Entrance into the River so deep, and for want of a strong Current of Water, to keep it open, they are forced to employ a large Engine work'd with Horses, to preserve the Entrance of the River navigable for small Vessels to come into the Canals of the City. It lies on a Bay in and about which there are 17 or 18 Islands, which so break off the Sea, that tho' the Road is very large, yet it is safe. The Banks of the Canals through the City are fac'd with Stone on both Sides; as far as the Boom, which is shut up every Night, at 9 a Clock, and guarded by Soldiers; there's Channels cut out of the main River for smaller Vessels, and every one that passes the Boom pays Custom. All the Streets run in a streight Line, most of them being above 30 Foot board, on each side clear of the Canals, and pav'd next the Houses with Bricks. All the Streets are very well built and inhabited, 15 of which have Canals, and they reckon 56 Bridges on them, most of them made of Stone. The Country Seats and Buildings round the City, are generally neat and well contriv'd with handsom Gardens for Fruit and Flowers, and adorn'd with Springs, Fountains, Statues, *etc.* The vast Quantity of Coco nut Trees, every where afford delightful and profitable Groves. They have fine Structures here, particularly the Cross Church, built of Stone, and the inside very neat. There are 2 other Churches for the *Dutch*, and 2 for the *Portuguese* Protestants; who are a mixed Breed of People. There is one Church also for the Protestant *Malayans*. The Town-house is built of Brick, in a Square, about the Center of the City; 'tis two lofty Stories high, and very finely built, where all Courts of Advice are held, and all Matters relating to the Civil Government of the City are determin'd, and the Senators and Directors of military Affairs meet. There's an inner Court inclos'd with a high Wall, and a double Row of Stone Pillars, where the Officers of Justice live. Here are Hospitals, Spin-houses, and Rasp houses, the same as in *Amsterdam*, with all other publick Buildings, equal to most Cities in *Europe* The *Chinese* have also a large Hospital in this City for their Aged and Sick Persons, and manage their Charity so well, that you never see a *Chinese* look despicable in the Street. The *Dutch* Women have greater Privileges in *India* than in *Holland*, or any where else; for on slight Occasions they are often divorc'd from their Husbands, and Share the Estate betwixt them. A Lawyer told me at *Batavia*, he has known out of 58 Causes, all depending in the Council-Chamber, 52 of them were Divorces. Great Numbers of the Natives, who are Criminals, and not executed after Condemnation, are chain'd by Pairs, and kept at hard Labour under a Guard, perpetually clearing the Canals and Moats round the City, or any other Labour for the publick. Three Leagues West from the Town, is the Island *Unrest*, where all the Company's Ships are refitted. There are great Magazines of Naval Stores, defended by Platforms of Guns; and the Castle at *Batavia* is Quadrangular, lies in a Level, and has 4 Bastions and Courtins, fac'd with white Stones, and provided with Watch-houses. In this Castle, or rather Citadel, the *Dutch* Governour-General, and most of the Members of the Council of *India*, with the other Officers of *Batavia*, have their Residence. The Governour's Pallace is of Brick, large and well built. In this Pallace is the Council-Chamber, the Secretary's Office and Chamber of Accounts. The great Hall is hung with bright Armour, Ensigns, Flags, *etc.* taken by the *Dutch* here. The Governour gives Audience to Strangers who are introduc'd to him by the *Sabandar*, who is chief Custom-master. Here is also a Church within the Castle, and an Armory with Apartments for all the Artificers belonging to the Castle, which has 4 Gates, and all the Avenues well defended, the whole being surrounded with Ditches, and the Works well mounted with Brass Cannon, as are the Bastions of the Town with Blockhouses within the Walls, so that they can fire upon Mutineers within, as well as upon an Enemy without. The Out-works of the Town, of which there are several every way at 4 Leagues Distance, are made of Earth, surrounded with Ditches and Quick-set Hedges, which render them Arbours for Beauty, and some of them fac'd with Brick. The Garrison on Duty is generally about 1000 strong, and all the Outworks are said to be furnish'd with a good Stock of Provisions as well as the Castle; but the Soldiers are kept much under, except the Governour's Guards, who have large Privileges, and make a fine Appearance. The Governour-General lives in as great Splendor as a King; he has a Train and Guards, having a Troop of Horse, and a Company of Foot, with Halberds, in Liveries of yellow Satin, richly adorn'd with Silver Laces and Fringes, to attend his Coach when he goes abroad. The Guards are as well equipp'd as most Princes in Europe: His Lady has also her Guards and Train. He is chosen but for 3 Years, out of the 24 Counselors call'd Rads of *India*, 12 of whom must always reside in the City. The *Chinese* have the greatest Trade here, farm most of the Excise and Customs, live according to their own Laws and idolatrous Worship, and have a Chief that manages their Affairs with the Company, who allow them great Privileges, and particularly a Representative in Council, who has a Vote when any *Chinese* is tried for Life: But these Privileges are allow'd only to such Chinese as inhabit here, for others are not admitted to stay above 6 Months in the Town, or on the Island *Java*. The other Strangers, who inhabit here, besides Europeans, are *Malayans*, with some People from most part of India. The *Javanese*, or ancient Natives are numerous, and said to be barbarous and proud, of a dark Colour, with flat Faces, thin short black Hair, large Eye-brows and Cheeks. The Men are Strong limb'd, but the Women small; the former have a Wrapper of Callicoe, 3 or 4 times round their Bodies, and the latter from their Arm-pits to their Knees. The Men have 2 or 3 Wives besides Concubines, and the *Dutch* say, they are much addicted to lying and stealing: Those on the Coast are generally *Mahometans*, but the others *Pagans*. The Women are not so tawny as the Men, and many of them handsom, but in general amorous, and unfaithful to their Husbands or others, being very apt to give Poison, which they do very cunningly. It would be too tedious for me to describe all the remarkable Things I saw at *Batavia*. In short, I was perfectly surpriz'd, when I came hither, to see such a noble City, and *Europeans* so well settled in the Indies. The Town is very populous, but not one Sixth of them *Dutch*. The *Chinese* here go all bare-headed, with their Hair roul'd up, and long Gowns, carrying Fans in their Hands. The *Dutch* say they are more industrious and acute in Trade than themselves. The Discipline and Order of the *Dutch* here, both in Civil and Military Affairs, is admirable. They have all Necessaries for Building and Careening Ships, as well as in *Europe*, and their Officers as regular as in her Majesty's Yards; whereas we have nothing like it in *India*. They keep the Natives very much in Awe, being perfectly despotical in their Government over them, because they say the Natives are naturally so treacherous that they are obliged to punish them severely, for small Faults; but they are favourable to the *Chineze*, because of the great Trade they have by their Means, and that they pay great Rents for their Shops, besides large Taxes, and from 16 to 30 per Cent. for Money, which they frequently borrow of the *Dutch*. I was told, there are about 80000 on the Island, who pay the *Dutch* a Dollar a head, each Month, for Liberty to wear their Hair, which they are not allow'd to do at home, since they were conquer'd by the *Tartars*. There comes hither from *China* 14or 16 large Junks yearly, being flat bottom'd Vessels, from 3 to 500 Tuns a-piece. The Merchants come along with their Goods, which are lodg'd in different Partitions in the Vessel, like Warehouses, for which they pay a certain Price, and not for the Weight or Measure of their Cargo, as we do; so that they fill them with what they please. They come in with an Easterly Monsoon, and generally arrive in *November* or *December*, and return the Beginning of *June*, so that the *Ducch* have all *Chineze* Commodities brought to them cheaper than they can fetch them; and being conveniently situated for the Spice Trade, they have all in their own Hands. *Batavia* wants no Commodities that *India* affords. 'Tis Pity our East India Company has no settlement to which the *Chinese* might resort; which I presume would turn to a much better Account than our going to *China* does, where our Traders are but indifferently us'd. 'Tis about y Years since we quitted *Benjar*, in the Island of Borneo, which, by all the Accounts I had here, might, if well improv'd, have been as serviceable to our *East India* Company as *Batavia* is to the *Dutch*, who have seldom less than 20 Sail of Ships at the Isle of *Java*, from 30 to 50 and 60 Guns each, with Men enough for them on all Occasions, so that they might easily drive us out of most Parts, if not all *India*, should we ever have an unfortunate War with them. Their Soldiers are very well train'd, and there's a Company always on Duty at every Gate of the City and Citadel; and they have 7 or 8000 disciplin'd *Europeans* in and about the City, who can be ready for Action, at a very short Warning; 'Tis the Metropolis of their *Indian* Settlements, and sends Governours and Officers to all the rest: The late General, before we came hither, had War with the Indians, which, I was inform'd, had like to have spoil'd their Settlements; but at last, they divided the Natives amongst themselves, brought them to a Peace on advantageous Conditions, and are now pretty secure of the Sea-Coasts, There are many pleasant Seats about the City, and the adjacent Country abounds with Rice, Sugar-Cane-fields, Gardens and Orchards, Mills for Sugar, Corn, and Gun-powder; so that this City is one of the pleasantest in the World. I don't think it so large as *Bristol*, but 'tis more populous: They have

Schools for *Latin*, *Greek*, *&c.* and a Printing House. They have lately begun to plant Coffee here, which thrives very well, so that in a little time they may be able to load a Ship or two; but I am told it is not so good as that of *Arabia*.

Chapter XIV

Octob. 12. We, according to Order from our Owners to keep cur Ships full mann'd, if the War continued till our Return, ship't here seventeen Men, most of them *Dutch*; the *Dutchess* and *Batchelor* near the same Number, so that we are all well mann'd; and tho' we look'd upon our Hardships to be over, several ran from us here that came out of *England* with us, being stragling Fellows that can't leave their old Trade of Deferring, tho' now they have a good Sum due to each of them, so that their Shares are by Contract due to those that continu'd.

Octob. 17. We got to the watering Place on the Main, within Princes Island at *Java* Head. The Chief of our Business here, was to get Water and Wood for our Passage to the Cape of *Good Hope*, which we compleated in 4 Days Time: But in the Interim a Misfortune befel us, which occasion'd our Stay longer on Account of a Boat lent us by Capt. *Pike*, Commander of the *Stringer* Gally, who followed us hither front *Batavia*, after a Servant of his who was brought away by Captain *Dover* in the *Batchelor*.

Octob. 23. The Boat was missing, but came back with all the Men safe, and we return'd her to Captain *Pike*, who had his Servant, and took his Leave of us.

We held the following Council just before we came to sail.

In a Committee on Board the *Duke*, *Octob.* 23. 1710. at *Java* Head.

It is agreed, that we make the best of our Way from hence to the Cape of Good Hope; and if through Misfortune any Ship should loose or part Company, either by bad Weather or otherwise, they are to go to the Cape of Good Hope, and if they don't find the other Ships, to stay there 20 Days: But if wit bin that Time the missing Ship or Ships don't appear, then to make their utmost Dispatch for the Island St. Hellena; and is not there, to proceed thence according to the Owners Orders for Great Britain.

Signed by the Majority of our Council.

Octob. 24. At 4 in the Afternoon *Java* Head bore N. E. by E. distant 10 or 12 Leagues, which being the last Sight we had of it, from that we took our Departure.

Octob. 25. A fresh Gale of Wind at S. E. with fair Weather, but an ugly swelling Sea. This Morning in Stowing our best Anchor, *Joseph Long*, a Sailor, fell over Board, and being no Swimmer, before we could get the Boat out to his Assistance, was lost.

Nothing remarkable happened till the 27th of *December*, but that my Ship prov'd so leaky, that on the 31st of October we had near 3 Foot Water in the Hold, and our Pumps being choak'd, we were in such Danger, that we made Signals, and fir'd Guns for our Consorts to come to our Relief, but had just suck'd her; as the *Dutchess* came up. The

10th of *October* she sprung a new Leak, which we could not sully stop, tho' we us'd all our Endeavours, and at the same time I had been for the most Part confined to my Cabbin by Illness, ever Since I left *Batavia*. The 28th of *December*, Mr. *James Wase* our chief Surgeon died, and we buried him decently next Day, with our Naval Ceremonies as usual, being a very honest useful Man, a good Surgeon, and bred up at *Leyden*, in the Study of Physick as well as Surgery. We made Land the 15th of *December*, came in with the Shoar the 18th, and had Soundings in 60 and 70 Fathom, the Ground grey Greet, with small Stones and Shells; had a strong Southerly Current, S. Lat. 34. 2. Lon. W. from *London* 334. 34.

The 27th of *December*, we came up with Cape *Falso*, betwixt which and the Cape of *Good Hope*, there's a deep Bay, and about a 3d over from the Cape, there's a Shold which breaks for a good Distance, but plain enough to be seen. By Noon we were a-breast of the Cape, and saw the Table-Land S. Lat. 34. 14.

The 28th We had very hard Flaws of Wind off the High Land, till we came within Sight of the *Lions Head* and *Rump*, two Hills over the Cape *Toun*. This Day we arriv'd in the Harbour of the Cape, saluted the *Dutch* Fort with 9 Guns, and were answer'd by 7. We anchor'd in 6 Fathom Water, about a Mile off Shoar, and found only one *English* Ship, call d the *Donegal*, Capt. *Cliff* Commander, homeward bound from *Mocha*, and 2 *Middleburgers* outward bound for *Batavia* in the Harbour, besides the Guard-Ship, and 2 or 3 Galliots.

The 29th. We moor'd our Ship, and got down our Yards and Topmasts to guard against the hard Flaws of Wind off the Table-Land, which frequently blow very fresh betwixt E. S. E. and S. E.

We sent 16 sick Men a-shoar. We spent till the 18th of *January*, 1710-11. in watering and refitting, and then held the following Committee.

On the 18th the Committee met a-shoar, and agreed as follows.

THE Three Ships wanting several Necessaries and Provisions, we agree, that Captain Rogers and Captain Courtney do bring 100 Weight of Plate a-shoar from either Duke or Dutchess, and 60 Ounces of unwrought Gold, with all the corned Gold or Silver that if in both Ships, We likewise empower them, in Conjunction with Captains Dover and Cook, to purchase what Necessaries we wanting for the Whole, and to sell what Goods are fit to be dispos'd of bere, if not too much to our Disadvantage rather than exchange more Gold or Silver, We also desir'd they would agree for a Cable and Anchor, now wanting for the Duke, in Place of her Sheet Anchor and Gable, lately put aboard the Batchelor for her Security.

Tho. Dover, Pres, Woodes Rogers, Steph. Courtney, Wm. Dampier, Robert Fry, John Connely, Lan. Appleby.

On the 1st of *February*, I offer'd some Proposals in Writing to Captains *Dover* and *Courtney*, with the rest of the Committee, wherein I told them 'twas my Opinion we should loose too much Time to stay for the *Dutch* Fleet, in order to have the Benefit of their Convoy to *Holland*, which would not only be out of our Way, but very tedious and chargeable; and we having large Quantities of decaying Goods on Board, the Tune we should loose by waiting for the *Dutch*, might be advantageously imploy'd in *Brazile*, where we could lie in very little Danger of the Enemy, and vend them at great Rates, and thence get to *Bristol* through the *North* Channel, having the Summer before us. Continuing in the Lat. of 55 or 56 Degrees, 2 or 300 Leagues, before we get the Length of the North of *Ireland*, and by that Means might avoid the Track of the Enemy. I earnestly press'd, that if they could not agree to this, one of our Privateers might take this Run alone, and the other keep with the *Batchelor* and *Dutch* Fleet, but the Majority was against any Thing, but going Home with the *Dutch* Fleet altogether, so that all I could do more was to remind them of examining the Goods aboard the *Batchelor*, and to take out of her so much Goods in safe Package, as would lie in the like Room of European Goods on Board the *Dutchess*, That if any Accident should happen to the *Bachelor*, we might have Part of her Value in another Bottom. I desir'd, if any amongst them were not of this Opinion, they would give their Reasons to the contrary in Writing; but we could agree to nothing. So I was forced to yield to the Majority of a Committee to go home with the *Dutch* Fleer, and having a good Conveyance by two Ships to advise our Owners, I wrote 'em a full Account of all our Transactions since we left *Grande*, and other Matters relating to the Voyage. And also lent what we had agreed in the Committee to our Owners, which was as follows.

Gentlemen,

This is to acquaint you of our safe Arrival at the Cape of Good Hope, December 29, 1710. with our Prize the Acapulco Ship, call'd Nuestra Senora de 'l Incarnation y Disengano, commanded by Monsieur John Pechberty, and now call'd by us the Batchelor Frigat, mounted with 20 Great Guns, and 20 Brass Puttereroes, and mann'd with 116 Men, a firm Ship, and each of our Ships are mann'd with 120 Men each, in Company with 3 English East-India Ships, and do expect 3 Sail more every Day: The Dutch Ships from Batavia (which are 12 Sail of stout Ships) are expected here every Hour, and fix Sail more from Ceylon, which Fleet we are resolved in Council to accompany to Holland, except we have an Account of Peace, or happen to meet with an English Convoy in crossing our Latitudes. Our Ships are all fitted with every thing necessary, and only wait for the Fleet, which we expect will sail by the last of March. Hoping God will so direct us, that we shall come with Speed and Safety to your selves, and the rest of our Friends, to whom we render all due Respects, and remain, Gentlemen,

Your most humble and most obedient Servants,

Tho, Dover, Pres, Woodes Rogers, Steph. Courtney, Edward Cook, Wm. Dampier, Robert Fry, William Stretton, Charles Pope, Tho. Glendall, John Connely, John Ballett.

We being now likely to spend so much Time here, and the *Duke* having been very leaky all the way betwixt *Batavia* and this Place, and considering the long Passage we had to *England*, I moved to the Council that we might go to *Sardinia* Bay to careen. 'Twas debated some time before betwixt me and Capt. *Courtney* pro and *con*; and to be farther satisfy'd, on the 13*th* Capts. *Cook*, *Fry* and *Stretton* were appointed to come aboard, and we had a Survey of Carpenters concerning the Leak. After some Rummage, they agreed 'twould be very dangerous to attempt any thing within-board, and no other way but Careening would do, which Capt. *Dover* and the Majority would not consent to; so that we are forc'd to lie in as bad a condition as ever, only now and then mitigate the Leak with a Bonnet, which is of no long continuance in the Harbour, much less when we come to Sea. This Day about Noon the *Batavia* Fleet came in, being 11 sail. The Fort saluted the Flag with 21 Guns, and all the *English* Ships saluted likewise, except mine, which being upon the Heel, could not do it.

Feb. 26. Having been very weak, and kept my Chamber for several Days, but now something better, I sent for most of my Officers ashore, that I might be thoroughly satisfied what was wanting aboard, in order to go home with the *Dutch* Fleet; and being too weak, and made uncapable of assisting to get any thing, I deliver'd in the said Account to Capes. *Dover, Courtney* and *Cooke*, with the rest of the Committee, that we might not be hurried to Sea without Necessaries for Subsistance.

On the 27*th* we made a Rummage for Bale Goods to dispose of ashore, having Leave of the Governour, and provided a Store-house, where Capt. *Courtney*, with the Owners Agent took their turns weekly during the Sale of them.

Nothing remarkable happen'd till the 3*d* of *April*, but that on the 13*th* of *March* 4 *Dutch* Ships came in from *Ceylon*, 3 of them having lost their Main Masts, and being otherwise much damaged by a violent Storm they met with in Lat. 18. S.

I took in more Water and Provisions, sent more Goods ashore to the Storehouse, and disposed of 12 Negroes.

On the 28*th* of *March* a *Portuguese* Ship from *Brazile* came in with advice, that 5 stout *French* Ships attempted *Rio Janiero*, but were repuls'd, and had a great Number of Men kill'd, and 400 taken Prisoners by the *Portuguese*.

April 3. Being in a readiness to sail, the Flag came off shore, was saluted first by the *Dutch*, and then by all the *English* Ships; but a Contrary Wind prevented our sailing. Most of the Goods sold at the Cape were taken out of the *Duke*, being in much worse Package than those aboard the *Dutchess* and *Batchelor*; so that most of our Bales that could be come at, have been open'd, and we find abundance of Damage, our Ship having been so long leaky, that we have not a tight Place in the Ship fit to secure dry Goods.

April 5. At Day-break this Morning the Flag hoisted a blue Ensign, loos'd his Fore-top-sail, and fired a Gun as a Signal to unmoor: As we were heaving in our Cable, it rubb'd against the Oakham, which had got into the Leak, and occasion'd the Ship to be as leaky again as ever, the having been indifferent tight for some time, and we were in hopes it would have continu'd. About Noon I came aboard very thin, and in no better Health than I was when I went first ashore at our Arrival here. Presently after I went aboard the Flag, there being a Signal made far all the *English* Commanders. We had before received our Orders, which were very particular, and as obligatory to be punctually observed. About 4 in the Afternoon the Flag, Vice and Rear Admirals weigh'd, with part of the Fleet, and fell down to *Robins* or *Penguin* Island, where they lay for the rest of the Ships.

April 6. In the Afternoon we all weigh'd from *Penguin* Island, 16 *Dutch* and 9 *English* Ships, having a fresh Breeze at S.S.E.

We buried ashore here, *George Russel*, a Foremastman, *Dec.* 30. 1710. *John Glasson*, d°. 5 *Jan.* Mr. *Carleton Vanbrugh*, Owners Agent, 3 *Feb.* Mr. *Lancelot Appleby*, 2*d* Mate, 21 d°. and four deserted.

Here follows a List of the Ships that arrived during our Stay at the Cape; all those homeward bound are now in company with us, except Capt. *Opie* in the *Olie*, and a *Dane* that sailed in *February*, designed home before us.

The Ships that arriv'd at the Cape while we were there.

Donnegall, Capt. *Cliff*, found here, from *Mocha* bound to *England*.
A *Dutch* Ship, arriv'd *Jan*. 6. from *Batavia*, and bound thither.
Loyal Bliss, Capt. *Rob. Hudson*, arriv'd *Jan*. 10.
from *Bengall*, bound to *England*.
A *Dane*, arriv'd *Jan*.15. from *Trincombar*, bound to *Denmark*.
A *Dutch* Ship, arriv'd *Jan*, 16. from *Zealand*, bound for *Batavia*.
Blenheim, Capt. *Parrot*, *Jan*. 22. arriv'd from *Mocha*, bound to *England*.
Oley, Capt. *Opie*, arrived *Jan*. 25. from *Batavia*, bound for *England*.
A *Dutch* Ship, arrived *Feb*. 4. from *Holland*, bound to *Batavia*.
The *Batavia* Fleet, 11 Ships, arrived *Feb*. 22. bound to *Holland*.
The *Ceilon* Fleet, 4 Ships, arrived *March* 7. bound for *Holland*.

Loyal Cook, Capt. *Clark*, arrived *March* 12, from *China*, bound for *England*.

Carloton, Capt. *Litton*, arrived *March* 17. from *Batavia*, bound for *England*.

King *William*, Capt. *Winter*, arrived *March* 26. from *Bengall*, bound to *England*.

A short Description of the Cape of Good Hope.

I Shall not trouble the Reader with what has been writ by others concerning this noted Place: And since I had neither Time, Health, nor Permission to ramble the Country, I can relate no Adventures that we had with Bears, Tygers or *Hottentots*; but what I shall say is from my own Observation.

The *Dutch* have here a well built small Town, containing about two hundred and fifty Houses, with a Church, and several line Gardens and small Vineyards near it. There are divers Villages in the Country, from 10 to 30 Miles distance, and scattering Plantations near a hundred Miles from the Cape; so that from the whole they are supposed to be capable of raising 3000 well armed Horse and Foot at a short warning. The Climate being in about 35 S. Lat. is excellent and healthful, and the Soil very fruitful. They have many pleasant Seats in the Neighbourhood, with Gardens, Vineyards, and Plantations of young Oaks; and other Trees raised by themselves; there being no large Timber nearer than 50 Miles off the Cape. I was inform'd that these Firms and Plantations bring in their *East India* Company a considerable Sum per *Annum*, besides Maintenance for the Garrison. They let the Land so cheap, for Encouragement of Planters, and it produces such a large Increase of Corn, Wine and Cattle, that it enables the People to say a great Excise for their Commodities, which are also continually exported for the *Dutch* Settlements in *India*, and spent in recruiting their Fleets that stop here: so that in a few Years they hope this Place will be so considerable, as to afford them Recruits on any Occasion for their Garrisons in *India*; and if they be pressed by a War these, they may always lodge such a Number of Men at this noble Settlement, which they esteem a second Fatherland, as may arrive at *India* in so good a Condition, that no *European* Power can be so capable of holding the *India* Trade as themselves. This makes me think it to have been a great Omission in our *East India* Company to quit this Settlement for St. *Hellena*, which is no way comparable to it, nor able to answer the same End, Amongst other Advantages, the *Dutch* have here a noble Hospital, furnished with Physicians and Surgeons as regularly as any in *Europe*; and this Hospital is capable of entertaining 6 or 700 sick Men at one time; so that as soon as the *Dutch* Ships arrive here, their distemper'd Men are put ashore, and they are supplied with fresh Men in their Stead. They have all sorts of Naval Stores here, with proper Officers to attend on all Occasions, which is a mighty Addition to their Strength, and enables them to preserve their *India* Trade. An Express comes hither annually from *Holland* by a small Ship, to meet their homeward bound *E. India* Fleet, which is generally from 17 to 20 great Ships. The Express brings a private Order to the Commander in chief, who is appointed by the Government in *India*; so that none knows where they are to meet their Convoy in the North Seas, but himself; and he gives it sealed up to each Ship, to be open'd in a proper Latitude near home. By this Method their Fleets have for many Years escaped the Enemy, and arrived safe in *Holland*. Their Form of Government, their Industry and Neatness abroad, is justly to be admired, and worthy to be imitated. I saw nothing I could blame, unless it be their Severity, for which no doubt they have very good reason, tho' it seemed harsh to me, who was born with *English* Liberty. They have an Island call'd Robin, which lies at the Entrance of the Cape Bay, about 3 Leagues from the Town, where they confine Mutineers, or other heinous Offenders, to hard Labour during Life, by Sentence of the Fiscal.

The *Dutch* generally send a Ship every Year from hence to *Madagascar* for Slaves, to supply their Plantations; for the *Hotentots*, who are very numerous, and love their Liberty and Ease so much, that they cannot be brought to work, even tho they should starve.

I spoke with an *English* and an *Irish*-men, who had been several Years with the *Madagascar* Pirates, but were now pardoned, and allowed to settle here: They told me, that those miserable Wrerches, who had made such a Noise in the World, were now dwindled to between 60 or 70, most of them very poor and despicable, even to the Natives, among whom they had married. They added, that they had no Embarkations, but one Ship, and a Sloop that lay funk; so that those Pirates are so inconsiderable, that they scarce deserve to be mentioned; yet if Care be not taken after a Peace to clear that Island of them, and hinder others from joining them, it may be a Temptation for loose stragling Fellows to resort thither, and make it once more a troublesome Nest of Free-booters.

The *Dutch* have seldom less than 500 Soldiers in the Cape Castle, which is very large, built with Stone, and has 70 Guns well mounted on its Ramparts, with convenient Dwellings for the Officers and Soldiers; but it lies too deep in the Bay to protect the Ships in the Road; therefore, they talk of erecting a Battery an the Starboard sandy Point, as you enter the Bay. The Road is so much exposed to the Sea, that in the Winter Months, where the Wind blows strong from thence, it is unsafe Riding, and Ships are very often lost here; so that whoever comes hither in that Season, ought to be well provided with Cables and Anchors to ride out a Storm: But in the Summer it seldom blows from the Sea; yet scarce a Day passes without very strong Flaws at S. E. which come down from the Table Mountains that lie over the Fort, so violently, that Boats cannot go to or from the Ships, but in the Morning and Evening, when it is generally very moderate and calm.

The *Dutch* have found out a noble hot spring of Water above 100 Miles up in the Country, which is of excellent virtue against all Distempers contracted in *India*; so that few have been carried thither, tho' in a desperate Condition, but they have recovered to admiration by drinking and bathing in that Water.

This Place having been so frequently describ'd by others, I shall only add, that I found the Character of the *Hottentots* to be very true, and that they scarce deserve to be reckon'd of the Human Kind, they are such ill look'd stinking nasty People: Their Apparel is the skins of Beasts, their chief Ornament is to be very greasy and black, so that they besmear themselves with stinking Oil, or Tallow and Soor and the Women twist the Guts of Beasts or Thongs of Hides round their Legs, which resembles a Tobacco-roll. Here's plenty of all sorts of Beasts and Fowl, wild and tame; and in short, there's nothing wanting at the Cape *of Good Hope*, for a good subsistence; nor is there any Place more commodious for a Retirement to such as would be out of the Noise of the World, than the adjacent Country in possession of the *Dutch*.

Nothing remarkable happened till the 1*st* of *May*, only I continued very ill, as my Ship did leaky, and sometimes we had Thunder, Lightning, Rain, and squalls of Wind. Yesterday Afternoon we had sight of the Island *St. Hellena*, bearing N. W. by N. about 6 Leagues, lying in S. Lat. 16.

On the 7*th* we made the Island of *Ascension*, S. Lat. 8. 2. Longit. W. from *London* 13. 20.

On the 14*th* at Noon we found we had just cross'd the Equator, being the 8*th* time we had done so in our Course round the World. There was a strong Current setting to the Northward, after the rate of about r Mite art Hour, Longit. W. from *London*. 21. 11. So that we have run much continually to the Westward, over and above the Circumference of the Globe,

The 17*th* in Lat. 3. 13. we found the Current still continuing to set to the N. W. 20 Miles in 24 Hours. The *Dutch* Commadore was very civil to us, and because our Prize sailed heavy, he allow'd her to keep a-head in the Night, which he did not to any other Ship. We and the *Dutchess* often tow'd her in the Day, to keep her up with the Fleet.

June 7. In the Lat. of 24°. 15". The 3 Admirals hall'd down their Flags, and hoisted Pennants at their Main-top-mast Heads, to appear more like Ships of War, every *Dutch* Ship doing the same. Now we draw near home, they scrape and clean their Ships, bending new sails, so that they look as if newly come out of *Holland*.

June 13. Yesterday Afternoon the Flag made a Signal for all the *Dutch* Commanders to go aboard with their Latitude and Longitude. We took the *Batchelor* in towe this Morning, having a fine moderate Gale at E. by N with smooth pleasant Weather.

June 14. We cast the *Batchelor* off about 5 Yesterday Afternoon, I being unwilling to run too far a head with her, now we are got so far to the Northward, where we may expect nor only the Danger of the Enemy, but also veerable Winds and thick Weather, by which means she may loose the Fleet. I advis'd Capt. *Courtney* the same in the Evening by a Letter. This Morning we rummaged our Hold, and found very little new Damage amongst the Bails, but all in general much decay'd by lying so long in ordinary Package.

June 15. The Admiral made a Signal this Morning for all the English Commanders, and some of the *Dutch* Skippers to come aboard him, where we found an excellent Entertainment, and the good Humour of the *Dutch* Admiral soon made all the Company understand each other without a Linguist, tho' we had much ado to get one at first Meeting. We parted before the Sun set, and had a fine Day.

June 28. Being got into the Latitude of 51 N. we had thick foggy Weather, so that the Flag fired two Guns every half Hour; each Ship answer'd with one. This continued several Days, which consumed a great deal of Powder, but by the Noise of the Guns it was easy to keep Company, tho' sometimes so thick for several Hours, that we could not see three Ships Lengths.

July 14. This Morning we fancied we saw Land, and some of the *Dutch* Ships made the concerted signal, but none was positive, having sampled, and 'found no Ground with above 100 Fathom of Line.

July 15. We saw 2 Ships yesterday Afternoon, one of which we spoke with, being a *Dane* bound for *Ireland.* She told us the Wars still continued, but gave a very imperfect Account of any other News: She informed us of the *Dutch* Men of War, that were cruizing for us off S*hetland* (being 10 sail,) whom she saw 4 or 5 Days ago, and reckon'd her self now about 40 Leagues from the Land. We had Soundings then in 70 Fathom Water, brown gravelly Ground. I just had time to send the Owners a Copy of my Letters from the Cape of *Good Hope*, and to let 'em know we were now got so far safe towards the Conclusion of a fatiguing Voyage. In the Morning we made Fair *Island* and Foul *Island* lying off of S*hetland*, presently after we saw the Men of War; but having little Wind, and they a good way distant from each other, we could join but one of them by Noon. Fair *Island* then bore S. S. E. distant about 2 Leagues.

July 16. All the Men of War join'd us Yesterday Afternoon, but one or two with the fishing Doggers, who were cruizing off to the North East of S*hetland*. After mutual Salutations both by the *Dutch* and *English* Ships, one of the Men of War was sent out to see for the missing Ships. Mean while the Fleet lay by, and having little Wind, the Boats came to and fro all Night, and supply'd us with what we wanted. The Inhabitants of those Islands came aboard with what Provisions they had, being very poor People, who subsist most by Fishing.

July 17. In the Morning we had a small Breeze, with which the Men of War got into the Fleet again having met with the other. About Noon we ail made Sail, steering away betwixt the S. S. E. and S. E. and the Wind at S. W. and S. W. by S. I wrote a single Letter to the Owners in general, by a *Scots* Fishing Boat belonging to S*hetland*, advising them of our joining the Men of War, who are order'd with the Fleet to the *Texel*, where I hope we shall soon meet an *English* Convoy. The *Dutch India* Admiral, tho' but a Company's Ship, wears his Hag, and gives signals and Orders to the *Dutch* Men of War, which is not suffer'd among the *English*, and in the whole Run from the Cape have kept an exact Discipline in the Fleet, not suffering any of the Commanders to go out of the Ships to visit each other at Sea without his Signal or Leaves

July 21. This Morning one of the Men of War was order'd away for the *Texel*, to give notice of the Fleet's coming; I again wrote to the Owners, for fear of any Miscarriage by the former Conveyances.

July 23. The Weather being close, the Commadore made a Signal about 10 a Clock for seeing Land, presently after all the Fleet answer'd him with their Colours. The Pilot-Boats coming off aboard the Ships, we had a aboard, who told us the *Texel* bore about S. E. by E. distant 15 or 16 Miles. Presently after Noon we parted with the *Rotterdam* and *Middleburgh* Ships, most of the Mea of War going with 'em to see 'em safe in. The Flag and all the *English* Ships saluted the Commadore, and after wards we saluted the Flag himself to welcome him in sight of *Holland*, and as soon as they got over the Bar, the *Dutch-men* fir'd all their Guns for joy of their save Arrival in their own Country, which they very affectionately call *Father-Land*. All the Ships bound into the *Texel* lay by from 2 till 5 a Clock, waiting for the Flood to carry us up. About 8 at Night we all came safe to an Anchor in 6 Fathom Water about 2 Miles off Shore.

On the 24*th* in the Morning the *Dutch* Flag weigh'd, in order to go up to the unlivering Place, As he pass'd by us, we gave him 3 Huzza's and 9 Guns. In the Afternoon I went up to *Amsterdam* where we had Letters from our Owners, to direct us how to act and proceed from Hence. On the 28*th* the *English East India* Ships had Orders to be in a readiness for sailing with the first *Dutch* Convoy for *London*. We got some Provisions aboard from *Amsterdam* oft the 30*th*. When I came aboard, on the Ist of *August* by Consent of our Council, we discharg'd what Men we ship't at *Batavia* and the Cape, and afterwards went a Way from *Amsterdam*. On the 4th the *Dutchess* and *Batchelor* went up to the Road, call'd the *Vlicter*, being a better Road than the *Texel*. In the Evening we had News of some of our Owners being at the *Helder*: Mr. *Pope* went to wait upon 'em, and in the Morning came aboard with them. After a short Stay they went for the *Dutchess* and *Batchelor*, designing thence for *Amsterdam*; we welcom'd 'em with 15 Guns at their coming and going; the *English East-India* Ships and others bound for *England* weigh'd with the *Dutch* Convoy to Day, having a fine Gale at N. E. On the 6th we weigh'd from the *Texel*, and went up to our Consorts, it being by a particular Order from the Owners for our better security; we being oblig'd to wait there, fearing the *India* Company would be troublesome, altho' we had dealt for nothing but Necessaries in *India*.

On the 10th in the Afternoon, the Owners with the Chief Officers came down, and the next Day went a-shoar to the Texel, where having an Abstract of our Voyage ready drawn up, we Went before a Notary Publick, and took our Affidavits, that what was therein contain'd was true to the best of our Knowledge, and that we had been at no other Places than therein mention'd. This was desir'd of us by *James Hollidge*, Esq. one of our Owners, to justifie our Proceedings to the Queen and Council, in Answer to what the *East-India* Company had to alledge against us, they being, as we were inform'd, resolved to trouble us, on Pretence we had encroached upon their Liberties in *India*. On the 12th, we return'd aboard again; and to keep ap a Form of Government, tho' the Owners were here, we held a Committee, where 'twas agreed to carry a Quantity of Gold to *Amsterdam*, to exchange for a supply of our Men and Ships, *viz*.

20 Guilders to a Sailor, 10 to a Land-man and to every Officer in Proportion as his Occasions requir'd. On the 13th we went away for *Amsterdam*, but did not carry any Gold out of our Ships, upon Consideration it might be prejudicial to the Insurance made on our Ships, if we took any Value out, and an Accident should afterwards happen so we agreed again, 'twould be better to take up the Money at *Amsterdam*

We had several Stores and Provisions from *Amsterdam* this Week, and likewise Money for the Officers and Men, which was paid 'em, and they had Liberty to go a-shoar by turns.

On the 23d in the Afternoon, the Owners came flown from *Amsterdam*, and the next Day examined the Prisoners aboard Us and the *Batchelor*, about raking the said Ship and other Prizes, having Notice of our going over for *England*, and that a Convoy was appointed to come for us.

We got all the Men off Shoar, who had been very troublesome to the Owners at *Amsterdam*, and every thing in Readiness for sailing. On the 31st Mr. *Hollidge* came aboard (the rest of the Owners being gone over for *England)* and took Account of what Plate, Gold, Pearl, *etc.* was in the Ship. The same being done aboard the *Dutchess*, he likewise took a List of our Men to get Protections for them, from being impress'd after our Arrival in the River of *Thames*. The next Day he went to the Texel to discharge the Custom due from our Ships, and on the 5th in the Morning he took his Leave of us.

On the 19th in the Afternoon, we had News of our Convoys lying without the *Texel*, which was very acceptable to the Crews of each Ship, who were in the utmost Uneasiness at our long stay, being just at Home, so that we had much ado to keep the Companies aboard till now. We got every thing in Readiness, in order for falling down to them.

On the 20th, about 5 in the Afternoon, we got down to the Texel, where we found our Convoy at Anchor, being the *Essex, Canterbury, Midway*, and *Dunwich* Men of War.

On the 22d in the Morning, the Wind being at N. E. we weigh d from the *Texel*, and by 10 of the Clock got clear of the Channel. In the Afternoon the *Commodore* took the *Batchelor* in Towe, and next Morning the Wind being against us, we bore away again for the Harbour as did likewise 4 *Dutch* Men of War that came out with us, bound for *London*; after seeing us safe in, he stood off to the Northward with the *Canterbury* and *Medway*, but came in the next Morning.

On the 25th our Officers met, where consulting that our 3 Ships wanted several Necessaries to keep the Sea, in case we should meet with bad Weather, we requested Captain *Roffey* our Commodore, that he would please to stay, should the Wind be fair, rill such Time as we could be provided with the said Necessaries from *Amsterdam*, which was granted

On the 13th the Wind continuing ac S. E. by S. and S. E. at Break of Day we weigh'd, as did likewise 4 *Dutch* Men of War.

On the 1st of October, about II of the Clock we came to an Anchor in the *Downs*, where several of our Owners came aboard, and after they had visited every Ship, went a-shoar with some Prisoners to examine 'em about our Capture, *&c.*

At 3 this Morning the *Essex* made a Signal to unmoar, and betwixt 9 and 10 weigh'd, he being order'd up to the *Buoy in the Noar*, and we to make the best of our Way to the *Hope*.

Octob. 14. *This Day at II of the Clock, we and our Consort and Prize got up to* Eriss, *where we came to an Anchor, which ends our long and fatiguing Voyage.*

finis.

APPENDIX,

CONTAINING

A DESCRIPTION OF THE COAST, ROADS, HARBOURS, ROCKS, SHOALS, ISLANDS, CAPES, WATERING-PLACES, CREEKS, COVES, MAKINGS OF LAND, COURSES, AND DISTANCES, FROM ACAPULCO IN THE LATITUDE OF 17 DEG. N. TO THE ISLAND OF CHILOE IN THE LATITUDE OF 44 DEG. S.

From the *best* Spanish *Manuscripts taken in the* South-Sea.

I Chuse to insert this Description as it is, without addition or diminution, because being taken on the respective Spots by the *Spanish* Pilots for their own use, I reckon it may be more useful as it is; therefore I have forborn intermixing it with the Descriptions of other Authors, which tho perhaps more pleasant to the Reader, are not so true, and by consequence cannot be so necessary for our Ships who may trade in those Seas.

If you fall to Leeward of Port *Acapulco*, and know not the making of the Lands which overshoot one another, you will see some white Rocks that the Sea breaks on over against Puerto *Marquis*, which is about two small Leagues from *Acapulco* to the Eastward.

It you go into *Acapulco* this way, take great care before you come to *Punta del Marquis*, which is a large sandy Strand. You must keep to the East-ward towards the high Land and the Ridges, and you will see Port *Mark's*; and as you run along, a white high Rock in the Entrance of Port *Acapulco*, and at the same time an Island full of red Hillocks, bring the Point East and West with the Island: and by these Marks you will know the Harbour, and steer right in for the white Rock, and then you'l see the *Griffo*, a Shoal above Water: Give it a small Birth, and you will have Water enough. Then steer for the *Punta Morrillio*, which is a small Precipice, and that will lead you unto the *Boca Chica* or little Entrance, when you will see the Town and Cattle, and may anchor before the Town; but if the Wind blows strong out, and you can-not get the Harbour, you must anchor and come in with the Land-breeze. 'Tis a very good Harbour, and clean Ground.

Coming right out of the Sea for *Acapulco*, you will see certain Moun-tains; the first somewhat high, the others ascending one behind the other, and the highest has a Volcano towards the S. E. and at the foot of these Mountains is the Harbour, with an Island before it towards the N W. between which and the Main lies a Channel. The S E. Entrance is wide; the greatest Danger is a small Shoal call'd *El Griffo*; some part of which is above Water: leave it on the Larboard Side a small space, and you will see two Rocks that stand high from the Water on the Shore.

I omit the Description of the Coves, *etc.* between *Acapulco* and *Puerto Escondido*, because it would be of no service; therefore shill only name them in course: I. *Pesquerias de Don Garcia,* a Cove or River, which by the name seems to have been a Fishery. 2. Rio de *Taquelamama* looks to be a Shoal-River. 3. Rio de *Massta* I take to be a small River. 4. *Isulas de Alcatraces,* Islands that lie before the River of *Massta.*

From the *Morro* or Head-Land of *Hermoso* to *Puerto Escondido* is 5 Leagues, Course E S E. and W N W. From *Puerto Escondido* S E. 18 Leagues lies *El Rio Galera,* or Galley River: this is a bold Coast, and lies E S E. and W N W.

From Port Acapulco towards the *Encenada de las Barraucanes,* i.e. the Bay of Hillocks, the Course is N W by W. and S E by E. 25 Leagues. The Hillocks are 15 or 16, and easily known. Parallel with them, lie several dangerous Shoals, which extend about 2 Leagues into the Sea: and all this Shore to *Puerto Escondido,* i.e. Hidden Harbour, so call'd because of a small Island which lies before it and covers it, is full of Hillocks and Strands of Sand, without any Harbour.

From Puerto *Escondido* in N. Lat. 16. to *Puerto de Angeles,* or the Harbour of Angels, is 31 Leagues, Course W by N. and E by S. from *Puerto Escondido* about 8 Leagues there's a low Point, and close to the Point a Rock. Three Leagues to the s E. is the River of Massia, with a small Island and some Rocks before its mouth.

From the River of *Massia* towards the S E. is high Land, and several small and great strands to *Puerto de Angeles.*

From *Puerto de Angeles* to the *Salinas,* or Salt-Pits, is 38 Leagues, Course E by N. and W by S. and 2 Leagues towards the S E. of *Puerto Angles* there's a Creek nam'd *Calleta,* before which there's a Ledg of Rocks which run a League out into the Sea. Three Leagues from Calleta S E. is the River of *Julian Caraco,* N W. and S E. from which there's a Shoal, some part of it above water, and appears like a Tortoise; 'tis about half a League from the Land: and mote to the S.E. is the Island *Sacrisios Puerto de Angeles,* in Lat. 15. 30. N.

Three Leagues from the Calleta or Creek before-mention'd lies *Guatulco,* N. Lat. 15. 40. the Course S E by E. and before you come to *Guatulco* there's a steep Point call'd *Bussadero,* and at the Entrance of *Guatulco* there's a Rock somewhat high and bald on the top.

More to the S E. lies *Tongolotanga,* a round high Island. Farther to the S E. there's a great River call'd *Capalita,* where the *Mexico* Road ends. Six Leagues S E. from hence is the *Morro* or Head-Land of *Ailea.* The Harbour of *Guatulco,* when you come out of the Sea, is known by some Plains and tall Trees which appear in em; and from hence to Tongolotanga is one League and half.

Seven Leagues more to the S. lies the Island of *Ittata,* and 3 Leagues further the *Morro* or Gape of *Bamba;* and N. and S. of this Cape for one League there's a great Shoal: All this Main Land is very high.

Two Leagues to the Eastward are the *Salinas,* or Salt-Pits, which have two Rocks near one another; by the said Rocks are the *Salinas,* where the high Land joins again, and runs home to *Puerto de los Angeles,* or Angels-Harbour. On all this Coast there's good Anchorage, and very clean.

From *Morro de Aytula* to the E. lies *Morro de Vanua.* 'Tis 4 Leagues from hence to the Isle of *Estata,* 3 Leagues from thence to *Morro de Massa-*

tian, and unto the *Salinas* it is 4 Leagues; and from the latter to *Morro de Massatian* two. The Isle of *Estata* is divided in the middle, which way soever you make it.

From the *Salinas* to *La Ventosa Porto de Tecoante Peque*, i, e. the windy Harbour of *Tecoante Peque*, 'tis 4 Leagues, and the Coast lies East and West. It is call'd Windy Harbour, because it blows harder here than in any Harbour of the Coast,

From the *Salinas of* the *Morro de Bernal* to the Gulph of *Tecoante Peque* is 20 Leagues, the Course N E. and S W. From the *Salinas* the Land is low as far as the Gulph. When you cross the Gulph, keep the Shore close on board, for the North Wind blows very hard; if you do not, you will meet a very rude Sea in the Offing with that Wind. But on all this Coast there's very clean Ground and good Roads, so that you may anchor in a Storm until you have fair Weather.

From the *Salinas* to the Bar of *Tecoante Peque* 'tis 7 Leagues E S E. W N W. low Land and good Anchorage. From the Bar to Port *Musquito* in N. Lat. 15. 'tis 9 leagues; and on the N W. part of *Port Musquito* there are Shoals which run a league out to Sea.

From *Porto Ventosa* of *Tecoante Peque* to the River *Tecoante Peque* is 4 leagues; the Coast lies N W. and S E.

From the River of *Tecoante Peque* to the Bar of Port *Musquito* 'tis 8 leagues, lying N W. and S E.

From the Bar of *Musquito* to the Mountain *Bernal* 'tis 8 leagues E S E. and W N W. From Port *Bernal* the Land grows low, and continues without any rising either in the Country or along the shore. This Gulph runs 40 leagues from the low Land to the other fide of the Land of *Tecoante Peque*, as far as *Guatulco*. From Port *Musquito* to Port *Bernal* is 9 leagues. In all this Gulph you may anchor near the Shore, because of the Northerly Winds as far as Port *Bernal*. From the Gulph of *Tecoante Peque to* the Bar of *Estapa* 'tis 75 leagues low Land, and the Coast lies N W. and S E.

From the Mountain of *Bernal* to the Mountain of *Incomienda* is 6 leagues, the Coast lies N W. and S E.

From the Mountain of *Incomienda to Volcano Soconesco* 'tis 6 leagues N W and S E.

From Port *Bernal* 5 leagues to the S E. lies *Incomienda*. and 12 leagues more to the S E. you find *Volcano' de Soconesco*.

From *Volcano' de Soconesco* to *Las Milpas* 'tis 12 leagues, the Coast N W and S W.

From *Las Milpas* to *Volcano de Sapotilan* 'tis 8 leagues, and the Coast runs N W. and S W,

From *Volcano de Sapotilan* to *Volcano de Sacatepeqque* 'tis 6 leagues, the Coast lies N W. and S E.

From *Volcano' de Soconesco* to *Milpas* 'tis 12 leagues, and from *Milpas* to *Anabacas* 25 leagues. These *Anabacasses* are small Plains, some of them with Hillocks divided in the top, others cover'd with low Shrubs. There are Trees on a Strand which make a Bay, and in the Rising-ground are three *Volcano's* within Land, about 8 leagues from one another, and the Mountain in the middle is N. and S. with those Palms, and call'd *Sapoticlan*.

From *Volcano de Sacatepeqque* to *Volcano* de *Atilan* 'tis 7 leagues, the Coast lies W by N. and E by S.

From the *Volcano of Atilan* to the *Anabacas* the Coast lies W by N. and E by S. From *Anabacas* to the *Volcano* of *Guatimala* 'tis 8 leagued, the Coast lying W by N. and S by E.

From the *Volcano* of *Guatimala* to the Bar of *Estapa*,tis 8 leagues, the Coast W by N. and E by S.

From the Bar of Estapa to the River of *Aloticalco* 'tis 10 leagues, the Coast N W by W, and S B by E.

From the last *Volcano* on the S E. side to the *Volcano of Guatimala* 'tis 10 leagues, and the Coast lies N and S. with the Bar of *Estapa*, which is the Port of *Guatimala*.

From the River of *Moticalco* to the Port of *Sonsonate* 'tis 18 leagues, the Coast W by N. and E by S.

From the Bar of *Estapa* to the Port of *Sonsonate* in N. Lat. 13. 'tis 36 leagues, and the Coast lies W by N. and E by S. 20 leagues to the S E. there's a great River, from whence to the River of *Moticalco* 'tis 6 leagues, from Port *Sonsonate* 'tis 10 leagues, and then you will see the *Volcano* of *Sonsonate* with two others; and if you would anchor here in *Sonsonate*, you must do it on the Starboard Side, which is the lowest Land, and keep your Lead till you have 12 fathom, and steer right in with the Warehouses, then anchor on the S E. part; but you must beware, for there are many Shoals all along to, and off from Point *Remedio*, which lies N and S. from this Harbour: and all on this Coast is low Land, with good Anchorage every where, in some places Sand, in others Mad or Owse.

From Port *Sonsonate* to *Volcano Isalcos* 'tis 4 leagues.

From the River *Lempa* to the low Land of *Ibaltique* 'tis 5 leagues, low Land, Shoal-Water, and a rude Sea.

Coming out of the River of *Sonsonate*, you must take great care of the Shoals and Rocks lying a-bout Point *Remedip*. In passing this Point Sail E by S. to the Bar of *Ibaltique*, which is 34 leagues. [Note, That about this Bar there are many Shoals more than 2 leagues off at Sea.] In sailing from the Point of *Remedio*, and 3 leagues East from it, you will see Mount *Vernel*; 'tis a middling Mountain, but the Coast is low Land, and 3 leagues farther to the Eastward is the *Volcano Cateculo*.

In the River of *St. Michael* at high Water 'tis 3 fathom deep, and from the Bar to *St. Michael* 'tis 4 leagues. From the *Volcano de Cateculo* to the Bar of *Ibaltique* 'tis 2 leagues: this Bar has many dangerous Shoals stretch'd out into the Sea. Two large Leagues N and S. of this Bar, there's a Volcano, which shews nearer than the others, and bears the name of *St. Michael*.

From the Bar of *Ibaltique* to Port *Martin Lopez*, 'tis 10 leagues, Course W by N. and E by S. You may know the Harbour by several white Banks and Ridges, there being no other such on this Coast, which joins with the Gulph call'd *De Fonseca*.

From Port *Martin Lopez*, where the Land joins With the Gulph *De Fonseca*, to Cocibina, it is 9 leagues; you may know this Gulph by certain Small Rocks join'd to the Point. From the Point of *Cocibina* to the *Mesa* (or Table) of *Voldan* 'tis 7 leagues, Course W by N. and E by S.

From the *Mesa* (or Table) of *Voldan* to the *Asexxadoes*, or Sawyers, 'tis 4 leagues. From the Point of *Cocibina* to the low Land of *Realejo* 'tis 13 leagues, Course E by S. and W by N. and between *Cocibina* and *Realejo* there's a small Hill call'd the *Mesa* (or Table) of *Voldan*.

Realejo in N. Lat. 12. 25. is the most remarkable Land on this Coast, for there is a high burning Mountain, call'd by the *Spaniards Volcano Vejo*, i.e. Old *Volcan*; which bring N E. and then steer with it, and the Harbour will appear: you go in with the Sea-Breeze. The *Volcano* is seen at a great distance, there being no Hill near it so high. By day it sends forth Smoke, and by night (particularly in bad Weather) it issues Flames, which you may see at least 20 leagues. When you have the Harbour open, and are about 2 leagues from it, you see a flat low Island about half a league in length, a mile from the Main, and near the middle of the Harbour, with a Channel on either side; that to the Westward is the best: but on the Northwest side you must take care of a dangerous Shoal, which when you have run by, keep the Wand close on board, to avoid a Sandy Point that extends it Self half Channel over from the Main. The East Channel is narrower, and rims with a great Tide. In this Harbour 250 Sail of Ships may lie Safe: you ride near the Main in 7,8,9 fathom Water at discretion, and your Anchors lie in firm hard Sand. From the Anchoring-place to the Town 'tis about 2 leagues, but as you go up, there are two Creeks, the Westermost goes by the backside of the Town, and the other goes directly to it; but there's Scarce Water for your Boat, if any thing big. The Creeks are very narrow, and the Land on either sides full of watry Plashes and Mangroves. About half a mile below the Town, on a Bank near the East Creek, there was formerly a strong Breast-work. *Realejo* is a sickly place, being in the midst of Plashes; but the adjacent Country produces Tar, Pitch, Cordage, Sugar, and Beef is very cheap here. They have Timber for Ships, which are sometimes built here. The Town is now more populous than ever, and is inhabited by some *Spaniard's* the rest are *Indians*, *Mulattoes*, *Mustices*, *Loboes*, *Zwartcrones*, and other Such Mixtures.

In this River are several Branches, and the Banks are full of Sugar-Works and Cattel. The City *of Leon* is about 4 leagues from *Realejo*, which was formerly taken by English Pirates; and about 3 leagues above *Realejo* is *Pueblo* Vejo, or the old Town, which was also taken and ransack'd by *French* Pirates. The River *Tosta* is sometimes dry, but when 'tis not, the Sea runs so rude that you cannot land.

From the *Volcano* of *Leon* to the City of *Leon* 'tis about 7 leagues; the way to it is thro a level Country of *Savannas*, and some Spots of Wood: There is only one River between 'em, which is fordable in several places. There's a small *Indian* Town about two miles from *Leon*, from whence there's a streight sandy Path thro a large Plain. The Houses in *Leon* are low, but very strong-built and large: They have many Orchards and Gardens, and fine Water-works, are very rich, have a great Trade with the North and South Seas, and a Governour under the Vice-Roy of *Mexico*.

From the Point of *Realejo* to *Rio de Tosta* 'tis 9 leagues S E by S. N W. from *Rio de Tosta* to the *Mesa* of *Sutiabo* 'tis 10 leagues, Course N W. S E. from this River, 3 or 4 leagues up in the Country, you see the *Volcano Anion*.

From the *Mesa* of Sutiabo to *Volcano de Leon* 'tis 4 leagues Course S E by E. N W by W.

From *Volcano de Leon* to *Telica* 'tis 4 leagues, and from *Volcano de Telica* to the *Mesa* de *Moliase* 'tis 2, and from the Table of *Moliase* to the high Land of *Sinotepe* 'tis 3 leagues.

From the high Land of *Sinotepe* to Port *St. John* 'tis 4 leagues.

From Port *St.* John to the Point of *Santa Catharina* 'tis 18 leagues, Course N W. S E. which is the breadth of *Gulfo Papagaio*, or Parrot-Gulph.

From the River of *Tosta* to Port St. *John* 'tis 7 leagues, Course N W. and S E. a very bold Coast, and a rude Sea. In Port *St. John* there's a smooth Table-Land about 2 leagues long. In this Gulph you must beware of the Northerly Winds, which blow very tempestuously, and strive to keep the Shore close on board. From this River to the Point of *Santa Catharina*, 'tis 18 leagues, and lies NW. and S E.

La Punta de Santa Catharina, or *St. Catherine's* Point, is in Lat. 11. 00. Off of this Point there's a large Rock, and within that, smaller ones. From this Point to *Punta de Guiones* 'tis 32 leagues N W. and S E. and from Point *St. Catharina* to *Porto de Velas* 'tis 8, E by S. and W by N. and over it there are two large Hills with a deep gap between them; and about a league or more towards the S E. there are certain Rocks which appear like Ships under sail.

From *Port de Velas* to *Morro Hermoso* 'tis 12 leagues N W by N. and S E by S.

From Cape *Hermoso* to Cape *Guiones* 'tis 12 leagues N W. S E. clean Ground.

From Cape *Guiones* to Cape *Blanco* 'tis 15 leagues, E S E. and W N W.

From Cape *Hermoso* to the Point of *Guiones* 'tis 12 leagues, N W. and S E. the Coast very clean: you may know the Harbour by a small Island at the point of it; and next the Shore from the Island there's a Ledg of Rocks, some above and some under water: and next the N W. Shore, and without the Island, 'tis very foul Ground. In the midway between *Guiones* and Cape *Blanco* there are two dangerous Shoals, a large league off at Sea. Cape *Blanco* is high Land home to the Water, and off the Point there's a small Island close to the Cape. Lat. 9. N.

From Cape *Blanco* to *Herradura* 'tis 18 leagues N W. and S E. Note, These two Capes make *Gulfo de Maya*; of which we have no Description.

From Cape *Herradura* to *Rio de la Stella* 'tis 11 leagues, N W. and S E. and from thence to *Rio del Cano* 8 Is, the Course N W. and S E. From Point *Mala* to *Golso Dulce*, 'tis 7 Is. N W. and S E. From Cape Blanco to the Island *Cano* 'tis 38 leagues, the Course is S E. and N W. and the Isle of *Cano* is from the main Land I league, in Lat. 8. 35' N.

From the Island of *Cano* to Point *Burica* the Course is N W by N. S E by S. Point *Burica* lies in Lat. 8. 20. From Point *Burica* to *Golfo Dulce* 'tis 4 leagues N W. S E. and from this Gulph to Point *Mala* 'tis 6 leagues, N W. S E.

From Point *Burica* to the Isles of *Coyba* 'tis 20 leagues S E. Run till you discover the island of *Quicara*, which lies before the Harbour on the South side, and is on the South of all the other Islands, in Lat. 7 25. N.

The Islands of *Coyba* or *Quibo*, in Lat. 7. 30. N. are several, but the big Island of that name is about 7 leagues long and 4 broad, and low Land. The N E. end is full of large tall Trees of divers sorts, and has good fresh Water: on the East and North-East side there are some Deer, black Monkeys, and green Guanoes, all good Food. Off the S E. Point there's a Shoal about half a league in the Sea; some of it appears above water the last quarter Ebb. There is no other Danger, so that you may go with your Ship within a quarter of a mile of the Shore, and anchor in 6, 7, 8, 10, or 12 fathom good clean Ground. This Island is distant from the Main about 10 leagues; the Air is temperate, and they have plenty of Cattel and Fowl, and excellent Oysters, some of which have Pearl; here are also green Tortoise, but not so good as those in the North Sea, and Timber for building.

A Description of the Coasts under the Mountains of Guanico, *near Point* Mariaco.

If any Ship be forc'd upon this Coast, they may safely enter thorow the *Canal Buena* (or good Channel) lying by Point *Burica*, and there come to an anchor at discretion. With your Boat you may enter the River of *St. Martin*, and go upwards, and you may find Inhabitants who will furnish you with Flesh, Maize, Fowls and Lemons; but remember it ebbs and flows here very much.

From Point de *Iquera* to Morro *de Porcos* (or the Cape of Hogs) 'tis 2 leagues, and from thence to Point *Mariaco* 10 leagues, the Coast E and W. with divers high Mountains and very deep Water under the shore, no Harbour nor Anchorage; and during the time of the *Vendavals*, or South-West, West, and North-West Winds, it is a very turbulent Coast. At Point *Mariaco* the Land runs to these. and makes a Bay of 8 leagues long, till you come to the River of *St. Martin*. *Morro de Porcos* lies in Lat.7. 15. N. and *Mariaco* in Lat. 7.30.

Malpelo is an Island in the Gulph of *St. Francis*: the Cape *St. Francis* the Isle of *Malpelo* and *Point Mala* lies in one Parallel N and S. and from Cape *Iquera* to Cape *St. Francis* 'tis 120 leagues. This is very near the middle of the Gulph, and lies in Lat. 4. 30 N.

From *Panama* in Lat.8. 40. N; to Porto *Perico*, 'tis 3 leagues, Course N E. and S W. and midway there's a very dangerous Shoal lying N and S. with *Paitilla* and *Vexico*, and with the River of *Grande*, N N W and S S E.

From the City of *Panama* to the Isle of *Chepillo* 'tis 7 leagues, E S E. and W N W. and one league from *Panama* is the River of *St. Juan de Dies*. The' Island of *Chepillo* is about one league in compass, and low Land next the Water, but farther up is the Hill 'call'd *Pacora*.

From *Chepillo* to Gulph *St. Michael* 'tis 5 leagues, and from *Chepillo* to the *Rio de Mastiles* 'tis also 5. This River is near the Point *Manglares*, off of which there are certain Shoals which run 2 leagues out to Sea. All this Coast is very dangerous; and to turn Windward from the Island *Chepillo* to the S E. between that and the Islands *del Rey*, you must keep the Lead, and come no nearer than 6 fathom, and tack and stand off with the Isle of *Pacheira*, which lies N and S. with Point *Manglares*; but you may borrow under the Isle *Pacheira*, for 'tis all round deep Water.

From the Island of *Pacheira* to *Perico* the Course is E S E. and W N W. 11 leagues. From *Pacheira* to the Island *de Chuche* the Course is N N W. and S S E. 4 leagues, and lies with *Taboga* N N W. and S S E. and with Panama N. 15 leagues dist. With *Otoque* it lies N E. and S W. and *Taboga* with *Otoque* N N E. and S S W. Those two Islands *Taboga* and *Otoque* are high Lands, and near *Taboga* lies another small Island call'd *Tabogilca*; on occasion you may pass between 'em, but there are some Shoals, therefore keep *Taboga* close on board: But if you can prevent it, come not near any of these Islands, for the Current makes Shoals about them, and so great, that many Times they are dry; and when you find the Current in a Calm or otherwise does carry you near them, let go your Anchor.

In going thro the Channel of the *Islas del Rey*, or the King's Islands, and the *Terra Firma*, or the Main Land, N N W. and S S. E. the nearer you range the Islands, the deeper the Water. Near the Main. Land there lies a Rock, and near this Rock the River *Maese* fells into the Sea. From this Rock to the S E. 'tis deeper Water than on all the Coast; but behind this Rock it is so shoal, Men pass it on foot. From the Rock *Chiman* to Cape *St. Lorenzo* it is deep Water, and you may anchor in 10 or 12 fathom and clean Ground; but behind it is all Shoals with Mangroves as far as the Gulph of *St. Michael*, where there are several small Islands and Rivers; you may anchor amongst them with care: in some places 'tis 15 fathom and upwards, but the Depth's uncertain; and the Current runs very strong on all this Coast.

Galley-Island bears from Point *Garachina* E S E. and W N W. dist. 5 leagues: 3 large ones from *Garachina* lies a Shoal call'd *St. Joseph*, and but 2 fathom Water on it. From thence upward all the Coast is low, and E and W. from Point *Garachina*, and E S E. and W N W. from the Isle *Galera* lies Shoals; but with the Lead and Care you may pass the Shoals of *St. Joseph*, where the Current runs very strong, occasion'd by the disemboguing of so many Rivers amble the Islands; observe that N E. and S W. two leagues from *Isula Galera* there's a Shoal that the Sea just washes over, but very near it to the Leeward is deep Water; and about the Isle *Galera* there are some stony Balks on the S W. side. Three months in the Year, *viz.* from August to *November*, the S W. W. and N W. Winds blow very bard, and the Current runs with great violence.

If you come with a great Ship into the Port of the King's-Isle (or *Isula del Rey*) take care you do not come by the small Isle on the South side, call'd *Elesante*, because there are many dangerous Shoals and Banks of Stones, which at low Water discover themselves: but to come in safe, range the great Island, and steer directly for two round Rocks lying on the North side of the Island, and you will see two small Islands, one call'd *Chupa*, the other *St. Pablo* (or St. *Paul*) and anchor between them in 8 fathom water. Here you will see the Town, and may be furnish'd with any Necessaries you want: it lies in Lat. 8. N. Note, That from the Point of *Garachina* there's another small Point call'd *El Sapo*, or the Toad.

From the Point *Garachina* to Port *Pinas* 'tis 7 leagues N by W. and S by E. and midway there's a small Cove or Bay, nam'd *Caracolos*. Port *Pinas* is high, double Land, and broken in chops, as is all that Coast, which you will see when you have Port *Pinas* N E. from you. A little without this Harbour there are two Rocks near each other; you may enter on either side, but the best Entrance is between the Rocks: Observe on the South side of this Harbour there are four or five small Islands, give them a good birth, and at the Entrance of the Harbour you will see a great Bay, in which there's good Anchorage and clean Ground; from thence towards the S E. you will see a Plain of Sand, in which Pinas lies, on your Starboard side, and Rio *Salada* on your Larboard: but up that River you will find fresh Water that descends from the Mountains, and divers Trees. You may careen securely in the Cove for the Weather, but there are divers warlike *Indians* whom you must take great care of; especially if you water above in the River, do not ground your Boat; and if you carry any Fire-Arms, hide 'em, and don't use them till you be provok'd. This Port is call'd *Pinas*, from, the great quantity of Pines that grow near it.

From Port *Quemado i.e.* burnt Harbour, in Lat. 6. 10. N. to Port *Pinas*, 'tis 12 leagues; the Coast lies N N W. and S S E. About half-way there's a small Bay with many Coco-Trees; it has a ragged Mountain over it, which, as you come in with the Land, is easy to be seen.

From Port *Quemado* to Cape *Corrientes* in Lat.4. 40. N. 'tis 29 leagues. All the Shore is very bold, but has no Harbour nor Anchoring. Cape *Corrientes* is a high round Mountain with two Hummocks near together. When the Cape is S E. from you, one of the Hillocks seems like an Island or great Rock.

From Cape *Corientes* to the River *Noaminas* 'tis 10 ls, the Coast lies N by W. S by E. The Land is low, and the River has two Entrances: It is inhabited by People that make War and Peace with one another at discretion. They man out Canoes, to rob Barks, Ships, or any thing they can get. Opposite to the Mouth of this Rivet lies *Palmas* a low Island, to Leeward of which there are many Shoals, particularly on the South-West side.

From *Rio Noaminas* to the River of *Bonaventura*, in Lat. 3. 15. N. 'tis 14 leagues. To go to this River you must enter a great Bay of the same name, in which there are two other Rivers, call'd Rio *del Agua* and *Rio del los Othones*, besides many Rivulets. In this Bay the Water is shallow, and there are many Shoals; there is one that comes from *Los Othones*, and reaches half the Bay over: the whole is very dangerous and little frequented. In this Bay Sir *Harry Morgan* was stranded, as the *Spaniards* report.

From Cape *Corientes* to the Isle of *Palmas* 'tis 20 leagues, the Coast runs N W. and S E. and along the Shore is low Land, but the inland is high, and seen at a great distance. The highest is about 8 leagues from Cape *Corientes*, and 12 from the Isle of *Palmas*: From thence to the River *Bonaventura* 'tis 11 leagues. To find the Port, observe a large Tree on the Larboard side at the Entrance; and in the River you will see a Rock, which you must steer right with till you discover a sandy Point on your Starboard side; then leave the Rock on your Larboard side, and sheer in within the Point, and you may anchor. From the Rock *St. Pedro* to the Point of Sand is one League. At this Point begins the Entrance of the River, and from the Tree at the mouth of it to the Fort 'tis 5 leagues; there you have 4 and 5 fathom Water, but in some places not above 2, Take care that you go not too near the Starboard side in the Entrance. After you are in, it is like a great wide Bay, and all round inhabited by warlike *Indians*. The highest Mountain, which is about 10 leagues up the Country, appears in clear Weather as it 'twere painted with divers Colours; and when you have the Rock of *St. Peter*, the Isle of *Palmas*, and the Mouth of *Rio del Aqua* in a parallel E and W. from you, you will find 7, 8, 9 fathom Water.

From Cape *Corrientes* to the Isle *Gorgona* in Lat. 3. N. 'tis 38 leagues, N by E. and S by W. The Island is 5 leagues from the Main, at the mouth of the River *Gorgona*. There are many Trees fit for Masts or Yards on its Bank; and on the S E. side there's a safe Harbour and very good Watering. You must anchor near the Shore, and an Hawser on Shore to guy your Ship. From this Port to *Rio de les Piles* 'tis 30 leagues, the Course N E and S W. On this

Coast you must keep your Lead if you are 2 leagues off, for it is very dangerous.

From *Rio Gorgona* to Point *Manglares* (or Mangrove Point) is 35 leagues, the Course N E. and S W. 'Tis inhabited by warlike *Indians*, who live near the Rivers, and war against one another, and fish in Canoes of Cedar: They often engage one another with great Clubs, and Darts made of hard Wood. All this Coast is full of their Tents and Barracks, from the River of *St. John* to *Mangrove-Point*.

Punt a del Morron de las Barbacoas, or Point *Barbacoas*, lies in N. Lat. 2. 45.

From the Isle of *Gorgona* to the Isle *Gallo* 'tis 24 leagues; all this Coast is low Land, with Mangroves and many dangerous Shoals occasion'd by numerous Rivers: the first is *Rio de los Cedros* the second *Rio de los Barbacoas*, which is near a low Point. The Land opposite to the Isle of *Calk* is very low, and all this Coast full of Shoals, at least 2 leagues out to Sea; so that you must anchor at least 3 leagues off Land, and stand no nearer than into 15 fathom, for the next cast you are aground. Before you come to the Isle *del Gallo*, there are the Rivers of *St. John* and *Tellembie*; and on the S E. side of the latter there's a small Mountain call'd *Barbacoas*. S E by E. from this River there are high Mountains to the Eastward, and you will see the Island *Gallo*, which seems to be two, one small, the other big, tho really but one: it lies in Lat. 2.15. N.

From *Ancon de Sardinas* to the River of *Santiago* 'tis 10 leagues, N E. and S W. From the River of *St. Jago* to the Bay of *St. Matteo* 'tis 8 leagues, N E. and S W. and about midway there's another small River, which you cannot see till very near the shore. From this River there lies a Shoal near 2 leagues out, on which Shoal was stranded *Juan Philippi de Corca*, the most noted Pilot of all the *South-Seas* in 1594.

Gorgonilla is a small Island, with a River where you may water and anchor in clean Ground. The Point of Mangroves lies 9 leagues N E. from the Island *Gallo*, 'tis low Land and full of Trees; you must give the Point a good birth, for there are Shoals two leagues off at Sea. Parting from this Point, you will see a great Bight of low Land call'd *Ancona Sardinas*: There are divers Shoals to the mouth of the River *Santiago*, and from thence the Land grows higher.

From Point *Manglares* to the River of *St. Jago* 'tis 15 leagues N E. This River is large and navigable for some leagues: about 7 from the Sea it divides it Self, and forms an Island which is 3 leagues broad. The widest Branch is that on the Southwest side of the Island: Both Branches are very deep, but the Mouth is choak'd up with Shoals; so that at low Water a Canoe cannot pass above the Island. The Mouth is, a league wide, the Stream runs streight and swift, the Tide flows up about 3 leagues; the Land on both sides is a black deep Mold, produces many tall Cotton and Cabbage-Trees, and Cedars. All this Country is Subject to very great Rains: There are no *Indians* within 6 leagues of the Sea; they feed much on Plantains and Maise, have some Hogs and Fowls, and are great Enemies to the *Spaniards*.

St. *Matthew's* Bay lies S E by S. 5 or 6 leagues from *St. Jago*, and has good fresh Water. There are many warlike *Indians* and *Mulattoes* upon this River and Bay, but very civil to Strangers. Here you may have Masts, Yards, or Canvas, great store of Fowls, Plantains, Bonanoes, and Nuts; but you must take great care not to meddle with their Women, nor offer any violence; but with civil Behaviour, you may have any thing the Country affords. The River where they inhabit lies between *Santiago* and St. *Matteo*; there are Shoals which extend from the Shore near 2 leagues.

In the River of *Atacames* there's good watering, and you may anchor at the Entrance near a small Rock, and to Windward of the Rock you may have Masts or Yards.

From Point *Galera* to the last of the three Rivers, nam'd *Coximes*, 'tis 16 leagues, keeping *Punta Galera* E N E. and about 2 leagues distance you will see the Entrance of Port Diego. From the first of these Rivers of *Coximes* to the last 'tis 6 leagues: about one from the Shore there are Shoals, but 3 leagues from the Coast you have 10 and 12 fathom Water.

From *Punta Galera* to Cape *St. Francis*, in Lat. I. N. 'tis 7 leagues: the Land is high, full of Trees, and about 7 leagues from the pitch of the Cape there's an high Island. This Cape has three Points, which as you run along you will see one after another: the third has two Rocks near together, and you will discover a Cove and very low Land. From Cape *St. Francis* to Cape *Passado* 'tis 20 leagues, the Course N by E. and S by W.

Coming from Cape *St. Francis* and going to Windward, you open a large Bight from one Cape to the other; but go not into it, for it is full of dangerous Shoals. From Cape *St. Francis* to *Persette* 'tis 5 leagues, the Course N by W. and S by E. anchor here in 5 fathom under the Cape. Here it blows very hard from Noon till Night, particularly from *May* to *December*. To go in here, you must keep the Lead. The Land over *Persette* is high, but to the Southward it is low. As you run along to *St. Juan de Quacos* in the low Land, are the three Rivers above-mention'd nam'd *Coximes*. When you go from Cape *St. Francis* or *Persette*, come not too near the Shore till you discover certain small red Hills, near which there are others high and steep.

The *Barrancas Vermillias*, or red Hills, are mix'd with white, which at Sea seems like Heaps of Salt; they are 10 leagues to windward of *Coximes*. If you want Water, go close to the Shore, leave 9 small Hills to Leeward, and anchor about one Musket-shot from the Shore, in good clean Ground and 14 fathom Water. On the broken Land there are several Lagoons, which furnish Water all the year, and in Winter plentifully; these Lagoons are under the Equinoctial. From these Hills to Cape *Passado* 'tis 10 leagues N E. and at the Point there's a small white Hill nam'd *Cavo Balena*, or Whale-Cape. *Passado* is high double Land, full of Shrubs and Brush on the top; and near the Point of this Cape there's a small Bay with several Hillocks, and to Leeward a small Harbour. Cape *Passado* lies in S. Lat. 8 min. If you come to windward of the Cape, and would anchor, you must keep about 4 Musket-shot from the Shore, where you will see a Cross planted; and there anchor in 8 or fathom. On shore you will find two Watering-places, one runs into the Sea amongst Rocks, and the other is a Lagoon about 3 or 4 Musket-shot from the first.

From *Cavo Passado* to the Bay *Carraoas* 'tis 4 leagues, high Land next the Sea, and some white Hillocks, which lie N W. and S E. You must not come in to Leeward, for in the middle of the Entrance there are Shoals; but you must pass to Windward of the white Hillocks of *Choropoto*, keep them close on board, go in with little Sail, and anchor in 4 or 5 fathom Water. You may come out to Leeward, but must keep your Lead, and go with a very easy Sail.

From the Bay of *Carracas* to *Manta* 'tis 9 leagues, Course N E. and S W. 'Tis high Land next the Sea, and there are several white Hillocks and broken Land to the River of *Choropoto*; from thence the Land grows lower, and makes like a Bay. Two leagues before you come to *Manta*, there's a low Point nam'd *Cames*; you must give it a good birth, for there's a great Shoal off of it; you may know it by a Mountain of broken Land in the Country over it: and farther to the Southward is that call'd *Monte Christi*, a very high and broken Land. On the S W. side the Land falls lower. If you come to the Windward of the Harbour of *Manta*, and would go in, you must keep your Lead going, for there is a Shoal at the Entrance, and you will see the little Mountain call'd *La Cerrillio de la Cruse*; bring this Mountain on the End of the Town, and you go clear of the Shoal, and may anchor in 7 fathom Water, bringing the Church S W.

From the Harbour of *Manta* to Cape *St. Lorenzo* 'tis 8 leagues, the Course E N E, and W S W. From *Manta* the land is low, but rises towards *St. Lorenzo*, which lies in Lat. I. S. and off of a Point near midway lies a Rock, and Shoals without it. Before you come to the Cape, there's a Bay in which there's a Shoal a league from the shore. The Cape of *St. Lorenzo* is high and steep, and near the Cape are 2 Rocks call'd *Los Frailes*, or the Fryars; one is bigger than the other, and both steep, no Danger near them.

When you have Cape *St. Lorenzo* South from you 4 leagues, and the two Rocks without it S W. you will see the Island *Plata*, Lat. I. 10. S. All the Leeward part of it is very clean Ground for anchoring, and all round this Island there's no manner of danger. It lies from Cape *St. Lorenzo* about S S W. 4 leagues. This Island has on the South side some small Rocks; when you first discover it, it seems round and high, and as you near it, looks like two Islands, tho but one. From *Isula de Plata* to Point *St Helena* 'tis 18 leagues N and S.

From Cape *St. Lorenzo* to Windward 6 leagues is *Porto del Callo*, N W. and S E. The Land falls lower gradually to the Port, in which there's a small Bay, and to the Leeward of it is a little Rock; bring that Rock South, and anchor in 6 fathom: but near the Rock there's some broken Ground, of which you must beware. This is a much better Harbour than that of *Manta*.

From Port *Callo* to the Island of *Salango* 'tis 4 leagues, the Course N and S. Between *Callo* and *Salango* there are two Harbours, about a league distant from one another. Those Harbours are known by white Hillocks, to the Leeward of which you will see the Harbour, and in either of them find Provisions, for they are inhabited. *Isula Salango* lies from *Isula de Plata* 6 leagues, N N W. the Land is somewhat high next the Sea; and in the Country above it there are some Mountains, and along shore divers small Sand-Bays and Coves.

From the Island *Salango* to the River *Colanche* 'tis 7 leagues, Course N by W. and S by E. The Coast is somewhat high near the Water-side, and in the Country are the Mountains of *Pisana*, which range along to the River of *Colanche*; they appear at Sea small and sharp at the end like a Knife. About midway 2 ls. from *Colanche* you will see two Rocks call'd *Aurcadoes*, i.e. the hang'd Men; and 3 leagues South from them lies an Island with a little Island or Rock, call'd the small Island of *Colanche*; you may anchor any where in the Bay of this Island, and sail round it without danger. In the River of *Colanche* there's good fresh Water, and from thence you will see the Town on the Point of *Santa Helena* 2 leagues, the Course N E. and S W. 'tis low Land next the Sea, with a few small Hills.

At Point *St. Helena*, Lat. 2. 20. S. you may find Provisions. You must come to an anchor in 4 fathom, right against the Town: there's the same Sounding all over the Road, but you must not anchor under that small Town on the Point, because of the Banks and Shoals. From this Town on the Point of *St. Helena* to the Harbour 'tis about a league and a half, and the Land is low next the Water-side.

Here enters the River of *Guiaquil*, of which having given a sufficient account in my Journal, I omit it.

From the Point of *St. Helena* to the Island of *Santa Clara*, in the mouth of the River of *Guiaquil*, 'tis 20 leagues, the Course N W. and S E. This Island is easy to be known; having describ'd it in my Journal, I say no more of it here.

From the Island of *St. Clara* to *Tombez* 'tis 6 leagues, the Course N N W. and S S E. which cross the River of *Guiaquil*. *Tombez* is low Land next the Sea, but the Country is high. The River of *Tombez*. is known by a very large Tree at the Entrance, much higher than any of the other Trees about it. When you wou'd approach this River, do not come too near the lowest Land, for there's a Shoal that reaches a large league out to Sea. About 2 leagues farther to Windward begin the Mountains of *Tombez*, that run along the Coast till you come to a low Point, call'd *Punta de Mero*. When you are in the Offing, you will see these Mountains of *Tombez*, which are easily known, being for the most part broken and ragged. From *Punta del Mero* to *Cavo-blanco* 'tis 10 leagues, the Course N E. and S W. Along great part of the Coast you have double Land, and about midway high Mountains call'd *Mancora*, under which there's a small Bay, and on the shore white Sand. To the Southward of this Bay you will see a high Point, and a little to Leeward of it, a curious Bay where you may anchor. On all this Coast: the Current always runs to Windward, and when it blows hard, there's a very great Sea; but you may corneas near the shore as you please, for it is steep, and here are divers Points and Bays that run from one to another. To know the Cape, observe that near the Water-edg there's a white Spot in the Clift. Cape *Blanco* is in S. Lat. 4. Oh this Coast from *May* to *November* there blow great Gales of Wind, for most part Southerly. Under Cape *Blanco* there's a small Bay to Leeward, where you may anchor in 14 fathom, and catch great quantities of Fish.

From *Cavo Blanco* to *Punta Parina*, S. Lat. 4. 22. 'tis 7 leagues, the Course N and S. You will see white Hillocks and several Coves and Bays, which seem to be Harbours: the principal and biggest is midway, call'd *Mallaca*, and lies a league and half from *Parina*. There is a steep Point with several white Hillocks before you come to it; and there's a very good Harbour call'd *Talara*, but frequented only by small Ships to load Salt. You must moor here by three Anchors, one to the S W. another to the S E. because of the Freshets, and the third to the N E. There are great Gusts from the Land. You may anchor here in 12 fathom or more, but close home to the Windward-most Point there's a Shoal that faces Point *Parina*, is low Land, and looks like two Islands: The Land within is hilly.

From Point *Parina* to the Harbour of *Payta* 'tis 10 leagues, Course N W. and S E. 'tis a large Bay and low Land, with some small white Hills to the River *Colana*. Take care how you come into this Bay, for it has frequent Calms, and off the River of *Colana* there are divers Shoals. From this River to *Payta* is 3 leagues; the Land is white with small Hills, and in some places doubled. As Marks for this Port, you will see several broken and ragged Mountains over it, but the Land in the Harbour is low: at entring, beware of Flaws. You may anchor here in 8 or 10 fathom, over against the Houses. From *Payta* to *Pena Oradada* is 2 leagues.

From *Pena Oradada* to the Island of *Lobos de Payta* 'tis 2 leagues, Course N. and S. Tis a small round Island, the Coast is not high, but very clean Ground near it. From this Island to the Point of *Aguja Sutavento*, or *Aguja* to Leeward, 'tis 15 leagues; midway there Is a great Bight, call'd *La Eucenanda de Cechusa*, which from *Lobos de Payta* is 12 leagues, the Course N. and S. the Land low, and all the Bay very clean Ground and good Anchorage; but not frequented by Ships, because it produces nothing for Trade.

From Point *de Aguja* to Leeward is white high Land, and from this Leeward Point to the Windward Point 'tis 4 leagues, Course W and by S, 'tis high Land, with a regular Descent towards the Shore. Go not too near the Windwardmost Point, for there's continually a very rude Sea. From Point *Aguja* to the Island of *Lobos*, and to Leeward of it is 5 leagues: this is a small Island in Lat. 6. 6, in compass about 2 leagues, lies N and S. is low ragged Land, and about it some small Rocks. From the Leeward part of the Island to the Windward Point on the Land 'tis 7 leagues, where you will see another small white and lower Island, which lies from *Punta del Aguja* N and S. From the said Point to *Morro* or Mount *Etten* 'tis 19 leagues. All the Coast is very low, with Shoal-Water and always a great swelling Sea.

In a Bay N by W. from the Point of *Lobos*, you will see a Cross as you come from the Windward; go directly in with that Cross, and when you have 6 fathom you may let go your Anchor, in clear sandy Ground, From the Island of *Lobos* to the Main 'tis 5 leagues, and between the Main and *Lobos* there's another small hilly Island 2 leagues from the shore; betwixt which and the Island there's a very good Channel, 8 fathom Water. On the East fide of this Island there's a sandy Bay, where you may anchor, and have plenty of Fish, but neither Wood nor Water. From Point *Aguja* to the Mountain of *Cherepe* the Course lies N W. and S E. all low Land, and is a very dangerous Coast. The Island of *Lobos de la Mar* being describ'd in my Journal, I shall omit it here.

If coming out of the Sea you would make *Cherepe*, and the Current or Calms set you into the Bay, you will see on the Mountain *Etten* a sharp Hill very high, which seems about 10 leagues from you; but if you find you are much to Leeward of *Etten*, you will see the Hill of *Requen*, which is ragged and broken on the top: and on the South side there's a spiry Peak like a Sugar-loaf. As you go more to the Eastward, you discover other Hills; but as you near the Land, the Hill *Requen* makes in divers shapes: and off of it you will see near the Water-edg, Land like a black Island, to the Southward.

From the Hill *Etten* to the Hills of *Mocupe* 'tis 4 leagues, the Land low, and Course E S E. and W N W. These Hills are black, and about one league in length: in the low Land between 'em are several Lagoons, or Ponds of fresh

Water; you may find them by high broken sandy Banks about a league to the Windward: but except Necessity force you, come not into this Bay, for here is always a great Sea.

From those broken sandy Banks to the Port of *Cherepe* in S. Lat. 7. for 2 leagues, the Land is higher towards the Water-side than inward, the Course is N. and S. You will see red Hillocks, and to Leeward of *Cherepe* a Mountain about one half league in the Country, higher and longer than the Hills of *Mocupe*; it makes in divers shapes, according to the Point of the Compass it is from you. If you would anchor in the Harbour of *Cherepe*, go to Leeward of a low Point, which at a distance shews like a black Island; but if it be clear Weather, you will see the Church at least 3 leagues at Sea. You must mind that at the Windwardmost Point there's a Shoal, which extends more than

A table of each Days Run between Cape St. Lucas in California, and the Island of Guam.

1709-10		Course.	Dist.	Lat. by Reck & Observat.	Long. W. from London	Diff. Lon. from Cape S. Lucas.	Variation Easterly.
				N.	W.	W.	
January							
12	E	S. 22 30 W.	45	22 16	114 09	00 09	03 00
13	F	S. 28 00 W.	66	21 18	114 42	00 42	02 50
14	G	S. 33 45 W.	54	20 24	115 15	01 15	02 50
15	A	S. 33 45 W.	52	19 25	115 45	01 45	02 50
16	B	S. 33 45 W.	68	18 56	116 24	02 24	02 45
17	C	S. 33 45 W.	72	18 00	117 06	03 06	02 45
18	D	S. 35 10 W.	41	17 11	117 30	03 30	02 15
19	E	S. 33 45 W.	62	16 32	118 05	04 05	02 00
20	F	S. 43 40 W.	68	15 44	118 54	04 54	01 50
21	G	S. 68 00 W.	83	15 00	120 15	06 15	01 30
22	A	W. 06 48 S.	94	14 49	122 05	08 05	01 10
23	B	W. 05 20 S.	152	14 36	124 25	10 25	00 50
24	C	W. 04 00 S.	142	14 24	126 45	12 45	00 40
25	D	W. 04 10 S.	151	13 14	129 05	1 05	00 45
26	E	W. 05 25 S.	147	13 50	131 23	17 25	00 50
27	F	W. 18 50 S.	97	13 29	132 58	18 58	01 00
28	G	W.	88	13 29	134 41	20 41	01 10
29	A	W. 03 00 S.	122	13 22	136 48	22 48	01 15
30	B	W. 04 00 N.	146	13 27	139 21	25 21	01 25
31	C	W. 04 00 N.	160	13 32	142 07	28 07	01 30
Feb. 1	D	W.	143	13 32	144 37	30 37	01 40
2	E	W. 04 00 N.	168	13 36	147 32	33 32	01 50
3	F	W. 06 00 S.	160	13 26	150 18	36 18	02 00
4	G	W.	156	13 26	153 02	39 02	02 10
5	A	W.	130	13 26	155 19	41 19	02 25
6	B	W.	137	13 26	157 43	43 43	02 30

7	D	W. 02 00 S.	161	13 25	160 31	46 31	02 50
8	C	W. 08 00 N.	144	13 41	163 00	49 00	03 00
9	E	W.	130	13 41	165 18	51 18	03 20
10	F	W. 01 00 N.	124	13 44	167 26	53 26	03 30
11	G	W. 03 00 S.	146	13 36	169 56	55 56	03 45
12	A	W. 01 00 S.	146	13 33	172 27	58 27	04 00
13	B	W. 01 00 N.	148	13 36	175 00	61 00	04 30
14	C	W. 02 00 S.	136	13 32	177 21	63 21	05 20
15	D	W. 04 00 N.	125	13 40	179 28	65 28	06 30
16	E	W. 04 00 N.	112	13 47	181 24	67 24	07 00
17	F	W. 04 00 N.	114	13 54	183 22	69 22	07 30
18	G	W. 01 00 S.	130	13 52	185 37	71 37	09 00
19	A	W. 07 00 S.	122	13 40	187 42	73 42	10 15
20	B	W. 07 00 S.	124	13 28	189 49	75 49	11 00
21	C	W. 04 00 S.	98	13 21	191 30	77 30	11 30
22	D	W. 05 00 S.	113	13 12	193 25	79 25	12 00
23	E	W 04 00 S.	70	13 07	194 37	80 37	11 50
24	F	W. 01 30 N.	72	13 10	195 51	81 51	11 00
25	G	W. 04 00 S.	118	13 03	197 51	83 51	10 00
26	A	W. 01 30 S.	70	13 00	199 03	85 03	9 50
27	B	W. 02 00 S.	71	12 57	200 16	86 16	9 30
28	D	W. 02 00 S.	120	12 54	202 20	88 20	9 00
Mar. 1	C	W. 02 00 N.	108	12 58	204 12	90 12	8 40
2	E	W. 03 00 N.	110	13 04	206 06	92 06	8 20
3	F	W. 01 00 N.	84	13 05	207 33	93 33	8 00
4	G	W.	88	13 05	209 04	95 04	7 50
5	A	W. 02 00 S.	106	13 02	211 54	96 54	7 30
6	B	W. 02 48 N.	105	13 07	212 07	98 42	7 10
7	C	W.	82	13 07	214 07	100 07	7 00
8	D	W. 03 00 S.	78	13 03	215 28	101 28	6 50
9	E	W. 03 00 N.	100	13 08	217 11	103 11	6 30
10	F	W. 06 00 N.	74	13 16	218 27	104 27	5 40

half a league to Sea; so that you must go with your Lead in 8 fathom, and when you are clear of the Shoal, steer right with the Church, bring it E S E.

and you will see a Cross which you must bring South, and anchor in 7 or 8 fathom.

From *Porto Cherepe* to *Pascamayo* 'tis 6 leagues, the Course N W. and S E. low Land and sandy, with some Hillocks; and towards the Inland about half a league are the Hills call'd *San Pedro del Toque*: where they join on the North side, there's a round Hill call'd *El Pan de Sucaro de Guadalupo*, i.e. the Sugar-loaf of *Guadalupo*; and when you have that Loaf to the East from you, you will see a Clift in the top of it. Porto *Pascamayo* resembles a great Strand, and about half-way in it shews white like a Rock in the Sea. All this Coast is bold, but not much frequented. Here's a very rude Sea that always runs here.

From *Pascamayo* to *Malabrigo* 'tis 5 leagues, low Land and sandy, with some white Hillocks. Before you come to *Malabeigo* about 3 leagues, there's a sandy Bay of very low Land, that reaches to *Malabrigo*; in some places 'tis Shoal-Water. To come to the place of anchoring, you must keep your Lead going, and keep in 5 or 6 fathom. When you near a small Hill to Windward, you will have but 4 fathom and half; and then you will see a Clift in the said Hill, which you must bring South, and come to an anchor. Off of this Hill come great Flaws of Wind, and often make a great Sea. If you come directly out of the Offing, you will see a small Bay on the South side at the end of that Bay. The Land to the Northward is ragged and broken, and about the middle of this broken Land you will see a round Hill, which is the Mark for the Harbour.

From *Malabrigo* to Port *Guanchaco*, in S. Lat. 8. 'tis 14 leagues: about midway there's a great River call'd Rio *Chicama*. Along the Coast the Ground is low and sandy, but up in the Country there are several great and little Hills. About 2 leagues before you come to *Guanchaco*, you will see a Point of Land which, rises gradually towards the Country, and then falls at once; so that at first it appears higher than those Hills within Land, and at last there seems to be a Pit between them. If you go into *Guanchaco*, keep the Lead going, and the Church in the Town, which you will see, and then you have 10 fathom. When you have the *La Cerra Campana* N E by N. anchor in 7, 8, 9, or 10 fathom. You must not neglect to under-run your Cables, and now and then to trip your Anchors; for the great Suff that comes in brings such quantities of Weeds, as will choke and bury both Cable and Anchor.

From *Porto Guanchaco* to the Hill of *Guanape*, S. Lat. 8. 30. 'tis 9 leagues, the Course N N W. and S S E. and midway there's a large Bay, and in the middle of that Bay a Hill call'd *Morro de Carretas*: It is a bold Coast, and low Land next the Water. Anchor not in this Bay, unless oblig'd by Necessity, for here runs a very rude Sea. Without *Guanape* you will see a great Rock call'd *Farrellon de Guanape*, and within this Rock a small Island, between which Island and the Rock there's a good Channel and all clean Ground. *Morro de Guanape* is about half a league round, encompass'd by the Sea, and has many small Rocks about it: from hence to *Porto Sancto* 'tis 9 leagues.

You may sail between the small Island of *Guanape* and the Shore without any danger, for all that can hurt you appears above Water. If from hence you would go for *Truxillo*, sail N W by N.

From the Cape of *Guanape* to that of *Chao* 'tis 7 leagues N W. and S E. low Land. The Cape of *Chao* is a high Precipice, and before it several small white Rocks; to Windward of the Cape there's a little blackish Island. There is no anchoring on this Coast.

From Cape *de Chao* to *Porto Santo* in S. Lat. 9. 'tis 6 leagues, Course N W. and S E. low Land; but before you come to *Porto Santo*, you will see divers small Rocks call'd *Los Corcobadoes*, or the Hump-backs: go not between those and the Shore, for there are several Ledges and Shoals; and before *Porto Santo* you will see an Island about a league long, it lies N and S. On either side this Island you may go into the Harbour without any danger; you anchor in 7 or 8 fathom, all clear Ground. At the Entrance you will see a small Spot of white Sand upon the shore, anchor right against that: and a little farther in you will see some Trees which look as if they were painted; behind them lies the Town.

From the Windwardmost Point of the Island *del Santa*, or Holy Island, to *Ferol*, 'tis one league; from thence to *del Acarma* 'tis 10, Course N W by N. and S E by S. high Land. *Porto Ferol* is a good safe Harbour: you go in among some small Islands in the middle of the Harbour, which is all very clean and safe. Within Land over the Harbour there's two great Hills of each side: over against these Hills are the Islands. The Hill to the Southward is round and large, and has several Spots; near the Main Land, over against this Mountain, there's a Shoal, but you have no occasion to come near it.

From *Ferol* to *Guanbacho* 'tis 6 leagues. If you would anchor here, remember that to Windward of the Hill call'd *El Morro* there lies a small Rock; and when you are within the Head-land, you will fee broken Land on the Starboard side: steer right in, and come to an anchor over against a Hill. On the same side you may go farther in, and anchor against certain Spots in the Land. Here you may have Wood and Water, but it 'will be proper to put a Hawser on shore, because of the Flaws from the Hills.

From *Guanchaco* to *Casma* 'tis 5 leagues, and between them are certain small Islands and Bays, in which there's very deep Water; but when you have an Offing, you cannot discern those Bays, because the Land overlaps them. *Casma* is a very good Harbour; and altho you have very hard Gales of Wind from Noon till Night, you have no great Sea. In the Bay there's a small white round Rock, but a little above the Water; it lies nearest the North Shore. On the South side there's a small Shoal about two or three Ships length, which you cannot discern but at low Water, when the Sea breaks on it, tho near a fathom and a half of Water. When you are pass'd between these, you may range the Main at discretion, and will find 14 or 15 fathom near Shore: anchor against the *Morro blanco*, or white Cape; carry a hawser or Stream-Cable on shore, and make it fast to the said Cape.

In Port *Vermejo* or red Harbour, S. Lat. 10.15. there are no Houses at the Water-side; the Land inwards is low, and there's a narrow Slip that leads to the Village, which is about 3 leagues from the Coast to the Southward. When Ships touch here, they send to this place for Provisions. Here's also a Rivulet of fresh Water, which in Summer runs into the Sea, but afterwards dries up for most part, only in some Pits you may then find Water. This Port is the best, and more Subject to Southerly Breezes than any other along this Coast; 'tis a very safe and bold Harbour. Going in, keep the bold Point close on board; and when you discover the small Creek, you may anchor in 7 or 8 fathom. Let your Anchor remain to the Northward, and carry your Stream-

Cable on shore to the Rocks. The Marks of this Harbour are red Hillocks, and an old *Indian* Fort.

From *Casma* to *Mongon* 'tis 4 leagues, and here the Coast alters, and the Current for most part runs to Leeward. The Mountain over this place is much higher and seen farther than any other Land thereabouts; if you see it S W. from you, it seems level on the top, and like a Table; and if E N E. it seems round with some broken Land on it; when you have it N E. from you the broken Land begins to open.

From *Mongon* to *Guarmey* 'tis 10 leagues, the Course N and S. and from *Mongon* to the Island of *Porto Vermejo* 'tis 4 leagues: 'tis a small white Island, and in the middle you will see a Bay which makes with two Points that resemble the Mouth of a Harbour, and is call'd *Sagietta de la Culebra*, or the Snakes Dart. The Land from *Mongon* to Port *Vermejo* is high and in heaps, with many Spots of white Sand: If you come near the shore, you will see a round Hill. You cannot pass between the Main and the Isle of *Porto Vermejo*, because of dangerous Shoals.

Puerto, or the Harbour of *Guarmey*, lies in S. Lat. 10. 30. When you would go into this Harbour from the *Bussaderos*, which is right under the Mountain call'd *Jaguci de la Corra*, you will see red Hillocks which seem very level on the top; they run as far as the Point call'd *Cabessa del Gatto*, or the Cats-head. Sail by that till you see a small Bay; having that open, let fall your Anchor in 12 fathom. A-stern of you there's a small Rock high out of the water, and about Musket-shot to Leeward is the Creek where the Barks load. Go not within this Bay or Creek with your Ship, for off of the Point there's a large Shoal. From *Bussadero* to *Cabessa del Gatto* 'tis 3 leagues: On the South side there's a very good Harbour; the Town is above half a league from the Strand, and inhabited by *Indians* and *Spaniards*.

From *Jaguci delta Corra* to the River *de la Barranca*, or of the Hillock, 'tis 9 leagues. The Land appears in heaps, but low next the Coast: in the middle there's a Hill call'd the *Cerro de Gramadal*, in the top of which there are two Clifts or Splits; that in the middle is the highest, the Hill to the Southward is lower, and that to the Northward the least and somewhat round. If it be thick Weather, and you have an Offing, these Hills seem to be Islands. One league before you come to *Rio del Barranca* lies *Paramonguilla*, which makes like a white Rock, and at some distance appears like a Ship under sail. To Leeward of *Paramonguilla* about a league, there's a low black Point that looks as it were cut right off, and to Leeward of that there's a large Strand: here you may anchor (in case of necessity for the Current) in 6 or 7 fathom.

From the River *Barranca* to *Soupe* 'tis 2 leagues. To Leeward of the Strand of *Soupe* there are red Hills next the Sea-side, to Leeward of these Hills make a small low Point, and to Leeward of that is the Port of *Barranca*, in S. Lat. II. there you may anchor in 6 or 7 fathom, and moor with an Elbow to guide your Ship between both for the Land-Breeze.

The *Playa* or Strand of *Soupe* makes a great Bay of loose Sand, and here only come Barks to load Corn. This Bay has always a great Swell, and when it blows, there's a very rude Sea.

From the Strand of *Soupe* to *Don Martin's* Island 'tis 3 leagues, the Land towards the Sea is low, but within Land are several small Mountains like Volcans. The Isle of *St. Martin* appears white, is about a quarter of a league from the Shore, and half a league in compass.

From the Island of *Don Martin* to the Harbour of *Guara*, S. Lat. II. 30. 'tis one league. Going to windward of the Island, you see another small one call'd *Isula de Lobos* (or Wolves-Island) near which there's a Shoal: go not near it, nor between them and the Shore, for there is little Water. To anchor in this Port, you must bring the Island of *Lobos* a-stern: upon the Headland there are two old Walls, which make like two Pillars; bring the one with the other, and the Island of *Lobos* a-stern, then let go your Anchor, but with care, for here are many sharp small Rocks that will hurt your Cables. You must moor with an Elbow; 'tis a rude Sea, but you have good Water, and may get all Necessaries at the Town, which is a league from the Harbour.

From the Point of *Guara* to *Guacho* 'tis one league; to this Harbour of *Guacho* come no Ships, but only Barks. To Leeward you see a Headland, and must give it a birth; for there lies a Shoal off it under water, and the Sea breaks on it.

On the Coast that comes from the *Salinas* to Windward, and near the Point *Remate* over against *Los Ferralones de Guara* (or the Rock of *Guara)* there's a small Bay call'd *La Herradura*; 'tis a good Harbour, and when you cannot weather the Rocks of *Guara*, you may anchor here, between the Point and the Main Land. In the Bay there's a small Rock call'd *Tambillio*; you may sail between it and the shore, but best without it. From this Point *Remate*, that makes the Coast which comes from *Tambo* and *Playa* de las *Perdices*, or Partridg-Strand, 'tis 3 leagues low Land; and a little in the Country there's a sandy Hill. In Partridg-Strand you have good clean anchoring-ground among high ridgy Sand-Hills, one of which is higher than the rest, and falls away lower to the Northward. When you come out of the Sea towards Partridg-Strand, they resemble a rising Covy of Partridges, being two large Rocks at some distance, and other smaller ones within them: but come not near the Hill *Chancaillo*, for it is very subject to Calms and a tumbling Sea.

From *Guaco* to the *Salinas* or Salt-Ponds 'tis 3 leagues, the Land low next the Sea. Here is a good Harbour, altho it blows hard, and a tumbling Sea, but neither Wood nor fresh Water; so that in case Ships are oblig'd to come hither for shelter, and are in want of Water, Wood, or Victuals, they fetch it from *Guara*. You must anchor here, before you come to those Rocks that are join'd to the Shore, in 7 or 8 fathom. Here is also another small Port call'd *Porto de la Barca*, but of little note or use.

From the Headland of *Salinas* to *Maltest*, which is the outermost: Rock of the Partridg-Strand, 'tis four leagues, the Course lies N. and S. from thence to the Main 'tis 4 leagues. These Rocks are seven or eight, and lie nearest. N. and S. All about them is clean Ground: you may pass between the two outmost in 40 fathom Water, but be sure to have your Anchors clear. They lie with the Isle of *Don Martin* N. and S. To *Los Ormigas* (or the Pismires) N and S. 7 leagues: to the Island *Callao* fifteen leagues N W. and S E. All the Coast from *Santa* to this place is clean Ground.

Port *Chancay* or *Chancaillo* lies in S. Lat. 12. 5. but little frequented, there being always a great tumbling Sea here. The Town is about half a league from the Water-side, and you may have Refreshments there.

From *Chancaillo* to *Chancay* 'tis 2 leagues ridgy Land. When you are in an Offing, it shews black, and thro those Ridges there fall great quantities of Water and Floods into the Sea. When you near the Shore, the Town appears white, and you see the Church of *St. Francisco*. Here is a very good Harbour for a Southerly Wind, only you have a tumbling Sea. To go in here, you must keep close to the Hill of *Chancay*; and to Leeward of that lies the Harbour: you may anchor where you please, for it is all clean. Come not too near the small Bay that you see at the Entrance, for it is full of sharp small Rocks.

From *Farelon Maltesi*, or (the outermost Rock of *Guara*, or the Partridges, to *Ormigas*, is 7 leagues, Course N and S. This Island *Ormigas* is small, appears white, and in the middle there's a small Clift. On the South side you have good Anchorage and clean Ground, but on the North side a Ledg of Rocks for above a league: at the end of this Ledg there's a bigger Rock than the rest, off which the Sea breaks. You must take great care of those *Ormigas*, for Ships have been lost about 'em. This Island *Ormigas* lies from *Maltesi* N and S. and bears from the Island *Callao* E by N. and W by S. 8 leagues, and from the *Pescadores* E by N. and W by S. 9 leagues.

From the Port of *Chancay* to the *Farelon Grande*, or great Rock of the *Pescadores* or Fishermen, 'tis 3 leagues, the Rocks high next the Sea, but in the middle there's broken high sandy Land. E. from the great Rock of the Fishermen there's a good Harbour call'd *ncon*; you must go in on the N W. side, where 'tis all clean Ground. Here you find Wells, but somewhat brackish. There goes no Sea in this Harbour.

These Fishermens Rocks are 6 or 7 small ones, and appear white; the Northwest Rock is the biggest. They lie in a range N W. and S E. and with the Headland of the Island *Callao* N N W. and S S E.

From the *Ferralones de los Pescadores* to the Harbour of *Callao* 'tis 5 leagues, Course N N W. and S S E. and from the Headland of the Island 5 more. From the *Pescadores* to the Rock of *St. Francisco* it is high Land, and from thence to *Callao* 'tis low. In this Bay between Los *Pescadores* and *Callao* you may turn to Windward, and anchor where you please; and all along this Coast unto *Chancay* there's good anchoring. When you would go into *Callao*, give the Headland a birth at least one league; for if you come nearer, you will find very strong Flaws: but here is clean Ground to anchor, and as I said before, you may turn to Windward, only take care of the Flaws, and of a small Ledg that lies off the Windwardmost Point. When you come before the Houses, anchor where you please, for all is clean, and no danger. *Callao* is in S. Lat. 12. 20. Here you may be supply'd with all manner of Necessaries.

From the Headland of the Island of *Callao* to Port *Paraca*, the Course is N N W. and S S E. 40 leagues; and from the Headland of the Island call'd *La Bihia* to *Morro* or Cape *Solar*, 'tis 2 leagues; from thence to the Rocks of *Pochacome* 'tis 3. Those Rocks are two great with several small ones, lying on the South side, run towards the Main Land, where they are all white. From those Rocks to the Point of *Chilca* it is 3 ls, and there's a low Point somewhat saddle-back'd. *Chilca* Harbour is the best in all the *South Sea*, and as still as a wet Dock; only the Entrance is narrow, and the Harbour so small that it will not contain above seven or eight Ships. To go in here, you must anchor in the Entrance; carry out a Warp, and warp in behind the small Island, and moor as you please.

From the Point of *Chilca* to *Mala* 'tis 4 leagues; from thence to the Island *Asia* 'tis 3. About midway of those 7 leagues there's a Bay, and in the midst of that three or four Mountains. As you go towards this Island, it appears white, and there are some small white Rocks within it. The Course from *Chilca* here is N W. and S E. all a bold Shore, This Island is about half a league in compass.

From the Island *Asia* to *Cannete* 'tis 7 leagues, the Course N W. and S E. low Land next the Sea, but farther in it is higher. Then you see a great Ridg of Hills nam'd *Cordillera*, with a great deep Gap. From thence comes down the River *Cerca*, and from the Coast rises another Hill, which descends again towards the S E. and joins over the Town to the Headland of *Cannete*, which is not very high, but runs out a great way into the Sea. Off the Head-land and Harbour there are some Rocks, but they are bold, and there's no danger but what is visible.

From the Headland of *Cannete* to the Port of *Chincha* 'tis 9 leagues and a bold Coast. In the Summer the Northerly Winds blow much, and for most part by night; near the shore it blows hardest, and all the Year the Current runs very strong to the Entrance of the Harbour, where Ships come to load Quick-silver. The Harbour is parallel with the River, where you may lie in 5 or 6 fathom; but the Barks that load Corn, go farther in near the Strand.

In the Harbour of Pisco you come to an anchor right against the Houses in 5 or 6 fathom. The Marks for anchoring in this Harbour, are to bring the Islands of *Chincha* N W. the Island of *Ballesta* W S W. and *Cangallon* S W. Along all this Coast you may safely anchor, for 'tis all clean Ground; only about one league and a half before you come to Pisco, you see a white Hill nam'd *Caucatta*. Come not too near this part, for the River *Pisco* throws out Sand, *&c.* which has caus'd some Shoals: but otherwise all over this Bay between the Islands of *Chincha* and *Pisco*, which is 3 leagues, you may turn to Windward, and anchor any where in clean Ground; you may also go between the Islands of *Chincha* and those of *Balesta* without fear. In *Pisco* there's Water, Wood, and all other Necessaries. From *Pisco* towards the S W. lies *Cangallon*, a high big Island with broken Land on the top; on some Points it makes more broken and ragged; the Land over against it, call'd the Headland of *Paraca*, is high. Within *Cangallon* it is all deep Water, but on the North side there are Rocks both great and small, and towards the South part some small ones. Between the Main Land and the Isle there's a good deep Channel, thro which the *Chili* Ships come into this Port; only on the S W. side there is some danger. *Cangallon* is in S. Lat. 14. 10. As you go from *Cangallon* to *Avasso*, it appears in divers Forms. From *Cangallon* to the Island *Carrate* 'tis 3 leagues N W. and S E. 'tis a small round low Island, and from the Main about 4 leagues.

From *Cangallon* to *Morro Quemado*, or the burnt Headland, 'tis 9 leagues. This Cape is reckon'd the worst in all those Seas for strong Gales. In this Harbour Ships load Wine and Coals for *Callao*. To get in here, coming from the Windward, furl all your Sails before you come to the narrow Entrance, and go in with your Fore-Sail low set; you may anchor under the Headland at discretion. When the Breeze is over, and it proves calm, weigh your Anchors again, and go farther in; but this Harbour shoots sometimes such Gusts of Wind, that Ships are forc'd back to Paraca, and when the Weather is settled, come back again to load.

Morro de Vejas, or the old Headland, is a high Cape, and lies from, the Isle of *Carrette* 2 leagues N and S. in S. Lat: 14. 20. The Head it self, when you have an Offing, seems like an Island, and to the Southward is low: In the top of the high part there's a Clift, which as you bring open, appears very deep and large. From *Morro de Vejas* to the Isle of *Lobos*, or Wolves, is about half a league, and on the N N E. side there's good anchoring; the S E. side makes like a Galley, and as you run by, it joins again, and then another Island shoots with it, that appears as if 'twere one Main Land. From *Morro del Vejas* begins a Bay that reaches to *Morro Quemado*.

Morro Quemado, or the burnt Cape, lies in S. Lat. 14. 30. 'tis high Land, but farther in the Country the Land is low, and shows in Hillocks. This Cape is often cover'd with the Clouds. To go in, you must range the Rocks (that you will see under the Cape) very near, and have all your Sails handed for the Flaws, only your Foretop-sail half-mast, and all your Anchors ready to let go; and when you let fall your Anchor, as soon as you are in the ground, give your Ship a sheer, and let go another for Security: and as the Wind slacks, go farther in, and anchor against the Strand, in what water you please; here you must moor with an Elbow: you have neither Wood nor Water here. When you come out, you may run between the Island and the Main without danger. If you are before the Harbour e'er the Breeze sets in, you may go in with more ease.

From *Morro Quemado* to Porto *Cavalla* 'tis 12 leagues, and from *Morro Quemado* to the Point of *Olleros* 'tis 6, Course N W and S E. high Land and level. To Leeward of this Point there are some Rocks near the Shore, and to Leeward of them you may anchor in a small Bay, which is very safe and secure; but this Place is little frequented, because it produces nothing to load.

From the Point of *Olleros* to *Porto Cavalla*, or Horse-Harbour, in S. Lat. 15. 'tis 6 leagues, Course S S E. and N N W. high Land next the Sea with Ridges of Sand. Midway is a large Bay, and in the middle of it some high steep Ridges, join'd to the high Land, and you will see a plain Hill like a Table call'd *Messa de Santa Maria*, or holy *Mary's* Table; then the Land appears low, till you come to the River *de Ica*. This is a dangerous Bay, subject to Calms and a tumbling Sea.

If you would harbour in *Porto Cavalla*, you must go in to Windward, your Boat out, Yards and Top-Masts struck, Anchors ready, and run in under your Sprit-sail and Mizen. Just off the Head going in there are some Rocks under water, therefore you must give them a birth: one of them is above the water, and call'd the *Fraily* or Fryar. Here you anchor in 8 or 9 fathom.

From Port *St. John* to Port *St. Nicholas* 'tis one league. Port *St. John* is little frequented: there's 8 fathom where you anchor, but no fresh Water nor Wood; nor is it inhabited, but sometimes Wine is loaden here that comes from the Country. 'Tis usual to have much Wind, but little Sea here.

From Port *Cavalla* to Port *St. Nicholas*, S. Lat. 15.30. 'tis 6 leagues and high Land, but level. About one league from the Headland of Port *St. Nicholas*, and to Windward, you may see a very deep Gap in the Land, out of which comes the River *Masca*. Farther to Windward in the Country you see two small broken Hillocks, the Windwardmost being the least; and coming in from the Sea, over this Land you will see Ridges of Hills; on the NW. side they seem to be steep, on the S W. side they fall away lower, and at the Point appear much in form of a Galley; in the high Land over it there are some broken Gaps. In this Port there's neither Wood nor Water, but 'tis a safer Harbour than *St. John*; in going into which, give the Windward Point a birth, for off of it lies a great Shoal. Between *St. Nicholas* and *St. John* there's 2 leagues low Land, and over it some reddish Hillocks. From Port *St. John* to Cape *Accari* 'tis 8 leagues, and in that run you have no manner of Port, Creek, nor Cove, nor any place to get Wood or Water.

From Port *St. John* to Port *del Loma*, S. Lat. 15. 20. or *Acari*, 'tis 8 leagues, N W. and S E. low Land, but in the Country 'tis higher. This is a very good Harbour, but not frequented; the Land producing nothing to load Ships with: but those that go for *Arica* and *Ariquipa* stop here in the rainy times, and when the Current runs to Leeward. From Port *Acari* to *Ariquipa* 'tis 8 leagues NE and SW. low Land; and under the Cape of *Ariquipa* you will see a Bay, which makes a good Harbour, and is call'd Port *Chala*. Near the Headland there are some sharp black Rocks. This Harbour is frequented by some trading Barks, and lies in S. Lat. 16.

From Cape *Ariquipa* to the Cape of *Attico* 'tis 14 leagues, Course NW. and SE. From Cape *Ariquipa* to Windward you will see a large Strand of Sand, which reaches to *Puerto Chala*. This Land is very high and full of Mountains. *Attico* is in S. Lat. 16. 30. From hence to *Ocona* 'tis 14 leagues, NW and SE. high Land, and up the Country snowy Mountains. Between *Attico* and *Ocona* there's a great broken Gap, from the River to the Sea, and close to the Water-side. About two Musket-shot from thence there's Water, and near the broken Gap are two Rocks call'd *Los Pescadores*, or Fishermen.

From *Ocona* to the Valley of *Quilca*, S. Lat. 17. 'tis 11 leagues, and a bold Coast; and from *Ocona* to *Camana* 'tis 6 leagues. *Camana* is inhabited by *Spaniards* and *Indians*. In this Harbour of *Quilca* you must anchor where you see the Gross about a quarter of a league from the Island, which is in the Entrance of the Port; and at the N E. of it you have 12 or 15 fathom. Ships may go into the Creek of *Quilca*, for the Water slows much there, and great store of Fish are taken here by Nets. If you have occasion to go into this Creek, and cannot get in, you may anchor till the Tide turns, or the Wind abates, in 20 fathom, good clean Ground; and when you have the Strand of *Camana* open, anchor, for it is all clean. *Camana* above-mention'd is an inland Town, and will appear in sight as you run along shore.

From the Creek of *Quilca* to the Port of *Xuli* 'tis 10 leagues, the Course N W and S E. From *Guilca* to the Island *Guano* 'tis 3 leagues, and from *Guano* to *Ylay* 'tis 4: in *Ylay* you may anchor within some Rocks call'd in the Draught the *Ferralones d'Ylay*, they are all bold above water, and here you have 40 fathom and upwards: the biggest of these Rocks are five, and all white, by them the Port is known. *Ylay* lies in S. Lat. 17. 15.

From *Ylay* or *Ilay* unto *Xuli* in S. Lat. 17.30. 'tis 3 leagues. This Harbour was the principal Port of *Arequipa*, and all the Coast of *Penasco*. As you come from *Ylay*, you may know this Port by a small narrow Creek of 20 fathom; and if you come out of the Sea for *Xuli*, you will see the *Volcano* of *Arequipa*, which lies from this Port N W and S E. 6 leagues in the Country: and if it be clear Weather, you will see other high Hills, one of which makes like a Sugar-loaf.

From *Xuli* to *Rio Tambo* or *Jambo* 'tis 12 leagues, Course SE by S. and NE by N. 'tis high Land; and 2 leagues to Windward of *Xuli* is *Rio Tambo*. Here you will see a Spot of low Land amongst the high, about one league long; all the rest of the Coast is bold high Land. You may anchor against the River *Tambo* in 20 fathom clean Ground: and from thence to *Yerba Buena* 'tis 2 leagues.

From the Island of *Yerba Buena* to *Porto Ylo* in S. Lat. 18. 'tis 8 leagues. To know where to anchor here, you will see in the high Land some broken Gaps; and when you have that East from you, and the Valley in the broken Gaps, you may anchor at discretion. There is good landing in the Harbour, and close to the Bar good fresh Water in a small River. The Point of Port *Ylo* is low, and reaches a great way out; you must give it a good large birth, for there is a great Undertow; and when you come out of the Sea, the Point appears like an Island. At the end of it there's a little rocky Island, and farther off are three or four Rocks out of the Water. From the Point of *Ylo* to *Rio de Sama* 'tis 8 leagues, the Course N W and S E. and midway is the Hill *Accacuna*. The River of *Ylo* is very good, and about one quarter of a league to Windward lies the Town of *Ylo*, inhabited by *Indian* Fishermen; from whom you may have Maize, Water, Wood, and other Necessaries.

From the Headland of *Sama* to that of *Arrica* 'tis 12 leagues, Course N W by W. and S E by E. and between 'em a great Bay; all along the shore 'tis low Land, and a sandy Strand, only the Land of *Guiaca* is high. From Cape *de Sama* to the River of *Sama* is 3 leagues; and half a league to Windward of the River of *Sama* is the Harbour of *Guiaca*; 'tis high Land, inhabited by *Spaniards* and *Indian* Fisherman, from whom you may have Wood, Water, and other Necessaries.

From the Port of *Guiaca* to the River of *Juan de Dios* 'tis 5 leagues, and from *Juan de Dios* to the Cape of *Arrica* other 5, and low sandy Land. In this Bay and all along shore you may anchor, the Ground being very clean; but on the shore there's for the most part a great Suff.

Cape *Arrica* in S. Lat. 19. is high Land and steep, with several white Spots. When you bring the Cape in sight of the Land to Windward of Cape *de Sama*, and *Guiaca* to be the highest, you are in a sort of Bay, and there appears lower Land. When you would anchor, you will see a small Island next the shore, and the Ware-houses on the Coast near a Strand; here you have 8 or 9 fathom, and you may anchor at discretion. You must moor with one Anchor right a-stern, for the Land-Breezes blow strong. Coming out of the Sea, you may know this Port by ridgy Land, and on those Ridges two Hills that shew like Volcans; they appear white, and if they bear N W. then you are to Windward of the Port; but if S E. you are to Leeward; and then you will see two other Hills, as white as if cover'd with Snow.

From Cape *Arrica* to Cape *Tarapaca* 'tis 25 leagues, high Land next the Water-side, the Course N by E. and S by W. About midway there are three Spots of broken Land in deep Gaps, and in each a River which falls into the Ocean. If you come out of the Sea, and have not had a good Observation; or if with the Current you have been horsed away, and made the Land of *Arequipa*; you may boldly run for the Shore by the said Marks, for there is no other Land that makes so on this Coast. When you are about these broken Hills to Windward, the first is call'd *Victor O Colpa*: these broken Lands are about 5 leagues in length; they have on the North side almost to the shore red Hillocks and Ridges about one league in length, and on the South side Ridges and Hillocks that are milk-white. From the broken Gap of *Victor O Colpa* to that of *Camarones* 'tis 7 leagues: The latter has a small white Rock close by it, and at some distance seems like a Ship under sail. These two Gaps, when East from you, are enclos'd; the broken Gap of *Pisagua* seems like a Bay. From the Gap of *Camarones* to that of *Pisagua* 'tis 8 leagues high Land, and lies N and S.

From the broken Land of *Pisagua* to Gape *Tarapaca* 'tis 6 leagues. This Gape is high, but inwards the Country is lower, and seems like the Entrance of two Harbours, over which the Land makes like a Hat, come in with it how you will; and under the Shore you see a small Island, but all the Coast very bold. From Cape *Tarapaca* to *Pica* 'tis 5 leagues, Course N and S. You see a small white Island, under which there's good Anchorage next the Shore, in 7 fathom water.

From *Pica* to *Rio de Lora* (or Loa) 'tis 12 leagues, high steep Land, and the Course N and S. On the shore there are some Ridges and white Hillocks, and where the Land is lower, the River is narrower: the Water of it is somewhat brackish; you may anchor about a quarter of a league to Windward of it near some small Rocks, that lie above water. When you are anchor'd, these small Rocks will be a-stern. From *Rio de Lora* to *Atacama* 'tis 15 leagues high Land, Course NNW and S S E. 'tis a rocky Coast and deep Water.

Five leagues from *Rio de Loa* to the Southward is *Paguisa*, in S. Lat. 21. 40. where you may have fresh Water; it lies behind a Point, and is known by white Spots in it. Right against this Watering-place there's a large Tree; you must anchor under the highest Land. Right over the Point there's a Mountain, and farther out some other Hills overgrown with Thistles. In case Water be wanting at *Paguisa*, 2 leagues from thence lie the *Agodonales*, which are known by several white Spots near the Sea: from those *Agodonales* you may get water for 8 leagues, but 'tis somewhat brackish.

From *Atacama*, in S. Lat. 22.30. to the Bay Of *Messillones* 'tis 5 leagues N E and SW. On the Point there's a Hill like a Sugar-loaf, and on the North side another somewhat less. The Bay of *Messillones is* deep, and the Anchoring-place to the Eastward, but the Entrance North and South.

On the South side the Point you may anchor near a large Rock in 15 fathom water clean Ground. The Bay of *Atacama* lies from Cape to Cape N by E. and S by W. and in the midst of this Bay is that of *Messillones*.

From the Point of the Bay of *Messillones* to Cape *Morreno*, in S. Lat. 23. 'tis 8 leagues, the Course N by E. and S by W. This Cape is high Land, and the N E. side is a Road near a small Island: Here's also a very commodious, but narrow Harbour, where you may careen. Give the Cape what birth you can, for here come off very great Flaws.

From Cape *Morreno* to Cape *de George*, in S. Lat. 23. 45. 'tis 15 leagues, the Course N by E. and S by W. Between the Cape there's a great Bay, which if the Wind come at S E. is dangerous, because it blows right in. If you are forc'd in here, and can get under *Morro de George*, you may anchor in 25 fathom good Ground, and no Danger but what appears above water. Here comes in a tumbling Sea.

From Cape *de George* to *Baya de nuestra Seniora*, or our Lady's-Bay, is 20 leagues, Course N N E. and SSW. The Land is high and mountainous, no Inhabitants, nor Water, till about 6 leagues before you arrive at the Bay. The highest and middlemost Mountain is over the Bay; under that there's Water and some plain Land, against which you may anchor in at least 25 fathom Water, in good clean Ground. From the Mountain the Land comes off like a Knife, and right against that Knife there's a large white Rock, in S. Lat. 24.30. about half a league from the Sea. You must have the Rock North of you, and lie to an anchor about one third of a league from the shore. If it be clear Weather, you may from hence see Cape *Morreno*. From this Rock to the

Bay of *Nuestra Seniora* about one half of the Bay is inhabited, and the other not: in the Bay there are very hard Gales of Wind.

From the Bay of *Nuestra Seniora* to Cape *Copiapo* 'tis 30 leagues, the Course N by E. and S by W. and from the Bay of *Nuestra, Seniora* to *Puerto Yrten* 'tis 6. In this Port there's good riding, but you must anchor in 30 fathom, that you may have room to sail if it blow Northerly. The Marks of the Harbour of *Bettas* is a Spot of white Sand, and in the middle of it a black Spot. This Port is in S. Lat. 25 and has no fresh Water.

From Bettas to *Juncal* 'tis 6 leagues: the Harbour is only good with the Wind at S W. it has no Water, and the adjacent Mountains are not inhabited.

From Juncal to General 'tis 6 leagues: this is a good Harbour, and has a small Island before it, but no fresh Water.

From *General* to Cape *Copiapo* 'tis 12 leagues, and all along shore good Anchorage, and Bays with shelter, as well against Southerly Winds as others. The Mountain of *Copiapo* appears like an Island, and the Point of St. *Helena*. Off the South part about one league from the shore there's a small Island, and under it good riding. On the Main there's some few Inhabitants.

From *Copiapo* to the Island *Salado* 'tis 10 leagues. Here is good Anchorage, and a Watering-place, but the Water not very good. The River lies between those two Islands. From this River towards the Sea there's an ugly Shoal, that lies off E and W. at a good distance.

From Baya Salado to Totoral, S. Lat. 27. 30. 'tis 15 leagues. On the North side of the Point there's good Anchorage. You must bring the Point S W by W. to get into the best of this Road, which is bad enough when the Wind is Northerly. Here is fresh Water.

From *Totoral* to Port *Guasco* in S. Lat. 28.45. 'tis 15 leagues. This Harbour is good from the S. to the NW. and is inhabited. You must anchor right against the River near a small low Island. The Point of the Main is encompass'd by 7 or 8 Rocks that appear out of the Water, and on the top of a Point there's a Sand-Hill somewhat ragged, where you anchor. You will see two or three more small Islands, and the Mountain over the Port is high, large, and round.

From *Guasco* to the Isle *Totoral* 'tis 12 leagues, and towards the shore a small Island. From the four biggest Islands, where the Road is, you may sail with the Wind Northerly from any part of the Road. The middlemost Island is the biggest of the 4, has 5 ragged Hills on the top; and that which is nearest the shore has some Rocks about it that appear above water. The two biggest of these Islands that lie near together, when they bear S S E. about 7 leagues from the Point of *Coquimbo*, appear but as one.

From the Port of *Coquimbo* in S. Lat. 30. there's a Point, and the Land not very high. At the Entrance there's two small Rocks above water, which you must leave on your Starboard side; and going in, you must go near the Point: for if the Current or Land-Flaws put you off, you will drive away, because you have no Ground, and cannot anchor. When you are in, you must anchor against the highest Land, right with a small Rock call'd *La Tortuga*, or the Tortoise. From the Road to the Town of *Coquimbo* 'tis 2 leagues.

From the Point of *Coquimbo* one league to windward is the Point of *Heradura*, a very good Harbour, clean Ground, and no Danger.

From the Point of *Coquimbo* to the Bay of *Longuey* or *Tangucy* in S. Lat. 30. 30. 'tis 7 leagues, Course S E. In the Road, which is right against a small River, there's a Headland which lies East with it; and all over the Bay there's good Anchoring, in clean holding Ground.

From *Limari* in S. Lat. 31. to *Choapa* 'tis. 10 ls, all very high snowy Mountains, and no Harbour, but a very bold Coast.

From Port *Governador* to Port *de la Liga* 'tis 5 leagues, the Course S E. We have no Description of this Harbour, but by the Draught it Seems to be very clean; and right before it lies a small Island in S. Lat. 32.12.

From Port *de la Liga* to Port *Papudo* in S. Lat. 32. 'tis 4 leagues: in the latter the Water is very deep, but good holding Ground, and the Entrance safe. In Port *Liga* near the Point there's a Shoal with 2 fathom water upon it: you must give it a good birth, run within it into 5 fathom, and anchor there. If your Boat go on shore, and the Swell runs high, you may run with her into a small Creek that leads to the River, and you are safe.

From *Papudo* to the Shoals of *Quintero* 'tis 5 ls. Most of those Shoals are above water and near the Point, but Ships may pass between them and the Main, there being a good Channel with 12 fathom water, clean Ground. From the Shoals to the Port of *Quintero*, S. Lat. 31.45. 'tis 2 ls. the Harbour is deep Water, and with Southerly Winds is very good, but the Northerly blow right in.

From Port *de Concon* to that of *Valparaysso* 'tis 10 ls. In that of *Concon* there's a great Shoal, which the Sea breaks on. To go in here, you must range close to the Point, and run in betwixt it and the Shoal.

From Port *Quintero* to Port *Valparaysso* 'tis 5 ls. the Course S E. With the Point of *Corunna* it lies S E by E. and with the River of *Chili S.* 3 ls. from *Quintero* in the River of *Chili* there's a great Shoal. Here begins the Kingdom of *Chili*.

From the River of *Chili* to *Porto Valparaysso*, or Port *Santiago*, S. Lat. 33. 'tis 2 ls. and in that Run you will see three Strands, and in the midst of them the River of *Minas* or *Margamorga*. The joining of the Land of the last Strand to Windward is Port *Santiago* or *Valparaysso*, where you will see a Gap and a small Strand. From the Point of this Strand comes a rocky Point, and behind that Point you anchor against the small Strand aforesaid. From *Puerto del Valparaysso* to *Punta de Corrona*, or Crown-Point, 'tis 2 ls. the Course WSW. and within that Point there's a Shoal, to which you must give a birth. There's a good Road near this Point, which lies SE. with *Coquimbo*, *Copiapo*, and Cape *Moren*.

From the Point of *Corrona* to *Puerto* de *Topocalma* 'tis 18 ls. About 6 ls. from *Corrona* are *Las Salinas*, or the Salt-Ponds, where there's fine Salt: there you may anchor near the high Rock, which is to the Southward. The Land hereabouts is low, and there are divers Shoals from where you anchor all along to the River *Rapel*, which you must take care to avoid. Several of the Heads of these Shoals stretch into the Sea two Musket-shot. If you anchor at the *Salinas*, and the Wind chop about Northerly, you must get to sail.

The Islands of *John Fernandez*, or the King's Islands, are two; that which is nearest the shore is 110 ls. from it, and lies SW. and from one Island to other 'tis 7 ls. the Course E. Here are two Harbours, one call'd by the name *of John Fernandes*, and the other *La Pescaria*. These Islands were discover'd by *John Fernandez*, a *Spanish* Pilot, in 1585. they lie in S. Lat. 33. 30.

Within the Cape of *Potocalmo* there's good anchoring with the Wind Southerly; but if you run about a quarter of a league within the Cape, you will meet terrible Flaws off the shore. You must anchor within the small Isle, in 25 fathom clean Ground. This Headland lies in S. Lat. 34.

From *Potocalmo* to *Quebrada de Lora* in S. Lat. 37. 40. 'tis 14 ls, the Course S E. The said *Quebrada*, or broken Land, much resembles that of *Lima*. About 7 ls off the Coast is low sandy Land, which reaches to the River of *Maule*; you may anchor here all along shore. From this Gap the Mountains begin to rise gradually, and are all full of great Trees. There's very much Timber all along this Coast to *Conception*.

From *Quebrada de Lora* to the River of *Maule*, in S. Lat. 35. 20. 'tis 7 ls. S E. On this River there's much Timber, and here they build Ships. At low Water the Mouth of this River is 3 fathom. At the Entrance there are two Rocks, and about half a league to Leeward is good anchoring with a Southerly Wind, the Northerly blows very hard here.

From the River *Maule* to the Point of *Ymos* or *Humos*, S. Lat. 35. 30. 'tis 10 ls. This Point is very dangerous because of the Shoals about it, upon which Ships have been lost. From the River of *Ymos* or *Humos* to this Point, the Course is SSE.

From the Point of *Ymos* to the River *Ytata* 'tis 9 ls. This River is much inhabited, and 'at the Mouth of it there's a good Road behind a Point that runs out. This River makes a great Gap in the Land, which is very high on each side. From the Point of *Imos* to the *Herradura* there's no anchoring, unless behind the Point before-mention'd. From the River of *Ytata* to *Herradura* 'tis 5 ls. *Herradura* is a Bay with a good Harbour, and at the Entrance there's 3 or 4 small Rocks above water.

From *La Herradura* to the Island of *Conception*, or *La Quiriquina*, S. Lat. 36. 15. 'tis 2 ls. Course N E. and S W. These 2 ls. make the Bay of *Conception*, and the Entrance is S. the North Wind blows right in. The *Spanish* Town lies close by the Water-side, where you will see a large sandy Strand. About one quarter of a league from *Conception* is the River *Andalica*, which you may enter with small Ships. You must anchor in *Conception*-Bay against a small River that runs thro the middle of the City, but at some distance, that you may have room to fail if the Wind blows Northerly.

All Ships that go from *Conception* to *Baldivia* or *Chiloe*, anchor at *Talanguana* in 12 fathom: here they wait for Northerly Winds. You must anchor about ½ league from the Rock of *Ollas*, bringing the Rock West from you. *Note*, That the Channel between *Talanguana* and the Island *Quiriquina* is narrow, and not to be pass'd thro but with the Wind large.

From the Point of *Talanguana* to the Isle of *Santa Maria* 'tis 10 ls. and from the Port of St. *Vincent* to the River of *Bobio* 'tis 2 ls. In the Entrance of this River there's two Rocks and two high Mountains of an equal size, call'd *Las Tetas de Viovio*, against which the Sea beats. From the River *Bobio* to *Punta de la Sappie* 'tis 7 ls. a good Coast for the Southerly Winds, but the Northerly blow right in.

From the Island of *Santa Maria* in S.Lat. 37.20. to *Porto Carnero* 'tis 10 ls. the Course S E. In this Island there are 2 good Roads, one to the Northward, the other to the Southward, If you enter the Road that shelters you from Northerly Winds, go not too near the Island, for there's little Water: you may anchor in 6 fathom with the Wind Southerly. Here's a great Sea, and on the North side a Suff and Undertow with a Southerly Wind. When you go in on the North side to *Porto Delicado*, beware of the Point, where there's a great Shoal, and at the N E. end of the Island there's Another, which extends half a league into the Sea, where Ships have been lost. This Island is about 2 ls. round, level on the top like a Table, and there's fresh Water in several places.

From the Island of *Santa Maria* to *Porto Carnero* 'tis 10 ls. In this Port there's a River, and a little within the Point a high Rock. Small Barks come hither with Provisions and Necessaries for the Fort of *Tecapel*, in Lat. 38. On the Mountain of that name the *Indians* meet to consultand be merry; from hence they began their March, when they kill'd the Governour of *Baldivia*.

From Port *Camera* to the Isle of *Mocha* 'tis 10 ls. the Course S W. From Port *Carnero* to the Cape of *Tecapel* 'tis 4 ls. The Harbour is bad with a Northerly Wind, and is not frequented but by Barks that bring, Provisions to the Forts on the Coasts, that curb the *Indians*.

The Island of *Mocha* lies from the main Land E by S. 4 ls. The River *Imperial* is right against it on the Main. This Island is high, and inhabited by *Indians*, who are always at war with the *Spaniards*. On the W S W. of this Island there are dangerous Shoals; it lies from the River of *Baldivia* 30 ls. the Course N and S. and from Point *de la Galera* E S E. and from the Islands of *John Fernandez* S E by S. 90 ls.

From *Quevete* to the River of *Boniface* 'tis 10 leagues, and from the Cape of *Boniface* to *Corral*, where Ships anchor, 'tis low Land. If you would go into *Baldivia*, you must anchor first about half a league without the Bar on the Starboard side. *Note*, That here are two Bars, the biggest lies on the Starboard side. If you would go in with your Boat, here is a small Channel, from which you have but one league to *Baldivia*; but where the Ships go in, it is 6 ls. The Entrances are two, parted by an Island; and farther up, and to the Southward, there's a small Island call'd *Constantino*. The other big Island that divides the Channel is inhabited' by *Indians*. The River *Saldivia* lies in S. Lat. 40. From this River to the Point of *Galera* 'tis 4 ls. and from the Point of *Quedar* 22, the Course S S E. Point *Galera* is low Land, and lies E by S.

From Point *Galera* to the River *Bueno* 'tis 5 ls. high Land with a Gap on the top.

From the River *Bueno* to Port *St. Pedro*, S. Lat. 41. 30. 'tis 9 ls. high Land with a Gap on the top, which you see from the River *Bueno*.

From Port *St. Pedro* to the Point *de Quedal*, in S. Lat. 41. 20. 'tis 8 ls. You may go in thro the Channel of *Carelmapo* on either side of the Rocks; there is also a good Passage between the Island *de Pedro Nuncy* an i the ocher Rocks. When the hithermost of the Rocks appears open with the Entrance, leave the Island of *Pedro Nuncy* on your Starboard side, and you may pass securely up thro the mid Channel till you come near Point *Remolinos*, which is 3 ls. from the Island of *Pedro Nuncy*. Give Point *Remolinos* a moderate birth, and you will see a curious Bay; anchor there in 12 fathom. The Bay is call'd *Puerto Chacoa*: lay your Anchor E and W.

From the Point of *Quedal* to that of *Godoy* 'tis 6 ls. Off of Point *Godoy* there are some small Rocks that appear out of the water. From the Point of

Godoy to *Carelmapo* there's the Bay of *Chika*; 'tis a bad Shoal-Harbour, and low Land.

Chiloe is an Island in S. Lat. 44. the Coast is very subject to Storms and tempestuous Weather, especially in *March*; for then the Winter begins, and People cannot put to Sea, the Northerly Winds blow so suriously: so that they must winter there contentedly till the Summer comes again, and the Norths are not so surious.

About the Ifland *Chiloe* there are 40 more, all taking their names from it, which is about 50 ls. in length and 7 in breadth. The Shape of it is like an Arm bow'd: the South part of it is divided from the Continent by a very narrow Sea, and the Continent there makes a Bay. All the Country here is uneven, abounds with Woods and Marshes, and very cold, lying all beyond 43 deg. S. Lat. In the Summer there are such cold Storms, that it resembles our Winter. There comes only one Ship in a Year hither, which is sent by the Governour of *Chili* to supply the *Spaniards*.

Maps and Sea-Draughts are always improvable; and altho this is an exact Copy of the *Spaniards* Coasting-Pilot Book, yet comparing the Writing with the Maps or their own drawing, I sound it differ in many places: which makes me sear there is yet some Error both in the Draughts of the Coast, and also in the written Descriptions, the *Spaniards* not being so exact as the *English* and *Dutch* in their Sea-Charts. But this being far better thin any yet publish'd, I was willing to annex it as an Appendix to this Book; and if it proves of any service to the Publick, it answers the End I intended it for.

THE NARRATIVE PRESS
TRUE FIRST-PERSON HISTORICAL ACCOUNTS

THE HISTORICAL ADVENTURE AND EXPLORATION SERIES

The *Historical Adventure and Exploration Series* from The Narrative Press are all first-hand reports written by the explorers, pioneers, scientists, mountain men, prospectors, spies, lawmen, and fortune hunters themselves.

Most of these adventures are classics, about people and places now long gone. They take place all over the world – in Africa, South America, the Arctic and Antarctic, in America (in the Old West and before), on islands, and on the open seas.

Some of our authors are famous – Ernest Shackleton, Kit Carson, Henry Stanley, David Livingston, William Bligh, John Muir, Richard Burton, Elizabeth Custer, Teddy Roosevelt, Charles Darwin, Osborne Russell, John Fremont, Joshua Slocum, William Manley, Tom Horn, Philip St. George Cooke, Apsley Cherry-Garrard, Richard Henry Dana, Jack London, and Buffalo Bill, to name a few.

One thread binds all of our books: every one is historically important, and every one of them is fascinating.

Visit our website today. You can also call or write to us for a free copy of our printed catalogue.

THE NARRATIVE PRESS LLC.
P.O.BOX 145
CRABTREE, OREGON 97335 U.S.A.
(800) 315-9005
www.narrativepress.com

Lightning Source UK Ltd.
Milton Keynes UK
06 April 2010

152371UK00006BA/34/P